W9-CJP-677

Religion
and Politics
in the
United States

Religion
and Politics
in the
United States

Kenneth D. Wald
University of Florida

St. Martin's Press
New York

© 1987 by St. Martin's Press, Inc.
All rights reserved.
Printed in the United States of America.
10987
fedcba
For information, write St. Martin's Press, Inc.
175 Fifth Avenue, New York, NY 10010

cover design: Darby Downey

ISBN 0-312-67058-3
ISBN 0-312-67056-7 (pbk.)

Library of Congress Cataloging-in-Publication Data

Wald, Kenneth D.
  Religion and politics in the United States.

  Includes bibliographies.
   1. Religion and politics—United States—History—
20th century.   2. United States—Religion—1960–
3. United States—Politics and government—1981–
I. Title.
BR526.W26 1986   332'.1'0973   86-60659
ISBN 0-312-67058-3
ISBN 0-312-67056-7 (pbk.)

BL
2525
.W35
1987

To Robin, Dara, and Jaina
with my love and gratitude

Contents

Preface

There is a sense, of course, in which religion is a subjective and personal matter but there is also a sense in which it is an objective fact and can be dealt with as such. It is a fact that there is such a thing as Christianity and that it has exerted a profound influence upon our thinking and institutions. To understand this influence is essential whether one is . . . a Christian or not.
—John H. Hallowell (1951)

I have written this book to show that religion is more important in American politics than most Americans realize but in different ways than they commonly imagine.

From reading the typical textbook on American government, one might think that religion has political relevance only on those rare occasions when church and state collide over issues like prayer in the public schools, abortion policy, or public observance of religious holidays. With only brief mention of such controversies, most textbooks imply that religious issues are at best secondary, that government's more serious tasks are such things as economic growth, public safety, world peace, and social justice. As I hope to show in the following pages, one cannot fully understand how America discharges the task of governing itself without recognizing the profound influence of religion.

Religion has penetrated public life in many ways. Not only has the American religious tradition contributed to some of the enduring principles that undergird the political system, but religious values and interests have helped to shape the political perspectives of individuals, probably affecting their reactions to both candidates and issues. Religious communities have entered the political process itself, in an organized effort to influence public policy on a wide range of issues. There is much more to the religious factor in American politics than just the church-state debate, as important as that is.

Of course, any time one highlights a particular factor in politics there is a risk of crediting that factor with too much influence. Even though religion is important in American politics and has been overlooked in the past, it is important to recognize at the outset that it is only one of many influences upon American political values, institutions, and policies. Thus, just as I will attempt to identify the conditions that enhance religious influence upon government and politics, so also will I note circumstances that limit the political impact of religious forces.

Although political observers are finally coming to recognize the political significance of religion in the United States, they have yet to give up another durable stereotype about religion in politics—namely, that religion is inevitably a force for conservatism and preservation of the existing social order. Recent attempts to enlist some religious denominations in conservative movements have reinforced the image of religion as a pillar of tradition. But in fact, the political implications of religion have been much too ambiguous to justify the image of uniformity among believers. Today, as always, deeply religious people can be found on different sides of most issues and at all points along the political spectrum. Around the globe, religion has inspired fervent loyalty to some governments and revolution against others. In the United States, the liberal Jesse Jackson and the conservative Jerry Falwell both draw upon a common theological tradition of evangelical Protestantism. I hope the reader will come away from the book with greater awareness of the political diversity associated with American religion.

Recognizing the political role of religion is not the same thing as judging it. Classroom experience makes me vividly aware that people reach different verdicts about the connection between religion and politics. Some people applaud it as necessary and proper; others denounce it as the root of mischief and evil. In this book I have tried to inform readers about both the noble and the unfortunate sides of the religious element in politics. In the intellectual minefield that is religion and politics, no one book can satisfy everyone or would be of much value if it did. This book is offered on the principle that good teaching prompts believers to question a faith and encourages skeptics to appreciate its value. In that sense, I hope to educate people who believe deeply in a religious faith as well as those who reject or do not care much about religion.

The reader should also know that this text takes a social scientific perspective on the subject of religion and politics. After trying to explain that thought in many different ways, I find that I cannot improve on the words of a scholar who began a book on the same topic by warning readers that "to be a historian is to seek to explain in human terms. If God speaks, it is not through him. If He speaks to others, the historian cannot vouch for it. In this sense the historian is necessarily secularist." (Strout 1974, xiv). As that comment suggests, the social scientific approach refuses to explain religion in terms of supernatural forces, insisting instead on finding human causes for patterns of human behavior. Likewise, most social scientists resist the opposite tendency to reduce religion to a biological or genetic trait. Supernaturalists may explain the survival of religion as God's will while some natural scientists might attribute the persistence of religion in society to the sound dietary principles and healthy lifestyles of believers (see National Research Council 1982, 6–10). While both these explanations may be true and useful, the social scientist prefers to emphasize the operation of human consciousness and choice. Thus Chapter 1 invokes neither the hand of God nor the principles of evolution to explain why religion prospers in America. Instead, consistent with the social scientific outlook, it calls attention to cognitive factors—humanity's apparent need to reduce uncertainty about its place in the universe—and elements of the social and political structure that encourage religious observance. The rest of the book follows suit.

The book begins with two chapters that establish the framework for studying the relationship between religion and politics in the United States. Chapter 1 demonstrates the continuing significance of religion in American life, and Chapter 2 identifies the features of religion and the American political system that promote regular interaction between the two spheres. In ensuing chapters I examine the potential political impact of religion on different levels of political life. Separate chapters are devoted to the influence of religion on fundamental American beliefs about politics and governance (Chapter 3); mass partisan and ideological orientations (Chapter 4); views about church/state relations (Chapter 5); and specific policy debates and issues on the public agenda (Chapter 6). The next two chapters explain the often puzzling changes that have taken place in the political behavior of major religious groups in the United States—Chapter 7 explores the theologically conservative Protestant churches, and Chapter 8 similarly analyzes the other major religious traditions, groups whose interesting patterns of stability and change have sometimes been lost in the glare of publicity devoted to the evangelical Protestants. I conclude with a chapter that weighs the positive and negative contributions of religion to politics and governance in the United States.

Because religion's role in politics is the subject of strong feeling, readers may want to know something more about the author's background and beliefs. Without revealing more than is necessary, I am Jewish, the child of Holocaust survivors and the grandchild of Holocaust victims. That heritage, which has shaped me in many ways I can only dimly comprehend, has certainly contributed to an abiding interest in the topic being examined and to a keen appreciation for the potential political consequences of religious belief. It may also account for my belief that religion should speak to public affairs. Though well aware that churches perform an important spiritual mission that might suffer from excessive political involvement, I nonetheless believe that religious institutions have a responsibility to remind the state of its ethical obligations. Accordingly, I am more comfortable when churches challenge the government than when they vest the state with a holy aura. Readers of different backgrounds may spot other assumptions that seem natural to me but are perhaps contentious to them.

Although I cannot be certain of all the ways my personal background has influenced the book, a good memory permits me to identify persons in the foreground who helped prepare the author for writing it. I owe a great debt to scholars who paved the way for this project with pioneering studies of religion and politics, and to contemporary investigators scattered among the academic disciplines of political science, history, sociology, anthropology, and religion. On a more individual level, some of the thoughts expressed here were forged in the heat of collaborative teaching and research with Mike Lupfer and Bill Marty of Memphis State University and with Sam Hill and Dennis Owen at the University of Florida. The manuscript itself benefited from the close reading and incisive suggestions of Clarke Cochran of Texas Tech, Jim Guth of Furman University, Corwin Smidt of Calvin College, and Robert Wuthnow of Princeton University and from the careful assessments of Marilyn Moller, Anne McCoy, and Dan Flanagan of St. Martin's Press. There was a manuscript to review only because Michael Weber and Peter Dougherty of St. Martin's showed a willingness to invest in a project with the potential of high intellectual payoffs but uncertain market prospects. Their confidence can never fully be repaid, but it will certainly help if lots of people buy the book.

I only wish my father had lived long enough to see the book and appreciate his influence on it. The values that were planted at home were further nurtured by teachers and clergy who continued my education, often without knowing it. My wife Robin and my daughters, Dara and Jaina, shared my life (and word processor) during the writing of the book, alternately helping me to keep going and distracting me from the task with various pleasant alternatives. The book was completed, on schedule, while Robin was writing a book of her own, one child was beginning school, and the other was teething. That should convince even the most skeptical person that supernatural forces work in the universe.

K.D.W.

REFERENCES

Hallowell, John H. 1951. *Religious Perspectives of College Teaching in Political Science.* New Haven, CT: Edward W. Hazen Foundation.

National Research Council. 1982. *Diet, Nutrition, and Cancer.* Washington, DC: National Academy Press.

Strout, Cushing. 1974. *The New Heavens and the New Earth.* New York: Harper and Row.

Religion
and Politics
in the
United States

1

A Secular Society?

When you introduce religion into politics, you're playing with fire.
Senator Lowell P. Weicker, Jr.

Religion and politics are necessarily related.
President Ronald Reagan

People are usually taught that it is impolite to argue religion or politics with strangers and dangerous to do so with friends. These topics are treated with such delicacy because they evoke strong passions; men and women have been known to discuss, debate, argue, organize, demonstrate, resist, fight, and kill—or be killed—on behalf of religious or political beliefs. What, then, could possibly justify an author's violating both taboos by writing a book about religion *and* politics?

The answer is simple: religion has become an extremely important factor in contemporary political life. The increasing religious overtones in recent presidential campaigns are one clear sign of the trend. The election of a Roman Catholic to the presidency in 1960 persuaded some observers that the electorate no longer cared about the religious affiliation of presidential candidates. But in 1976, candidate Jimmy Carter's strong profession of religious faith drew close attention from a national media and an electorate largely unfamiliar with the phenomenon of "born-again" or evangelical Christianity. Four years later, all three candidates on the presidential ballot were evangelical Protestants, and several ministers with large television audiences drew national headlines for their organized efforts on behalf of the Republican nominee. In 1984, many conservative Protestant ministers drummed up support for Ronald Reagan, and the Democrats chose among three major contenders with strong religious credentials: an ordained Baptist minister (Jesse Jackson), a former divinity student (Gary Hart), and the son of a Methodist minister (Walter

All biblical citations are from the King James Version as edited by Roy B. Chamberlin and Herman Feldman under the title *The Dartmouth Bible* (Boston: Houghton Mifflin, 1961).

Mondale). And in 1986, a prominent television minister declared a strong interest in seeking the 1988 Republican nomination. In the nation's single most important political ritual, the selection of a president, the religious emphasis has been plain.

In recent years, moreover, the national political agenda has included a host of controversial questions that touch upon deeply held religious beliefs and outlooks—issues such as abortion, women's role in society, pornography, homosexuality, and the arms race. Contemporary controversies over prayer in public schools and government recognition of religious holidays exemplify the continuing debate over church-state relations. Even economic policy questions, which traditionally were deemed beyond the sphere of religious concern, increasingly have been looked at from a "moral" perspective. During 1985, for example, the official body representing Roman Catholic bishops in the United States released a searching theological critique of the U.S. economy, and the Reagan administration proposed changes in tax laws that, it was claimed, would strengthen the biblically ordained institution of the family.

The growth of religious controversy around the globe has also reverberated in American political life. In response to a powerful resurgence of Islamic fundamentalism, the United States has attempted to play peacekeeper in Lebanon, has been held hostage in Iran, and has supplied weapons to Moslem rebels in Afghanistan. During the 1980s, revolts by religious minorities have threatened various governments friendly to the United States, raising the possibility of U.S. diplomatic or military intervention. United States government support for anticommunist governments and movements in Latin America has roused opposition from some religious leaders concerned about human rights abuses by American allies and support by other churchmen in the name of anticommunism. Some churches have pressed the government to negotiate reductions in nuclear weapons, to admit more political refugees from Central America, and to cut economic ties with the government of South Africa.

On the basis of this evidence, a strong case can be made for studying the impact of religion on national political life. We may applaud it, deplore it, be repelled or fascinated by it—but the first imperative is to understand how and why religion has become such an important factor in American politics. Despite the evidence, scholars and citizens alike have been slow to recognize the political impact of religion in the United States. The underestimation stems in large part from a mistaken belief in the "inevitable" secularization of modern life. As the next section shows, the widespread belief that religion will recede from the mind of humanity has prompted observers to discount religious influences in the political realm.

THE PUZZLE OF RELIGIOUS VITALITY

A recent survey of social studies textbooks concluded what many observers have long suspected; namely, that in studies of the American experience, religion has not received the attention it deserves (Vitz 1985). Scholars may have underestimated the religious dimension in American life because they were personally untouched by religious sentiment or preferred a society in which religion played a smaller role. For the most part, however, the deemphasis on religion stemmed from widespread acceptance of social theories that predict the virtual extinction of religious forces in modern life (Warner 1979). The novelist who wrote that "a man's eyes can only see what they're learnt to see" understood well that expectations can become blinders, prompting us to overlook important information and developments. The persistence of religion in American society may have gone unappreciated precisely because it violated widely held expectations.

The contemporary strength of religion, let alone its powerful impact on political life, runs counter to the two most influential theories of social change—the *modernization* approach, associated principally with the sociologists Emile Durkheim, Max Weber, and Talcott Parsons; and the *class conflict* model developed by Karl Marx and Friedrich Engels. Influenced by these two approaches, scholars "learnt to see" the decline of religion as a significant force in advanced societies; consequently, they expected the decline of religious controversies in politics. The influence of these theories has not been limited to scholars; when a *Time* magazine cover story of several years ago posed the stark question "Is God Dead?" it showed how the ideas about religion circulating among intellectuals had filtered into public awareness.

The modernization approach predicts transformations in life and thought because of the rapid growth of cities; the rise of factory production; the spread of education, communication, and technology; and the emergence of vast administrative apparatuses, or bureaucracies. Sociological observers of the late nineteenth and early twentieth centuries believed that these developments, which define our concept of "modern," had wrought massive changes in the place of religion in society. Before the onset of the modernization process, most people lived in small, geographically isolated settlements and were preoccupied by the daily task of producing life's necessities. Interacting almost exclusively with other members of their close-knit communities, the people of these settlements were enmeshed in a network of shared beliefs, customs, and traditions. These primitive conditions may conjure up images of a Stone Age pygmy tribe in a rain forest, but the portrait would be just as appropriate for the Irish villages, Norwegian communes, and East European *shtetls* whose migrants eventually populated much of the United States.

Dependent for survival upon forces beyond their control or understanding—natural forces like weather and disease, human forces such as war and political repression—people in premodern settlements attributed great power to supernatural forces. The myths and folk religions of primitive cultures are commonly thought to have originated in fear of the unknown, in dread and awe (Goodenough 1972). According to moderization theory the forces of modernity have acted to shatter such cultures. Migration to a city in search of work removes the villagers from traditional influences and brings them into regular contact with persons from different backgrounds. The values of the village, particularly the emphasis upon fate and the supernatural, are undermined by what the uprooted learn about scientific cause and effect in school, in the factory, and through the mass media (Inkeles 1983).

Modernization theory holds, further, that contact with modern institutions inevitably erodes traditional religious sentiments. Modernization is built upon the notion that people can understand nature and master it through science and technology. The "demystification" of the natural world—the sense that people rather then unseen gods shape human destiny—undermines belief in the supernatural. When held up to scientific standards of proof and evidence, religious claims and, therefore, religious faith may falter. In primitive societies, moreover, relations between people are governed largely by custom and tradition. Divinely inspired rules prescribe deference, obedience, and obligation, depending upon one's inherited social standing. But under the impact of modernism, exchange, bargaining, and negotiation become the accepted mode of human interaction, with law and reason—not religion—determining the framework. Loyalty is given not out of reverence but as repayment for services rendered. As a consequence, people come to define their personal identities and political interests not in terms of religion but as a function of their standing in the marketplace—as owners, workers, small businessmen, and so forth.

According to the predictions of modernization theory, societies that have been fully exposed to the currents of modern life will accord religion a minor role (Halebsky 1976, chaps. 1–4). Except among the elderly, raised in a more devout age, and the residents of cultural backwaters, the *practice* of religion will diminish. The *institutions* of religion will suffer a similar fate unless they are transformed into agencies of social welfare and service centers—and even then churches must compete with the state to perform these tasks. An even more telling sign of religious decay, as Bryan Wilson (1966, 10) stressed, is the erosion of religious *thought:*

> Men act less and less in response to religious motivation: they assess the
> world in empirical and rational terms, and find themselves involved in
> rational organizations and rationally determined roles which allow small

scope for such religious predilections as they might privately entertain. Even if . . . non-logical behaviour continues in unabated measure in human society, then at least the terms of non-rationality have changed. It is no longer the dogmas of the Christian Church which dictate behaviour, but other quite irrational and arbitrary assumptions about life, society and the laws which govern the physical universe.

This change in the terms of thought, from a God-centered to a human-centered world, may be less apparent than the withering of worship and churches; but to modernization theorists such as Wilson, it is the great testament to the victory of secularization in the modern world.

The forecast of religious decline in the modern world has been reinforced by another influential theory of social change—Marxism. For Marx and Engels, no less than for modernization theorists, religious sentiments reflected a human response to forces that defy understanding, and belief in the supernatural was likely to be a casualty of economic development (Aptheker 1968; Bonino 1976, chap. 3; Vree, 1976, chap. 4). Though the sociological model first outlined by Marx and Engels differs considerably from that of modernization theorists, both theories forecast the decay of religion as a social force and its removal from politics.

Writing in the middle of the nineteenth century, Marx began his analysis with the paradox that the human conquest of nature, which ought to have put an end to hunger and oppression, seemed instead to have intensified inequality. The sources of wealth, differing from one era to the next, had always been monopolized by and used to enrich the few at the expense of the many. But with the coming of industrialization and factory-based economies, he argued, the process of exploitation became more severe. Once subordinate to the forces of nature, workers now found themselves subordinate to economic elites. Unemployment replaced natural calamity as the scourge of human existence.

In this setting, Marx suggested, religion appealed most strongly to those who are most oppressed and most in need of an explanation for their plight. Christianity found its pioneers among slave populations because it promised them the solace of a better life to come; psychologically, the Christian religion was a balm, an alternative to despair. Subsequently, the growth of Christianity was encouraged by the dominant groups in society because it might teach the "lower orders"—be they slaves, serfs, or industrial workers—to accept their condition as God's will and to look for solace in the afterlife. In this way, Marx argued in a famous passage, religion became the "opiate" of the people.

In Marx's view, a society built upon exploitation could not long endure, because the oppressed majority would eventually recognize the nature of its exploitation. As conditions worsened, the working class would realize the inequity of prevailing economic arrangements and their source in man-made doctrines and practices. When this occurred, Marx expected an uprising, the seizure of power on behalf of the previously oppressed majority and the creation of a more just and humane social order. In this new world, the mass of humankind would reclaim its proper place as the maker of its own destiny and all the artificial doctrines developed to support the dethroned system—including religion—would be consigned to the dustbin of history. Religion, which had persisted because of intolerable social conditions, would simply evaporate with these social transformations.

Marx's argument that religion must lose influence in economically advanced societies has been tremendously influential, even among non-Marxists. Bolstered by social theories that confidently forecast the demise of religion, many students of politics have predicted that religious controversy will eventually disappear from the political agenda, as conflicts over religious questions are replaced by disputes rooted in economics and the basis of political loyalty shifts from "premodern" factors such as religion, ethnicity, and region to more modern factors like social class, occupational standing, and socioeconomic status (Epstein 1967, 88; Hechter 1975). What most political observers never expected to find was an advanced industrial society in which religion would exercise a tenacious hold upon the public mind and strongly influence the conduct of political life.

THE SURPRISING PERSISTENCE OF RELIGION

By most conventional yardsticks, the United States was one of the first nations to achieve modernization, and it continues to lead the way in many aspects of social development. If modernization leads inevitably to secularization—to the decline of religious institutions, practices, and feelings—then the erosion of religion ought to show up first in such a mobile, affluent, urban, and industrialized society as that of the United States. Yet American religion, like Mark Twain, has obstinately refused to go along with reports of its imminent death.

Just how poorly the modernization and Marxist theories of religion fit the United States is demonstrated graphically in Figure 1.1, which reflects information from fifteen different countries. The diagonal line in Figure 1.1 shows the relationship between level of economic development and the proportion of a representative national sample who told interviewers that religious beliefs were "very important" to them.[1] The downward slope of the line as the level of "modernization" increases generally confirms the prediction that economic development goes hand in hand with a decline in religious sentiment. The United States, however, is a conspicuous exception to the generalization. This country, with by far the highest score on the index of economic development, was also the most "religious" of countries as shown by the answers its citizens gave to the

Figure 1.1 The Relationship Between Economic Development and Religious Beliefs

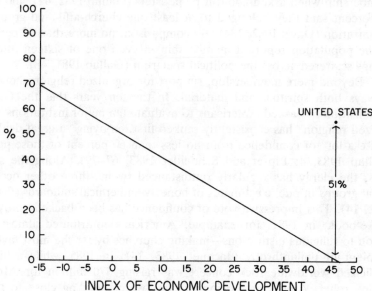

interviewers. The magnitude of American "exceptionalism" can best be gauged by comparing the proportion of Americans who actually assigned great importance to religious belief—51 percent—with the proportion that should have done so on the basis of the pattern in other countries—a mere 5 percent.

By all the normal indicators of religious commitment—the strength of religious institutions, practices, and belief—the United States has resisted the pressures toward secularity. Institutionally, churches are probably the most vital voluntary organizations in a country that puts a premium on "joining up." A 1980 tabulation by the National Council of Churches listed approximately 340,000 churches in the United States with a total membership of about 135 million (Jacquet 1983, 238). Denominational differences in the meaning of "membership" make it impossible to come up with precise proportions, but the 135 million church members amount to somewhere between 60 and 75 percent of all Americans old enough to join. Despite all the talk about decline, the proportion of church members among persons aged fifteen and older is virtually the same today (76.9 percent) as it was in 1950 (78.5 percent) and, with due allowance for the raggedness of historical data, seems to be higher now than in 1890, when the first official census of churches was undertaken.[2]

Sample surveys, the modern barometers of public opinion, also have revealed a population strongly attached to institutional religion. In the early 1980s, just under 70 percent of the adult population claimed church membership when asked about it by pollsters (Gallup 1982, 41), and over 30 percent said they belonged to at least one church-affiliated group or organization (Davis 1982, 134). By comparison, no more than 13 percent of the population reported membership in even one of sixteen interest groups scattered across the political spectrum (Gallup 1981, 48).

Beyond mere membership, support for organized religion shows up in ways both spiritual and material. In the ten years that the Gallup organization has asked Americans to evaluate ten major institutions, "organized religion" has consistently ranked first, enjoying "a great deal" or "quite a lot" of confidence from no less than 60 percent of those polled (Gallup 1983, 4; Lipset and Schneider 1983, 67–79). Along the same lines, the clergy has regularly outdistanced twenty-three other occupational groups in public estimates of honesty and ethical standards (Gallup 1982, 14). This impressive vote of confidence has been backed up by the pocketbook: in 1981, for example, Americans contributed almost $25 billion to religious institutions—making churches by far the most favored recipient of philanthropy (Jacquet 1983, 14). In 1985, while a highly publicized worldwide rock concert was raising $70 million for African famine relief, American religious groups were spending close to three times that sum in the same effort (Capuzzo 1985).

Surveys of church practice—another presumed casualty of the modern age—have shown an equally high level of attachment to religion. What anthropologists call rites of passage—formal celebrations of an individual's progress through life, such as naming ceremonies, attainment of adulthood, marriages, and funerals—are still monopolized by the churches in the United States, as they are in many other cultures. But as a recent national survey revealed, devotion is hardly limited to such occasions. The people surveyed were presented with a list of religious activities and asked how often they practiced each one (Research and Forecasts 1981, 42). Even the least common of the activities listed—encouraging other people to turn to religion—was performed frequently or occasionally by more than half the respondents. More than three-quarters claimed to read the Bible, pray, and attend worship services on at least an occasional basis.

It is instructive to compare these figures with those measuring individual participation in the country's great secular rite of passage—the presidential election. Figure 1.2 pairs particular forms of religious practice with equivalent acts in the 1980 presidential election campaign.[3] It may seem debatable to link, say, attendance at church with voting in a presidential primary or those who pray frequently with those who claim to follow public affairs "most of the time." Yet the particular pairings do not matter very much, for only five out of eleven political acts are performed as frequently as the least common religious activity. Any remain-

Figure 1.2 Religious and Political Participation in the United States

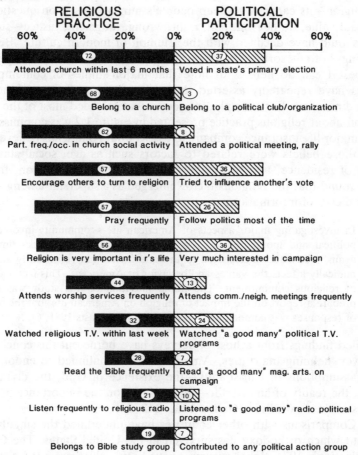

RELIGIOUS PRACTICE — POLITICAL PARTICIPATION

Religious Practice	%	%	Political Participation
Attended church within last 6 months	72	37	Voted in state's primary election
Belong to a church	68	3	Belong to a political club/organization
Part. freq./occ. in church social activity	62	8	Attended a political meeting, rally
Encourage others to turn to religion	57	36	Tried to influence another's vote
Pray frequently	57	26	Follow politics most of the time
Religion is very important in r's life	56	36	Very much interested in campaign
Attends worship services frequently	44	13	Attends comm./neigh. meetings frequently
Watched religious T.V. within last week	32	24	Watched "a good many" political T.V. programs
Read the Bible frequently	28	7	Read "a good many" mag. arts. on campaign
Listen frequently to religious radio	21	10	Listened to "a good many" radio political programs
Belongs to Bible study group	19	7	Contributed to any political action group

ing doubts about the extent of religious practice in the United States can be put to rest by two comparisons not presented in Figure 1.2. The proportion of Americans claiming to speak in tongues, a fairly exotic form of religious activity practiced by about 4 percent of the adult population, exceeded the proportion who worked for a party or candidate in 1980 and came within a percentage point of the share of the population who used the federal income tax form to steer $1 to the presidential campaign fund (Gallup 1982, 110; Miller 1982, 479–80). At the other end of the scale, the recorded level of church membership among *all* Americans apparently has been greater than the turnout among voting-age Americans in all postwar presidential elections (Asher 1984, 33).

If the continuing vitality of religious institutions and practices in

American society is easy enough to demonstrate, it is much more challenging to prove the persistence of religious feeling. Precisely that aspect
of religion—its capacity to keep people's minds focused on questions of
ultimate value, on heaven, hell, right, wrong, judgment, justice—supposedly should have declined with the triumph of modern culture. Because
"feelings" of any sort are notoriously slippery things to measure, perhaps
the best I can do here is to note that major studies of contemporary
values have repeatedly asserted the underlying importance of the religious dimension. For example, the report that provided most of the information about religious practice presented in Figure 1.2 was commissioned
by a major life insurance company to assess what Americans believed and
how those beliefs were related to factors such as age, social standing,
place of residence, and so on. Despite this secular orientation, the authors found that the religious factor emerged as a superstar among all the
other pieces of information:

> In investigating major aspects of American life—community involvement,
> political and moral beliefs, personal relationships, and work—time and
> again, systematic analysis led to the one factor that consistently and dra-
> matically affects the values and behavior of Americans. This factor is level
> of religious commitment. The initial intention of this study was not to
> prepare a report on the impact of religion on American life, but the pattern
> of responses was compelling. (Research and Forecasts 1981, 6).

Detailed findings from a host of surveys have borne out this conclusion.
By overwhelming majorities, Americans have continued to endorse the
core assumptions of Christianity—the existence of God, the divinity of
Jesus, the reality of an afterlife—and to insist on the importance of these
values in their own lives (Gallup 1982, 112–27).

Comparisons with other countries have underlined the singular degree to which orthodoxy has survived in the United States. The Gallup
organization's 1974 global surveys about basic values provided a benchmark for this kind of comparison. When asked about belief in an afterlife
and belief in a deity who keeps a watchful eye on the world, Americans
stood out from people in other advanced societies by their tenacious
commitment to the supernatural (Hastings and Hastings 1979, 333). Just
under 70 percent of Americans surveyed said they believed in life after
death—a proportion of believers greater than that in Europe, Latin
America, and the English-speaking world, and equal to that in the Far
East and sub-Saharan Africa. And as for the concept of an active God,
more than two-thirds of the Americans polled endorsed such a belief,
making the United States closer to the Third World than to societies that
it resembles economically. Subsequent investigation of the content of
these beliefs about God and an afterlife has underscored the continued
strength of traditional religion in American society (Davis 1984, 114–26).

When Americans think about God, they conceive of a creator and healer; the image of heaven carried in the minds of modern Americans depicts a place of union with God and reunion with loved ones.

To the extent that such things can be measured, religious feeling, like religious institutions and practices, has survived intact in probably the most "modern" society in history. Statistics must be used to make the point because numbers are the currency of argument in a scientific culture. But because national statistics often have a numbing effect, they should be supplemented with a local example. The stability of a religious texture to American life has been demonstrated forcefully by a continuing study of one American community, a small industrial town in eastern Indiana. In the 1920s and 1930s, a pair of gifted social observers decided to put Muncie, a typical town they called "Middletown," under the microscope of social analysis (Lynd and Lynd 1929, 1937). Curious about the changes wrought by the passage of fifty years, a team of social scientists set out in the 1970s to repeat the study of Muncie (Caplow et al. 1983). In the half century since the first study, Muncie had experienced all the changes that are supposed to encourage secularization—rapid population growth, relentless technological advance, the spread of education, increasing bureaucracy, the penetration of mass media, an expanded governmental presence. Could the vibrant religious tradition of the town possibly have survived the corrosive effects of these changes?

Despite the odds against it, traditional religion was found to be doing quite nicely in modern Muncie. In the words of the most recent study of the town, "The Reverend Rip Van Winkle, Methodist minister, awakening in Middletown after a 60-year sleep, would hardly know he had been away" (Caplow et al. 1983, 280). He might be surprised by the growth of tolerance among religious groups, but little else had changed since the 1920s. The Middletown residents of the 1970s seemed every bit as pious as their grandparents and great-grandparents. Most people still subscribed to the core beliefs of Christian theology and, whether measured by the numbers of clergy and buildings, by financial contributions, or by attendance at worship, the churches still flourished. But surely, it may be argued, the survival of religion was purchased at a high price—by sacrificing the traditional emphasis on the emotional and spiritual for a more modern style that stresses reason and social reform. This is certainly a plausible suggestion, but it collapses under the evidence of growth in the most theologically conservative churches, a renewed emphasis on emotional forms of worship in all denominations, and the continuing priority placed by the clergy on the spiritual well-being of their flocks. Against all expectations, the most recent study of Muncie uncovered a community with reverence for the sacred and faith in religion as a source of strength and guidance. As the case of Muncie illustrates so well, there can be little doubt about the durability of religion in the United States.

In trying to counter the widespread myth that religion is dead or declining in the United States, I have set out the arguments for persistence in the starkest possible way. By making the case so emphatically, I do not want to suggest that American religion is altogether immune to the forces of modernity. The appeal of the "old-time" religion remains strongest among certain population groups—housewives, the elderly, inhabitants of rural areas and small towns, Southerners, persons with low levels of education—that share limited exposure to such major institutions of modernization as the marketplace, cities, industry, and schools. People who are deeply embedded in those institutions are less likely to maintain a commitment to religious orthodoxy. It is also true that religion has adapted to modern thought by recasting God. In the vision of some religious authorities, God now appears not only as the almighty power of the universe and source of redemption, but also as a psychologist, economic adviser, athletic trainer, and friend (Hunter 1983, chaps. 4, 6).

It is one thing to acknowledge these changes, but quite another to overinterpret them as signs of the imminent extinction of religious sentiment in American life. The greater appeal of traditional religion to persons on the margins of modernity—probably the rule in American history—is a matter of degree rather than of kind. Although the form of worship may differ from what is common in the periphery, religion retains impressive strength at the center. Similarly, the recasting of God to meet modern needs and anxieties is hardly a new development. Throughout history, religion has frequently been called upon to answer human needs in areas that seem far removed from the traditional concerns of theology. Religion has certainly been influenced by the modern world, but it is more accurate to view secularization as adjustment and adaptation than to employ the image of decline and fall.

POSSIBLE EXPLANATIONS
FOR THE VITALITY OF RELIGION

Apparently, religion has not disappeared from that most "developed" of societies, the United States. Where did modernization theorists and Marxists go wrong in predicting that it would? Both types of social theory appear to have underestimated both the need for religion, even in the most advanced societies, and the capacity of American religious institutions to adapt to changing circumstances.

For an increasing number of students of religion, the durability of beliefs about the supernatural stems from basic human needs (Bell 1977; Greeley 1972; Greeley and Baum 1973; Prozesky 1984). Alone among creatures, human beings possess the capacity to think in a sophisticated way, and this to wonder about themselves and their place in the universe. They wonder particularly about the meaning of life, the reality of death, the basis of ethical behavior and human cooperation. They ask, among other questions, why some people commit evil; why the good and innocent should suffer from it; and how, apart from instinct, they can even think to know what is good and what is evil. To answer these questions about life—to give meaning to human existence—humans develop systems of belief that include religion. So long as the world requires some explanation, it is argued, human beings will create faiths to live by. In this view, the durability of religion is rooted in human nature itself.

Nothing about this notion would bother most modernization theorists or Marxists. They would argue, merely, that the need for a system of meaning will eventually be satisfied fully by science or by a comprehensive body of political ideas, at which point religion will become unnecessary.

The experience of the modern world suggests, however, that science and ideology need not inevitably displace religious belief. Unquestionably, science has reduced the human misery that was supposed to encourage religious belief. In practice, however, liberation from want seems to have encouraged humanity to think more intently about questions of ultimate value. People who have been freed from the threat of economic insecurity are likely to have the time, leisure, and inclination to ask questions about spirituality. To put it rather crudely, the issue of justice and the meaning of life are most likely to interest persons (and societies) with full stomachs. As basic material needs are fulfilled, societies increasingly turn their attention to questions of values in which religion is accorded an important role (Inglehart 1971).

The decline of religion has also been predicted on the assumption that when human beings understood nature, they would not need religion. This assumption seems questionable, because there are some questions about life on this planet that no scientific advance can ever settle. It is hard to see how familiarity with, for example, the third law of thermodynamics can ever comfort troubled people or improve upon religious faith in enabling them to cope with the inevitability of mortality.[4] Science is simply irrelevant to such questions. In other cases, the progress of science may reinforce concern for spirituality. The more Albert Einstein learned about the beauty and symmetry of nature, the more he appreciated what he saw as God's hidden hand—and he has not been the only scientist to be so moved (Tracy 1973). Finally, in certain cases science may actually intensify concern about questions of value. The spectacular growth of medical technology has raised agonizing moral dilemmas about the nature and conditions of life, dilemmas that appear on the political agenda in the form of issues such as abortion, euthanasia, organ transplantation, in vitro fertilization, genetic engineering, embryo experimen-

tation, life extension, and "living wills." Progress in weapons development has underlined dramatically the problem of human evil and the
need for human cooperation.

In advanced technological societies, paradoxically, there has been a
striking loss of faith in reason as a solution to all human problems. Consider this assessment of the current mood:

> These are gloomy times. People are fatalistic and death possessed. There is
> a conviction that we have been collectively asleep at the wheel, that the
> path of so-called reason has taken us far along the road to hell, probably
> past the point of no return. More and more, the feeling is taking hold that
> we are on the edge of a volcano that is about to explode. (Frankel 1984,
> 162)

This comment, all the more remarkable because it comes from the pen
(or word processor?) of a man described as "a business consultant who
specializes in information and telecommunications technologies," illustrates how a society built upon science may generate profound discontent
with the consequences of scientific activity. For some people, the reaction
to a technological society apparently run amuck is a return to spirituality,
a greater respect for the religious values that science once seemed to
render unnecessary. Odd as it may seem, science has restored questions
of value to the center of public concern. In so doing, it has prompted a
renewed interest in the religious traditions that speak to questions about
right and wrong.

If not science, will politics perhaps substitute for religious faith? The
quest for justice through political movements may well take on the form
of a religious crusade. But in the end, when political movements have
triumphed, the perennial problems remain, and the perennial solutions,
including religion, offer themselves. This cycle of disillusionment has
been illustrated most clearly by the saga of Marxism.

As a political movement, Marxism is one of the great success stories
of the twentieth century. What began as the doctrine of an obscure German writer has captured the imagination of many intellectuals and the
apparatus of power over a sizable part of the globe. Where Marxism has
been harnessed to the unlimited power of government, it has brought
about remarkable social transformations, often at a terrible price and
usually accompanied by systematic efforts to banish religious thought
from the minds of the people. Yet within such societies, the abuses and
inadequacies of the system have prompted some of the most devoted
Marxists to wonder anew about human nature and even to look at traditional religious dogma as a source of explanation (Machovec 1976).
Among ordinary people, as the case of Poland so vividly illustrates,
Marxism sometimes proves to be no match for the power of religious
orthodoxy (Pomian-Srzednicki 1982; Szajkowski 1983).

In the United States, too, political faith has not yet managed to supplant religious commitment. Whereas some political activists discard their religious faith as an impediment to achieving social change, others see no conflict between the two spheres and no necessity to choose between them. When religious and political loyalties do appear to collide, the choice may actually favor the former. During the turbulent political era of the late 1960s and early 1970s, the extremes of the American political spectrum were symbolized by two divergent public figures: Eldridge Cleaver, the eloquent and angry spokesman for black nationalism; and a conservative political operative named Charles Colson, who once said that he would have sacrificed his own grandmother to gain political advantage. In the 1980s, disillusioned with the consequences of their political activism, these two firebrands have shared public platforms to preach for a return to biblical Christianity. With less publicity, other intellectuals have traveled the same path from political activism to religious commitment (Schumer 1984). A few conversions may not indicate a social trend, but they do dramatize how politics may prove to be an ineffective alternative to religion.

WHY THE UNITED STATES?

The inadequacy of science and political ideology is only part of the explanation for the persistence of religion in the United States. Theories about intrinsic human needs and failed alternatives are global concepts that cannot fully explain why the United States, in particular, has remained so much more deeply tied to religion than have societies with even less exposure to modern currents.

According to some theorists, the persistence of religion in the United States can be related to the remarkable diversity of denominations in the country (Salisbury 1983). Whereas most countries are dominated by a single religious group that may well receive financial support from the state, the American religious pattern has been accurately described as pluralist. The early settlers subscribed to a variety of faiths, and Americans have since taken advantage of the freedom of religion to found literally hundreds of new sects (Marty 1984). The diversity among the early settlers was compounded by the importation of new faiths through the global population migration to America. As a result of this heterogeneity of outlook, no single denomination today comprises more than about 40 percent of the church membership (Quinn et al. 1982, 1–3); thus, it is correct to say that all Americans belong to minority religions. What is true of the nation as a whole also holds at the local level. According to a recent study, nearly half the U.S. population resides in counties in which no single denomination has majority status (Salisbury et al. 1984).

The multiplicity of denominations in the United States has had important ramifications on the persistence of religious attachment in the face of modernization. Pluralism has forced the churches to compete for members and so has encouraged them to adapt to new social realities. To an extent possibly unparalleled in the modern world, the American citizen is confronted with a range of denominational options. Protestants, who make up a majority of religious adherents in the United States, have had and continue to enjoy a particularly wide choice among numerous denominations offering what seem like slight variations on a common theology. Given the availability of alternatives, the churches, in order to survive, must compete for followers. In religion, as in politics and economics, competition has stimulated the participants to bid for support with all manner of incentives.

Adaptation to a competitive situation has taken many forms. Denominations have had to master the latest techniques in persuasion and recruitment as they reach out to potential "consumers"—hence the churches' use of sophisticated means of communication, marketing skills, and information technologies. The emphasis on attracting members from the religious marketplace has also prompted the churches to offer attractive benefit packages and services that in other countries might be provided by government.[5] As part of this effort to embrace a wider community, the churches have also struggled to become compatible with dominant social values. Far from standing apart from society or condemning it, American churches for the most part have labored to integrate themselves into the American way of life (Herberg 1960). As noted above, even the message of religion has been tailored to modern times, through an emphasis on the relevance of religion to worldly pursuits as diverse as sports, the stock market, and mental health.

In countries lacking religious diversity, churches may well remain attached to symbols, rituals, and patterns of behavior that cannot withstand the social forces that promote secularity. Not having the luxury of a monopoly, the American churches have deliberately attempted to adapt to social realities and, in the process, have cultivated skills and qualities that almost certainly have contributed to the persistence of religious attachment. (Whether they can make these adjustments without sacrificing the core of belief is an important issue beyond the scope of this book.)

A second way pluralism promotes religious vitality is by emphasizing the American tradition of governmental neutrality toward denominations. Paradoxically, the "wall of separation" between church and state may have served not only to free the political system from dangerous religious conflict, but also to strengthen the churches. A church or religion that is closely associated with a worldly power runs the risk of suffering from guilt by association if the regime turns repressive or promotes injustice. Conversely, a church that is insulated from government may thrive by avoiding entanglement with an unpopular government.

Marx had expected religion to collapse when the workers recognized it as a prop of capitalism that justified exploitation as God's will and conveniently postponed justice until the next life. But American religion has not always served the purpose of the dominant economic powers. Slaveowners found support for servitude in the Bible, but the slaves could and did read the Old Testament as a call to resistance and revolt. The religious impulse that could be used to justify the worst abuses of capitalism could also fuel movements against the oppression of industrial workers. Even today, when many Roman Catholics have joined the ranks of the wealthy and powerful, their church continues to speak out against poverty and to remind Americans about the plight of the oppressed.

Unlike the churches in many other societies, those in the United States appear to have avoided an exclusive association with any particular political affiliation. This conclusion has been supported by a study of public opinion in eight Western European societies. In several countries in which a particular religion enjoyed the support of the state, surveys revealed moderately strong statistical associations between the religiosity of individuals and their self-professed political beliefs as measured on a left-versus-right continuum (McDonough, Barnes, and Pina 1984, 661–63). Political conflict in those societies was fairly strongly defined by a "secular" left wing confronting a "religious" right. In the United States, by contrast, a much weaker relationship was found between a person's personal religious attachment and self-described ideological position. By remaining apart, reserving the right to pass judgment, American religion has avoided becoming an adjunct of the political system and so can remain unscathed when the political system itself is in disrepute. The high regard for churches in the United States also may owe something to their avoidance of too close an identification with any political party or administration—although that positive image may be threatened by the growing political activism of churches.

*   *   *   *   *

I have gone to such lengths to stress the staying power of religion for a reason. Religious conflicts in politics are commonly treated as a throwback, an interesting diversion from the "real" issues of the modern era. But if religion remains a vital force in this day and age, then one cannot claim to understand the contemporary era without appreciating the religious factor—especially in terms of politics, a realm in which the persistence of religion may have significant implications. The remainder of the book delineates the many ways religion intersects political life in the United States.

NOTES

[1]Figure 1.1 is an ordinary least-squares regression equation using data from fifteen countries: Canada, Britain, France, West Germany, Italy, Brazil, Mexico, India, Japan, Australia, Holland, Belgium, Finland, Norway, and Denmark. The independent variable was Cole's (1979, 209–10) economic development index compiled on the basis of twenty-two separate statistics. The dependent variable, the proportion of the national sample who described their religious beliefs as "very important," was obtained from Hastings and Hastings (1979, 333). The aggregate values Gallup reported for Scandinavia and the Benelux nations were assigned to the individual countries. Because of different assumptions and the inclusion of Canada, regression results diverge somewhat from Burnham's (1981, 135) findings.

[2]For a summary of church membership over the years, see Jacquet (1983, 242), but note that the entry for 1890 should be 21.7 rather than the 41.7 million printed erroneously. The denominator—the number of persons aged 15 and older—was calculated from data supplied by the U.S. Bureau of the Census (1960, 71–73; 1950, xx; 1981, 26).

[3]The data on religious practice in Figure 1.2 are from Gallup (1982) and the Connecticut Mutual study (Research and Forecasts 1981). All political participation items except for attendance at community meetings, which came from the Connecticut Mutual survey, were calculated from data in Miller (1982). These questions were posed to a cross-section of Americans in November and December 1980.

[4]For a fascinating account of how religious values may fill a void where science appears to fail, see duBarlay's (1984) study of a British hospice. A journalist reported of the hospice, "Religion plays a central part in the life of St. Christopher's. It is not compulsory, nor is it thrust upon patients. 'But I don't think any could work here for long without the support of some faith,' she [the founder] says firmly. The pressure and intensity of the work, the great demands of the dying and their relatives means that those who work there need answers, or at least partial answers in order to sustain themselves" (Toynbee 1984).

[5]My local newspaper recently printed a story that illustrates how the churches may outperform secular authorities. After a storm blew a tree onto an elderly woman's property, cutting off the electricity, she contacted the local utility to restore service. Because the damage occurred on private property and to equipment that was legally the responsibility of the woman, the company had no authority to fix the problem. Over the course of the next day and a half, the woman's problem was brought to the attention of a dispatcher for the utility company, a representative from the Older Americans Council, several officials from the local office of the responsible state agency, a citizen advocate, and her church. By the time the public officials had begun to investigate the situation, the

church had sent over volunteers to repair the damage and to look after the woman until family members could arrive to help. Theologians used to refer to a "God of the gaps," a deity that was invoked when other resources had failed; this example illustrates how a "church of the gaps" can fill in the cracks where secular authorities fail (Knight 1984).

REFERENCES

Aptheker, Herbert, editor. 1968. *Marxism and Christianity*. New York: Humanities Press.

Asher, Herbert. 1984. *Presidential Elections and American Politics*. Third edition. Homewood, IL: Dorsey Press.

Bell, Daniel. 1977. "Return of the Sacred? Argument on the Future of Religion." *British Journal of Sociology*. 28: 419–449.

Bonino, Jose Miguez. 1976. *Christians and Marxists: The Mutual Challenge to Revolution*. Grand Rapids, MI: William B. Eerdman's

Burnham, Walter Dean. 1981. "The 1980 Earthquake." In *The Hidden Election*, ed. Thomas Ferguson and Joel Rogers. New York: Pantheon, 98–140.

Caplow, Theodore, Howard M. Bahr, Bruce A. Chadwick, and associates. 1983. *All Faithful People: Change and Continuity in Middletown's Religion*. Minneapolis, MN: University of Minnesota Press.

Capuzzo, Michael. 1985. "Churches Act in Concert for African Aid." *Miami Herald*. July 26: 1C, 5C.

Cole, J. P. 1979. *Geography of World Affairs*. Fifth edition. Harmondsworth, Middlesex, England: Penguin Books.

Davis, James A. 1984. *General Social Surveys, 1972–1984: Cumulative Codebook*. Chicago, IL: National Opinion Research Center, University of Chicago.

Davis, James A. 1982. *General Social Surveys, 1972–1982: Cumulative Codebook*. Chicago, IL: National Opinion Research Center, University of Chicago.

duBarlay, Shirley. 1984. *Ciceley Saunders*. London: Hodder and Stoughton.

Epstein, Leon D. 1967. *Political Parties in Western Democracies*. New York: Praeger.

Frankel, Carl. 1984. "A Legacy." *American Scholar*. 52:159–166.

Gallup Organization. 1983. "Confidence in Institutions." *The Gallup Report*. #217: 3–14.

Gallup Organization. 1982. "Religion in America." *The Gallup Report*. #201–202.

Gallup Organization. 1981. "Special Interest Groups." *The Gallup Report*. #191: 45–55.

Goodenough, Erwin R. 1972. "Religion as Man's Adjustment to the Tremendum." In *Ways of Understanding Religion*, ed. Walter H. Capps. New York: Macmillan, 45–48.

Greeley, Andrew. 1972. *Unsecular Man: The Persistence of Religion*. New York: Schocken Books.

Greeley, Andrew, and Gregory Baum, editors. 1973. *The Persistence of Religion*. New York: Herder and Herder. Volume 81 of "Concilium: Religion in the Seventies."

Halebsky, Sandor. 1976. *Mass Society and Political Conflict: Toward a Reconstruction of Theory*. New York: Cambridge University Press.

Hastings, Elizabeth Hann, and Philip K. Hastings, editors. 1979. *Index to International Public Opinion*. Westport, CT: Greenwood Press.

Hechter, Michael. 1975. *Internal Colonialism: The Celtic Fringe in British Na-*

tional Development, 1536–1966. Berkeley, CA: University of California Press.

Herberg, Will. 1960. *Protestant, Catholic, Jew.* Second edition. Garden City, NY: Doubleday-Anchor.

Hunter, James Davison. 1983. *American Evangelicalism: Conservative Religion and the Quandary of Modernity.* New Brunswick, NJ: Rutgers University Press.

Inglehart, Ronald. 1971. "The 'Silent Revolution' in Europe: Intergenerational Change in Post-Industrial Societies." *American Political Science Review.* 65: 991–1017.

Inkeles, Alex. 1983. *Exploring Individual Modernity.* Cambridge, MA: Harvard University Press.

Jacquet, Constant H., editor. 1983. *Yearbook of American and Canadian Churches, 1983.* Nashville, TN: Abingdon Press.

Knight, Sidney, 1984. "Belated Good Thinking Finally Halts a Tragedy of Errors." *Gainesville Sun.* April 6: 4A.

Lipset, Seymour Martin, and William Schneider. 1983. *The Confidence Gap: Business, Labor, and Government in the Public Mind.* New York: Free Press.

Lynd, Robert S., and Helen Merrell Lynd. 1937. *Middletown in Transition.* New York: Harcourt, Brace and Company.

Lynd, Robert S., and Helen Merrell Lynd. 1929. *Middletown: A Study in Contemporary American Culture.* New York: Harcourt, Brace and Company.

Machovec, Milan. 1976. *A Marxist Looks at Jesus.* Philadelphia, PA: Fortress Press.

Marty, Martin E. 1984. *Pilgrims in Their Own Land.* Boston: Little, Brown.

McDonough, Peter, Samuel H. Barnes, and Antonio López Pina. 1984. "Authority and Association: Spanish Democracy in Comparative Perspective." *Journal of Politics.* 46: 652–688.

Miller, Warren E., and the National Election Studies. 1982. *American National Election Study, 1980: Pre and Post-Election Surveys.* Second edition. Ann Arbor, MI: Inter-University Consortium for Political and Social Research.

Pomian-Srzednicki, M. 1982. *Religious Changes in Contemporary Poland: Secularization and Politics.* London: Routledge and Kegan Paul.

Prozesky, Martin. 1984. *Religion and Ultimate Well-Being: An Explanatory Theory.* New York: St. Martin's.

Quinn, Bernard, Herman Anderson, Martin Bradley, Paul Goetting, and Peggy Shriver. 1982. *Churches and Church Membership in the United States, 1980.* Atlanta, GA: Glenmary Research Center.

Research and Forecasts, Inc. 1981. *The Connecticut Mutual Life Report on American Values in the 1980s: The Impact of Belief.* Hartford, CT: Connecticut Mutual Life Insurance Company.

Salisbury, Robert H. 1983. "American Politics: Religion and the Welfare State." In *Comparative Social Research,* ed. Richard E. Tomasson. Greenwich, CT: JAI Press, 56–65.

Salisbury, Robert H., John Sprague, and Gregory Weiher. 1984. "Does Religious Pluralism Make a Difference? Interactions Among Context, Attendance, and Beliefs." Paper prepared for delivery to the Caucus for Faith and Politics, American Political Science Association, Washington, DC.

Schumer, Fran. 1984. "A Return to Religion." *New York Times Magazine.* April 15: 90–98.

Szajkowski, Bogdan. 1983. *Next to God . . . Poland: Politics and Religion in Contemporary Poland.* New York: St. Martin's.

Toynbee, Polly. 1984. "In the Midst of Death We Are in Life." *Manchester Guardian Weekly.* March 4: 19.

Tracy, David. 1973. "The Religious Dimension of Science." In *The Persistence of Religion,* ed. Andrew Greeley and Gregory Baum. New York: Herder and Herder, 128–135.

U.S. Bureau of the Census. 1981. *Statistical Abstract of the United States: 1981.* Washington, DC: Government Printing Office.

U.S. Bureau of the Census. 1960. *Historical Statistics of the United States, Colonial Times to 1957.* Washington, DC: Government Printing Office.

Vitz, Paul C. 1985. "Textbook Bias Isn't of a Fundamentalist Nature." *Wall Street Journal.* December 26: 6.

Vree, Dale. 1976. *On Synthesizing Marxism and Christianity.* New York: John Wiley and Sons.

Warner, R. Stephen. 1979. "Theoretical Barriers to the Understanding of Evangelical Christianity." *Sociological Analysis.* 40: 1–9.

Wilson, Bryan. 1966. *Religion in Secular Society: A Comment.* Baltimore, MD: Penguin Books.

2

Religion and Politics: Points of Contact

To his followers, who willingly signed over their lives and fortunes, the leader of the cult was a new Messiah, possibly even a God. Under his direction, they would march out of spiritual bondage to achieve harmony and social justice. Even critics who doubted his honesty and regarded him as a manipulator admitted that the leader was a spell-binding orator whose doctrines had a magnetic appeal to poor blacks in urban ghettos. At the height of its popularity, his movement had its own churches, newspapers, schools, and social welfare agencies. Even though he was recognized as a potentially significant political force in America, the leader decided to move his society to the wilds of another continent. The jungle settlement ended in tragedy.

Victims of a catastrophe that wiped out thousands of their coreligionists, the survivors fled across the Atlantic to the United States. Despite the distance, they did not forget the events that had made them refugees. To enlist the American government on behalf of an independent homeland for their persecuted brethren, they have organized powerful national associations, raised enormous amounts of money, and tried to pressure public officials by threats of electoral retaliation. Having gained special strength and influence in New York and the Democratic party, the group has nonetheless managed to achieve a national consensus on American support for the beleaguered new nation. Though the cause continues to enjoy considerable sympathy among Americans, the group's single-mindedness occasionally draws the charge that members put the well-being of the foreign homeland above the broader interests of the United States.

A small group of men and women, motivated by intense Christian faith, call on America to mend its evil ways. They are outraged by national policies that deny legal standing to other human beings, policies that have been approved by the U.S. Supreme Court. While willing to try changing the law through normal political activities, some on the fringe of the movement resort to violence against people and institutions committing what they consider the great sin. To their critics, these crusaders for public morality appear narrow-minded, intolerant, and uncompromising. The group responds to such accusations by insisting that America return to the religious values that have long sustained the republic.

Another group of American Christians sees the arms race as the paramount threat to world peace and human survival. Persuaded that nations will use weapons if they are available, these activists call on their government to stop its weapons buildup and negotiate treaties of arbitration with its military adversaries. They are also worried about America's growing military involvement in Latin America and urge the government to send teachers, medical supplies, and economic assistance instead of troops.

The attentive citizen should have no difficulty attaching names to the groups described in these passages. The cult is obviously the "Peoples' Temple" of Jim Jones, which ended in 1978 with a mass suicide or massacre in Guyana. The second vignette, of course, describes the efforts of the American Zionist movement to build public and governmental support for a Jewish homeland in the Middle East. For thirty years, Zionist leaders have helped to persuade Congress and various presidents to provide strong military and diplomatic assistance to Israel. The third group is immediately recognizable as the "New Christian Right," a label for the religious conservatives who have challenged the liberalization of abortion, changes in long-established sex roles, and other policies regarded as departures from traditional moral values. The final passage clearly deals with the growing support for nuclear disarmament in the Roman Catholic church and other denominations.

Or so it may seem! As closely as the labels appear to fit the facts of each case, the four groups just described are *not* Jim Jones and the Peoples' Temple, the American Zionist movement, the Moral Majority, and the contemporary Catholic peace movement. Whatever the similarities to recent religiously based political actions, the vignettes actually refer to four earlier episodes from American history in which religious enthusiasm fused with political action: the back-to-Africa movement of Marcus Garvey, nationalist political agitation by Irish-American Catholics, the abolitionist crusade against slavery, and the Christian pacifism of William Jennings Bryan.[1] As these examples from the nineteenth and early twentieth centuries make clear, religious activity in politics is neither new nor unprecedented in American experience. To the contrary: a close look at American history reveals a durable tradition of interaction between religious and political activity, arising from and strengthened by several factors.

To understand why religion and politics are so frequently tied together in this country, it is necessary to examine the *incentives* for political activism by religiously committed people and groups, the *opportunities* for involvement, and, finally, the *resources* that enable the religious to participate effectively. Any coherent explanation of the persistent linkage of religion and politics in the United States depends on close examination of all three factors.

CAUSES OF RELIGIOUS INTERVENTION IN POLITICS

Visitors to the United States are often struck by the readiness of Americans to enter the political arena in pursuit of moral causes and to interpret complicated public issues in terms of good versus evil (Brogan 1960, chap. 5). Although moral crusades are not unique to the United States, they seem to occur more frequently here than elsewhere. In most other advanced industrial societies, political conflict commonly centers on questions about the distribution of economic resources and burdens. Such issues are hardly unknown in American political life, but they must share the national agenda with controversies that touch more directly upon moral values and religious doctrine. The passion that suffuses such issues as abortion, school prayer, equal rights, pornography, and other moral concerns seems notably lacking when Americans confront questions such as tax rates, national health insurance, labor union rights, or tariff protection. Moreover, at a time when the politics of religious concern seems to be weakening in other advanced societies, it has gained a renewed foothold in American politics.

Why should religion become an element in political controversy in the first place? Part of the answer to this question lies in those forces within religion that encourage political activism. In all, three aspects, or "faces," of religion may promote an interest in politics—creed, institution, and social structure (Wald 1983, chap. 5). Although these three elements may not constitute the essence of the concept of religion, they do represent the major "manner and form in which religious phenomena appear in human experience" (Capps 1972, 135), and each provides an incentive for religious groups to enter the political arena.

As used here, *creed* refers to the fundamental beliefs, ideas, ethical codes, and symbols associated with a religious tradition, including what others call a theology or belief system. The emphasis here is on the content of religious teachings and the values that the tradition encourages. As comprehensive systems of belief, religious traditions may provide guidance for believers about appropriate behavior in secular realms, such as politics.

Churches differ in the degree to which they assert a connection between religious faith and political principles. Some, such as Mennonite congregations, are quite explicit about the political lessons of their faith, announcing that the church is committed to nonviolence, separation of church and state, and mutual service. In most churches, however, political orientation has to be inferred from the beliefs and ethical codes of the religious tradition. When a church lacks an authoritative statement of political principles, its members may disagree about how (or even whether) the faith applies to political questions. Whether the cues are direct or indirect, religious belief systems may send messages that influence political outlook and behavior.

Religion and politics can also be linked through the tie of interest. Religious communities are represented in concrete form by specialized *institutions,* the second face of religion pertinent to political activism. In the United States, churches are not merely buildings that provide places for worship; rather, they have become multipurpose agencies providing an astonishing array of services, including formal education, social welfare, pastoral counseling, publishing, charitable fund-raising, recreational facilities, medical care, cemeteries, libraries, and summer camps. Several of the largest churches have become hubs for worldwide operations, complete with the organizational complexity of a major corporation. Ties to a common denomination and to interchurch movements of various kinds have further enmeshed the churches in a web of formal institutions.

As a result of these extensive responsibilities and activities, churches often acquire a strong and immediate interest in policies determined by the government. A church day school, for example, is subject to governmental regulations on zoning, taxation, health and public safety, professional standards, wages and working conditions, racial integration, curriculum, and standardized testing. Religious broadcasting, like its secular counterpart, is regulated by the Federal Communications Commission. A church that offers counseling services or engages heavily in charitable fund-raising may unwittingly expose itself to legal action. Because of the potential impact of governmental decisions upon their many activities, religious groups frequently find it valuable—or necessary—to take an active role in the political process.

Religion also denotes a *social group,* or community of believers. The members of a congregation may share regular social interaction, a common status, and a distinctive way of life. Of course, churches differ in the demands they place upon members and in the degree to which they constitute genuine communities, as opposed to casual associations. Nonetheless, the communal nature of religion may induce a particular pattern of political activity by members of a congregation. If a church attracts people who experience similar conditions of life, whether poverty or affluence, that shared status may lead congregants to develop a common outlook on politics and social issues. Underlying political tendencies can be brought to the surface by messages from the pulpit and reinforced by continued social interaction with like-minded church members. In some cases—the black churches, for example—political solidarity is virtually imposed on the group members by the hostility of outsiders. The larger the role played by the church in defining the lives of its members, the greater the church's potential impact upon their political activities.

A revealing example of how these incentives can affect the level of political involvement is that of the U.S. Roman Catholic church, which has repeatedly attempted to relate Catholic religious thought to important issues on the national political agenda. Through homilies, sermons, pastoral letters, and the dissemination of papal encyclicals, church leaders have attempted to educate Catholics about how to apply the principles of the faith to such diverse public problems as abortion, national defense, economic policy, and the position of women in society. The church has also taken a strong public stand on issues that affect the immediate welfare of its institutions. To ease the financial burden of the church's comprehensive system of religious day schools, Catholic leaders have sought public assistance in the form of textbook sharing, public transportation, and tuition tax credits. As individuals, Catholic laypeople have shown a traditional attachment to the Democratic party. This linkage was formed at the turn of the century, when the predominantly immigrant and working-class Catholic population found Democrats far more receptive than Republicans to their needs and aspirations. The historical memory of how the Democratic party provided a path of upward mobility for ambitious young Catholics kept the alliance intact even after many Catholics had moved into the social and economic mainstream.

Creed, institutional interest, and social standing have also been responsible for the political actions of other religious groups in American life. To some extent, the Catholic church has only followed in the footsteps of other religious groups (Handy 1984). During the nineteenth century, many Protestant churches took public stands on such vital issues as slavery, tariffs, and imperialism, justifying their preferences as an outgrowth of religious beliefs. In the attempt to defend institutions or public practices that supported Protestant interests, moreover, the churches frequently intervened in the legislative process—trying, for example, to mandate the holy character of the Sunday sabbath or to adjust immigration quotas so as to encourage migration from Protestant nations. Like Catholics, the Protestants have tended to form alliances with political groups that represent their social and economic interests. For Protestants, no less than for Catholics, creed, institutional self-interest, and social bonds have encouraged political involvement.

In the current period, new or revitalized religious groups have been drawn into political action by the same incentives that have motivated the well-established churches. The forces that encourage an intersection of religion and politics are numerous and diverse. The Mormon church has urged its membership to follow church doctrine in public disputes over abortion, school prayer, pornography, and the like. Evangelical Protestant churches, many of which have become imposing organizations that sponsor broadcast networks, school systems, and major publishing houses, have entered politics to safeguard these institutions from governmental regulation. Because an increasing proportion of the American Roman Catholic community comprises poor and deprived Hispanic immigrants, the Catholic church has become far more aggressive in advocating government spending to address social problems.

How Government Structure
Encourages Political Action of Churches

In order for churches to act upon the incentives just described, the political system must be open to them. At a minimum, this requires opportunities for participation without legal restriction. Whereas some democratic societies severely limit the political activities of churches and religious leaders, the United States historically has given religious groups relatively free reign to participate in public affairs.[2] The federal tax code does require churches to refrain from endorsing candidates if they want to retain exemption from the income tax, but this provision has not been strictly enforced. The political system is thus open to U.S. churches, in the sense that few formal barriers keep them from political activity.

In another sense, the U.S. political system actually encourages organized groups to compete for influence over public policy (Truman 1962). As political scientists have long recognized, the complex structure of the U.S. government encourages groups to undertake political activity. In this regard, religious groups are no different from the many other organizations that attempt to influence public policy at all levels of society.

Decentralization is fundamental to American political life. Rather than concentrate power in the hands of one institution, the founders of the nation divided political authority among three autonomous branches of government. Advocates of any particular policy thus have three separate routes open to them: they can try to achieve their goals by legislation, by legal action, or through the administrative process. Because political power is further subdivided among at least three separate levels of government (national, state, and local), a group with political goals has additional freedom to choose the ground on which it fights. Governmental fragmentation, accordingly, gives groups multiple points of access to the policy-making process. Such a complex governmental structure may or may not be conducive to good policy-making, quick reaction to pressing problems, or clear direction, but it certainly keeps the decision-making process remarkably open to causes that can find an effective advocate.

The way in which structure makes a difference for religious groups can be seen by the different outcomes of the antiabortion movements in the United States and Canada (Schwartz 1981). In Canada, as in the United States, the penalties for abortion were reduced or eliminated from the late 1960s to the early 1970s. Liberalization brought forth the same vociferous objections from Catholics and conservative Protestants that it produced in the United States. But there the similarity between the two nations comes to an abrupt end.

Organized on the British parliamentary model, the Canadian governmental system offered the opponents of liberalized abortion few opportunities to challenge official policy. Because the criminal code was the exclusive responsibility of the national government, the provincial authorities and local governments could do little to restrict the availability of abortion services. At the national level, the governing Liberal party easily defeated antiabortion efforts originating in the courts or in the Parliament. Political leaders who might have disagreed with the decision to relax restrictions on abortion largely toed the line, lest they endanger their careers in a system that rewards loyalty to party. Thus, despite strong objections from a large Catholic population, the Canadian government was able to persevere in its policy of making abortion more widely available to the population.

The different outcome of the abortion debate in the United States, where antiabortionists have won a number of significant victories, testifies to the many avenues of attack provided by the complex and multifaceted U.S. system of government. When national abortion policy was liberalized through the *Roe* v. *Wade* decision handed down by the Supreme Court in 1973, critics sought to use the amending power of the Constitution to restore restrictive policies. Failing in that and in attempts to remove abortion from the Court's jurisdiction, they proceeded to chip away at the decision in several other arenas. Congress has been persuaded to reduce or eliminate federal payments for abortion under various programs of health insurance and foreign assistance. Using ordinances covering zoning, the regulation of public health, and parental rights, some states and localities have tried to restrict access to abortion facilities, and several such restrictions have been sustained by the Supreme Court. The critics of abortion can also claim a symbolic victory—and potentially much more—in the 1985 decision of the Justice Department to petition the Supreme Court for a wholesale reconsideration of the *Roe* v. *Wade* decision. Although limits on abortion remain much less stringent than they were before 1973, the opponents of abortion have capitalized upon the separation of powers and upon the federal structure of government to partially offset the Supreme Court's 1973 ruling.

Few of the options used by the religiously motivated opponents of abortion in the United States are available to persons of similar belief in other countries. In most nations, the policy decisions of a national government are not routinely subject to review by an outside agency, nor can they be overturned by appeal to a higher law as embodied in a constitution. In most circumstances the party in government has a relatively free hand to shape legislation without competition from other national institutions. Similarly, because of concentration of lawmaking authority and administrative power in the central government, provinces and localities usually are powerless to block the implementation of national policy.

These differences in structure account for the willingness of American politicians, unlike their Canadian counterparts, to join political crusades sponsored by religious groups (Grodzins 1960). The typical political career in the United States is rooted in a locality or state. Because nomination to public office is determined by the residents of the district, to stay in office or win promotion to a higher post an official must satisfy public opinion in the district. Candidates are required to develop personal electoral organizations, raise most of their own campaign resources, and emphasize whatever issues will resonate most powerfully in the constituency. Once in office, they enjoy considerable leeway from the party line. This decentralized system of representation has produced a recurrent pattern of behavior among American elected officials on issues with great emotional potential: they display great sensitivity to the views of constituents on such highly charged issues, and they are willing to advocate the district's opinion even if it conflicts with national party policy.

For American politicans in general, loyalty to district opinion on a moral issue will pay electoral dividends. It does not impugn the sincerity of U.S. legislators to note that moral advocacy may contribute to a successful political career. Where nomination to office, campaign finance, and promotion to higher office depend upon the party, ambitious politicians have strong reasons to conform to the party line. The absence of these weapons in American political parties helps explain why public officials feel free to take up moral causes if they judge that such issues will advance their political standing.

RELIGION AS A POLITICAL RESOURCE

Many groups, not just those motivated by religion, have incentives to participate in and opportunities to pursue their goals through political action. Religious groups, however, are especially likely to participate effectively because of their resources: that is, qualities possessed by religiously motivated activists that can prove valuable in political action. These resources grow out of the three faces of religion already examined in this chapter.

Religious ideas are potentially powerful sources of commitment and motivation. As history repeatedly has taught, human beings will make enormous sacrifices if they believe themselves to be driven by a divine force. When the power of the churches is applied to a political issue, the message is likely to exert substantial influence over attentive parishioners. Until quite recently, the major American churches largely restricted their political preaching to questions involving personal behavior. The "social" message from the pulpit tended to stress public solutions for individual problems, such as drinking, gambling, drug use, and licentious sexual behavior. It is precisely on such issues that the attitudes of churchgoers differ most substantially from those of persons who do not regularly encounter church preaching on politics (Hoge and De Zulueta 1985).

The potential political strength of religious ideas has been displayed repeatedly in local, statewide, and national movements against pornography, homosexual rights ordinances, the Equal Rights Amendment, liberalized abortion laws, and other policies that challenge practices traditionally regarded as sinful. The capacity of these issues to ignite political action was nicely demonstrated in a recent study conducted by political scientists Paul Allen Beck and Suzanne Parker (1985). In interviewing a group of adult Floridians in 1981 and again in 1982, they found that many people shifted their positions on political issues from one interview to the next. This high degree of inconsistency suggested that citizens do not have firm or deep convictions about many of the issues that dominate political conflict. Beck and Parker did find three exceptions to this generalization, all of which involved issues touching upon moral values. The members of the sample were most consistent in their views about abortion, school prayer, and the Equal Rights Amendment. Because these issues apparently tap into opinions of great intensity and durability, it is not surprising that they have generated sustained political action by persons with traditional religious beliefs.

In addition to what might be called their intellectual resources—the capacity to motivate people to action—the churches also enjoy substantial organizational advantages. Success in politics depends in part on the ability to mobilize citizens behind a common goal, for which purpose it helps greatly to have public credibility, access to citizens, and a means for communicating ideas. The churches, with precisely these traits, are natural political organizations. As observed in the previous chapter, the churches enjoy a very positive image in American society—a level of prestige that can yield political credibility. In terms of access and communication, churches are powerful organizations with formal membership, headquarters, regularly scheduled group meetings, publications, and full-time professional leadership. Because of patterns of association in American society, the church is often the only such well-organized group to which a citizen is likely to belong. If the church wants to transmit political messages, it has the apparatus to do so with great efficiency.

As a social system or subculture, the church has yet other resources that can contribute to a powerful political role. By virtue of participating in a social network, the church member may encounter messages about political issues and interact with fellow members who adhere to the church's line. A person surrounded by church members who participate actively in a campaign is likely to learn about the issues from a religious point of view, to receive encouragement about joining in the activity, and to observe and acquire social skills that may promote political success. Though not intended for that purpose, congregational organizations may serve as leadership training institutes for people who lack other means of exposure to organizational skills.

These social factors help to explain the positive relationship many observers have found between church attendance and voter participation in presidential elections (Hill and Cassel 1984; Hougland and Christenson 1983; Macaluso and Wanat 1979). These studies infer a connection between religious and political involvement by comparing the attitudes and behavior of people with different levels of exposure to church influence. Political scientists Theodore Macaluso and John Wanat (1979, 160–61) have argued that churches promote a sense of civic responsibility by teaching members that social obligations have a sacred character. This sense of stewardship toward public affairs should translate into higher rates of participation. Treating churches just like other social formations, sociologists (Hougland and Christenson 1983, 406) have contended that participation in associations of any kind provides "the social contacts and organizational skills necessary to understand political action and to exert effective influence." It is also possible that participation in a religious community breaks down the individualist tendency in contemporary society and leads people to regard themselves as part of a larger group with legitimate claims upon public policy. Whatever the exact factors involved, the churches serve as social networks that seem to draw participants into public affairs.

Although churches possess imposing political resources and the opportunity to participate in politics combined with the incentive to do so, there are three potential limits on religious-group activism.

To begin with, certain types of faith actually depress political involvement. Some religious traditions refuse to get involved with politics, which they see as irrelevant to their primary task of saving souls. A belief about the futility of political action also can be a potent deterrent to political participation (Quinney 1964)—as I once learned when, while I was canvasing for a candidate, a church member slammed a door in my face with the shout, "No politics on Sunday!" Other religious groups have gone even further, insisting that members separate themselves completely from the corrupting influence of all secular institutions and activities. Even if a church does not condemn political participation, it might make such heavy demands upon the members' time, energy, and resources that congregants have nothing left to devote to political action. One of the few studies of the impact of religious involvement on a variety of forms of political participation—not just voting—found that churchgoing did *not* encourage more active forms of political involvement, such as making campaign contributions or undertaking volunteer work for candidates (Hougland and Christenson 1983). British studies also have uncovered a negative relationship between the level of involvement in church life and active participation in political parties and campaigns (Stark 1964; Cheal 1975). Hence, the link between religion and participation seems to be restricted to the least demanding form of political action—the casting of a vote.

Another limitation on church political activity is the fear that political clout will be purchased at the expense of spiritual influence. It has long been suspected that churches enjoy such a positive image in the United States because they are regarded as places apart, a refuge from the corruption of other secular institutions. According to polling data, the public generally prefers the churches to remain "above" politics and reacts negatively to clergy who become agents of a particular party or candidate. If the church enters the political world as an active participant, it risks losing some of the prestige and social influence that makes it such a respected institution. That outcome is particularly likely when a church or religious group takes a political position that alienates members who might otherwise remain loyal.

Finally, it is important to remember that churches do not enjoy a monopoly on political resources. Other associations—labor unions, professional groups, service clubs, business networks—possess communications and mobilization capacities. Membership in such organizations also contributes to electoral participation, whether or not there is an explicit political purpose (Hill and Cassel 1984, 24). If church impact is greater than that of other similarly advantaged organizations, that is because church affiliation is so much more widespread than membership in other kinds of associations.

*   *   *   *   *

A combination of incentives, opportunities, and resources serves to draw churches into politics at several different levels. Religion may play a role in forming the fundamental assumptions and outlooks that channel public thinking about government and politics. When it operates to affect such basic orientations about politics, religion has an impact on "political culture." At a second level, religion may contribute to political identity and partisan loyalties. The traditional tie between Catholics and the

Democratic party illustrates this effect. The third level at which religion interacts with politics involves specific policy debates. The remainder of the book will examine religious influence in those spheres.

It is important to emphasize at this point that the traffic between religion and politics in the United States runs two ways. Religious groups may take the initiative in political action, but they may also react to the decisions of government and other political actors. Roman Catholic doctrine about abortion did not draw the church into political activity until the United States Supreme Court struck down most legal restrictions on the availability of abortion. The politically conservative pastors of the New Christian Right have characterized their entry into politics largely as a response to government actions that left traditional churches aggrieved. Such a reactive posture by the churches may well be more common today because of changes in the scope of governmental authority. The state now claims more regulatory power than it used to—power that may be used to establish policies that affect the major functions of religious groups. If there truly is greater political involvement by religious institutions, that situation may reflect a defensive reaction to an expanded government rather than any desire to impose religious values upon a reluctant society.

NOTES

[1]For information about these movements, consult the accounts in Burkett 1978; Carroll 1978; and Clements 1982.

[2]It is common for nations to prohibit members of the clergy from holding public office. In Mexico, where the church was identified with the losing side in a civil war, no religious labels are allowed for political parties. Trying to keep the lid on simmering religious conflict, authorities in Egypt have banned bumper stickers containing any religious expression.

REFERENCES

Beck, Paul Allen, and Suzanne Parker. 1985. "Consistency in Policy Thinking." *Political Behavior*. 7: 37–56.

Brogan, D. W. 1960. *Politics in America*. Garden City, NY: Doubleday-Anchor.

Burkett, Randall K. 1978. *Garveyism as a Religious Movement*. Metuchen, NJ: Scarecrow Press.

Capps, Walter H., editor. 1972. *Ways of Understanding Religion*. New York: Macmillan.

Carroll, F. M. 1978. *American Opinion and the Irish Question, 1910–1923: A Study in Opinion and Policy*. Dublin, Ireland: Gill and Macmillan.

Cheal, David. 1975. "Political Radicalism and Religion: Competitors for Commitment." *Social Compass*. 22: 245–259.

Clements, Kendricks. 1982. *William Jennings Bryan: Missionary Isolationist*. Knoxville, TN: University of Tennessee Press.

Grodzins, Morton, 1960. "American Political Parties and the American System." *Western Political Quarterly.* 13: 974–998.

Handy, Robert T. 1984. *A Christian America?* Second edition. New York: Oxford University Press.

Hill, David B, and Carol Cassel. 1984. "Voting and the Rest of Life: A Social Exchange Theory of Electoral Turnout." Paper presented at the annual meeting of the American Political Science Association, Washington, DC.

Hoge, Dean R., and Ernesto Zulueta. 1984. "Salience as a Condition for Various Social Consequences of Religious Commitment." *Journal for the Scientific Study of Religion.* 24: 21–38.

Hougland, J. G., and J. A. Christenson. 1983. "Religion and Politics: The Relationship of Religious Participation to Political Efficacy and Involvement." *Sociology and Social Research.* 67: 405–420.

Macaluso, Theodore F., and John Wanat. 1979. "Voting Turnout and Religiosity." *Polity.* 12: 158–169.

Quinney, Richard. 1964. "Political Conservatism, Alienation, and Fatalism: Contingencies of Social Status and Religious Fundamentalism." *Sociometry.* 27: 372–381.

Schwartz, Mildred. 1981. "Politics and Moral Causes in Canada and the United States." In *Comparative Social Research,* ed. Richard F. Tomasson. Greenwich, CT: JAI Press, 65–90.

Stark, Rodney. 1964. "Class, Radicalism, and Religious Involvement in Great Britain." *American Sociological Review.* 29: 698–706.

Truman, David. 1962. *The Governmental Process.* New York: Alfred A. Knopf.

Wald, Kenneth. 1983. *Crosses on the Ballot: Patterns of British Voter Alignment Since 1885.* Princeton, NJ: Princeton University Press.

3

Religion and American Political Culture

In hunting for evidence of religious influence in American political life, most observers examine church-state controversies or search for indications that religious groups vote in solid blocs. Another kind of religious influence is not quite so apparent. As William Lee Miller recognized, religion may contribute to the basic political values shared by citizens of a nation:

> There is also a still more important, if less measurable, *indirect* and long-term effect of the religious tradition upon the nation's politics. This is the impact of ways of thinking, believing, and acting in religious matters upon the shape of the mind, which impact affects the way other fields, like politics, are understood. Such effects, seeping down into the national character, may be discernible not only in clergymen and church people but in members of the society at large. (Miller 1961, 83)

By forming an important strand in American culture, religion has helped to define the context of American political life. This chapter will trace the connections between the religious ideas and practices prevalent in the American colonies and subsequent American thought about important political questions.

To assert that religion contributed to the development of national political ideals is not to claim a monopoly for it. In the development of something as complex as a national political creed, secular thought and material interests of many kinds also play vital roles. The modern era has taught us to doubt the purity of motives, especially when they are expressed in terms of idealism, and to look for self-interest as the source of most human action.[1] Recognition that human beings undertake activity for diverse reasons, however, should not mislead a careful observer into ignoring altogether the impact on social conduct of abstract forces such as religion. In the colonial period, when religious creeds, institutions, and communities exerted a major impact on life and work, there was bound to be some spillover to politics. Because the contribution of religion to American political culture covers such important beliefs as obedience, the design of government, and the national mission, the religious roots of American political culture merit close investigation.

THE PURITAN IMPRINT ON COLONIAL THOUGHT

Although Americans often think of their country as a "new nation," its history and development largely untouched by the rest of the world, much that appears unique about American culture can be traced to the European heritage of the colonial settlers. In terms of religious influences upon American political thought, the critical element of that heritage was the commitment of the colonial settlers and their descendants to a particular form of Christianity that emerged from the Protestant Reformation (Bercovitch 1975; Niebuhr 1959).

Throughout sixteenth- and seventeenth-century Europe, dissatisfaction with the established churches fueled revolts against ecclesiastical authorities and the civil officials who sustained them. The leaders of the revolt in England, recognized today as the spiritual inspiration of American Protestantism, regarded themselves as nothing less than God's agents, engaged in a desperate struggle for the liberation of the church from "centuries of superstition and error" (Simpson 1955, 17). Convinced that they could not reform or replace the state church, many Puritans, Pilgrims, and other so-called Dissenters from the official Church of England chose to separate themselves from "an unregenerate government which persisted in maintaining a corrupt church" (Simpson 1955, 14–15), leaving England for places where they could practice a religion consistent with their version of Christian faith. The impulse to create societies that would honor God in what they saw as the one true Christian fashion took the Puritan settlers across the Atlantic to found the American colonies. In America, a land without religious traditions, they were free to build a culture in which the Protestant images of God, humanity, and the church became the core assumptions of everyday thought.

The influence of the Puritan outlook on American thought did not depend solely upon the weight of numbers. The denominations most closely identified with the Puritan wing of the Protestant Reformation, the Congregationalists and Presbyterians, were dominant only in New England. The Church of England, though a minority faith in most of the settlements, enjoyed official status at one time or another in the southern colonies of Virginia, Georgia, and North and South Carolina. Roman Catholicism was a force to be reckoned with in Maryland. The Middle Atlantic colonies were settled principally by members of the Dutch Reformed church, the Quakers, and adherents of several German Protestant traditions. Even in New England, the dominance of the Puritan congregations soon was challenged by the strength of newer sects like the Baptists and the Methodists, and weakened by internal conflicts over questions of theology and politics. Despite this high degree of formal religious diversity in the colonies, most of the denominations appeared to share the outlook and assumptions that characterized Puritanism. Many foreign observers have viewed the Puritan outlook as the root of American culture (Hudson 1965a, 7–10), a judgment widely shared by historians of American religion (Ahlstrom 1965; Heimert 1966).

As difficult as it may be for twentieth-century minds to understand one another, the difficulty is compounded many times over when a twentieth-century mind confronts one of the seventeenth and eighteenth centuries. Yet the attempt is essential to any understanding of the perspectives that shaped the early political thought of Americans. In the century and a half that elapsed between the establishment of the first permanent settlements on the continent and the founding of the republic, the theology of the Reformation was continually adapted and adjusted to the American situation. Though the religious impulse may have waned over time, its preeminence challenged by new intellectual currents and commercial considerations, periodic revivals kept it very much alive in the American mind.

The Puritan impulse focused the American mind on the Bible. Under the doctrine that ordinary people need no intermediary between themselves and the word of God, Puritanism encouraged individuals to look for divine guidance in the Scriptures. Up to the time of the Revolution and perhaps for sometime thereafter, it is safe to assume, the Bible was the only book familiar to the typical inhabitant of America. To judge from a recent study by Donald Lutz (1984), the biblical tradition seems also to have played a major role in the thought processes of those who led the Revolution and created the Constitution. In an intensive study of nearly 1,000 political documents issued to the public from 1760 through 1805, Lutz found that the single most frequent source of citations was the Bible. Though such a pattern hardly shows (and Lutz does not claim) that the Bible determined what the founders believed, it does suggest strong familiarity with the Christian tradition among influential writers and, presumably, their readers.

The imprint of Protestant Christianity upon the era of the founders and, through time, upon contemporary U.S. political life is apparent in several respects. From the body of Puritan thought come three elements that proved especially important for subsequent American political practice: covenant theology, the emphasis on original sin, and the concept of a chosen people. Each of these doctrines was applied by the Puritan thinkers and their successors to the earthly realm of politics. Covenant theology helped Americans decide under what conditions governments deserved obedience. The Puritan image of human sinfulness provided clues about the best design for maintaining stable government. And the idea of "chosenness" encouraged Americans to think about their nation in missionary terms. Despite the passage of two centuries since these ideas were formulated, they continue to cast a long shadow over the conduct of American political life.

COVENANT THEOLOGY
AND THE RIGHT TO REVOLT

Most Americans take it for granted that citizens owe allegiance to governments that respect their basic rights and liberties; they also seem to accept without question the assertion in the Declaration of Independence that citizens have a right to revolt against governments that deny fundamental freedoms. The idea of conditional allegiance, of a "contract" between citizens and rulers that can be voided when the government misbehaves, is a cornerstone of American political thought.

This concept of government as compact gained such ready acceptance among colonial Americans because it bore a close resemblance to a central element in Puritan theology, the *covenant.* Puritan thinkers gave considerable warrant to this model of association, which appears at several different points in the Bible (Elazar 1980, 12–20). In the most influential of biblical covenants, Abraham and God were joined together by bonds of mutual obligation as Abraham accepted the promise of God's blessing for himself and his heirs, the people of Israel, and in turn pledged to do God's work in the wilderness (Genesis 12:3). This was not an obligation imposed upon Abraham by fiat but a "conscious contract with God" in which Abraham "promised to do certain things for God in return for which God pledged Himself to recompense Abraham" (Miller 1956, 119). The defining characteristic of a covenant, as the Puritans understood it, was that of a voluntary agreement, sanctified by God, in which individuals freely surrendered autonomy in exchange for something of greater value. God hovered over covenants either as a partner or, in the case of contracts among individuals, as the sanctifier and guarantor in whose name the agreement was forged.

This model of social organization was applied by the Puritans to all manner of human associations. Under the image of the covenant, the "church" was redefined: rather than an institution with authority in a particular geographical area, it was seen as a community of the elect, a gathering of those who received the promise of eternal salvation in exchange for accepting a mission to act as God's agents in this world.

Extended to civil societies, the covenant provided a basis for human governance. In crossing the Atlantic, the Puritans envisioned themselves as a latter-day people of Israel, re-creating the Hebrew covenant in their pilgrimage to the New World. The most famous reenactment of the covenant ritual was the Mayflower Compact, in which the Pilgrims (a Puritan congregation) aboard the ship pledged to create a holy, Bible-based commonwealth in the wilderness in exchange for God's blessing upon them. The settlements that spread throughout the New England colonies during the seventeenth century were founded upon similar compacts (Schecter 1980).

The political implications of the covenant idea became especially important when Americans sought to justify their decision to cut all legal ties with Great Britain. The crucial link between politics and religion was forged when the idea of a covenant was extended to encompass an entire nation. If the relationship between colonist and king was a contract sealed by the authority of God—in other words, a covenant—then the terms of that contract bore divine authority. The citizens owed allegiance to the ruler and the ruler, in turn, was committed to honor the contract by acting within its limits. In the view of the colonists, "Rulers who violate the agreed-upon forms are usurpers and so to be legitimately resisted" (Miller 1967, 98).

The implications of this type of reasoning were revolutionary. Whereas others interpreted the Bible as saying that God had ordained obedience to government, a view that promoted absolutist rule, the Puritans understood the relationship between people and government as one of mutual obligation. The basis for this revised interpretation was the model of the biblical covenants. Through agreements with Adam, Noah, Abraham, and others, God had entered into binding contracts with human beings. Though surely not the equal of the mortals in these partnerships, God nonetheless promised to behave in accordance with the terms of the contract, acting as a kind of constitutional monarch in the universe. If God had agreed to be bound in this manner, how could any earthly monarch presume to claim exemption from limits or obligations?

Fortified by biblical precedent, the colonists insisted that the monarch respect their universal rights as creations of God, along with the specific rights due to them as citizens of the British empire.[2] Because obedience was conditional on the ruler behaving in conformity with agreed-upon standards, it could justly be withdrawn whenever the standards were violated. Thus, when King George III clearly abridged the rights to which the colonists felt entitled, they claimed that the colonies no longer owed him loyalty. Resistance to a government that violated God's law could even be seen as a religious obligation. The covenanting impulse that prompted their forebears to separate physically from England helped propel the colonists out of the British empire.

The colonists repeatedly invoked the covenant tradition to justify the breaking of their bonds with Great Britain. Almost a year to the day before the Declaration of Independence was made public, the Continental Congress called upon Americans to observe a day of national confession, marked by "publick humiliation, fasting, and prayer." After promising this confession and pledging repentance, the colonists asked God for help in persuading the British to respect the terms of the compact that bound the colonies to the mother country (Miller 1967, 90-91). When the British proved resistant to these prayers, the colonists once again stressed the breaking of the covenant as justification for revolt. The Declaration of Independence begins with the assertion that the colonists deserved independence under "the Laws of Nature and Nature's God." Consistent with covenant theory, the colonists asserted that the bond between rulers and ruled was dependent on the ruler's respect for those rights that God granted to men. Once the terms of the compact had been violated by a despotic King George (as the colonists attempted to demonstrate in great detail), the people of America could claim a divine mandate to dissolve their ties. The Declaration concludes with the submission of the purity of the rebels' claims to "the Supreme Judge of the World."

The breaking of the covenant not only entitled the people to withdraw authority from a corrupt government, but, as the Declaration also emphasizes, authorized them to form a new system of rule. Once independence was secured, the colonists went about the task of building a new state on the promise that a new covenant was required. After a false start, they settled on what is sometimes called the American national covenant—the Constitution of the United States. Although the Constitution does not explicitly recognize God as a partner or invoke divine blessing, the document bears the mark of covenant thinking in a number of important respects (Riemer 1980, 138–43; Rothman 1980).

Following the original Hebrew conception of covenant as a voluntary undertaking, the Constitution was a contract freely entered into by the people of the thirteen states. It was presented to them as a document that they were free to accept or reject. The biblical covenant created a "people" who, if they accepted the agreement, were promised God's blessings; similarly, the Constitution was presented in the name of the "People of the United States" to achieve for them such beneficent ends as justice, order, welfare, and liberty. Covenants, as the Puritans understood them, routinely set limits on the power of authorities. The privileges of power were legitimate only insofar as they were carried out with respect for the God-given rights of the contracting parties. Commentators have called attention to the corresponding emphasis on limits in the U.S. Constitution. The document is replete with provisions spelling out what government may *not* do and holding government subject to strict rules and standards in the performance of its duties. Then, too, the Constitution seems to enjoy something of the hallowed status of a covenant. It is treated as a holy relic—encased in a shrine to which citizens make pilgrimages—and its authors are revered by some as saints or demigods.

PURITANISM AND DEMOCRACY: A QUALIFICATION

To associate the spread of democratic thinking with Puritan ideas about the covenant is not to absolve the Puritan heritage of antidemocratic tendencies. At various times in American history, the popular image of the religious pioneers has been one of intolerance of dissent, hostility to science, and lukewarm support for the spread of representative institutions. As Sydney Ahlstrom (1965, 95) succinctly summarized this interpretation, "Puritans were insufferable, self-righteous precisionists with narrow minds and blue noses, authoritarian, clericalist, intolerant, and antidemocratic." Even more sympathetic critics have recognized that Puritanism harbored both pioneers of democratic thought and its determined enemies (Berk 1974).

The contribution of the Puritan heritage to democracy involved more than direct translation of religious values such as the covenant into political principles. If Puritanism was, on balance, a force that encouraged Americans to protect human liberty, it was so because the democratic elements in Puritan thinking were reinforced by institutional self-interest and by the social practices of Protestant Christianity in the New World. All three elements of religion—social and institutional as well as creedal—must be considered in discussing the linkage between Puritanism and democracy.

Many leaders of reformed Protestant churches were drawn so wholeheartedly to the cause of the Revolution out of the fear that Great Britain would withdraw both political and religious liberties from the colonies. The original migration to New England had been motivated by the desire to escape from an oppressive national church that maintained its power through an alliance with civil authorities. Having recognized the sovereignty of individual conscience as the basis for religious affiliation, the early Puritan settlers found it impossible to impose an effective unity of outlook in religious matters. Almost in spite of itself, the Puritan ethic thus contributed to religious diversity and to a grudging acceptance of toleration in matters of faith. The colonists came to regard the preservation of religious pluralism as a matter of the highest importance.

During the century or so leading up to the Revolution, the efforts of the British government to assert greater control appeared to strike at the hard-won religious liberty of the colonies. In the 1760s, colonists were particularly agitated by plans to appoint Anglican bishops in America. Such an aggressive attempt by the Church of England to gain favored legal status brought back painful memories of the persecution that Puritan dissenters had once suffered at the hands of the Anglican establishment. To persons steeped in a tradition of congregational autonomy and religious pluralism, a system in which religious leaders enjoyed minimal civil authority, the prospect of a centralized system of church government seemed to be the opening wedge in a campaign to undo the legacy of their Puritan forefathers. As Carl Bridenbaugh (1962) demonstrated in a convincing analysis of the continuing conflict between the Church of England and the colonies, fear of losing religious liberty played a major role in the development of American nationalism and helped stimulate the drive for independence from Great Britain.

The colonists themselves had learned much about the actual practice of democracy from the remarkably high degree of individual and congregational freedom in colonial religious life. In most of Europe, local churches were held accountable to centralized national hierarchies that prescribed a code of belief, determined the acceptable forms of worship, and provided ministers charged with ensuring that local practice conformed to national standards. Membership in the church, determined solely by place of residence, was essentially a matter of passive acceptance rather than active involvement. Colonial religious life, in contrast, developed on the bases of the principles of voluntary participation and of congregational autonomy. The initiative for starting a church rested with individuals rather than a central source of authority. Because the church was their creation, the founders could prescribe conditions of membership, formulate a code of belief and practice, and select a minister who served at the pleasure of the congregants. Membership in a church was an option, rather than an automatic function of status, and carried with it an obligation to participate actively in the running of the congregation.

The tradition of self-rule that grew up in the churches seems to have encouraged the development of a vigorous democratic spirit in the political realm. From governing their own churches, Americans acquired both a taste for and competence in self-government. In the judgment of the historian Sydney Ahlstrom (1975, 1:424), the experience of membership in a self-governing church "prepared men to regard the social compact as the proper basis of government." This conclusion gains support from the mutual development in New England of the congregational principle in church governance and democratic practices in civil life. To a degree unparalleled elsewhere, the New England colonies had achieved high levels of suffrage, powerful representative institutions, and a marked respect for the rule of law (Brown 1977). Religion further encouraged the spirit of self-government by its contribution to the spread of education, science, cultural institutions, and civil associations (Shipton 1947).

The link between democracy and religion thus turned upon all three dimensions of religion. If the creed of Protestant Christianity was ambiguous about democracy as a system of government, the fear of Anglican assaults upon the reformed churches and the training in self-government provided by autonomous congregations tipped the scales in favor of the Revolutionary cause. For these institutional and social contributions, as much as for covenantal theology, the heirs of the Protestant Reformation deserve recognition as precursors of the democratic spirit in America.

HUMAN DEPRAVITY
AND INSTITUTIONAL RESTRAINT

Along with the covenant tradition, another aspect of Puritanism helped guide the founders of the Republic in building a new political system. The Puritan emphasis upon the inherently sinful nature of humankind (a strong theme in Protestant thought) provided principles of governance that the founders observed in constructing their constitutional alternative to the colonial framework. Though we are apt to think of their creation, the Constitution, as a neutral set of institutional arrangements, the system they fashioned is infused with a moral architecture that still guides the conduct of American political life.

The American governmental system was designed by political architects who assumed that human beings could not be trusted with power. To keep government safely under control, they divided authority among three separate branches, giving each leverage to use against the others, and they added additional safeguards such as powerful territorial governments (the states). As a consequence of that framework, the great challenge to any U.S. political leader is to overcome the inherent division of authority by mobilizing all institutions and levels of government on behalf of a common purpose. Compromise, delay, and deadlock are characteristic of normal American political life, to the frustration of advocates of rapid change.

The ultimate explanation for this aspect of U.S. political life lies in the image of humanity that guided some of the founders in their deliberations at Philadelphia. Far from adoring "the people," many of the founders appraised them with a cold eye and found more to say about the defects of popular will than about its virtues. In emphasizing their suspicions about humanity, the founders repeated a theme found in Reformation theology. For the Puritans, the fate of mortals was symbolized by the story of Adam. In sinning against God, Adam forfeited eternal happiness for a life of toil and sorrow that would end in death. Puritans interpreted this as a statement of the inherent depravity of human beings who, given a choice between good and evil, would often choose the latter. Unlike Catholic doctrine, which taught that the church could offer an escape from damnation, or that of religions that held out some hope for mass human regeneration through good behavior, Puritan theology offered little prospect of escape from the curse of Adam. Though a few would enjoy the light of God's grace and become saints on earth, the mass of humankind would know only depravity and sinfulness on earth and eternal torment thereafter.

This perspective led to two important political conclusions. First, because governments were the creations of fallible mortals, no government could be expected to act with rectitude. Quite the contrary, a government that reflected the sinful nature of its human creators would be prone to exceed its rightful authority. Under those circumstances, prudence dictated that the power of government be limited—or, in the words of one Protestant clergyman, "We should leave nothing to human virtue that can be provided for by law or constitution" (Strout 1974, 61). Second, because God was the only source of redemption, it was not the task of governments to make people good. The highest aspiration of government should be merely to subdue the most blatant excesses of human behavior. Puritan thought acknowledged that these rules could be softened if those who constructed and ran the government happened to be members of God's elect. But even then, it would be wise to put restraints on government, lest it fall into the hands of the unregenerate. And even a government of saints, unlikely as that would be, could do no more than promote the conditions under which men and women might have the opportunity to live righteously.

These assumptions weighed heavily in the deliberations of the Constitutional Convention and were offered to justify the document that emerged from that conclave. Although revered as the foundation of a democratic republic, the Constitution was crafted by politicans who made no secret of their faith in the Puritan image of human sinfulness (Wright 1949). In a series of newspaper articles written to encourage ratification by the states and now regarded as an authoritative reflection of the founders' intentions, Alexander Hamilton, John Jay, and James Madison outdid one another in trumpeting their belief that human beings should not be trusted with unlimited power. The authors of what came to be known as *The Federalist Papers* presented countless historical examples to show that people were inherently prone to choose evil over good, self-interest over the public good, and immediate gratification over prudent delay. Previous attempts at republican government had foundered because organized groups destroyed the institutions of representation in their single-minded pursuit of power and wealth. With its wealth of examples of past failures, *The Federalist Papers* reads like a catalog of human imperfections. This jaundiced (or to some, realistic) assessment of humankind was accepted as a basic condition, rooted in human nature, revealed in history, and impervious to changing social conditions.

Like the early Puritan settlers, the founders identified the innate corruption of humankind as the root problem of government and the great challenge to stable democracy. The task of the Constitution they crafted was to permit republican government in spite of human tendencies to destroy liberty. To accomplish this, the founders broke with traditional political thought by viewing human depravity both as a barrier to liberty and, under the right circumstances, as a republican asset. The problem, they agreed, was to secure a government capable of providing order yet limited enough to maintain a large degree of freedom. In practical terms, this meant that the national or central government must be given greater power than it had been allowed in the aftermath of the Revolution. The question was how to harness and control the power a strong central government would require.

The founders' principal solution to this problem was to partition the major powers of government by embedding them in distinct and separate institutions. Given an independent base of power, the founders thought, the three branches of government could be expected to resist encroachments by each other. They would pool their authority to achieve a common goal only when that goal was clearly in the national interest. By dividing power in this way, John Adams had written earlier, "the efforts in human nature toward tyranny can alone be checked and restrained, and any freedom preserved in the Constitution" (quoted in Wright 1949, 9).

Paradoxically, then, the weaknesses of humankind were called upon to power the engine of free government. The human shortcomings that other theorists had perceived as the stumbling block to any plan for durable republican government were enlisted by the founders as a bulwark against tyranny. What would keep the branches independent of one another, the framers predicted, were precisely those less-than-noble qualities that reposed in typical human beings: ambition, envy, greed, lust for power, and so on. Jealous to preserve its own power and status, Congress would never cede to the president the absolute authority of a monarch. Recognizing that their perpetuation depended on preservation of the Constitution, the state governments would use their veto power over constitutional amendments to retain their role. Judges and executive branch officials would be restrained by the recognition that they could lose their exalted status by impeachment. All in all, as one scholar has written (Diggins 1984, 53), the founders believed "that the Republic would be preserved by the 'machinery of government,' not the morality of men."

Considering that the Constitution had to be submitted to the people for evaluation, it may seem remarkable that the founders were so explicit in denouncing the trustworthiness of human behavior. In one of the most important of the *Federalist Papers,* number 51, Madison did little to flatter the citizens whose votes he sought. To control the government, he wrote, it was not enough to rely upon the best instincts of the people; it required "auxiliary provisions" such as the various limiting mechanisms of the Constitution. The great hope for the preservation of liberty was to equip each branch of the new government with "the necessary constitutional means and personal motives to resist encroachments of the others." Then, in a phrase that nicely encapsulated the Federalist philosophy of humankind, he reiterated the principal rationale for the various devices that controlled the exercise of governmental authority.

> It may be a reflection on human nature that such devices should be necessary to control the abuses of government. But what is government itself but the greatest of all reflections on human nature? If men were angels, no government would be necessary. If angels were to govern men, neither external nor internal controls on government would be necessary. (Rossiter 1961, 322)

Precisely because mortals fell short of angelic standards and angels did not deign to rule, prudence demanded that government be restrained from acting on its worst impulses.

That the framers felt free to defend the Constitution in those terms suggests that their image of human depravity was widely shared by the American people. In the fight over ratification, the most effective opposition came from critics who accepted the Puritan diagnosis but doubted that the proposed remedies for it were strong enough to control the weaknesses of human nature (Kenyon 1955). The Antifederalists, for example, believed that the framers of the Constitution were naive to imagine that any strong, centralized government could withstand the depradations of greedy and ambitious human beings. Whatever the differences between the proponents and enemies of the new governmental framework, however, the important point is that the entire debate was conducted within the bounds defined by the Puritan vision of human sinfulness.

Skepticism, rooted in the Puritan view of original sin, also led the founders to a negative view of government that is still widely shared by American citizens. For all their veneration of the American way of life, Americans are quite cynical about politics and tend to hold its practitioners in low regard. There is a pronounced distrust of the motivations of politicians and an enduring yearning to purify politics by bestowing leadership on persons who have achieved eminence in other fields—astronauts, businessmen, soldiers, engineers, farmers, and the like. These people, untainted by contact with a corrupting system, supposedly must be prevailed upon to give up the pleasures of life and enter the sordid world of political combat. There they are supposed to save the citizenry from "politics" by restoring a measure of sanity and common sense to political life.

The traditional American view of politics as a sordid endeavor derives in part from the founders. As we have just seen, they perceived government as a necessary evil, an institution that had to exist to preserve order but was not a good thing in itself. By embracing so wholeheartedly the Puritan image of man, emphasizing human bellicosity as the constant threat of liberty, they essentially reduced government to the status of a nightwatchman. Believing that government could just as easily threaten liberty as safeguard it, they called for as little governmental authority as was necessary to prevent society from collapsing into disarray. As for the higher task of cultivating human virtue, that was to be left to private institutions, such as the church; it did not belong in the government's sphere of responsibility (Diamond 1977).

The founders' concept of government would have astounded the ancient political thinkers, to whom politics, which Aristotle called "the master science," was the highest expression of human capacity (Will 1983). To the ancients, the state was a moral tutor, whose task was to promote certain virtues among its citizens. According to this conception, politics was the realm in which people could overcome narrow self-interest by searching for the best interests of the community. "Citizenship" was not a term denoting a dry legal status, but a title of honor reserved for those who cared deeply about the community and cultivated the public good. A republican form of government could not survive unless it inculcated such virtuous qualities in its inhabitants. According to classical republican thought, the very maintenance of the state depended on its commitment to elevate, to ennoble, to advance the interests of the community by promoting exemplary behavior. To accomplish those ambitious goals, the state had to possess substantial means, even the ability to coerce recalcitrant people to conform to what the community defined as acceptable conduct. Participation in that enterprise was seen as important and honorable.

Nothing could be further from the American conception, which equates good government with limited government. Most Americans operate from the assumption that the inherent rights of individual citizens normally take precedence over the claims of the state or those of any broader social purpose. Because such individual rights can be threatened by an overbearing government, Americans put a premium on protecting individuals from the heavy hand of the state. Following the founders, Americans have routinely denied government the right or authority to regulate belief or to limit most forms of conduct. Outside a very limited sphere, "personal virtue" is simply not seen as the proper concern of government.

Such a negative interpretation of authority has had a corresponding impact on the image of politicians. Those who are most deeply involved in conducting the business of the state, it has commonly been assumed, do so in pursuit of nothing more than self-interest. The vocation of politics, perceived in the classical tradition as the pursuit of public welfare, appears to the modern age as merely a struggle for power and personal advantage. Under this modern image, the status of the practitioners of politics has been reduced significantly. There is a widespread suspicion that politics attracts people because, as careers go, it is a fairly good way to make a living.

Limitations on government power can certainly be defended by reference to the terrible damages inflicted on other societies by governments that saw themselves as agents of God or history, charged with remaking humanity in a new image. Just as certainly, it presents problems when government tries to persuade the citizenry to undertake actions that contribute in the long run to the public good but run against immediate self-interest. As Robert Horwitz (1977, 133) asked, "How can a republic based solely on the principle of individual self-interest continue to defend itself against its external enemies if its citizenry has not an iota of patriotism, public spirit, or any element of that sense of duty that leads men to make sacrifices in defense of their country?" By teaching that government is a threat to the liberty of free-born citizens, that it is a necessity born of human imperfection, the founders unwillingly made it difficult for their successors to motivate behavior in the public interest.

ONE NATION UNDER GOD: A CIVIL RELIGION

Yet another aspect of American political life, a pronounced tendency to approach political issues in moral terms, owes much to the Puritan inheritance. Commentators have long noted that American political rhetoric is infused with religious symbols and references, and that debates about contending policy choices are frequently couched in terms of competing moral values. According to some scholars, this constant recourse to religious images and symbols in American political culture provides evidence of the existence of what has variously been called a public theology, a political religion, a religion of democracy, a public philosophy, or, most commonly today, a civil religion.

At the core of the rich and subtle concept of a civil religion is the idea that a nation tries to understand its historical experience and national purpose in religious terms (Bellah 1975; Bellah and Hammond 1980; Richey and Jones 1974). In the same way that religion may endow the life of an individual with a greater meaning than mere existence, so a civil religion reflects an attempt by citizens to give their nation a transcendent value.[3] The nation is recognized as a secular institution, but one that is somehow touched by the hand of God. British author G. K. Chesterton recognized this tendency in the United States, which he referred to as "a nation with the soul of a church."

The term *civil religion* does not refer to any formal code of beliefs that is fully developed and authoritatively encapsulated by a single written document. Because there is no formal statement of it, the content of a civil religion has to be inferred from the speeches and writings of political leaders. It lacks the status of a state religion, so citizens are not obliged to assent to it. A civil religion is neither the religion of a particular church nor, at the other extreme, a fully articulated religion that competes with existing denominations. Rather, it is a code subscribed to, in varying degrees, by all religions in the nation. Accordingly, it closely resembles one anthropologist's definition of a creed: "A constellation of ideas and standards that gives people a sense of belonging together and of being different from those of other nations and cultures" (cited in Mead 1974, 45–46). By imparting a sacred character to the nation, a civil religion enables people of diverse faith to harmonize their religious and political beliefs.

In thinking about the transcendent purpose of their nation, Americans traditionally have been drawn to the biblical metaphor of the "chosen people" (Cherry 1972). As noted in the section on covenant theology, the early Puritan colonists were prone to interpret their passage to the New World as a reenactment of God's covenant-making with the people of Abraham. Like the ancient Jews, the Puritans felt that they had been selected by God for the purpose of bringing redemption to humankind (Lienesch 1983). If they succeeded in establishing Christian communities in the wilderness, creating "God's New Israel," the rest of the world would see how the faithful were rewarded with good fortune. Even though the reality of Puritan settlements strayed far from the Christian models that motivated their founding, the inhabitants were constantly reminded that their success or failure had implications for all of humankind. That the existence of the United States is still viewed as part of a divine plan shows up in the "Pledge of Allegiance" in the phrase "one nation under God"—which was added only in the 1950s.[4]

Ever since the concept of a civil religion was first suggested, in the late 1960s, its existence has been the subject of a sustained debate among scholars of American society (see Gehrig 1979 for a good summary). Some observers have discounted civil religion as nothing more than a universal tendency among nations to endow themselves with supernatural attributes. Robert Bellah, the sociologist who did more than anyone else to popularize the concept, has argued that the national traumas of the 1960s and 1970s largely eroded American faith in the nation's higher purpose (Bellah 1975; Bellah et al. 1985). Against this backdrop, social scientists have tested for the existence of civil religious sentiments with a variety of research tools. Although their findings have not been entirely consistent, most studies have detected in public attitudes something very much like a civil religion.[5] A content analysis of the national magazine published by the Masonic fraternal organization identified a large number of statements emphasizing the nation's divine purpose (Joliceur and Knowles 1978). Using questions such as those listed in Table 3.1, Ronald Wimberly and his colleagues demonstrated a high level of public assent to statements that seem consistent with the civil religion theme (Christenson and Wimberly 1978; Wimberly 1976, 1979). Responses to these questions, which have been asked to divergent audiences, do not simply reflect commitment to general religious values or any other background factors. Rather, just as predicted by the scholars who first called attention to an American civil religion, civil religious feelings have been widely diffused among the persons interviewed in the polls. A similar survey among elementary school children in the Midwest yielded comparable support for the civil religion hypothesis (Smidt 1980). On the basis of these studies, it does appear that Americans expect their nation to fill a spiritual purpose.

Evidence of a civil religion may also emerge during national tragedies. When President John F. Kennedy was assassinated in 1963, sociological investigators noted a marked increase in prayer, worship, and other forms of religious activity. Despite the formal secularization of the governmental system and President Kennedy's membership in a minority faith (Roman Catholicism), many Americans reacted to the assassination by expressing intense religious commitment. To the political scientist Sidney Verba (1965, 354), the public response revealed that "political commitment in the United States contains a prime component of primordial religious commitment." In mourning the slain president,

Table 3.1 Measuring Civil Religion Sentiment

The existence of an American civil religion has been inferred from the citizens' responses to statements such as the following.
1. It is a mistake to think that America is God's chosen nation today.
2. I consider holidays like the Fourth of July religious as well as patriotic.
3. We need more laws on morals.
4. We should respect a president's authority since his authority is from God.
5. National leaders should affirm their belief in God.
6. Good patriots are not necessarily religious people.
7. Social justice cannot only be based on laws; it must also come from religion.
8. To me, the flag of the United States is sacred.
9. God can be known through the experience of the American people.
10. If the American government does not support religion, the government cannot uphold morality.
Positive responses to items 2–5 and 7–10 indicate a civil religious orientation, as does disagreement with items 1 and 6.
SOURCE: Wimberly 1976, 343.

Americans were honoring a sacred symbol. The discovery that a political leader could take on a religious significance for the public provided further evidence that the nation is viewed in transcendent terms.

Widespread public affirmation of a civil religion has important consequences in political life. In what social scientists call "legitimation," or its "priestly" aspect, civil religion helps cement loyalty to the nation. God blesses the nation because it serves a sacred purpose. So long as the nation conducts its affairs according to some higher purpose, it warrants allegiance from its citizens on grounds other than mere self-interest. By giving the nation a mission to which citizens are emotionally attached, civil religion may thus counter the tendencies to elevate self-interest into the only basis for loyalty and obedience. The "legitimation" function of civil religion has been confirmed by Corwin Smidt (1982) who found that the children most likely to develop a very positive image of political authority were those who perceived the nation in transcendent terms.

Also, as illustrated by the statements of two every different political commentators quoted in Table 3.2, civil religion provides standards by

Table 3.2 Expressions of Civil Religion

>   It is true that, by and large, the press in Indochina wrote stories critical of the American policy there. But it was not because reporters were unpatriotic. It was, rather, because reporters saw America slipping toward the habits of totalitarian powers whose activities we deem as less than moral.
>   What we did was to hold this country to a greater standard. Since our Government says that it stands on higher moral ground than the Communist powers, that it is different, it must behave differently, not just say so. That is the standard by which the press measured its country.
>
>   Sidney Schanberg, The New York Times,
23 April 1985, 312

Q. Who's side *is* God on?
A. Well, I think He's on the side of Right, Justice, and Goodness—all those things. And I think the side anti-ERA is on.
Q. Is God American?
A. No, but He certainly blessed America more than any other country. And with that goes the responsibility to do the right thing and assume that leadership. If America abandons that responsibility, it could face a terrible destruction.
Q. Who is God against? Who's on the other side?
A. The Devil.
Q. Represented by whom?
A. . . . the Devil is a very intelligent creature, who appears in a lot of forms. I do think he's in the Kremlin, among other places.

Phyllis Schlafly, Ms. magazine, January
1982, 92

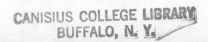

which to judge the behavior of a nation. It suggests that there are things higher than the nation and that it is permissible to criticize the nation for its departures from moral codes. As the New Testament taught, a nation "under God" is deemed responsible to God and will be held by God to a high standard of behavior. Because transgressors suffer severe punishment from a just God, citizens have an incentive to keep the nation firmly on the path of righteousness. This is the ethical or prophetic function of civil religion.

Critics of American policy, such as the journalist quoted in Table 3.2, have usually invoked the prophetic side of civil religion, by calling on America to honor its own aspirations and standards. When he admonished American Christians to challenge racial segregation, the Reverend Martin Luther King, Jr. (1963, 128), imagined what St. Paul would have said to them:

> You have a dual citizenry. You live both in time and eternity. Your highest loyalty is to God, and not to the mores or the folkways, the state or the nation, or any man-made institution. If any earthly institution or custom conflicts with God's will, it is your Christian duty to oppose it. You must never allow the transitory, evanescent demands of man-made institutions to take precedence over the eternal demands of the Almighty God.

The deep hold this concept has had on the American mind is evidenced by the fact that it has recurred with equal intensity among those who have resisted the changes sought by King. In their indictment of American policies, conservative critics such as Phyllis Schlafly (see Table 3.2) have stressed that God's blessing on the United States is contingent on the country's adherence to biblical morality. Although they are more prone than King to cite biblical passages that appear to annoint the political system with divine sanction, right-wing leaders such as Schlafly and the Reverend Jerry Falwell also have reserved the right to disobedience when they see human law in conflict with divine law.

No American politician expressed the priestly and prophetic themes of civil religion more eloquently than Abraham Lincoln (Morgenthau and Hein 1983). Although relatively untouched by "church religion," Lincoln saw the United States as a nation with a divine purpose that had been most clearly revealed in the noble principles of the Declaration of Independence. For Lincoln, the commitment to secure free government, which had been sanctified by the sacrifices of the revolutionary generation, was the higher purpose that the United States represented. By adhering to the principles of the Declaration, he told Congress late in 1862, the nation was nothing less than "the last, best hope of earth." Because the Union was the concrete embodiment of that continuing commitment to liberty, Lincoln made its maintenance and eventual restoration his highest priority. At Gettysburg, he interpreted the deaths of

Union soldiers in transcendent terms, saying that their sacrifice in the cause of liberty had reaffirmed the sacred character of the American mission. He then asked Americans to respond with "increased devotion" to the cause for which the soldiers had given the "last full measure of devotion" (Lincoln 1959a).

If Lincoln enunciated civil religious themes to sanctify the Union, he was equally willing to call down the wrath of God upon the nation when he thought it had strayed from the path of righteousness. Although favoring moderate solutions to slavery, he clearly regarded the maintenance of that institution as a great national sin—perhaps the American equivalent of Adam's fall from God's grace. In his second inaugural address, delivered only a month before his assassination, Lincoln (1959b) chided Northerners and Southerners alike who claimed God's support for their cause. Quoting from Scripture, he noted that God punished those who committed offenses in the world. Those responsible for the "offense" of American slavery included all Americans, both the Southerners who kept slaves and the Northerners who had acquiesced in its continued existence. He saw the bloodshed and violence of the war as God's retribution: "He gives to both North and South this terrible war as the woe due to those by whom the offense came." Rejecting complacency and self-righteousness, Lincoln called upon the nation to accept its punishment and then to rededicate itself to the principles of the Declaration.

Lincoln was far from alone in his invocation of civil religion; in fact, students of political rhetoric have demonstrated its recurrence in the public statements of nearly all American presidents (Hart 1977). In a systematic content analysis of inaugural addresses delivered from George Washington to Ronald Reagan, Cynthia Toolin (1983) found the speeches replete with reference to the nation's divine origin and its corresponding moral obligation to light the way for the remainder of the earth. To judge from the utterances of the two most recent occupants of the office, the priestly and prophetic strains of civil religion have retained potency. Jimmy Carter's first speech as president encouraged Americans to develop "full faith" in their country—wording that signifies dedication to a transcendent force—and contained numerous references to the country in religious terms (Hahn 1984). Carter also emphasized the prophetic side of civil religion in urging upon the nation the biblical injunction "to do justly, and to love mercy, and to walk humbly with thy God." In declaring at his inauguration that "I believe God intended for us to be free," Ronald Reagan (1981, 4; also Shannon 1982) made an even more explicit statement of belief in a civil religion. The prophetic side of Reagan's faith can be inferred from his frequent suggestions that the United States has strayed from the intentions of the founders in asking government to do too much (1981, 3). Though he did not say directly that God had punished Americans by sending an economic recession, that line of reasoning would be consistent with the view that violations of a sacred covenant bring retribution upon transgressors.

Civil religion is a double-edged sword. It can ennoble a people by prompting generous instincts and a resolute commitment to the nation's principles. Yet the two streams of civil religion—legitimation and prophecy—can also be vulgarized. Attributing a sacred purpose to the nation can degenerate all too easily into idolatrous worship of the state. The belief that a nation is the perfect embodiment of God's will can inhibit the skepticism and self-criticism so important to democratic politics (Lipsitz 1968). Similarly, in holding the nation to high standards of conduct, the civil religious tradition may produce a frame of mind that disdains the compromises necessary for an orderly political life. If the standards are rigid and unbending, the system one of moral absolutes, then all deviations are equally reprehensible—a view that does not encourage a sense of proportion.

Although civil religion has been degraded in this manner in domestic politics, the dangers of extremist versions have been most visible in American interactions with the rest of the world (Tiryakian 1982). To the constant irritation of many nations, including allies, the United States often has acted as if God had granted it an exclusive franchise to regenerate the world. Some critics have argued that this sense of mission, coupled with a tendency to view international politics as a clash of moral opposites, has undermined the development of an effective foreign policy. An approach to the world built on moral absolutes can distort judgment by blinding policymakers to important subtleties.

Consider, for example, the U.S. government's behavior toward international communism in the tense period following World War II. When the wartime alliance between the United States and the Soviet Union broke down in the aftermath of victory, American policy reverted to a position of unrelenting hostility. Whatever the real provocations in Soviet behavior, the U.S. foreign policy leadership was prone to treat the Soviet Union as a moral leper that had to be isolated from the world community (Hoopes 1973). Many thoughtful critics who harbor no illusions about Soviet intentions have wondered if this policy served American interests. They have noted that the moralistic approach to international communism, including denunciation of it in theological terms, may have prevented American policymakers from recognizing and exploiting the split in the late 1950s between the Soviet Union and the People's Republic of China. In this view, an opportunity to assert the national interest by maneuvering between the rival communist powers was passed over in favor of a crusading approach. If these critics are right—and their views are still being debated—the moralistic approach impeded a realistic assessment of American interests.

Such a crusading mentality may also have encouraged the very bar-

barism it was meant to counteract. As George Kennan (1951) charged, a moralistic streak that stigmatizes opponents as the embodiment of evil will be satisfied with nothing less than total victory over the enemy. The result, a "total war" mentality, impedes compromise and thus excacerbates tension. Persons and nations who believed God was on their side have been responsible for some of the most unspeakable horrors of world history (as have people who rejected the notion of God or any higher spiritual realm). Little wonder, then, that civil religion should be regarded as a two-edged sword. Like religion in general, it may call forth the best and worst instincts in human behavior—and there is ample evidence of both in the impact of the American civil religion.

* * * * *

It would surely be an exaggeration to state flatly that religion alone *caused* important political attitudes—including the social contract, limited government, and American destiny—to take hold of the American imagination. The link between the ideas of sixteenth-century religious thinkers and eighteenth-century political activists is a tangled and meandering path, not a straight line. Religion, in its various guises, should be recognized as only one of the forces operating in the development of American political culture.

At least two other influences shaped the American political system in its formative period—a new intellectual force and the lure of economic advantage. The foremost intellectual rival to the ideology of the Protestant Reformation was a body of thought developed in seventeenth- and eighteenth-century Europe under the name of the Enlightenment (May 1976).[6] This movement, characterized above all by a belief in human progress through the systematic application of reason, supplied a heavy dose of optimism to counterbalance the negative image of humanity derived from Calvinism. Without some sense that humans could engage in reasonable conduct under the proper institutional arrangements, the founders could not have contemplated constructing a democratic political system. Their attempt to create a written constitution alone bespeaks a tremendous confidence in the human capacity to discover eternal truths by reflection and debate. The influence of the Age of Reason, as the Enlightenment era has been called, was apparent in the thought and behavior of political activists throughout the revolutionary period and during the early history of the nation.

In addition to the sway of intellectual currents from Europe, the colonists were also moved by material forces. Clearly, key elements of the political culture served to advance the economic interests of powerful groups in early American society. As generations of schoolchildren have learned, a major incentive to break with Great Britain were economic grievances about taxation and other matters. The founders' strong commitment to the idea of limited government may have also been the product of economic self-interest, for a government with limited authority was a government incapable of redistributing income from the wealthy to the poor. The founders generally came from the more affluent stratum of colonial society, and material interests may well have disposed them to accept the Calvinist argument on the need to keep governmental authority tightly reined in. Similarly, the missionary impulse in American political culture permitted the nation to fuel its economic expansion by the constant acquisition of new land, raw materials, sources of labor, and markets.

Given the many factors at work in forming the American political culture, the appropriate conclusion is that certain patterns of religious thought, habitual ways of reasoning about God and humankind, made it easier for some political ideas to take root in American society. Accustomed to thinking about God and mortals in contractual terms, Americans were receptive to a political theory that treated government in a similar fashion. The widespread belief that humans behave sinfully disposed the colonists to accept the doctrine of limited government. Trained by their religion to see God at work in the daily lives of men and women, Americans could easily imagine a divine hand guiding the destiny of their country. In this way, religion was one of the factors that facilitated the development of a common political outlook.

This qualified judgment, recognizing religion as one among several sources of the American founding, should also provide a perspective on the debate about the nation's path since the Revolution. Among some contemporary descendants of the Puritan heritage, there is a tendency to treat recent American history in terms of a decline and fall. As three evangelical scholars recently conveyed this image, it begins with the assumption that the United States "emerged from the generally Christian actions of generally Christian people [who] . . . bequeathed Christian values, and a Christian heritage, to later American history" (Noll, Hatch, and Marsden 1983). By loosening legal constraints on items as diverse as abortion, school discipline, sexual behavior, drug use, and sex roles, it is charged, the government has betrayed its heritage and abandoned its Christian foundations. But if Christianity certainly played a prominent role in the American founding, the evidence presented herein does not sustain the claim that colonial America was exclusively influenced by Christian values.[7] Whether or not early America was morally superior to present-day society is a question that will continue to be debated; beginning the debate with the image of a golden age, a one-time "Christian America," is a dubious strategy.

When examined from the perspective of political culture, religion has generally been a unifying force in American politics, helping to generate a national consensus on basic political values. Even if the religious inspiration of these core ideas has been forgotten, the political concepts of social contract, limited government, and American destiny remain integral elements of American political culture. As the next several chapters will show, religion can divide as well as unite. Some important fractures in the body politic originate in differences among religious groups over theology, social standing, and institutional interests. I will first examine how these differences affect mass attitudes on policy issues and behavior in the voting booth.

NOTES

[1]As a student once remarked to me, perfectly revealing the cynicism of the age, "People are rich or poor before they are anything else."

[2]The development of contract thought among the colonists has traditionally been credited to the "secular" influence of the English philosopher John Locke. But as Winthrop Hudson (1965a) argued, Locke drew upon the ideas of the Puritans to formulate his doctrine of government by consent of the governed.

[3]In a review of the civil religion concept, Richey and Jones (1974, 14–18) identified five overlapping uses of the term. I have adopted the definition of civil religion as a sense of national transcendence because that is the manner in which the "chosen people" metaphor has entered the political culture.

[4]The degree to which this type of civil religion is the unique property of American culture or a more universal phenomenon has yet to be fully addressed. Michael Walzer (1985) has found the Exodus metaphor throughout political history. For some suggestive thoughts on civil religion in comparative perspective, see Coleman (1970) and Bellah and Hammond (1980, chaps. 2–4).

[5]The exceptions include Thomas and Flippen (1972), who found few references to any divine plan for the United States in newspaper editorials published during "Honor America" week. In interviews that Benson and Williams (1982) conducted with members of the U.S. Congress, most legislators proved unwilling to endorse statements that interpreted the nation's destiny in transcendent terms.

[6]Since the Christianity of the Protestant Reformation was skeptical about the capacity for human regeneration and emphasized revelation as the key to understanding, it may be tempting to portray religion and rationalist thought as incompatible. In practice, the two traditions at times found common ground and at times competed for influence—often within the mind of the same individual.

[7]Noll, Hatch, and Marsden (1983) have made a strong case that a "Christian culture" is generally unlikely and that colonial America was a considerable distance away from a scripturally based commonwealth. They also raise doubts that the Christian influence in early America was uniformly positive.

REFERENCES

Ahlstrom, Sydney. 1975. *A Religious History of the American People.* 2 volumes. New York: Image Books.

Ahlstrom, Sydney. 1965. "The Puritan Ethic and the Spirit of American Democracy." In *Calvinism and the Political Order,* ed. George L. Hunt. Philadelphia, PA: Westminister Press, 88–107.

Bellah, Robert, Richard Madsen, William M. Sullivan, and Steven M. Tipton. 1985. *Habits of the Heart.* Berkeley, CA: University of California Press.

Bellah, Robert N. 1975. *The Broken Covenant: American Civil Religion in a Time of Trial.* New York: Seabury Press.

Bellah, Robert N., and Phillip E. Hammond. 1980. *Varieties of Civil Religion.* New York: Harper and Row.

Benson, Peter L., and Dorothy L. Williams. 1982. *Religion on Capitol Hill: Myths and Realities.* San Francisco, CA: Harper and Row.

Bercovitch, Sacvan. 1975. *The Puritan Origins of the American Self.* New Haven, CT: Yale University Press.

Berk, Stephen E. 1974. *Calvinism Versus Democracy.* Hamden, CT: Archon Books.

Bridenbaugh, Carl. 1962. *Mitre and Sceptre: Transatlantic Faiths, Ideas, Personalities, and Politics, 1689–1775.* New York: Oxford University Press.

Brown, Katherine B. 1977. "The Controversy Over the Franchise in Puritan Massachusetts, 1954 to 1974." In *Puritan New England,* ed. Alden T. Vaughan and Francis J. Bremer. New York: St. Martin's Press, 128–154.

Cherry, Conrad E., editor. 1972. *God's New Israel: Religious Interpretations of American Destiny.* Englewood Cliffs, NJ: Prentice-Hall.

Christenson, James, and Ronald C. Wimberly. 1978. "Who is Civil Religious?" *Sociological Analysis.* 39: 77–83.

Coleman, John A. 1970. "Civil Religion." *Sociological Analysis.* 31: 67–77.

Diamond, Martin. 1977. "Ethics and Politics: The American Way." In *The Moral Foundations of the American Republic,* ed. Robert H. Horwitz. Charlottesville, VA: University Press of Virginia, 39–72.

Diggins, John P. 1984. *The Lost Soul of American Politics: Virtue, Self-Interest, and the Foundations of Liberalism.* New York: Basic Books.

Elazar, Daniel J. 1980. "The Political Theory of Covenant: Biblical Origins and Modern Developments." *Publius.* 10: 3–30.

Gehrig, Gail. 1979. *American Civil Religion: An Assessment.* Storrs, CT: Society for the Scientific Study of Religion. Monograph Series, #3.

Hahn, Dan F. 1984. "The Rhetoric of Jimmy Carter, 1976–1980." *Presidential Studies Quarterly.* 14: 265–288.

Hart, Roderick. 1977. *The Political Pulpit.* West Lafayette, IN: Purdue University Press.

Heimert, Alan. 1966. *Religion and the American Mind: From the Great Awakening to the Revolution.* Cambridge, MA: Harvard University Press.

Hoopes, Townshend. 1973. *The Devil and John Foster Dulles.* Boston, MA: Atlantic–Little, Brown.

Horwitz, Robert H. 1977. "John Locke and the Preservation of Liberty: A Perennial Problem of Civic Education." In *Moral Foundations of the American Republic,* ed. Robert H. Horwitz. Charlottesville, VA: University Press of Virginia, 129–156.

Hudson, Winthrop S. 1965a. "John Locke: Heir of Puritan Political Theorists." In *Calvinism and the Political Order,* ed. George L. Hunt. Philadelphia, PA: Westminister Press, 108–129.

Hudson, Winthrop S. 1965b. *Religion in America.* New York: Charles Scribner's Sons.

Joliceur, Pamela M., and Louis K. Knowles. 1978. "Fraternal Organizations and Civil Religion: Scottish Rite Freemasonry." *Review of Religious Research*. 20: 3–22.

Kennan, George F. 1951. *American Diplomacy, 1900–1950*. Chicago, IL: University of Chicago Press.

Kenyon, Cecelia. 1955. "Men of Little Faith: The Anti-Federalists on the Nature of Representative Government." *William and Mary Quarterly*. 12: 3–43.

King, Martin Luther, Jr. 1963. *Strength to Love*. New York: Harper and Row.

Lienesch, Michael. 1983. "The Role of Political Millennialism in Early American Nationalism." *Western Political Quarterly*. 36: 445–465.

Lincoln, Abraham. 1959a. "Second Inaugural Address." In *The Search for Democracy*, ed. Harry W. Kirwin. Garden City, NY: Doubleday-Anchor, 203–205.

Lincoln, Abraham. 1959b. "The Gettysburg Address." In *The Search for Democracy*, ed. Harry W. Kirwin. Garden City, NY: Doubleday-Anchor, 102–103.

Lipsitz, Lewis. 1968. "If, as Verba Says, the State Functions as a Religion, What Are We to Do Then to Save Our Souls?" *American Political Science Review*. 62: 527–535.

Lutz, Donald S. 1984. "The Relative Influence of European Writers Upon Late 18th-Century American Political Thought." *American Political Science Review*. 78: 189–197.

May, Henry. 1976. *The Enlightenment in America*. New York: Oxford University Press.

Mead, Sidney A. 1974. "The 'Nation with the Soul of a Church.' " In *American Civil Religion*, ed. Russell E. Richey and Donald G. Jones. New York: Harper and Row, 45-75.

Miller, Perry. 1967. *Nature's Nation*. Cambridge, MA: Harvard University Press.

Miller, Perry. 1956. *Errand into the Wilderness*. Cambridge, MA: Harvard University Press.

Miller, William Lee. 1961. "American Religion and American Political Attitudes." In *Religious Perspectives in American Culture*, ed. James Ward Smith and A. Leland Jamison. Princeton, NJ: Princeton University Press, 81–118.

Morgenthau, Hans, and David Hein. 1983. *Essays on Lincoln's Faith and Politics*. Lanham, MD: University Press of America.

Niebuhr, H. Richard. 1959. *The Kingdom of God in America*. New York: Harper Torchbooks.

Noll, Mark A., Nathan O. Hatch, and George M. Marsden. 1983. *The Search for Christian America*. Westchester, IL: Crossway Books.

Reagan, Ronald W. 1981. "Inaugural Address of President Ronald Reagan." *Weekly Compilation of Presidential Documents*. Washington, DC: Government Printing Office, January 26: 1–5.

Richey, Russell E., and Donald G. Jones, editors. 1974. *American Civil Religion*. New York: Harper and Row.

Riemer, Neal. 1980. "Covenant and the Federal Constitution." *Publius*. 10: 135–148.

Rossiter, Clinton, editor. 1961. *The Federalist Papers*. New York: New American Library.

Rothman, Rozanu. 1980. "The Impact of Covenant and Contract Theories on Conceptions of the U.S. Constitution." *Publius*. 10: 149–163.

Schecter, Stephen L. 1980. "The Founding of American Local Communities: A Study of Covenantal and Other Forms of Association." *Publius.* 10: 165–185.

Shannon, W. Wayne. 1982. "Mr. Reagan Goes to Washington: Teaching Exceptional America." *Public Opinion.* 4: 13–17, 55.

Shipton, Clifford K. 1947. "Puritanism and Modern Democracy." *New England Historical and Genealogical Register.* 101: 181–198.

Simpson, Alan. 1955. *Puritanism of Old and New England.* Chicago: University of Chicago Press.

Smidt, Corwin. 1982. "Civil Religious Orientations and Children's Perceptions of Political Authority." *Political Behavior.* 4: 147–162.

Smidt, Corwin. 1980. "Civil Religious Orientations Among Elementary School Children." *Sociological Analysis.* 41: 25–40.

Strout, Cushing. 1974. *The New Heavens and New Earth.* New York: Harper and Row.

Thomas, Michael C., and Charles C. Flippen. 1972. "American Civil Religion: An Empirical Study." *Social Forces.* 51: 218–225.

Tiryakian, Edward A. 1982. "Puritan America in the Modern World: Mission Impossible?" *Sociological Analysis.* 43: 351–368.

Toolin, Cynthia, 1983. "American Civil Religion from 1789–1981: A Content Analysis of Presidential Inaugural Addresses." *Review of Religious Research.* 25: 39–48.

Verba, Sidney. 1965. "The Kennedy Assassination and the Nature of Political Commitment." In *The Kennedy Assassination and the American Public,* ed. Bradley S. Greenberg and Edward S. Parker. Stanford, CA: Stanford University Press, 348–360.

Walzer, Michael. 1985. *Exodus and Revolution.* New York: Basic Books.

Will, George F. 1983. *Statecraft as Soulcraft: What Government Does.* New York: Simon and Schuster.

Wimberly, Ronald C. 1979. "Continuity in the Measurement of Civil Religion." *Sociological Analysis.* 40: 59–62.

Wimberly, Ronald C. 1976. "Testing the Civil Religion Hypothesis." *Sociological Analysis.* 37: 341–352.

Wright, Benjamin F. 1949. "The Federalist on the Nature of Political Man." *Ethics.* 59: 1–31.

4

The Religious Dimension of American Political Behavior

By the side of every religion is to be found a political opinion, which is connected with it by affinity. If the human mind be left to follow its own bent, it will regulate the temporal and spiritual institutions of society in a uniform manner, and man will endeavor . . . to harmonize earth with heaven.
—*Alexis de Tocqueville*

Even in colonial America, a land with a common theological tradition, people did not always see eye-to-eye on the appropriate political applications of religious ideas. The potential for religiously based political conflict in the United States was further encouraged by the subsequent fragmentation or national religious life. Along with the massive eighteenth- and nineteenth-century migrations from Europe came challenges to Protestant supremacy from perspectives inspired by Catholic and Jewish thought. And just as it began facing competition from immigrant religions, Protestant unity started to decay from within. As new denominations spread rapidly on the expanding southern and western frontiers, the more established branches of Protestantism split into competing denominations over a variety of issues. Thanks to these internal fractures, the differences within Protestantism eventually came to rival the differences between Protestants and non-Protestants. The presence of the new religious groups and the widening fissures within Protestantism undermined the capacity of religion to unite Americans in a common body of thought. During much of the nineteenth and early twentieth centuries, religion was a source of continuing social conflict and political dispute.

Despite subsequent convergence on some issues and the decline of overt religious conflict in politics, differences between religious groups continue to mark political behavior in the United States today. Whatever Americans believe about how religion and politics should interact, their behavior does not always reveal a strict "wall of separation" between religious and political loyalties. Individuals hold opinions and cast votes, but they do so subject to the tug of group tradition and influence. Global studies have revealed that religion, in concert with such factors as social class, race, ethnicity, and region, has continued to exert a major influence on a variety of political orientations (Lijphart 1971; Rose and Urwin 1969). After reviewing numerous studies of voting patterns in different countries, one leading expert on mass political attitudes was forced to conclude that "religious differentiation intrudes on partisan political alignments in [an] unexpectedly powerful degree wherever it conceivably can" (Converse 1974, 734). The use of the word *unexpectedly* reveals that modern observers have been surprised to find political differences tied to "primordial" religious cleavages rather than to thoroughly "modern" inequalities such as social class.

In recognition of the importance of religion in contemporary political loyalties, this chapter describes how religious groups agree or disagree on a variety of political orientations and explains major differences between groups by reference to creedal, institutional, and social characteristics. Of course, American political attitudes bear the imprint of many factors aside from religious group loyalties. This chapter will not argue either that other group loyalties are absent from the public agenda or that religion intrudes on every political issue of importance. Rather, by charting the contours of denominational differences and evaluating explanations for the link between religious group membership and mass political behavior, it will explore the religious roots of some contemporary political controversies.

PATTERNS OF RELIGIOUS AFFILIATION

A valuable perspective on the contemporary relationship between religion and political attitudes in the United States can be gained through a series of public opinion surveys conducted periodically by the National Opinion Research Center at the University of Chicago. Known as the General Social Survey, these periodic interviews with representative national samples of the adult population contain a broad range of data about social and political attitudes. Because the surveys identify the religious preferences of the participants, they make it possible to compare religious groups with one another.[1] In the following analysis, respondents in surveys conducted in 1980, 1982, 1983, and 1984 are combined, so as to obtain a data set large enough to permit examination of religious groups that are normally excluded from study because of small representation in any single poll.

For purposes of group analysis, I have divided the American population into six major religious categories: Catholic, Jewish, black Protestant, white "mainline" Protestant, white "evangelical" Protestant, and persons who report no religious preference or preference for a nontraditional faith.[2] Catholics and Jews form distinctive religious communities, so their treatment as separate categories should come as no surprise. Similarly, in a society in which there is strong social pressure to claim attachment to some religious tradition, those who report no affiliation obviously require separate analysis. The reason for singling out black Protestants stems from the unique historical tradition, social situation, and political role of the predominantly black religious denominations.[3] An equally significant line of division separates the white Protestants into two camps with different religious beliefs, styles of worship, and attitudes toward the role of the church in society. Because the contrasting orientations of evangelical and mainline Protestants seem to be taking on increased political relevance, it seems appropriate to consider the two groups as different religious types.[4]

The evangelical camp includes Protestants who have also been described as conservative, traditional, old-time, and fundamentalist. They are distinguished by a style of religious commitment that stresses loyalty to the traditional orthodoxy of Protestant Christianity. Historians of American religion trace this tradition to the great waves of Protestant revivalism in the eighteenth century. The contemporary evangelicals have retained the religious intensity and passionate, emotional commitment to faith that characterized the Puritan settlers. In theological terms, today's evangelicals are distinguished by three core items of faith: "(1) the belief that the Bible is the inerrant Word of God, (2) the belief in the divinity of Christ, and (3) the belief in the efficacy of Christ's life, death and physical resurrection for the salvation of the human soul" (Hunter 1983, 7; see also Quebedeaux 1978). Evangelicals also emphasize the importance of personal religious experience, as leading to individual salvation, and see the church principally as an agent for guiding nonbelievers into the embrace of a forgiving God. Beyond this basic unity of theological outlook among evangelicals, the conservative religious tradition in Protestantism habors great variety in styles of worship, form of church governance, points of doctrine, and other features.

The mainline camp in American Protestantism, also known as the modernist, liberal, or moderate camp, consists principally of denominations with quite different historical traditions. Descended from religious groups that were relatively unaffected by revivalism, preferring instead to trust reason as the key to approaching God, mainline Protestants have relaxed some traditional beliefs that used to distinguish Protestants from

other types of Christians. Unlike the evangelicals, who are prone to interpret biblical injunctions as absolute statements, the moderates tend to
interpret many Christian beliefs in symbolic terms. Apart from liberal
theology, what has held the mainline camp together and distinguished it
from evangelicalism has been a certain vision of the church's role in
society (Kelley 1977). Supporters of this Protestant wing call on the
church primarily to enhance fellowship among its members and to improve the social conditions of society at large. By visualizing the church as
provider of fellowship, entertainment, guidance, and knowledge for its
members and as an advocate for the poor and oppressed outside its walls,
the mainline churches keep their gaze simultaneously on heaven and
earth. Like evangelicalism, the mainline tradition represents a tendency
rather than a rigid position: that is, there remain significant differences
among churches sharing the label.

In practice, the dividing line between evangelical and mainline Protestants is not always neat or easy to trace; it cuts right through some
denominations and churches, even the minds of individual church members (Hoge 1976). Participants in the General Social Surveys have not
regularly been asked the types of detailed questions sufficient to classify
individuals as either mainline or evangelical. In the absence of such data,
I have categorized white Protestants on the basis of denomination and
place of upbringing.

As a common rule of thumb, churches affiliated with the National
Council of Churches are regarded as mainline. Following that rough-but-
ready definition, the mainline category includes the approximately 40
percent of white Protestant respondents who described their religious
preference as Congregationalist, Methodist, Episcopalian, Presbyterian,
Disciples of Christ, American Lutheran, American Baptist, Unitarian,
Friends, or any of several smaller denominations. Most of the remaining
Protestants belong to denominations affiliated with the National Association of Evangelicals or have otherwise been identified as predominantly
evangelical in theology. The denominations so classified in this analysis
include Missouri and Wisconsin Synod Lutherans, Southern Baptists, the
Churches of Christ, the Assemblies of God, and several smaller churches
commonly regarded as fundamentalist and/or pentecostal.[5] Like any
scheme for putting human beings into separate categories, this method of
apportionment should be regarded as an approximation—a simplifying
device for reducing complexity to a manageable level. It is useful only
insofar as it aids in the discovery of different tendencies in the political
behavior of religious groups.

Figure 4.1 shows the distribution of the more than 6,000 survey
participants among the six basic religious categories. The size of the slices
confirms the extent of religious pluralism in the United States. No single
religious group comes close to claiming a majority of the population; and

Figure 4.1   U.S. Religious Preferences in the 1980s

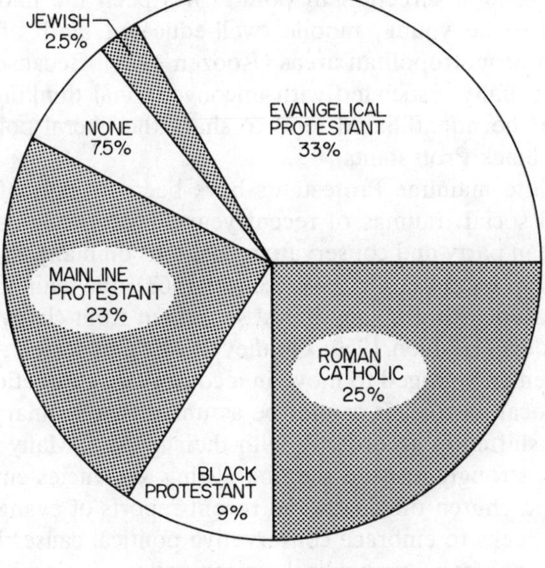

Source: 1980-84 General Social Survey. N=6400

were the groups to be subdivided to reflect their internal diversity on issues of theology, worship, and church organization, the sense of religious fragmentation would be reinforced. The largest single chunk of the population, about one-third of the adult population, comprises white evangelical Protestants. The Roman Catholic church follows evangelicalism in size, claiming the adherence of roughly one-quarter of those who voiced a religious preference. The mainline Protestants make up a slightly smaller share of the population than Catholics. The remainder of the adult population is divided among black Protestants (9 percent of the total), persons who claimed no religious preference (7.5 percent), and Jews (2.5 percent).

Previous research has identified some basic political tendencies of the six religious groups. American Jews, like their coreligionists in other countries, have long been identified with left-wing political causes (Dawidowicz and Goldstein 1974; Elazar 1969; El Azhary 1980; Fuchs 1956; Guysenir 1958; Liebman 1979; Rischin 1962). Black Protestants have usually supported the same liberal policies and candidates as Jews. Since the 1960s, some commentators have professed to see (and others have hoped for) a movement toward more conservative positions in both groups and the uncoupling of their political alliance. Even with these purported changes, most experts still find black Protestants and Jews on the left side of the political spectrum (Fisher 1976, 1979). Although religious nonaffiliates have not been subject to much research, one clue about their general direction in politics has been the finding that such people tend to be young, mobile, well-educated, and affluent, and to live in urban or metropolitan areas (Roozen 1978). Because such characteristics are usually associated with unconventional thinking, it has been thought that the nonaffiliated tend to share the liberal political outlook of Jews and black Protestants.

The white mainline Protestants have been strongly affected by the political and social traumas of recent years. Historically associated with the Republican party and conservative positions on many issues (Berelson et al. 1954; Lazarsfeld et al. 1948; Lenski 1963), the mainline Protestants have been faced with growing liberal sentiment from clergy and denominational leaders (Hadden 1969; Quinley 1974). Conversely, the evangelicals have been encouraged to move in a conservative direction by some of their most vocal pastors. It cannot be assumed that ordinary members of these camps shifted in accordance with their leaders. Many mainline Protestants have strongly resisted the liberalizing tendencies emanating from the pulpit and church officials. And recent reports of evangelical leaders urging their flocks to embrace conservative political causes have diverted public attention from evangelical voices calling for social justice and world peace through cooperative disarmament (Fowler 1982; Rifkin 1979). The opinion data will reveal how mainline and evangelical white Protestants have responded to these conflicting messages.

Like Jews and black Protestants, Catholics coalesced around the Democratic party in the 1930s; the Catholic commitment to the party was reinforced in 1960, when the Democrats conferred their presidential nomination on a Catholic candidate (Converse 1966; Scoble and Epstein 1964; Greer 1961; Fenton 1960; Baggaley 1962). Some observers have doubted the depth of this commitment, arguing that attachment to the more liberal political party was a transient stage, reflecting the immigrant and working-class background of Catholics. Under conditions of economic parity with Protestants, it has been suggested, Catholics will embrace the political conservatism that appears to be a more natural outgrowth of church doctrine (Phillips 1969, 140–75; Lipset 1964; Crosby 1978; Whyte 1981). Although many Catholics have moved into the economic mainstream and the Republicans have courted them aggressively on the basis of opposition to abortion and other policies, it remains open to debate whether the Catholic masses have moved to the right side of the political spectrum (Hanna 1979; Fee 1976; Greeley 1977). Except on the issue of abortion, members of the Catholic religious elite—priests, bishops, and lay leaders—appear to have moved in just the opposite direction (Hanna 1984).

Expectations about religious group patterns do not always distinguish among different political issues. It is quite possible that a group may stand out as relatively conservative on one type of policy but adopt a much more liberal position on another. To take account of this possibility, I have grouped the questions on the General Social Survey into three categories. The first set relates to political identity: preference for a political party, choice of presidential candidates, liberal versus conservative self-image, and general attitude toward government spending. The second taps attitudes toward several political issues of recent import—crime, civil liberties, race relations, and spending for social purposes. The final category is reserved for the "moral" or "social" issues involving behavior that challenges traditional Christian teaching.

POLITICAL IDENTITY

The most basic component of political identity is preference for a major political party. Despite a decline of formal party membership, a rise in the proportion of citizens declaring themselves independent of the parties, and a greater willingness to cross party lines in voting, most Americans still classify themselves, in greater or lesser degree, as supporters of one or the other major political party. The selection of a particular partisan label (including "independent") remains a useful predictor of basic political attitudes, electoral choice, and a wide array of related attitudes and forms of behavior. Though finer distinctions are possible, I have divided the participants in the General Social Survey simply into Democrats (39 percent), Republicans (24 percent), and independents (36 percent).[6] Figure 4.2 shows the partisan breakdown within each of the six religious groups.

Figure 4.2 Party Preference by Religious Preference

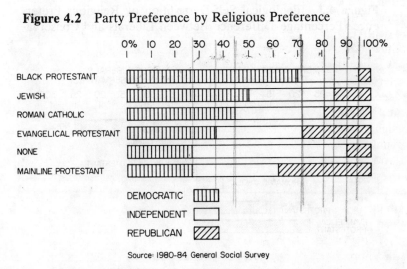

Source: 1980-84 General Social Survey

Pronounced differences among religious groups in patterns of partisan allegiance were apparent. The two most strongly Democratic groups—the only groups giving that party a clear majority—were black Protestants and Jews. At the other extreme, the mainline Protestants, remaining true to reputation as the most Republican of groups, were the only denominational category with a plurality of Republican identifiers. Of the remaining groups, pluralities of Catholics and white evangelical Protestants preferred the Democrats but were less committed to that party than were black Protestant and Jewish respondents. Persons with no religious preference turned out to be predominantly independent in politics as well; of the religiously uncommitted who did adopt a party label, Democrats outnumbered Republicans.

Another important element of political identity, ideological self-image, can be measured by asking individuals to characterize their political views on a scale from "extremely liberal" to "extremely conservative," with "moderate, middle of the road" as the neutral midpoint. Taken as a whole, the respondents were more comfortable with the neutral designation (41 percent) than with any other classification; after the moderate plurality came persons on the conservative side of the spectrum (35 percent) and then liberals of various degrees (24 percent). With the moderate option so attractive to Americans of all religious preferences, differences among groups can best be gauged by the balance of support between the remaining liberals and conservatives. On that measure, as portrayed in Figure 4.3, Jewish respondents, black Protestants, and persons with no religious affiliation were the three most liberal groups, whereas both types of white Protestant leaned heavily to the right side of the political spectrum.

Figure 4.3   Ideological Self-Description by Religious Preference (Percentage Difference Between Liberals and Conservatives)

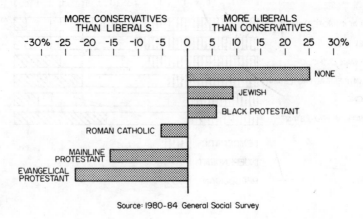

Source: 1980-84 General Social Survey

Catholics mirrored the national distribution, with a plurality in the middle and conservatives outnumbering liberals by a clear margin.

The choice between presidential candidates gives citizens an opportunity to act on their more abstract political leanings. Participants in the 1980 survey were asked about their preferences in the 1976 presidential election; in the three General Social Surveys conducted after the 1980 election, interviewers canvassed the preferences of participants for the three major candidates on the 1980 presidential ballot. Because the choices of actual voters were supplemented with the preferences of the large number of nonvoters, the surveys exaggerate Democratic strength. In 1976 the balance of support favored the Democrats by the healthy ratio of 57 percent for Democratic candidate Jimmy Carter to 43 percent for Republican Gerald Ford. The distribution of preferences was much closer in 1980, when 48 percent of survey participants endorsed the Democratic standard-bearer (Carter), 44 percent supported the Republican Ronald Reagan, and 7 percent voiced support for independent candidate John Anderson.

Figure 4.4 reports the percentages of each group preferring Carter to Ford in 1976 and either Carter *or* Anderson over Reagan in 1980.[7] Consistent with their party and philosophical leanings, Jews, black Protestants, and persons with no religious preference proved substantially more likely to prefer the Democratic presidential candidate in 1976 and the Democrat or the independent in 1980. The white mainline Protestants, the only group with a plurality of Republican identifiers, gave a correspondingly lopsided proportion of their support to the GOP candidate in 1976 and 1980. For white evangelical Protestants and Catholics, the patterns were more complicated. The white evangelicals gave Jimmy Carter slightly less support than did the rest of the nation in both 1976 and 1980. In percentage terms, Carter won evangelical support by 55 percent to 45 percent in 1976 but fell behind the Republican candidate by a ratio of 44 percent to 52 percent in 1980.[8] Typical of their centrist position on other questions, Catholic respondents were very close to the overall national pattern in both 1976 and 1980: a three-to-two preference for the Democrat in 1976 declined to a narrow margin of 49 percent to 42 percent just four years later.

The traits of party preference, ideological placement, and voting record can be taken to reflect judgments about how extensively the national government should intervene in daily life—an issue at the root of American politics since at least the 1930s. The General Social Survey does not inquire directly about this principle, but it does ask respondents about their support for spending on health, the environment, education, and cities. These relatively noncontroversial programs can serve as general indicators of support for government activity (Pollock 1983). Because Americans generally endorse high levels of public spending in opinion

Figure 4.4 Presidential Preference by Religious Preference, 1976 and 1980

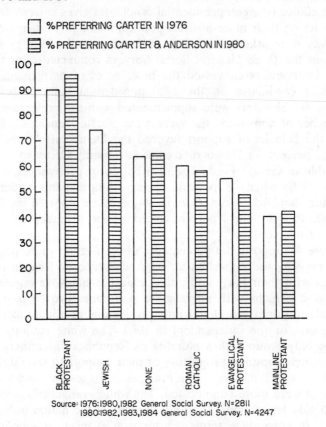

□ %PREFERRING CARTER IN 1976

▤ % PREFERRING CARTER & ANDERSON IN 1980

Source: 1976:1980,1982 General Social Survey. N=2811
1980:1982,1983,1984 General Social Survey. N=4247

polls, however, the most meaningful division is that made on the basis of degree of enthusiasm for *increased* spending on the four problem areas. As a benchmark, about a third of all respondents favored spending more money for at least three of the four activities.

In Figure 4.5 the religious groups are arrayed according to support for additional spending in at least three of the four areas. Not surprisingly, given the pattern up to this point, black Protestants, Jews, and those with no religious preference were the strongest proponents of increased federal spending. Only one-quarter of white Protestants, evangelicals and mainline alike, shared that liberal view. Roman Catholics were close to the overall distribution, with about one-third of the community calling for increases in government spending.

Overall, then, black Protestants and Jews were consistent supporters of the liberal option. Except for the partisan dimension, in which

Figure 4.5 Support for Increased Governmental Spending on Health, Education, Urban Areas, and the Environment by Religious Preference

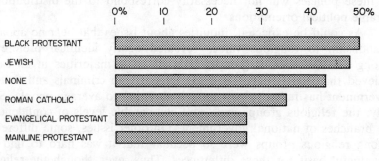

Source: 1980-84 General Social Survey

they exhibited a pronounced aversion to any party label, the respondents with no religious preference were usually as liberal as the black Protestants and Jews. The views of Catholics tended toward the middle position, suggesting neither a pronounced liberal nor conservative tilt. Catholics were slightly more Democratic than the nation in party identification and presidential choice but slightly more conservative in self-image and attitudes toward government spending. The two groups of white Protestants anchored the conservative side of the political spectrum. Members of mainline denominations were strongly pro-Republican in both psychological preference and choice of presidential candidates. They shared with evangelicals an aversion to increased government spending but were somewhat less inclined to see themselves as right-of-center than were members of the most traditional Protestant churches. The evangelicals were most likely of all to picture themselves as right-wing and to express a strong desire to hold government spending to its current level. Although conservative in that sense, evangelicals tilted toward a Democratic self-image and were substantially more likely to favor that party's presidential candidate than were mainline Protestants.

CONTEMPORARY POLITICAL ISSUES

Do religious group differences in political identity extend to more specific issues and controversies? Analysis of the collective opinions of the religious groups on several issues that have ranked high on the recent American political agenda should shed some light on that question. These issues should not be expected to produce precisely the same patterns of religious group difference as produced by the political identity questions.

Since many political issues cannot be defined exactly on the liberal-to-conservative spectrum, and since many Americans react to specific problems without regard to any broad ideological orientation, group opinions on these policies will not necessarily correspond to the distribution of durable political orientations.

As could be expected, inquiries about issues that bear no apparent relationship to religious values revealed nearly identical preferences among the six religious groups. Overwhelming majorities in all camps believed that courts have been too lenient with criminals and that the government has failed to pay enough attention to average people. Similarly, the religious groups expressed comparable levels of confidence in the branches of national government. On other issues, some differences among religious groups were so peculiar that it was hard to find any meaningful basis for those differences. Thus, even though the religious groups evinced varying opinions on communism as a form of government and on the advisability of police permits for gun ownership, the group differences conformed to no coherent pattern.

On yet other issues the dividing line ran between religious groups but reflected racial differences. On the death penalty for murder, to take a clear example, black Protestants were divided almost equally for and against, whereas all other groups favored capital punishment by overwhelming ratios. Black Protestants also stood out from all other denominations by a greater sympathy for governmental action to reduce income differences through progressive taxation and other devices. What best accounts for this type of pattern, I would venture, is not that black religion has some unique message about these themes, but rather that blacks are represented disproportionately among the poor and among those sentenced to capital punishment.

Thus, religion was not—nor should it have been expected to be—relevant to all controversies or as relevant as it was for political identity. With several issues covered by the General Social Survey, however, ties to the core of political identity were apparent, for the patterns uncovered mimicked precisely the patterns of religious differences observed for partisanship and related factors. Providing the best examples of this consistency were attitudes toward race relations and toward federal spending for social welfare programs.

In one series of questions, respondents were asked if they objected to any or all of five forms of racial integration.[9] As can be seen in Figure 4.6, in which answers to the five are combined and arrayed on a scale, the religious groups followed a by-now familiar pattern of responses: the trio of black Protestants, Jews, and respondents with no affiliation were most receptive to integration, the two Protestant camps were least receptive, and Catholics, as usual, fell midway between the clusters.[10] In another question series, respondents were asked about the adequacy of federal

Figure 4.6 Support for Racial Integration by Religion Preference

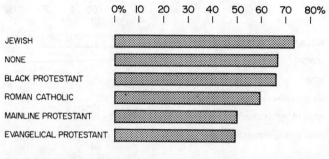

Source: 1980, 1982, 1984 General Social Survey. N = 4374

spending for programs to aid the disadvantaged, including foreign aid, assistance to blacks, and welfare.[11] Compared with public spending on behalf of general social purposes such as education and health, support for these group assistance programs was lower and the denominational differences were much narrower. Nonetheless, as Figure 4.7 demonstrates, the denominational families lined up in a predictable way. With blacks in the lead, the three religious groups with the most consistent liberal political identities emerged as greater-than-average supporters of increased funding for aid programs. Following the black Protestants, Jews, and nonaffiliates, Catholics were almost exactly at the national average. The two Protestant camps exhibited the least enthusiasm for expansion of these governmental programs. On this issue, as on racial matters, then, attitudes reflected fairly closely the forces that divided religious groups in terms of basic political identity.

THE "SOCIAL ISSUE"

In the late 1960s, a new type of political issue appeared on the national political agenda. What was labeled the "social issue" was actually a packet of controversies revolving around drug usage, new patterns of sexual behavior, equal rights for women, and similiar matters. At base, these issues all raised questions about the place of traditional social and moral values in public policy. Even though they do not touch upon the formal role of the churches in American society, the social issues have frequently been debated with reference to religious values. For many observers, the phrase "religion and politics" has come to encompass matters such as abortion, pornography, drug use, and nontraditional sexual practices. Any comprehensive discussion of religious group differences in

Figure 4.7 Support for Increased Government Spending to Help the Disadvantaged by Religious Preference

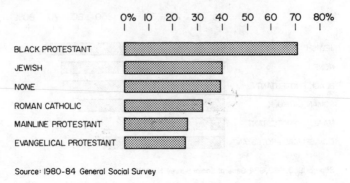

Source: 1980-84 General Social Survey

American politics must consider this newer type of conflict, in addition to the long-standing debates examined above.

Apart from abortion—a complicated issue that requires separate treatment—the issues involved here are drug usage, homosexuality, extramarital sexual relations, and pornography. Attitudes toward the first three were evaluated on the basis of answers to single questions. For pornography, individuals were given the chance to respond to several claims about its consequences and to select a preference among several policy options. The pornography questions produced one set of respondents who gave negative or restrictive responses to sexually explicit materials and another set who seemed to prefer a public policy of neutrality.

On the four issues involving sexuality and drug use, Figure 4.8 reveals massive and striking religious group differences. These issues pitted Christians of all churches, races, and denominations against the two groups of non-Christians—Jewish respondents and persons with no stated religious preference. It was not simply that one set of respondents favored certain practices and others opposed them just as strongly; instead, the two sets of non-Christians were internally divided and the Christians were strongly skewed toward one pole. Jews and nonaffiliates disagreed among themselves over whether nontraditional forms of behavior were acceptable or objectionable, whereas Christian respondents overwhelmingly affirmed traditional moral values in each case.

Almost half of the nonaffiliates and about three-fifths of Jews thought marijuana should not be legalized; more than three-fourths of each Christian groups opposed a more permissive policy. About half of the non-Christians declared that extramarital sex was "always wrong," a position endorsed by no less than 70 percent of respondents in any other religious classification. About four in ten of the Jewish and religiously unattached respondents thought that sex between persons of the same

Figure 4.8   Conservatism on Social Issues by Religious Preference

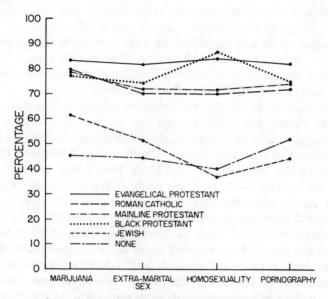

Source: Marijuana: 1980,1983,1984 General Social Survey, N=4221
Extra-marital sex: 1980,1982,1984 General Social Survey, N=4533
Homosexuality:1980,1982,1984 General Social Survey, N=4402
Pornography: 1980,1983,1984 General Social Survey, N=4374

gender could never be right. That might sound like a high degree of opposition to homosexuality, but it did not come close to the outright condemnation of gay sex by about three-quarters of the Christians. On pornography, the same pattern showed up: about half of the Jews and religious independents lodged some objection, a figure that the Christians exceeded by 20 percent or more. Those who accepted the New Testament have apparently taken to heart its condemnation of sensuality outside certain prescribed forms; for groups less strongly tied to Christianity, the moral status of certain kinds of behavior remains a matter of debate and disagreement.

Then there is abortion. Since the Supreme Court's historic ruling of 1973, this contentious issue has been the subject of intense debate and even more intense action. Experts have found that mass attitudes toward abortion depend heavily upon the circumstances of the case (Granberg 1978; McIntosh, Alston, and Alston 1979). The different circumstances that might prompt a woman to terminate a pregnancy can be evaluated on two separate scales. The first scale measures support for abortion on grounds that the woman is single, poor, or has already had a family and wants no more children. On this scale of support for abortion on "social" grounds, the American public has proven to be almost equally divided between persons who reject abortion under any of these circumstances and respondents who endorse the availability of abortion under one or more of the conditions. Public support for legalized abortion is much higher when there is a likelihood of birth defects, health threats to the mother, or pregnancy as a result of rape. The "health" scale that includes these three situations drew wholehearted support from 70 percent of the persons surveyed in the General Social Survey.

The placement of the six religious groups on the two scales is shown in Figure 4.9. Even though the level of support for abortion differed significantly according to the justification offered, the religious groups placed in the same order on both scales. A majority of Roman Catholics, white evangelicals, and black Protestants rejected all social reasons for abortion—poverty, the mother's marital status, or the desire to limit family size. The same three groups were relatively the least supportive of abortion even in circumstances of birth defects, threats to the mother's health, or rape. Although majorities of the three groups said abortion should be permitted under these circumstances, their support for abortion on health grounds was markedly lower than the support registered by Jews, mainline white Protestants, and nonaffiliates. The last-named groups were not indiscriminantly proabortion; rather,

Figure 4.9   Support for Legalized Abortion by Religious Preference

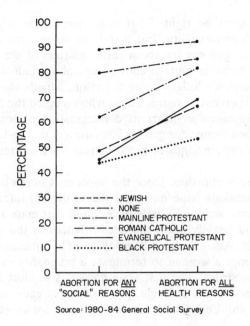

Source: 1980-84 General Social Survey

they were divided equally between opponents and supporters of abortion for social reasons. They were, however, virtually unanimous in approving abortion if health considerations or rape were factors in the pregnancy.

Does religion affect public opinion on social issues? Yes, but not simply or consistently. The restrictive versus permissive camps shifted from one issue to another. On drug use, pornography, and heterosexual sex outside marriage, Christians and non-Christians parted company. On abortion, one important body of Christians shared the more permissive attitude of non-Christians. And within any particular religious community, members were not in complete agreement—a reminder that religious group differences on political issues are not always present, consistent, or clear.

RELIGIOUS DIFFERENCES
AND SOCIAL STANDING

To understand why religion may influence mass political opinions and behavior, it is necessary to consider several factors that could account for the group patterns delineated in previous sections. This task would be much easier if social scientists had thought more systematically about the role of religion in the political outlooks of individuals and religious communities. Because relatively little such work has been done, knowledge about the sources of linkage between religious and political loyalties must take the form of hypotheses, offered tentatively and with caution.

One common reaction to revelations of some of the more dramatic political differences between religious groups, such as the pronounced disagreement between denominations on public spending or the equally significant variations in partisan identification, is denial that these patterns "really" have anything to do with religion per se. Skeptics tend to view the ties between religious and political views as spurious; members of a religious group, they argue, think alike about politics not because of their religion but because they share other characteristics that directly influence political attitudes.

The most commonly cited sources of unity linked to religion have been historical experience and economic or social standing. Jews tend toward liberalism, it is argued, becaue of their experience as an oppressed people whose emancipation was part of the liberal agenda and was frequently resisted by conservative movements. Jews are said to have inherited from this tradition a sympathy for liberal values and a suspicion of conservatism. Similarly, proponents of an economic explanation would attribute the conservatism of mainline Protestants to their high social status and economic privileges, not to religious convictions. In this view, differences in political orientations between religious groups generally can be reduced to social characteristics that happen to be associated with membership in the various denominational families (Allinsmith and Allinsmith 1948; Ebersole 1960).[12]

Attempts to trace denominational political distinctiveness back to social standing are based on the discovery of major variations in the profiles of American religious groups. The denominational groups have been shown to exhibit striking differences in ethnic and racial composition, geographical distribution and concentration, and, most importantly, social and economic achievement (McKinney and Roof 1982; Roof 1979b). Figure 4.10 compares the six religious categories in terms of educational achievement, a major influence on social status and political outlooks in the United States. Consistent with many other studies, the figure shows Jewish respondents with much the highest level of formal education in the population, followed at some distance by the participants who did not report any religious affiliation. These two groups are followed by another two groups with very similar educational profiles, the mainline white Protestants and Roman Catholics; then, clustered at the lowest level of educational achievement, come white evangelicals and black Protestants. Analyses of religious group differences on related indicators of social standing such as income and occupational attainment have disclosed very similar patterns.

The claim that political differences between religious groups reflect only the social composition of denominations can be tested by a comparison of religious group attitudes with social standing held constant. Using party identification as an example of a political difference, one would try

Figure 4.10   Education by Religious Preference

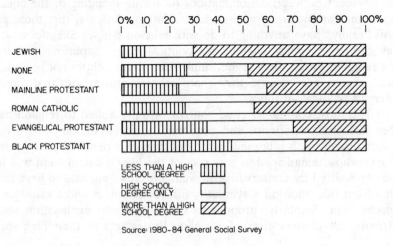

Source: 1980–84 General Social Survey

to discover if, for example, Jews of high education reported the same level of attachment to the Democratic party as did persons with similar educational levels but different religious preferences. If religious group differences were shown to narrow at each level of education, then education apparently could contribute to political variations. But if the political differences were shown to persist—if, sticking with the same example, college-educated Jews were to be still more strongly attached to the Democratic party than were college-educated Catholics, evangelical Protestants, or other groups—then religious differences in politics could not be attributed wholly to a factor such as education.

The test results for the six denominational groups appear in Figure 4.11. Members in each group were subdivided by education into three categories: no high school degree, a high school degree only, and a high school degree with some additional schooling. The central vertical line represents a condition of perfect party balance, in which the percentage of Democrats and Republicans is identical. Where the bar extends to the right of the line, as it does for most of the groups, Democrats outnumber Republicans. If the proportion of Republicans is greater, the bar extends to the left. Expressed simply as one number, party balance indicates the

Figure 4.11 Party Balance by Religious Preference With Education Held Constant (Percentage Difference Between Democrats and Republicans)

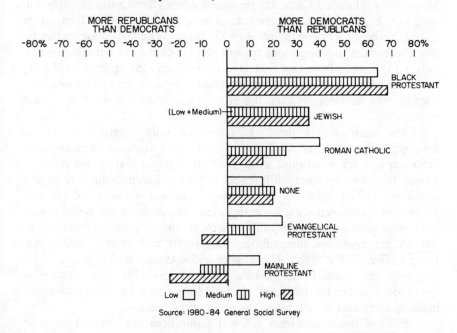

Source: 1980-84 General Social Survey

difference obtained by subtracting the percentage of Republicans in a group from the percentage of Democrats.

The figure shows social status to be an important but not altogether complete explanation for denominational differences in partisanship. For some groups—most clearly, white Protestants from both mainline and evangelical denominations—gains in education were clearly associated with movement toward Republicanism. Most white Protestants with low levels of education were Democrats, but a plurality of those Protestants with some postsecondary schooling were Republican. Catholics followed much the same pattern, although the differences were not quite so pronounced as with the Protestants. The party balance favoring the Democrats declined by 24 points between the least and most educated segments of the Catholic population. The trend for these groups is consistent with a general finding that high levels of education, like other sources of high social status, are associated with a preference for Republican over Democratic party identification.

Yet if social status clearly influences party loyalties, it does not eliminate the full measure of religious group differences. Status had virtually no effect on the partisan orientation of three of the religious categories—Jews, blacks, and persons without religious preference. In each of these groups, the pro-Democratic balance was relatively unaffected by educational level. Moreover, the general level of the party balance differed among denominations even with educational level held constant. Moderately educated Catholics remained more Democratic (a party balance of +25) than white Protestants of comparable education from either the evangelical (+11) or mainline (−12) camps. The least educated mainline Protestants inclined more toward Republicanism (a party balance of only +13) than did the best educated Catholics (+15) or Jews (+35). By the same token, pro-Republican attachment among mainline white Protestants was far stronger than the group's educational level alone would predict.

The analysis in Figure 4.11 represents only a partial test of the influence of social characteristics. When more rigorous controls have been applied for additional social traits that might distinguish religious groups from one another, differences in political identity have remained significant (Wald 1986). Many scholars, studying a variety of political orientations and outlooks, have reported that controls for social conditions may narrow intergroup differences in various political orientations but do not eliminate them altogether (Beatty and Walter 1982, 1983, 1984; Cohen and Kapsis 1977; Glantz 1959; Grupp and Newman 1973; Laumann and Segal 1971; Maddox 1979; Miller 1974). That conclusion has stood whether the indicator of social status used has been education, income, urbanization, ethnicity, or occupational status.

Even if denominational political differences are affected to some degree by social forces—the strongest conclusion warranted by current research—that still does not mean that religion is irrelevant to political attitudes and orientations. If religion confers an economic disadvantage or advantage upon members of a group, it contributes in a major way to the shaping of political outlooks. From both the world and the American experience, it is not hard to identify religious groups that have suffered from economic discrimination because their creed differed from that of the majority of the community. The informal restrictions that once confined most Catholics to the working class probably go a long way toward explaining why Catholics were so receptive to Democratic party efforts to build social programs such as unemployment insurance, workmen's compensation, federal aid to education, and the like (Buenker 1973). Membership in a high-status church may provide individuals with social ties, business connections, and opportunities to gain considerable position in society. With such a strong stake in the existing order, members of prestigious denominations may develop a conservative outlook on social change (Baltzell 1964; Domhoff 1983).

To make the argument more strongly: religious values may be critical element in determining the social status of the denomination and, thus, a powerful if indirect influence on political orientations. In one of the classic (and most controversial) works of modern sociology, the German scholar Max Weber (1928) advanced a theory linking certain religious values to success in the economic realm. Trying to explain why Protestants had surpassed Catholics in economic achievement since the advent of capitalism in Europe, Weber suggested that the cause lay partly in the different social values inspired by the two traditions. The Protestant emphasis on discipline and self-control, born of the Puritan desire to illustrate God's blessing, was nicely suited to the demands of work life in a capitalist economy. By comparison, Weber argued, Catholic values encouraged behavior that was not conducive to economic achievement. In particular, the tendency to regard life on earth as mere preparation for the next world and to equate material poverty with spiritual grace handicapped Catholics in competitive economic struggle. If this "Protestant ethic" thesis is correct—and there has been enormous controversy about it—then the economic standing of religious groups is even more strongly connected with denominational values. Thus, although it is possible to apportion some of the credit for denominational differences in politics to economic factors, the pattern of economic status itself may ultimately have much to do with religion.

In addition to the relatively "hard" differences shown on objective measurement scales of education, income, and so forth, religious groups may also differ from each other in subjective social standing. High income does not necessarily confer social acceptability, and advanced education does not invariably correlate with prestige. Too, such subjective assessments may influence the perspectives of group members and thus help to account for unique political traditions. Subjective social standing is frequently invoked to explain the persistence of Jewish liberalism. Why should Jews, by objective standards one of the highest status groups in the United States, maintain such a firm commitment to liberal political values—a commitment that seems, contrary to all common sense, to *increase* with economic achievement (Maller 1977; Fuchs 1955)? As measured by social attitudes, Jewish standing in society has not matched the level of Jewish economic and educational attainment. Because of a strong collective memory of persecution, it has been claimed, Jews tend to think of themselves not as part of the established elite, but rather as a group on the margin of society, defensive and vulnerable to attack by the majority. The social insecurity of American Jews has been said to make Jews especially wary of any political movements that appear to encourage intolerance and bigotry (Cohn 1957; Liebman 1973; Petrusak and Steinart 1976; Rothman and Lichter 1982). Hence, Jews make common cause with other subordinate groups in clear defiance of their immediate economic interests.

The concept of subjective status can be extended to explain the political activism of the black Protestant churches. Denied the most elementary forms of family life, access to education, and any opportunity to develop an independent community life, black slaves were allowed only the church as a focus of collective loyalty. Not surprisingly under such conditions, the church developed into the social, cultural, and intellectual center of black life. To a degree unmatched in white society, the black church provided its members some protection from a hostile outside world, a durable source of collective identity, training in organizational skills, and the opportunity to nurture native leadership (Colombo 1984, 23). When blacks began to challenge the system of segregation that remained in place a century after the passing of slavery, the church became the crucible of action, and it continues today as the principal agent in black political action. Even though race produced the ghetto, the black political response was heavily conditioned by the intense religious commitment that developed in social isolation. For black Protestants, Jews, and other religious groups, subjective social standing may be as important in the forging of political views as factors that can be measured in dollars or years of schooling.

RELIGION AND POLITICAL VALUES

Some observers have not been reluctant to attribute religious group differences in politics to the values, teachings, and ideas of the various traditions. The application of religious creeds to politics is most visible when the leaders of a faith assert that their religion demands a particular political stance. In the United States, where official political announcements by churches traditionally have been comparatively rare, the overt linking of religious ideas with political positions has recently become much more common among almost all denominations.

The Catholic hierarchy, for example, has insisted that church teachings about the nature of life impose upon Catholics the obligation to reject artificial birth control and to resist abortion. As these are medical procedures governed by public policy, Catholic doctrine has drawn some members of the faith into political action. The Catholic hierarchy has not been alone in translating faith into political principles. Members of the clergy who participated in the drive for civil rights insisted that segregation was incompatible with Judeo-Christian values. In the 1960s and 1970s, some leaders of mainline white Protestantism urged on biblical grounds that members of the churches oppose the Vietnam War and work for a broad-ranging program of social reform and welfare services. Most recently, some leaders of the evangelical wing of Protestantism have asserted biblical support for programs on the conservative agenda. Each basic plank in the program put forward by the Moral Majority, an organization supporting conservative social policy on moral grounds, has been accompanied by a reference to a specific passage in Scripture. In excommunicating a supporter of the Equal Rights Amendment for disobedience, the elders of the Church of Jesus Christ of Latter-Day Saints (the Mormons) surpassed other groups in enforcing compliance with political doctrine as a condition for church membership. Nonetheless, it would be hard to think of a religious group whose leaders have not defended some political position on theological grounds.

The connection between doctrine and politics may also draw upon theological tradition in more subtle ways. Rather than speak directly to political issues, it has been suggested, certain common ways of thinking about religion spill over into politics (Laitin 1978). According to most observers, the differences in style and approach between a "conservative" and a "liberal" orientation in religion may well correspond to the political orientations of the same name.[13] Michael Parenti (1967, 268) suggested four key dimensions on which the conservative and liberal religions differed:

(a) The extent to which divine teaching is considered fixed, final, and unchallengeable, as opposed to being susceptible to rational investigation and modification; and consequently, the extent to which intellectualism and many of the values associated with it are opposed or welcomed.

(b) The extent to which the drama of redemption and atonement is defined as a personal battle waged for one's soul for the sake of eternal salvation, rather than as a moral commitment to a worldly social betterment of mankind.

(c) The extent to which sin and evil are defined as inherent in human nature (e.g., original sin) and inevitable in human behavior (e.g., concupiscence), rather than as social effects of widespread environmental causes.

(d) The extent to which human well-being and natural pleasures are manifestations of a "lower," corrupting realm of nature—something to be repressed as the contamination of the spiritual, rather than responsibly cultivated as the fulfillment of God's beneficence.

Recent research has suggested another major difference between conservative and liberal religions—their images of God. According to Andrew Greeley (1982), the concept of God evokes for some people a "warm" image of friendship, nurturance, caring, and love, but for others a "cold" image of discipline, order, and punishment. Additional research on the same theme has revealed that religions may convey different messages about God's presence in the world and responsibility for the flow of human events (Piazza and Glock 1979; O'Grady 1982).

How might these dimensions of religious belief take on political significance? Because of their emphasis on faith in fixed authority over the free play of intellect, persons of a conservative orientation are more likely than religious liberals to stress the need for obedience than to encourage skepticism or dissent (Rokeach 1969). If redemption is interpreted to mean bringing the Kingdom of God to realization on earth, as liberal religions seem to argue, movements for political change are infused with a transcendent purpose. But if, as in conservative religion, life is seen as a mere preparation for the next world or the imminent return of God to earth, then little can be done except to live as righteously as possible and to guard the integrity of one's soul from temptation and corruption (Kleppner 1970). An emphasis on sinfulness as the essential condition of mankind seems quite compatible with a skeptical orientation toward the prospect of improving conditions through political action (Rosenberg 1956). Similarly, if human pleasures are judged inferior to spiritual rewards, there is little urgency about improving material conditions. The liberal belief in "social" sin and the dignity of earthly existence, which contrasts sharply with conservative religious assumptions, spurs efforts to eradicate structural barriers to justice and to improve the material conditions of life. Belief in a warm, caring God who is part of the world tends to enhance commitment to social welfare, whereas the image of a cold and authoritative deity lends support to government's role in securing order and property.

These contrasting modes of thought are illustrated by the way in which Jews and Lutherans apply their differing religious styles to the political realm. A classic example of a liberal faith, Judaism venerates learning and charity as major virtues and is relatively silent about the origin of sin and the prospect of life after death. That combination of values encourages optimism about the human condition and a sense of urgency about the application of reason to human problems. As described by some experts, the Jewish outlook seems almost to demand social and political involvement on behalf of liberal causes.

> Implicit in this style is the view that man and his environment are malleable, that he is much more the creator of history than its creature. Implicit, too, is the notion that man's environment and his polity are made for him. Implicit is a dynamic view of law, that it is changing and made for man. . . . And especially implicit in such a style is the belief that what happens in this life on this earth is very important, what happens here and now matters very much. (Fuchs 1984, 70)

Subject to the influence of this body of assumptions, Jewish voters not surprisingly have been strongly attracted to political leaders and movements that promote social change—drawn so strongly, in fact, that they have occasionally preferred activist liberals from Christian denominations to more conservative Jewish candidates (Leventman and Leventman 1976). For a people normally given to such a high level of solidarity, crossing denominational lines is strong evidence for the political impact of a liberal religious style.

The Jewish stress on human capacity to remake the world through political action finds barely an echo in Lutheran doctrine. Martin Luther taught that salvation would come only to the person who submitted thoroughly and wholeheartedly to the will of an omniscient God. In sharply contrasting the evil of mortals to the perfection of God, Lutheran thought treats humans as creatures of passion and sin who should not interfere with the divine plan for the world. Based on an extensive survey of Lutheran laypersons in the Detroit metropolitan area, Lawrence K. Kersten (1970, 31) found that Luther's spiritual descendants accepted his counsel to take the world as it is.

> Lutheran social philosophy suggests that true happiness for man and total release from the bondage of sin are not possible until after death. If earthly conditions are undesirable, man should patiently endure them, for they may actually be a test of his faith. Man must trust that God will change the social structure or social conditions when He sees fit.

Such religious beliefs may help to account for the pronounced economic, social, racial, and political conservatism exhibited by Lutherans (Weber 1983).

At this point, it should be emphasized that links between political attitudes and religious orientations have been more often asserted than proven. Attempts to assess direct connections between religious belief and political outlook have yielded mixed results. The most consistent relationships between theological beliefs and political outlooks have been found with samples of the clergy, a group that should have the firmest grasp of the political implications of religious thought. In almost every study of the clergy I have located, commitment to a conservative religious style correlated with conservative outlooks on politics and social issues (Balswick 1970; Hadden 1969; Hero 1973; Driedger 1974; Jeffries and Tygart 1974; Johnson 1966, 1967; Schindeler and Hoffman 1968; Zehner 1967). As for surveys of more typical people, some empirical studies have reported a relationship between commitment to the tenets of conservative religion and (1) conservative beliefs about race and ethnic relations, (2) Republicanism, (3) resistance to liberal initiatives on environmental and social welfare policy, (4) support for traditional beliefs about sexual roles and behavior, and (5) a low level of toleration for "deviant" political ideas (Johnson 1962, 1964; Rokeach 1969; Orum 1970; Glock and Stark 1966; Hendricks 1977; Stellway 1973; Hand and Van Liere 1984; Steiber 1980). Similarly, "image of God" studies have for the most part linked the Old Testament image of a stern and vengeful deity with various manifestations of political conservatism (Hoffman 1982, 1985—but see Jelen 1985).

Nevertheless, this type of relationship between theological and political outlooks has not always been sustained by empirical research. On the basis of an exhaustive review of previous research, Robert Wuthnow (1973) pointed out that well-designed studies were just as likely to report no relationship between religious beliefs and political attitudes as they were to find a positive association. Focusing exclusively on studies about racial beliefs, Gorsuch and Aleshire (1974) discovered that persons committed to religion for its intrinsic value were the least likely to hold prejudiced views of blacks. Responding to the emergence of organized political activity by leaders of the evangelical Protestant churches, several studies have found that in general, church members tie religious and political attitudes together only in the domain of sexual and social roles (Wald and Lupfer 1983). The idea that Jewish political values derive from the content of the religion has been challenged by the discovery that the most religiously observant Jews, who should have the greatest exposure to the implicit liberal messages of Judaism, in fact constitute the most politically conservative element of the community (Cohen 1983, 143–53; Liebman 1973, 139–44). An inverse relationship between attachment to traditional religion and racial militance has also been reported in studies of black Protestants (Marx 1967, chap. 4; Madron et al. 1974; Nelsen et al. 1975). Even when survey findings have appeared to support connections between denominational belief and political outlook, the conclusions have been challenged on grounds that they really represented social background influences of the kind examined in the previous section (Anderson 1966; Henriot 1966; Jay 1981; Rojek 1973; Roof 1974; Summers et al. 1970).

Those who would insist on drawing too strong a connection between religious orientations and particular forms of political belief should remember the many exceptions to the rule. Left-wing movements for social reform have frequently been inspired by Christian doctrine (Murchland 1982; Littell 1970). William Jennings Bryan, the defender of religious conservatism par excellence, had no difficulty combining a deep commitment to fundamentalist theology with passionate conviction in international arbitration, the rights of urban workers, women's suffrage, public ownership of utilities, and, in general, support for an extensive government effort to secure social and economic justice. The same Bryan who condemned evolution, in large part for its pernicious social implications, saw his commitments to social reform as the logical outgrowth of Christian morality (Levine 1975). Like Bryan, many black Protestants, white evangelicals, and Roman Catholics find no contradiction between theological conservatism and political liberalism. Even the Pentecostal movement, normally regarded as the politically most regressive wing of Protestantism, has found biblical sanction for racial integration (Elinson 1965, 414–15). The confluence of liberal theology with conservative politics can also be found in American political life. Despite a traditional commitment to liberalism, some Jews have enlisted on behalf of conservative programs and policies. Milton Friedman, the dean of laissez-faire economists, is Jewish; so is Howard Phillips, leader of the Conservative Caucus and a long-term activist in right-wing political movements. Much to the dismay of many liberals in the Jewish community (see Shorris 1982), the principal leadership of the American "neoconservative" movement comprises Jewish intellectuals disillusioned by events in the 1960s and 1970s.

These exceptions suggest that there are limits to simple theological explanations of political attitudes. On the one hand, the lack of an authoritative source of interpretation for most American religions leaves believers free to develop their own understanding of sacred texts and teachings. And even where the religious tradition seems clearly to point to a logically related political position, church members may keep the religious values segregated in their minds, limiting the application to politics. Perhaps that is why Lupfer and Wald (1985) found in their Memphis study that evangelicals did not judge humanity in the harsh manner that seems to follow from the doctrine of original sin.

On the other hand, most religious traditions are elastic enough to support very different political applications. Drawing on a common sacred text, for example, the Reverends Jerry Falwell and Martin Luther King, Jr., ended up in remarkably different places. Elasticity also shows up when denominations or individuals change political behavior despite an unchanging religious outlook (Balswick et al. 1975). Where influential leaders of evangelical Protestantism once read the Bible as a blueprint for the Social Gospel, in the 1920s the predominant interpretation shifted to emphasize biblical passages that promoted political withdrawal. Before then, evangelicals provided many of the leaders of progressive causes such as the antislavery movement and Populism and supported other policies, such as Prohibition, that can now be understood as sincere attempts to improve social conditions (Clark 1976; Smith 1965; Hammond 1974).

In recognition of these limitations, the apparent compatibility of religious with political thought must be treated with caution. Even when religious orientations are found to be consistently in league with corresponding political outlooks, the links should be treated as dispositions that allow some room for exceptions. If one should not claim too little for religion, in the manner of those who always see social standing as the "real" cause for denominational political differences, neither should one claim too much. Tocqueville and Weber were correct in using the term *affinity* instead of *cause* to examine how different religions related the Kingdoms of God and humanity.

RELIGION AND GROUP INTERESTS

Institutional interest provides the last major line of explanation for denominational differences in political attitudes and behavior. At first glance, churches may not appear to fit in with other organized institutions that make claims upon government. The principal concern of churches, after all, is to minister to the spiritual needs of the membership. Yet because their wide scope of activity inevitably brings them into contact with government, churches, like secular groups, develop interests that may require defense in the political realm. Of concern in this regard is how the assertion of institutional interests may affect the basic attitudes and loyalties of the church and its supporters.

In the United States, as in other countries, the issue of education has frequently drawn churches into the political realm. Partly in an effort to maintain themselves (although for other reasons as well), American churches have supported extensive systems of elementary, secondary, and postsecondary education. These schools provide both instruction in basic skills and training in religious traditions and practice. The Catholic parochial schools provide the best known example of religious education, but many denominations have built their own facilities in locations where their members are concentrated. As of the early 1980s, approximately 11 percent of school-age children attended church-related elementary and secondary institutions, and churches supported almost 800 institutions of higher learning in the United States (Vance and Snyder 1983, 46, 105).

The maintenance of these institutions is an enormous drain on the financial resources of the churches, and so several efforts have been undertaken to relieve the burden. In each case, the relief efforts have impinged on the public sector. One persistent line of attack has been to seek some sort of state support, either through direct payments to church schools for the nonreligious part of their efforts (salary supplements, supply of textbooks for secular subjects) or through requirements that public schools share resources with their nonpublic counterparts. The interests of the private schools also have touched on the public systems when taxation levels have been set to support the latter. Most recently, supporters of religious education have tried to persuade Congress to grant tax relief for tuition payments.

In each of these cases, the affected churches and their members have a straightforward financial incentive to support policies that favor the religious schools. With state support, churches can maintain an institution that helps ensure continuity of belief across generations. Under these circumstances, it is hardly surprising that polls have shown very strong support for various forms of state aid among denominations that maintain schools and much more resistance in churches in which the bulk of children attend public institutions (Menendez 1977, chap. 11; Rothenberg and Newport 1984, 58–61). Conversely, studies of voting on urban bond issues dedicated to financing public education have revealed a high level of opposition from Catholics—who have a financial interest in minimizing the cost of a school system many do not utilize (Cataldo and Holm 1983).

Interests do not have to be restricted to the financial sphere nor to single issues. In the late 1920s and 1930s, a convergence of interests brought first- and second-generation Catholics and Jews, previously inactive or pro-Republican, into the New Deal Democratic coalition fashioned by Franklin D. Roosevelt. Part of Roosevelt's appeal to these groups lay in his commitment to economic policies that addressed their economic needs; at the same time, however, Roosevelt was also looked upon as a defender of the religious minorities from attack by the Protestant culture. As the immigrant presence in urban areas grew from the late nineteenth century onward, Protestants more and more looked askance at the challenge to their norms and beliefs posed by the influx of Catholics and Jews. The period from approximately 1880 to the 1920s was marked by Protestant efforts to preserve their image of the Christian America by invoking the force of law to support pious behavior in matters of personal conduct (Handy 1984). For their part, the immigrants grew increasingly to resent Protestant crusades for immigration restriction, the prohibition of liquor, and the imposition of Sunday closing laws. The implementation of these policies represented a victory for Protestant ideas of morality, which were far more restrictive on such issues than were Jewish or Catholic ideas.

As the minority party in the United States, the Democrats had a strong incentive to court the as-yet unattached potential voters. The party's urban organizations proved highly receptive to the interests and concerns of the immigrant workers, and this receptivity was finally matched at the national level at the 1928 presidential nominating convention. There, the party formally repudiated the Ku Klux Klan, then principally an extremist Protestant group attacking Catholics and Jews, and conferred the presidential nomination upon New York governor Alfred E. Smith, a Catholic who embodied "the revolt of the underdog, urban immigrant against the top dog of 'old American' stock" (Lubell 1965, 53). Although he lost badly to Herbert Hoover in the 1928 presidential election, Smith brought over to the Democratic side the votes of Catholics in urban America (Lichtman 1979; Burner 1967). Four years later, Roosevelt would capitalize upon that cultural conflict and on the nation's economic disarray to claim the presidency for the Democrats.

Roosevelt's policies in 1932 and thereafter cemented the alliance of Jews and Catholics with the Democratic party (Flynn 1968). Catholics were favorably disposed toward a presidential candidate who had denounced religious bigotry in the heated 1928 campaign and who quoted a papal encyclical in support of his plans for economic recovery. Roosevelt further recognized the church by appointing two Catholics to cabinet positions (half the number who had held such positions in all previous administrations combined), naming Catholics to other important positions in government, and, in an important symbolic gesture, opening up direct contacts between the church and the White House. Roosevelt cultivated Jewish support with similar actions but earned the highest degree of loyalty for his leadership of the war against Hitler. Jews thereupon embraced the Democratic party with a tenacity matched by few groups—a commitment that was redoubled when Roosevelt's successor made the United States one of the first countries to recognize and endorse the formation of a Jewish state in Israel.

By means of such actions, political leaders attempt to convey to members of religious groups their understanding of the group's situation and sympathy for its goals. Eventually, if the conditions are ripe and the romance is conducted with sufficient skill, political elites can forge strong ties between a party and the members of denominations. Unlike some political parties in other countries, the major American parties have never appealed for support solely as the representatives of a specific religious interest. But American parties have sent signals to religious groups indicating their willingness to make room for members of the denomination in the party coalition. Through the process known as political socialization, group members may even come to regard affiliation with a particular party as one element of their religious identity (Irvine 1974). Support for the party becomes, in essence, a natural reflex for members of the religious group. Studies of group-based political loyalties have underscored the durability of the associations between religious commitment and political loyalties. Despite the obsolescence of many of the issues that prompted Jewish and Catholic support for the Democratic party under Franklin Roosevelt, the connection has persisted. Political commitments by denominations based initially on common interests thus may broaden into durable loyalties that outlive their original causes.

THE ROLE OF SOCIAL INTEGRATION

Very little has been said thus far about how members of groups acquire the outlooks characteristic of their religion. By what process do adherents of a denomination learn about its theology, institutional interests, and subjective social standing—the principal routes by which political traits are forged? In order to answer the question, it is important to think of "religion" as an activity pursued (usually) in groups by human beings. The same principles that govern the organization and maintenance of other groups apply equally well to groups defined by a religious purpose:

> Members of religious groups have a common identity, interact with one another regularly, and expect each other to think and act in certain ways. These expectations, which are commonly called group norms, are enforced by sanctions, i.e., rewards and punishments which group members administer to each other. The norms of a religious group constitute its special culture, a culture that is usually distinct in some ways from the culture of other groups in its environment. (Johnson and White 1967, 31)

In that description, Johnson and White called attention to the means by which religious groups create a common consciousness that may extend to political ideas.

By participating in a religious group, the individual learns what is expected of him or her and the behavior patterns required for maintaining membership. When attending church, the affiliate enters a world with a communication network that reinforces the sense of group awareness. Both inside and outside the church, the member may come to have more and more social contact with like-minded persons from the religious community. In the case of the young, the church creates special educational institutions for the express purpose of transmitting group norms. These formal networks are supplemented by informal messages from various agents, especially parents, about what constitutes appropriate behavior for members of the denomination. The minister is an additional source of cues about norms. In most churches the clergy is recognized as the source of spiritual leadership and is expected, as an integral part of worship, to provide guidance about church doctrines. When these elements are put together, they provide the church with impressive potential to influence the outlooks of the membership.

Through each of these routes—restricted communication, social interaction, formal training, informal education, ministerial guidance—the church impresses on the individual member a commitment to its norms. In American churches, these norms may include informal commitment to a party or political outlook, or at least agreement on some of the elements that can influence political perspectives: theological assumptions, a sense of social status, and a belief that group members share certain interests. Through these avenues of influence, churches may provide cues that reinforce political differences between denominations (Converse and Campbell 1969; Kaplan 1969). Most Americans, while frowning upon explicit political direction from the clergy, are less resistant to the relatively subtle means of political education that may emanate from the church.

Because individuals are not equally involved in churches, they are not equally receptive to the political messages flowing from them. The extremes of involvement run from the person with no religious background or connection to any denomination to the cult member whose immersion in the internal life of the religious community cuts off all outside sources of political information. Not surprisingly, the nonaffiliate is likely to develop political ideas independent of traditional church doctrine, whereas the cult member is likely to follow the church's political guidance with complete loyalty. Between these poles lay a wide range of religious commitments and, presumably, of responsiveness to the political cues given out directly or indirectly by the religious group. This factor accounts for the consistent finding that commitment to the denomination strengthens conformity to the political norm of the religious group and accentuates attitude differences between persons from different groups. Hence the discovery, to cite only one of the many available from the literature, that religious group differences in party identification and presidential voting are greatest among persons with the strongest involvement in their respective religious families (Anderson 1973; Knoke 1974).

Strength of commitment to the religious group has been measured in different ways—frequency of attendance at worship, involvement in the organizational life of the church, level of social interaction with church members, length and intensity of exposure to church doctrine, even the individual's subjective assessment of the importance of religious identity relative to other group loyalties. Whatever the measure of commitment, research both in the United States and elsewhere has suggested, political loyalty to a denominational pattern builds as the individual's life becomes more nearly encapsulated by the religious group (Wald 1986).

Levels of religious participation may also minimize the impact of nonreligious factors upon the political loyalties of church members. The church is an arena that frequently brings together people from different social backgrounds. Although the point should not be overstated, a strong sense of collective religious identity, with its associated political messages, may override the other sources of political cues available to the church members. Instead of picking up political orientations from newspapers, neighbors, coworkers, or other secondary organizations, the individual may imbibe loyalties from the church members and leaders who are the principal partners in social interaction. The muted level of class differences in politics found between members of the same religious denomination appears to confirm the operation of this process (Bochel and Denver 1970). To the extent that they actually forge a common political approach among persons of diverse social standing, churches may account for the persistence of political differences independent of social forces such as income, occupation, and education.

* * * * *

Religion is relevant to some types of political conflict but not to others. When they do appear, political differences among denominations cannot be reduced to a single source, be it theology, social standing, or institutional interest. All these factors may play a role in forging the patterns of belief observed at the beginning of the chapter. Whatever the source of political identity, the transmission of group-based political ideas appears to depend upon the individual's level of involvement in the religious community. For individuals whose lives are the most deeply merged with the church, politically distinctive behavior appears to be the rule.

Most of the political differences examined in the chapter do not touch directly on religion. However, American history is rife with conflicts about the place of the church in public life. In the next chapter, these traditional church-and-state issues will be examined.

Notes

[1]In the General Social Survey (Davis 1984), the participant is asked to identify his or her "religious preference" from a list of "Protestant, Catholic, Jewish, some other religion, or no religion." Those who pick the Protestant option are asked a follow-up question about their specific denomination. It is important to recognize that such denominational labels, and the categories based on them, fall far short of perfection. However, the difficulty of developing meaningful schemes for classifying religious preferences is no greater than the obstacles facing researchers who seek to categorize people by social class, ethnicity, regional background, or political loyalty. All measurement schemes are approximations of the concept they are meant to represent. Provided that the purpose of the exercise is kept in mind—to identify religious group tendencies in the political realm—the religious preference questions on the General Social Survey are ade-

quate to the purpose. For an extended discussion of techniques for assessing the religious orientation of individuals, see the excellent essays by Roof (1979a) and Wilson (1978, appendix).

[2] Even with a large sample size, the numbers of respondents from nontraditional faiths and Eastern religions are too small to analyze with reliable results. They have thus been combined with the vastly larger category of people who indicate no current religious affiliation.

[3] Blacks who subscribe to non-Protestant faiths are not numerous enough to support reliable analysis, and hence have been excluded from the analysis.

[4] Differences of similar scope can easily be noted in the other religious categories. Judaism is divided into Conservative, Reform, Orthodox, and Reconstructionist wings, and both Catholicism and black Protestantism are divided between a charismatic and pentecostal wing and a more traditional and centrist approach to faith. Even though these divergent orientations may have political relevance, and may diminish the cohesion of the group, the emphasis here is on tracing differences of political tendency between broad religious traditions.

[5] For some denominations known to be split internally by the evangelical-mainline axis, principally the Methodists and Presbyterians, the region of residence at age 16 was taken as the likely indicator of theological leaning. Under this scheme, residents of Southern states in those denominations were assigned to the evangelical grouping and non-Southerners from the indeterminate denominations were grouped with the mainline Protestants. See Grupp and Newman (1973) and Hougland and Lacey (1981) for precedents justifying the entire classification scheme.

[6] Since polling began in the late 1930s, the Democrats have retained a healthy lead over the Republicans in mass political identification. A sharp shift to Republicanism in the wake of the 1984 presidential election brought the two major parties much closer together. Whether this Republican surge will persist remains unknown.

[7] Although Anderson voters rejected both major party candidates, their opinions put them closer to the Democrats, and so they have been grouped with supporters of the Democratic candidate.

[8] That Carter even did this well probably reflects the appeal of his regional identity to the many evangelicals located in the South and his own association with the evangelical tradition.

[9] For evidence showing that these five items hang together in the minds of respondents, see the factor analysis performed by Chalfant and Peek (1983).

[10] That Jews were found to be more supportive of civil rights than blacks reflects some cooling in the ardor of blacks for integrationist solutions to racial problems. Had the items tapped the question of affirmative action, there is little doubt that black respondents would have been by far the most supportive.

[11] Pollock (1983) has shown that these distinct programs form a common dimension in the minds of the mass public.

[12] The low level of support for capital punishment by black Protestants can also be used to illustrate the concept of spurious association. Their standing as the minority group most likely to suffer capital punishment, not their religious values, was offered to explain why blacks expressed the greatest resistance to the death penalty.

[13]Even though the differences are frequently used to characterize entire religious traditions as conservative or liberal, they constitute tendencies that may divide people of a common heritage.

REFERENCES

Allinsmith, Wesley, and Beverly Allinsmith. 1948. "Religious Affiliation and Politico-Economic Attitude: A Study of Eight Major U.S. Religious Groups." *Public Opinion Quarterly.* 12: 377–389.

Anderson, Charles H. 1973. "Religious Communality and Party Preference." In *Research in Religious Behavior,* ed. Benjamin Beit-Hallahmi. Monterey, CA: Brooks-Cole, 336–352. Originally published in 1969.

Anderson, Donald. 1966. "Ascetic Protestantism and Political Preference." *Review of Religious Research.* 7: 167–171.

Baggaley, Andrew. 1962. "Religious Influence on Wisconsin Voting, 1928–60." *American Political Science Review.* 56: 66–70.

Balswick, Jack, Dawn McN. Ward, and David E. Carlson. 1975. "Theological and Socio-Political Belief Change Among Religiously Conservative Students." *Review of Religious Research.* 17: 61–67.

Balswick, Jack O. 1970. "Theology and Political Attitudes Among Clergymen." *Sociological Quarterly.* 11: 397–404.

Baltzell, E. Digby. 1964. *The Protestant Establishment: Aristocracy and Caste in America.* New York: Vintage.

Beatty, Kathleen Murphy, and Oliver Walter. 1984. "Religious Preference and Practice: Reevaluating Their Impact on Political Tolerance." *Public Opinion Quarterly.* 48: 318–329.

Beatty, Kathleen Murphy, and Oliver Walter. 1983. "The Religious Right and Electoral Change." Paper delivered to the annual meeting of the Midwestern Political Science Association, Chicago, IL.

Beatty, Kathleen Murphy, and Oliver Walter. 1982. "Religious Belief and Practice: New Forces in American Politics?" Paper presented to the annual meeting of the American Political Science Association, Denver, CO.

Berelson, Bernard, Paul F. Lazarsfeld, and William N. McPhee. 1954. *Voting: A Study of Opinion Formation in a Presidential Campaign.* Chicago, IL: University of Chicago Press.

Bochel, J. M., and D. T. Denver. 1970. "Religion and Voting: A Critical Review and a New Analysis." *Political Studies.* 18: 205–219.

Buenker, John D. 1973. *Urban Liberalism and Progressive Reform.* New York: Charles Scribner's Sons.

Burner, David. 1967. *The Politics of Provincialism: The Democratic Party in Transition, 1918–1932.* New York: W. W. Norton.

Cataldo, Everett F., and John D. Holm. 1983. "Voting on School Finances: A Test of Competing Theories." *Western Political Quarterly.* 36: 619–631.

Chalfant, H. Paul, and Charles W. Peek. 1983. "Religious Affiliation, Religiosity, and Racial Prejudice: A New Look at Old Relationships." *Review of Religious Research.* 25: 155–161.

Clark, Norman H. 1976. *Deliver Us From Evil: An Interpretation of American Prohibition.* New York: W. W. Norton.

Cohen, Steven M. 1983. *American Modernity and Jewish Identity.* New York: Tavistock Publications.

Cohen, Steven M., and Robert E. Kapsis. 1977. "Religion, Ethnicity, and Party Affiliation in the United States: Evidence from Pooled Election Surveys, 1968–1972." *Social Forces.* 56: 637–653.

Cohn, Werner. 1957. "The Politics of American Jews." In *The Jews,* ed. Marshall Sklare. New York: Free Press, 614–626.

Colombo, Furio. 1984. *God in America: Religion and Politics in the United States.* New York: Columbia University Press. Translated by Kristin Jarrat.

Converse, Philip E. 1974. "Some Priority Variables in Comparative Electoral Research." In *Electoral Behavior: A Comparative Handbook,* ed. Richard Rose. New York: Free Press, 727–745.

Converse, Philip E. 1966. "Religion and Politics: The 1960 Election." In *Elections and the Political Order,* ed. Angus Campbell, Philip E. Converse, Warren E. Miller, and Donald Stokes. New York: John Wiley, 96–124.

Converse, Philip E. 1964. "The Nature of Belief Systems in Mass Publics." In *Ideology and Discontent,* ed. David Apter. New York: Free Press, 206–261.

Converse, Philip E., and Angus Campbell. 1969. "Political Standards in Secondary Groups." In *Readings in Reference Group Theory and Research,* ed. Herbert H. Hyman and Eleanor Singer. New York: Free Press, 473–489.

Crosby, Donald F. 1978. *God, Church, and Flag: Senator Joseph R. McCarthy and the Catholic Church, 1950–1957.* Chapel Hill, NC: University of North Carolina Press.

Davis, James A. 1984. *General Social Surveys, 1972–1984: Cumulative Codebook.* Chicago, IL: National Opinion Research Center, University of Chicago.

Dawidowicz, Lucy S., and Leon J. Goldstein. 1974. *Politics in a Pluralist Democracy: Studies of Voting in the 1960 Election.* Westport, CT: Greenwood Press. Reprint of the 1963 edition.

Domhoff, G. William. 1983. *Who Rules America Now? A View For the '80s.* Englewood Cliffs, NJ: Prentice-Hall.

Driedger, Leo. 1974. "Doctrinal Belief: A Major Factor in the Differential Perception of Social Issues." *Sociological Quarterly.* 15: 66–80.

Ebersole, Luke. 1960. "Religion and Politics." *Annals of the American Academy of Political and Social Sciences.* 332: 101–111.

El-Azhary, M. S. 1980. *Political Cohesion of American Jews: A Reappraisal of Their Role in Presidential Elections.* Washington, DC: University Press of America.

Elazar, Daniel. 1969. "American Political Theory and the Political Notions of American Jews: Convergence and Contradictions." In *The Ghetto and Beyond,* ed. Peter Isaac Rose. New York: Random House, 203–227.

Elinson, Howard. 1965. "The Implications of Pentecostal Religion for Intellectualism, Politics, and Race Relations." *American Journal of Sociology.* 70: 403–415.

Fee, Joan L. 1976. "Party Identification Among American Catholics, 1972, 1973." *Ethnicity.* 3: 53–69.

Fenton, John H. 1960. *The Catholic Vote.* New Orleans, LA: Hauser Press.

Fisher, Alan. 1979. "Realignment of the Jewish Vote?" *Political Science Quarterly.* 94: 97–116.

Fisher, Alan. 1976. "Continuity and Erosion of Jewish Liberalism." *American Jewish Historical Quarterly.* 66: 322–348.

Flynn, George Q. 1968. *American Catholics and the Roosevelt Presidency, 1932–1936.* Lexington, KY: University of Kentucky Press.

Fowler, Robert Booth. 1982. *A New Engagement: Evangelical Political Thought, 1966–1976.* Grand Rapids, MI: William B. Eerdmans.

Fuchs, Lawrence. 1984. "The Political Behavior of American Jews." In *American Political Theology,* ed. Charles W. Dunn. New York: Praeger, 70–78.

Fuchs, Lawrence H. 1956. *The Political Behavior of American Jews.* Glencoe, IL: Free Press.

Fuchs, Lawrence H. 1955. "American Jews and the Presidential Vote." *American Political Science Review.* 49: 385–401.

Glantz, Oscar. 1959. "Protestant and Catholic Voting Behavior in a Metropolitan Area." *Public Opinion Quarterly.* 23: 73–82.

Glock, Charles Y., and Rodney Stark. 1966. *Christian Beliefs and Anti-Semitism.* New York: Harper and Row.

Gorsuch, Richard L., and Daniel Aleshire. 1974. "Christian Faith and Ethnic Prejudice: A Review and Interpretation of Research." *Journal for the Scientific Study of Religion.* 13: 281–307.

Granberg, Donald. 1978. "Pro-Life or Reflection of Conservative Ideology? An Analysis of Opposition to Legalized Abortion." *Sociology and Social Research.* 62: 414–429.

Greeley, Andrew M. 1982. *Religion: A Secular Theory.* New York: Free Press.

Greeley, Andrew M. 1977. "How Conservative Are American Catholics?" *Political Science Quarterly.* 92: 199–218.

Greer, Scott. 1961. "Catholic Voters and the Democratic Party." *Public Opinion Quarterly.* 25: 611–625.

Grupp, Frederick W., and William M. Newman. 1973. "Political Ideology and Religious Preference: The John Birch Society and the Americans for Democratic Action." *Journal for the Scientific Study of Religion.* 12: 401–413.

Guysenir, Maurice G. 1958. "Jewish Vote in Chicago." *Jewish Social Studies.* 20: 195–214.

Hadden, Jeffrey. 1969. *The Gathering Storm in the Churches.* Garden City, NY: Doubleday-Anchor.

Hammond, John M. 1974. "Revival Religion and Anti-Slavery Politics." *American Sociological Review.* 39: 175–186.

Hand, Carl M., and Kent D. Van Liere. 1984. "Religion, Mastery-Over-Nature, and Environmental Concern." *Social Forces.* 63: 555–570.

Handy, Robert T. 1984. *A Christian America: Protestant Hopes and Historical Realities.* Second edition. New York: Oxford University Press.

Hanna, Mary. 1984. "From Civil Religion to Prophetic Church: The Bishops and the Bomb." In *American Political Theology,* ed. Charles W. Dunn. New York: Praeger, 144–153.

Hanna, Mary T. 1979. *Catholics and American Politics.* Cambridge, MA: Harvard University Press.

Hendricks, John S. 1977. "Religious and Political Fundamentalism: The Links Between Alienation and Ideology." Ph.D. thesis, Department of Political Science, University of Michigan.

Henriot, Peter, S. J. 1966. "The Coincidence of Political and Religious Attitudes." *Review of Religious Research.* 8: 50–58.

Hero, Alfred O., Jr. 1973. *American Religious Groups View Foreign Policy: Trends in Rank-and-File Opinion, 1937–1969.* Durham, NC: Duke University Press.

Hoffman, Thomas J. 1985. "Religion and Political Change: The Impacts of Institutional Connectedness and Religious Imagery." Paper delivered to the Annual Meeting of the American Political Science Association, New Orleans, LA.

Hoffman, Thomas J. 1982. "Religion and Politics: An Empirical Inquiry." Ph.D. thesis, Department of Political Science, University of Arizona.

Hoge, Dean R. 1976. *Division in the Protestant House*. Philadelphia, PA: Westminister Press.

Hougland, James G., and William B. Lacy. 1981. "Membership in Voluntary Organizations and Support for Civil Liberties." *Sociological Focus*. 14: 97–110.

Hunter, James Davison. 1983. *American Evangelicalism: Conservative Religion and the Quandary of Modernity*. New Brunswick, NJ: Rutgers University Press.

Irvine, William P. 1974. "Explaining the Religious Basis of the Canadian Partisan Identity: Success on the Third Try." *Canadian Journal of Political Science*. 7: 560–563.

Jay, Evelyn D. 1981. "Religious Commitment: Its Origins and Its Consequences for Social Conservatism." Ph.D. thesis, Department of Political Science, University of California, Berkeley.

Jeffries, Vincent, and Clarence L. Tygart. 1974. "The Influence of Theology, Denomination, and Values upon the Positions of Clergy on Social Issues." *Journal for the Scientific Study of Religion*. 13: 309–324.

Jelen, Ted G. 1985. "Images of God as Predictors of Attitudes on Social Issues Among Fundamentalists and Non-Fundamentalists." Paper presented to the Annual Meeting of the Society for the Scientific Study of Religion, Savannah, GA.

Johnson, Benton. 1967. "Theology and the Position of Pastors on Public Issues." *American Sociology Review*. 32: 433–442.

Johnson, Benton. 1966. "Theology and Party Preference Among Protestant Clergymen." *American Sociological Review*. 31: 200–208.

Johnson, Benton. 1964. "Ascetic Protestantism and Political Preference in the Deep South." *American Journal of Sociology*. 69: 359–366.

Johnson, Benton. 1962. "Ascetic Protestantism and Political Preference." *Public Opinion Quarterly*. 26: 35–46.

Johnson, Benton, and Richard H. White. 1967. "Protestantism, Political Preference, and the Nature of Religious Influence: Comment on Anderson's Paper." *Review of Religious Research*. 9: 28–35.

Kaplan, Norman. 1969. "Reference Groups and Interest Group Theories of Voting." In *Readings in Reference Group Theory and Research,* ed. Herbert H. Hyman and Eleanor Singer. New York: Free Press, 461–472.

Kelley, Dean M. 1977. *Why Conservative Churches Are Growing*. Second edition. San Francisco, CA: Harper and Row.

Kersten, Lawrence K. 1970. *The Lutheran Ethic*. Detroit, MI: Wayne State University Press.

Kleppner, Paul. 1970. *The Cross of Culture*. New York: Free Press.

Knoke, David. 1974. "Religious Involvement and Political Behavior: A Log-Linear Analysis of White Americans, 1952–1968." *Sociological Quarterly*. 15: 51–65.

Laitin, David D. 1978. "Religion, Political Culture, and the Weberian Tradition." *World Politics*. 30: 563–592.

Laumann, Edward O., and David R. Segal. 1971. "Status Inconsistency and Ethnoreligious Group Membership as Determinants of Social Participation and Political Attitudes." *American Journal of Sociology*. 77: 36–61.

Lazarsfeld, Paul F., Bernard Berelson, and Hazel Gaudet. 1948. *The People's Choice: How the Voter Makes Up His Mind in a Presidential Campaign*. New York: Columbia University Press.

Lenski, Gerhard. 1963. *The Religious Factor.* Garden City, NY: Doubleday-Anchor.

Leventman, Paula Goldman, and Seymour Leventman. 1976. "Congressman Drinan, S. J., and His Jewish Constituents." *American Jewish Historical Quarterly.* 66: 215–248.

Levine, Lawrence W. 1975. *Defender of the Faith: William Jennings Bryan—The Last Decade, 1915–1925.* New York: Oxford University Press.

Lichtman, Allan J. 1979. *Prejudice and the Old Politics: The Presidential Election of 1928.* Chapel Hill, NC: University of North Carolina Press.

Liebman, Arthur. 1979. *Jews and the Left.* New York: Wiley Inter-Science.

Liebman, Charles. 1973. *The Ambivalent American Jew.* Philadelphia, PA: Jewish Publication Society.

Lijphart, Arend. 1971. "Class Voting and Religious Voting in the European Democracies." Survey Research Centre, University of Strathclyde, Glasgow.

Lipset, Seymour Martin. 1964. "Three Decades of the Radical Right: Coughlinites, McCarthyites, and Birchers." In *The Radical Right,* ed. Daniel Bell. Garden City, NY: Doubleday-Anchor, 373–446.

Littell, Franklin H. 1970. "The Radical Reformation and Revolution." In *Marxism and Radical Religion,* ed. John C. Raines and Thomas Dean. Philadelphia, PA: Temple University Press, 81–100.

Lubell, Samuel. 1965. *The Future of American Politics.* Third edition. New York: Harper and Row.

Lupfer, Michael, and Kenneth D. Wald. 1985. "An Exploration of Adults' Religious Orientations and their Philosophies of Human Nature." *Journal for the Scientific Study of Religion.* 24: 293–304.

Maddox, William S. 1979. "Changing Electoral Coalitions From 1952–1976." *Social Science Quarterly.* 60: 309–313.

Madron, Thomas W., Hart M. Nelsen, and Raytha L. Yokeley. 1974. "Religion as a Determinant of Militancy and Political Participation Among Black Americans." *American Behavioral Scientist.* 17: 783–796.

Maller, Allen S. 1977. "Class Factors in the Jewish Vote." *Jewish Social Studies.* 39: 159–162.

Marx, Gary T. 1967. *Protest and Prejudice: A Study of Belief in the Black Community.* New York: Harper and Row.

McIntosh, William Alex, Letitia T. Alston, and Jon P. Alston. 1979. "The Differential Impact of Religious Preference and Church Attendance on Attitudes Toward Abortion." *Review of Religious Research.* 20: 195–213.

McKinney, William, and Wade Clark Roof. 1982. "A Social Profile of American Religious Groups." In *Yearbook of American and Canadian Churches, 1982,* ed. Constant H. Jacquet. Nashville, TN: Abingdon for the National Council of the Churches of Christ in the U.S.A., 267–273.

Menendez, Albert J. 1977. *Religion at the Polls.* Philadelphia, PA: Westminister Press.

Miller, Abraham, 1974. "Ethnicity and Party Identification: Continuation of a Theoretical Dialogue." *Western Political Quarterly.* 27: 479–490.

Murchland, Bernard. 1982. *The Dream of Christian Socialism: An Essay on Its European Origins.* Washington, DC: American Enterprise Institute.

Nelsen, Hart M., Thomas W. Madron, and Raytha L. Yokeley. 1975. "Black Religion's Promethean Motif: Orthodoxy and Militancy." *American Journal of Sociology.* 81: 139–146.

O'Grady, John F. 1982. *Models of Jesus.* Garden City, NY: Image Books.

Orum, Anthony M. 1970. "Religion and the Rise of the Radical White: The Case of Southern Wallace Support in 1968." *Social Science Quarterly.* 51: 674–688.

Parenti, Michael. 1967. "Political Values and Religious Cultures: Jews, Catholics, and Protestants." *Journal for the Scientific Study of Religion.* 6: 259–269.

Petrusak, Frank, and Steven Steinart. 1976. "The Jews of Charleston: Some Old Wine in New Bottles." *Jewish Social Studies.* 38: 337–346.

Phillips, Kevin P. 1969. *The Emerging Republican Majority.* New York: Double-day-Anchor.

Piazza, Thomas, and Charles Y. Glock. 1979. "Images of God and Their Social Meanings." In *The Religious Dimension: New Directions in Quantitative Research,* ed. Robert Wuthnow. New York: Academic Press, 69–91.

Pollock, Philip H. 1983. "Are There Two Liberalisms? The Partisan and Demographic Influences on Two Dimensions of Political Belief." *Sociological Focus.* 16: 227–237.

Quebedeaux, Richard. 1978. *The Worldly Evangelicals.* San Francisco, CA: Harper and Row.

Quinley, Harold E. 1974. "The Dilemma of an Activist Church: Protestant Religion in the Sixties and Seventies." *Journal for the Scientific Study of Religion.* 13: 1–22.

Rifkin, Jeremy, with Ted Howard. 1979. *The Emerging Order: God in the Age of Scarcity.* New York: Ballantine Books.

Rischin, Moses. 1962. *The Promised City: New York's Jews, 1870–1914.* New York: Harper and Row.

Rojek, Dean. 1973. "The Protestant Ethic and Political Preference." *Social Forces.* 52: 168–177.

Rokeach, Milton, 1969. "Religious Values and Social Compassion." *Review of Religious Research.* 11: 24–39.

Roof, Wade Clark. 1979a. "Concepts and Indicators of Religious Commitment: A Critical Review." In *The Religious Dimension: New Directions in Quantitative Research.* ed. Robert E. Wuthnow. New York: Academic Press, 17–45.

Roof, Wade Clark. 1979b. "Socioeconomic Differentials Among White Socioreligious Groups in the United States." *Social Forces.* 58: 280–289.

Roof, Wade Clark. 1974. "Religious Orthodoxy and Minority Prejudice: Causal Relationship or Reflection of Localistic World View?" *American Journal of Sociology.* 80: 643–664.

Roozen, David A. 1978. *The Churched and the Unchurched in America: A Comparative Profile.* Washington, DC: Glenmary Research Center.

Rose, Richard, and Derek Urwin. 1969. "Social Cohesion, Political Parties, and Strains in Regimes." *Comparative Political Studies.* 2: 7–67.

Rosenberg, Morris. 1956. "Misanthropy and Political Ideology." *American Sociological Review.* 21: 690–695.

Rothenberg, Stuart, and Frank Newport. 1984. *The Evangelical Voter.* Washington, DC: Free Congress Research and Education Foundation.

Rothman, Stanley, and S. Robert Lichter. 1982. *Roots of Radicalism: Jews, Christians, and the New Left.* New York: Oxford University Press.

Schindeler, Fred, and David Hoffman. 1968. "Theological and Political Conservatism: Variations in Attitudes Among Clergymen of One Denomination." *Canadian Journal of Political Science.* 1: 429–441.

Scoble, Harry M., and Leon D. Epstein. 1964. "Religion and Wisconsin Voting in 1960." *Journal of Politics.* 26: 381–396.

Shorris, Earl. 1982. *Jews Without Mercy: A Lament.* Garden City, NY: Double-day-Anchor.

Smith, Timothy L. 1965. *Revivalism and Social Reform: American Protestantism on the Eve of the Civil War.* New York: Harper and Row.

Steiber, Steven R. 1980. "The Influence of the Religious Factor on Civil and Sacred Tolerance." *Social Forces.* 58: 811–832.

Stellway, Richard J. 1973. "The Correspondence Between Religious Orientation and Socio-Political Liberalism and Conservatism." *Sociological Quarterly.* 14: 430–439.

Summers, Gene F., Richard L. Hough, Doyle P. Johnson, and Kathryn A. Veatch. 1970. "Ascetic Protestantism and Political Preference: A Re-examination." *Review of Religious Research.* 12: 17–25.

Vance, Grant W., and Thomas D. Snyder. 1983. *Digest of Education Statistics, 1983–1984.* Washington, DC: National Center for Educational Statistics.

Wald, Kenneth D. 1986. "The Persistence of Religious Influence in American Electoral Behavior." Paper presented to the Annual Meeting of the Midwest Political Science Association, Chicago, IL.

Wald, Kenneth D., and Michael B. Lupfer. 1983. "Religion and Political Attitudes in the Urban South." In *Religion and Politics in the South: Mass and Elite Perspectives,* ed. Tod A. Baker, Robert B. Steed, and Laurence W. Moreland. New York: Praeger Special Studies, 84–100.

Weber, Mary Cahill. 1983. "Religion and Conservative Social Attitudes." In *Views from the Pews: Christian Beliefs and Attitudes,* ed. Roger A. Johnson. Philadelphia, PA: Fortress Press, 103–122.

Weber, Max. 1958. *The Protestant Ethic and the Spirit of Capitalism.* New York: Charles Scribner's. Translated by Talcott Parsons.

Whyte, John H. 1981. *Catholics in Western Democracies: A Study in Political Behavior.* New York: St. Martin's Press.

Wilson, John. 1978. *Religion in American Society: The Effective Presence.* Englewood Cliffs, NJ: Prentice-Hall.

Wuthnow, Robert. 1973. "Religious Commitment and Conservatism: In Search of an Elusive Relationship." In *Religion in Sociological Perspective,* ed. Charles Y. Glock. Belmont, CA: Wadsworth, 117–132.

Zehner, Paul. 1967. "Beliefs and Political Behaviors of Chicago Clergymen from Nine Denominations." Unpublished Ph.D. thesis, Department of Political Science, Northwestern University.

5

Religion
and the State

When Caesar, having exacted what is Caesar's, demands still more insistently that we render unto him what is God's—that is a sacrifice we dare not make.
—Alexander Solzhenitsyn

It may not be easy, in every possible case, to trace the line of separation between the rights of religion and the Civil authority with such distinctiveness as to avoid collisions and doubts on unessential points.
—James Madison

Because Americans frequently fail to recognize the subtle religious influences on political life, I have devoted two chapters to examining the contributions of religion to important themes in American political culture and to political differences among the major religious groups. It is now time to move on to an analysis of those open conflicts between government and religion that often come to mind with the phrase "church and state."

Popular discussions of this topic often reveal deep disagreements over the meaning of provisions of the Constitution relating to religion and how the Constitution has been interpreted by the Supreme Court and other government agencies.[1] This confusion frequently extends to basic claims about the role of religion in American political history. Consider, for instance, the perennial debate over the religious motivations of the American founders. In a column that appeared in my campus newspaper (Miles 1984), a contributor confidently described the founders as deists and free thinkers who were highly skeptical about traditional forms of religion and who "really were not that concerned with the opinion of God and his agents." In his view, they wrote a Constitution intending to subdue political activism by churches. That interpretation clashes sharply with the view of another writer, who has portrayed the founders as deeply religious men, Christian statesmen who would have been "amazed" by the claim that the state should not support the institutions of religion (Schaeffer 1984, 135). If it is hard to gain agreement on the question of what a particular group of men thought about the relationship of religion to the government, it is doubly difficult to interpret the motives and consequences of subsequent decisions about church-state relations.

This chapter supplies some perspective on these issues by discussing the reasons for church-state tension and how the solution worked out by the founders has been modified by the Supreme Court to fit the changing circumstances of the country. Government policy on the subject is not fixed in stone. The United States may now be entering a new phase in church-state relations under the leadership of a more conservative Supreme Court. The chapter concludes with an examination of the new approach taken by the Court and how it might affect the shape of church-state relations in coming years.

THE GENESIS OF CHURCH-STATE CONFLICT

The relationship between church and state presents two sets of problems for all governments. On the most fundamental level, governments must decide what legal status to grant to churches, the institutional expressions of religion. Should government take account of religious sentiments, treat churches as just another type of interest group, or try to restrict the public role of the churches? The problem is particularly severe when, as in the United States, many types of churches compete for the loyalty of the citizens. In such a situation, "taking account" of the public's religious sentiment may inflame members of religious minorities and persons who are not religious. Yet by ignoring religion or limiting its public role in the interest of preserving harmony, the government runs the risk of alienating citizens for whom religion is an important source of personal identity.

The second type of church-state problem stems from possible conflicts between religious motivation and behavior in secular realms. Religions provide guidance about how people should live their lives. In some cases, religious beliefs may counsel individuals to undertake actions that violate the duly established laws of the state. Government may demand behavior that a church forbids or may prohibit actions that the church requires. In either case, the citizen is forced to choose between loyalty to the public law and loyalty to religious faith. What should be done when church and state provide conflicting guidance about appropriate or permissible behavior?

Because it involves the rights and privileges of two different institutions, the question of the legal status granted to churches is known as the boundary problem, or, from the phrase first used by Thomas Jefferson, that of the "wall of separation" between church and state. The second type of church-state problem, collision between the teachings of church and state, is usually described as the free exercise controversy—a label that recognizes the possibility that the free exercise of religious belief may run afoul of limits established by secular law. Both types of problem have repeatedly found their way onto the American political agenda. From any number of possible examples, two recent incidents will be used to illustrate each type of church-state problem.

The national news media recently focused attention on two court cases that raised in the starkest possible way the religious basis of disobedience to secular law (Zlatos 1984; Associated Press 1984a, 1984b). On February 16, 1984, an Indiana infant named Joel David Hall died of pneumonia. Less than four months later, in a neighboring town, nine-month-old Allyson Bergmann died of bacterial meningitis. The parents of both children had refused to seek medical care because of religious convictions. The Hall and Bergmann families belonged to Faith Assembly Church, a large congregation in northern Indiana that preaches faith in God as an alternative to medical care. Believing that God will conquer disease and pain if souls are pure, church members regard illness as a sign of defective spiritual commitment by individuals and their families. They also believe that any resort to professional medical care will only hasten death, because God will interpret it as evidence of diminished faith. Consistent with their understanding of life as a divine gift dependent on intense spiritual devotion, the church members avoid hospitals, reject medical devices such as eyeglasses and hearing aids, refuse immunizations, and do not maintain life insurance or use seatbelts. For failing to seek timely medical care, the parents of the two infants were charged under Indiana laws with reckless homicide and child neglect, convicted in jury trials, and sentenced to prison terms. The cases currently are being appealed.

The Indiana cases represent, in extreme form, the free exercise basis of church-state conflict. Government and religion came into conflict because each claimed the authority to set standards for human behavior. The right of government to limit what citizens may do is widely accepted by most modern societies. The authority of government is recognized in codes of law that state which types of behavior are unacceptable and define the penalties for disobedience. Religions also take positions on what behavior is permissible, and they embody their beliefs in sacred documents and religious codes. Recognizing the authority of government in most spheres, churches frequently urge the state to make religion the basis for deciding what types of behavior should be encouraged or forbidden. But when the laws do not agree with the doctrines of a church, the religious may claim for themselves a right to follow what they see as God's "higher law." That was the premise of Martin Luther King, Jr., when he openly defied laws on racial segregation as incompatible with Christianity; that was also the premise of the parents of Allyson Bergmann and Joel David Hall for not seeking medical care.[2]

In the Faith Assembly cases, government demanded one standard of behavior and the church another. Based on the widespread belief that government should protect children, who usually cannot defend themselves, the state of Indiana invoked laws calling for heavy fines and jail terms for parents who do not seek timely medical care for sick children. In moving against the parents of the Bergmann and Hall infants, the state was particularly alarmed by evidence that infant mortality rates among Faith Assembly members were three times the state average, even though church members could have afforded professional treatment. According to the prosecutor, the substitution of prayer for effective medical care constituted "negligence and criminally reckless conduct" under secular law. On their part, the Halls and Bergmanns claimed that faith healing was a legitimate exercise of their religion and that the state of Indiana had no legal basis on which to force them to act against their beliefs by calling in a physician. The bedrock of their defense, however, was the claim of moral superiority for church doctrine over state laws. Asked by the judge if she would ever seek medical treatment for her children, the mother of Joel David Hall declared, "On the basis of my convictions, and of my fear of God almighty, I could not provide medical care." What the state required as evidence of reasonable behavior by a parent, the church denounced as a form of blasphemy. In such a case, the parents asserted the right to follow their conscience.

The boundary problem does not usually appear in so dramatic a form, but it probably arises more frequently. A typical illustration of the boundary problem was the controversy that arose in the central Florida town of Sanford over the recognition of religious holidays in public schools (Associated Press 1984c). During the week before Christmas in 1983, Olivia Myers bought cards for her second-grade classmates at Pine Crest Elementary School and put a Jesus sticker on each of the cards. Concerned that such a religious symbol might violate school regulations about religious practices, Olivia's teacher consulted with the school's assistant principal and was told not to allow distribution of the cards during class. Like many public school systems, that of Seminole County had a policy of forbidding celebrations on religious themes. Under this policy, religious holidays could be studied as cultural events, but calling attention to the theological basis of holidays was prohibited as constituting an endorsement of a particular religion. Hence, although cultural symbols such as Christmas trees or Santa Claus were acceptable under the guidelines, a religious symbol, such as a picture of Jesus, appeared to touch on matters of personal faith that public schools were supposed to avoid. The decision to prohibit distribution of Olivia's cards and similar attempts to minimize religious themes drew criticism from some churches in the county.

In focusing on these two major types of church-state conflict, I do not mean to suggest that the two institutions are permanently locked into a battle for supremacy. Though conflicts occur, not all church-state interaction is marked by hostility. On some occasions, churches have actually called in government agencies to resolve situations beyond their power to remedy. Thus, church members and the diocesan hierarchy of the Lutheran church in America asked the police and the court system to remove a Pennsylvania minister who refused to accept dismissal from his pulpit (Wilhelm 1985). As corporate institutions, churches are entitled to the protection of government in such matters of property.[3] Government may also be asked to help individuals secure religious liberty from threats posed by other, nongovernmental institutions. For example, the federal courts have been petitioned to require businesses to recognize the conscience of employees whose faith does not permit them to work on certain days of the week or to perform certain responsibilities (Greenhouse 1984). But in most cases, and particularly in those that draw headlines, controversies arise over where to draw the proper line between the institutions (boundary) and the moral authority (free exercise) of church and state. This source of the controversy may be as seemingly trivial as an eight-year-old's wish to distribute Christmas cards to her classmates in public school or as significant as a parent's decision to withhold medical care from a critically ill child.

PRINCIPLES OF CHURCH-STATE RELATIONS

The American approach to the boundary and free exercise problems is governed by the famous phrase from the Constitution's first amendment: "Congress shall make no law respecting an establishment of religion, or prohibiting the free exercise thereof. . . ." That statement and a prohibition on "religious tests" for holding public office are the only formal references to religion in the Constitution. This brevity in the discussion of religion has inspired continuing debate over what kinds of government action toward religion are permitted and how far individuals may go in claiming religion as justification for violating secular law. The constitutional language on religion, like that on so many other subjects, has been interpreted differently from one generation to the next. The debate over the precise meaning of the words in different circumstances, a source of passionate controversy and fierce argument, is examined in later sections. Despite its intensity, however, that debate should not disguise what has been a strong American consensus on the role of religion in the state.[4]

For the more than 200 years it has existed as an independent nation, the United States has pursued what might best be described as a partial separation of church and state. There has been virtually unanimous agreement that the establishment clause ("Congress shall make no law respecting an establishment of religion") forbids the government to grant preference to any particular religion. Together with the corresponding free exercise clause (". . . or prohibiting the free exercise thereof"), it also seems clearly to rule out the possibility of the government imposing one religion as the official faith or prosecuting members of another because their beliefs are repugnant. But if "separation of church and state" is interpreted to mean that government should make no allowances for religion or belief, then the United States is a long way from complete separationism. In numerous ways, the government has recognized the strong religious beliefs held by many citizens of the nation and made it clear that separation does not require state hostility to religious influence (Kirby 1977).

The currency, national seal, "Pledge of Allegiance," national anthem, legislative prayers, and oaths sworn in federal courts all make explicit reference to a belief in God. Most of these practices have been upheld in court challenges. In such political events as a presidential inauguration, the religious motif is readily apparent through the Bible on which the oath is sworn and the prominent participation of clergy in the ceremony. In addition, the churches on occasion have been asked to participate in the formation of public policy. Until the Supreme Court broadened the grounds for "conscientious objection" to military participation, it was customary for members of the clergy to sit in judgment on the moral basis and the sincerity of persons who applied for exemption from military service. Even today, the clergy may be sought out to review public policies that raise moral issues. Pursuing a middle ground between the available alternatives, the United States on the one hand has avoided the option of submerging the state to the church, as in a theocratic system of government, and on the other has refused to restrict the church to a nonpolitical role.

The scheme of partial church-state separation, as worked out in the First Amendment to the Constitution, reflected a compromise between persons who disagreed about the political value of religion. Rather than fit neatly into the categories of religious supporters or opponents, most of the influential founders recognized religion as a force with the potential both to enhance and to undermine political stability. Hence the particular arrangement of church-state relations in the United States constitutes neither a wholehearted endorsement of religious influence on government nor unremitting hostility to it. To appreciate the American solution to the boundary and free exercise problems, it is essential to examine the circumstances under which it evolved.

THE FOUNDERS AND RELIGION

When the founders prohibited "religious tests" for holding federal office, the establishment of a national religion, and governmental interference with religious belief, they were reacting against both their understanding of British history and common practices in the colonies. From the Reformation, which had inspired the settlement of America, they acquired the belief that alliances between a powerful church and an absolute state would corrupt both institutions. More immediately, they observed how some of the North American colonies appeared to court that same danger by providing religion with the sanction of government in the form of religious requirements for public office, the establishment of an official faith, and denial of religious freedom to members of minority religions.

Many colonies demanded that public office be filled only by persons who could pass some test of acceptable faith. Even where a relatively wide range of religions were recognized, as a rule Christianity was the basis for these religious tests. Pennsylvania reserved public office for persons who would swear, "I do acknowledge the Scriptures of the old and New testiment [*sic*] to be given by divine inspiration" (Schappes 1971, 68). Belief in God was not sufficient in Maryland, which, although one of the most tolerant colonies, further demanded that officeholders accept the concept of the Holy Trinity (Kirwin 1959, 24–29). North Carolina also went one step further than Pennsylvania, excluding not only Jews but also Catholics from holding executive or judicial office (Schappes 1971, 598). In addition to such religious tests, most of the colonies formally recognized one religion as the official faith. Under this system, citizens could be obliged to attend services at a church of the favored denomination and were taxed to provide revenue for the dominant religion. Besides enjoying material support from the government, the clergy of the established church often were granted legal privileges such as exemption from certain types of civil laws. Competing faiths were put at a further disadvantage by laws making worship the privilege of the established church. As an example, the charter for the New York colony limited the right of public worship to all "who profess faith in God by Jesus Christ" (cited in Schappes 1971, 18–19).

The degree to which legal support of one church hampered the free exercise of other faiths was apparent in several restrictive features of colonial law. In some colonies, conformity to the official faith was a condition of residence and dissent the grounds for expulsion or worse. The "worse" in Massachusetts was death. According to that colony's charter of 1641 (cited in Dunn 1984, 22), "If any man after legal conviction shall have or worship any other god, but the lord god, he shall be put to death." What it meant to "have any other god" was spelled out by another law that warranted the death penalty for anyone who cursed or blasphemed "the name of God, the father, Son or Holy ghost." This law was invoked in 1660 to hang a Quaker woman who had refused repeated orders to stay out of Massachusetts (Marty 1984, 86–87). For denying the divinity of Jesus, the doctrine of the resurrection, and the occurrence of miracles, a Jewish resident of Maryland faced the possibility of death and the loss of property (Schappes 1971, 13–15). Under these conditions, the "free exercise" of religion applied only to the established religion of the colony.

Although differing over how far the government might go in recognizing religion, the men who most influenced the Constitution and operated the new system of government in its first years were virtually unanimous in rejecting state support for a national faith. Such support was deemed bad for the state because it promoted false values, undermined respect for the law, and introduced an unhealthy fanaticism to public affairs. As men of strong if unorthodox faith, the founders also shared a belief that establishment of a national religion or government support for religions would do religion more harm than good. Because each of these objections is relevant to current debates over church-state relationships in the United States, the founders' logic demands careful review.[5]

For some of the founding generation, notably Thomas Jefferson and John Adams, organized religion deserved no government support because, among other reasons, it perverted the true meaning of religion. Their extended correspondence shows that the architects of the Declaration of Independence and Washington's successors to the presidency both agreed that true religion consisted of benevolent conduct toward one's fellow human beings. They outdid one another in denouncing the irrelevance and superstition of the dogmas that priests and clergy had encrusted over the simplicity and beauty of religion's moral content (85, 139, 283; see also the comments of Ben Franklin, 25–26). All that was important in Christianity and the other religions, Adams wrote (81, 281), could be found in the Sermon on the Mount and the Ten Commandments. Jefferson agreed heartily: years before, he had tried to rewrite the Scriptures by pruning away all the doctrines that he saw as unnecessary—including the divinity of Jesus, the Holy Trinity, and the structure of the church (173–216). Precisely because formal religion appeared to give more attention to such mystical concepts than to the essential truths of the Golden Rule, it evoked little enthusiasm from Adams and Jefferson. Hence, they believed that organized religion would not contribute to the public good if it enjoyed the patronage of government.

Establishment was also considered unwise by some of the founders because it seemed likely to bring the law into low esteem. As deeply held matters of personal belief, religious views could move people to take extreme actions in defense of conscience. History seemed to demonstrate that attempts to impose a uniform faith by government action would inevitably unleash passion and violence. With so many different religious groups in the colonies, each offering its own distinct version of the truth, any national establishment would be certain to offend the many citizens who subscribed to different faiths. Under these circumstances, a law commanding support for an established church could not realistically be enforced. According to Madison, the consequence of an unenforceable law would be a striking demonstration of government's impotence and a reproach to its authority (108). In the absence of consensus, he thought, it would be better to pass no law at all than an unpopular statute that would be widely disobeyed.

The final political problem connected with establishment was the founders' firm belief in the inevitable degeneration of a state church into a system of religious tyranny. The experience of the colonies suggested to them that although establishment might begin as a mild and benign preference for one church, the privileges of governmental support would almost certainly encourage attempts to suppress alternate views. John Adams, whose skepticism of the churches earned him an unwarranted reputation for irreligion, asked rhetorically, "When or where had existed a Protestant or dissenting sect who would tolerate a free inquiry?" Answering his own question, he noted that the clergy would accept all manner of brutality and ignorance in the name of preserving the one true faith. "But," he wrote from personal experience, "touch a solemn truth in collision with a dogma of a sect, though capable of the clearest proof, and you will soon find you have disturbed a nest, and the hornets will swarm about your legs and hands and fly into your face and eyes." Having experienced similar condemnation for his attempt to reduce all religions to a common core of moral commands, Jefferson echoed Adams's appraisal of the tendency of churches to persecute those who did not fully accept their doctrines. To give such an institution access to the full powers of the state, they agreed, would create a powerful engine of oppression.

The harmful political consequences of a national religion were not the only reasons the founders rejected establishment. They also argued that political support would make for bad religion. As Jefferson observed, a government that compelled religious exercises could dictate other terms to a church, reducing it to a servant of power (137). More fundamentally, the founders concurred that religion was meaningful only when it was a sincere expression from the heart and mind of a free people. Second to none in his admiration of religion as a spur to upright conduct, George Washington repeatedly emphasized the need to keep religion a matter of personal conscience, free of government intervention. To do otherwise, Washington argued, was to put human beings in God's role as the judges of other people's conscience (49). Jefferson advised his nephew to "question with boldness" even the existence of God, because if a Supreme Being existed, "he must more approve of the homage of reason than that of blindfolded fear" (128–29). Although the government could force people to swear loyalty to a public faith, it could not make their hearts pure or their behavior any better. From this evidence, it seems clear that resistance to establishment did not grow out of hostility to faith. Even Tom Paine, the founder most widely regarded as an enemy of Christianity, believed that the practice of true religion would improve if churches were separated from the state.

All these supposed defects of establishment would be turned into benefits if government refrained from endorsing a religion or trying in any way to regulate acceptable belief. Freed from state support, political leaders of the early nation predicted, the false churches would collapse as humanity returned to the essentials of religion (320). Instead of undermining respect for the law by insulting the conscience of dissenters, a government that respected religious freedom would enjoy widespread popular support and obedience in the legitimate exercise of its power. In fact, citizens watchful of their religious freedom would be equally sensitive to safeguard their other fundamental and natural liberties. Finally, in the absence of attempts to enforce a single faith, the founders expected an even greater number and diversity of churches. In religion, as in politics, they thought that diversity would make tyranny less likely, and so they welcomed the prospect of growth in the number of denominations. On top of these political benefits, of course, rested a firm belief that religion would be purified as its practice was freed from compulsion and hypocrisy.

So long as it was "universal, noninstitutional, and uncoerced" (Diggins 1984, 80), religion could contribute to good government by teaching men restraint and instilling in them a commitment to good works (see Tocqueville, 1945, vol. I, chap. 17; vol. II, book 1, chap. 5). It was that kind of faith that was endorsed when, for example, Washington in his farewell address referred to the importance of religion to morality. In that sense, the founders treated religion as a factor with the potential to stabilize republican government. Yet they remained aware that religion in a particular, institutional, and coerced form could do as much damage to the stability and reputation of republican government as any other source of social conflict (67). That is why they attached so much importance to denying any religion a favored status.

At a minimum, the founders did not want the national government to prefer any one religion or faith over another. Some writers have suggested that that was *all* they wanted or meant. In particular, it has been argued recently, the First Amendment to the Constitution was written only to prohibit the establishment of a *national* faith and governmental preference for one particular denomination (Malbin 1978; Curry 1986). In this view, nothing in the Constitution prohibits the states from endorsing a particular faith or the national government from providing nondiscriminatory support for religion in general. In terms of the specific intentions operating at the time of the First Amendment, this narrow interpretation has much to commend it. Many states maintained a religious establishment and other forms of official recognition of religion at the time the Constitution was passed. Because these establishments were not challenged on legal grounds, it has been contended, the First Amendment must not have been intended to limit the states. Moreover, the founders accepted a level of official recognition for religion far beyond what is tolerated today.

None of the founders appeared to believe that government must ignore religious feeling in its official actions. Thinking that God's blessings would be important in the outcome of the Revolutionary War, Washington ordered officers and soldiers in the Continental Army to maintain "punctual attendance" at worship services (50). Samuel Adams, the least reluctant of the founding generation to limit religious expression, used his position as governor of Massachusetts to issue religious proclamations (355–56); Washington did the same when he called for the first day of "thanksgiving" by the new nation (71–72). Even Jefferson, who provided the famous (or infamous) interpretation of the First Amendment as building "a wall of separation" between church and state, had no objection to the use of municipal buildings for worship by the different congregations in his village (163). Though he steadfastly recommended against paying for religious instruction at the state university he founded in Charlottesville, Jefferson advised the Virginia legislature to encourage the denominations to fund professorships of their own (164). By accommodating the claims of different churches in this manner, he thought the university could counter the false impression that it stood "against all religion." James Madison, usually portrayed as the strictest separationist among the founding generation, also apparently conceded religion an important public role (Weber 1982).

If one looks beyond the immediate circumstances of the adoption of the First Amendment, however, it becomes more difficult to sustain the very narrow interpretation of motives that some have ascribed to the founders. Although they conceded the continuation of establishment at the state level, Jefferson and Madison had made clear their opposition to official religion by waging a continuing battle for disestablishment of the Episcopal church in their native Virginia. Other members of the founding generation were involved in similar struggles throughout the states. It appears that Madison accepted limiting the disestablishment clause to the national government only as a way of strengthening support for the Constitution as a whole.

Just as important, some of the founders appeared to have doubts about the very idea of governmental aid to religion, even if it were to be allocated on a nondiscrimatory basis by state governments. Washington objected on principle to a bill introduced in the Virginia legislature to pay religious teachers from tax revenues. Rather than rankle the consciences of dissenters and so "convulse the State" with religious conflict, he much preferred a scheme like Jefferson's compromise on religious instruction at the state university. In a letter to a political friend, Washington expressed himself as favoring the obligation of all religions—Christianity no less than Islam or Judaism—to pay for their own religious instruction (64–65). "I wish an assessment had never been agitated," he wrote, "and . . . that the Bill could die an early death." Madison, the most relentless critic of public aid to religion, responded with vehemence the same year to a proposal in Congress that would have set aside a section of the Northwest Territory to support the church favored by a majority of the inhabitants. He denounced the proposal as "unjust" and "hurtful," a bill "smelling so strongly of an antiquated Bigotry" that it would reduce international respect for the country (306–7). Neither Washington nor Madison might have considered such proposals as unconstitutional under the terms of the First Amendment, but they did declare them to be unwise.

The strongest evidence that the founders did not favor even nondiscriminatory aid or noncoercive state recognition lay in their expressed sensitivity to the feelings of religious minorities. Their apparent awareness of how state recognition might injure the feelings of religious minorities can be interpreted to support preference for governmental aloofness to any religious expression, however bland and noncontroversial. A deeply religious man who served several terms as president of the American Bible Society, John Jay of New York objected to opening the sessions of the Continental Congress with a prayer. Citing the diversity of belief and custom among the delegates, he doubted that a prayer could be found that would not offend some member of the assembly. To the commander of a military expedition in Canada, General Washington stressed the need "to avoid all disrespect to or contempt of the religion of the country" (49). More than just a tactic designed to neutralize the French-Canadian Catholics, Washington's statement reflected his belief that one nation seeking freedom of conscience should not infringe the same right of another. As president, Washington showed the same sympathy to the religious groups that suffered the brunt of exclusion under state laws of establishment. He told a general meeting of Quakers that he believed that "the conscientious scruples of all men should be treated with great delicacy and tenderness" and wrote to the Jewish community in Newport, Rhode Island, of his belief that religious freedom was a "natural right," not a mere "indulgence" of toleration to minority faiths that the majority could grant or withdraw at will (60–61). Jefferson provided the clearest display of sensitivity to the implications of state recognition of religion when, as president, he was asked to proclaim a religious holiday (136–37). Reluctant to assume an authority that was, if it existed at all, reserved for state governments, he refused to issue even a watered-down proclamation encouraging national prayer with nothing more than the force of public opinion behind it. Challenging the proponent of such a plan, he asked, "Does the change in the nature of the penalty make the recommendation less a *law* of conduct for those to whom it is directed?" Jefferson doubted that the Constitution gave the president "the authority to direct the religious exercises of his constituents" even if such "direction" was nothing more than bland verbal encouragement.

Given their belief that taking note of any denomination or even recognizing something as broad as Christianity might offend the sentiments of good citizens, it seems unlikely that the founders would have approved what the Constitution may have permitted. Their approval of religious freedom extended to almost any form of faith that did no harm to the public good (61). As political scientist Michael Malbin (1978) has emphasized, the leaders of the new government thought that the state should judge religions not by their beliefs but by the behavior those beliefs produced.[6] In his *Notes on the State of Virginia*, Jefferson made the point very clearly.

> The legitimate powers of government extend to such acts only as are injurious to others. But it does me no injury for my neighbor to say there are twenty Gods, or no God. It neither picks my pocket nor breaks my leg. If it be said his testimony in a court of law cannot be relied on, reject it then, and be the stigma on him. Constraint may make him worse by making him a hypocrite, but it will never make him a truer man. It may fix him obstinately in his errors, but will not cure them. (123)

The state had a just interest in religion, Madison concurred, only when faith impelled a believer to "disturb the peace, the happiness, or safety of Society" (301). Even then, it was actions, not beliefs, that constituted an offense. On this reading the founders appear to have been as eager to keep the state from limiting religious expression as they were to keep the government from promoting it.

The prevailing attitudes about church and state in the early republic were reflected in the thoughts and actions of political leaders other than the major participants in the Constitutional Convention. A more complete sense of how early American political leaders understood the Constitution's religious policy can be gained through examination of an instructive controversy that began in the early years of the nineteenth century.[7] Since the founding of the nation, the government had always permitted the mail to be transported between communities on Sunday, the Christian Sabbath. In 1810, Congress enacted a law requiring post offices that received Sunday mail to stay open on that day and directing postmasters to make deliveries the same day they received shipments. Despite numerous protests from Christian organizations over defamation of the Lord's Day, Congress not only repeatedly refused requests to repeal the law, but also extended it on several occasions. Early reports from the House committee with jurisdiction over the Post Office stressed that suspension of Sunday mail would impede the efficient performance of a major and legitimate government function. But as the protests mounted, the committee increasingly cited religious considerations as the basis for refusal to end Sunday delivery of posts.[8]

The language of a report issued in 1830 made the case for continued Sunday delivery in terms that would probably have pleased the founding generation. By acceding to requests to end mail delivery on Sunday, it was argued, Congress would effectively be granting official recognition to the Christian Sabbath. Withholding the mail on Sunday would force non-Christians to respect a holiday that they did not recognize in their hearts. In strong language, the House committee reminded the petitioners that the Constitution gave religious equality to all people by denying privileges to any—even if the faith in question was shared by the vast majority of the population. Echoing the fear of the founders that even slight concessions to one faith might open up a wedge for greater government regulation in the future, they wrote that

> the conclusion is inevitable, that the line cannot be too strongly drawn between Church and State. If a solemn act of legislation shall, in *one* point, define the law of God, or point out to the citizen one religious duty, it may, with equal propriety, proceed to define *every* part of divine revelation; and enforce *every* religious obligation, even to the forms and ceremonies of worship; the endowment of the church, and the support of the clergy. (Committee on Post Offices and Post Roads 1830, 1).

Rather than coerce individuals by using the authority of government, the committee recommended that petitioners try to "instruct the public mind" on the evils of the practice that they condemned. If all men and women truly came to believe in the evil of Sunday mail, the practice would wither instantly; so long as people did not unanimously share the views enunciated by critics of Sunday mail, governmental intervention could only inflame religious passions.

Whatever their merits or demerits, the committee reports reveal a view of church-state relations that appears to have prevailed in the minds of early legislators. As the 1830 report emphasized, any governmental recognition of religion appeared to be forbidden under the First Amendment. Although this view was not unanimously accepted, as indicated by dissents from the 1830 report and by language in earlier committee documents, the ideas of the founders were interpreted as supporting the "wall of separation" that Thomas Jefferson sought between the institutions of government and the churches.

THE WIDENING WALL OF SEPARATION

Despite the constant potential for controversy, neither the boundary problem nor the free exercise concept excited much national attention in the first 150 years under the Constitution. Over that span, the controversy over Sunday delivery of mail was one of the few church-state items to engage Congress. At the state level, fierce battles were fought over proposals to drop establishment and soften other forms of official support for religion. Although denominational competition and conflict remained important elements of political controversy, the constitutional status of religious institutions and belief was simply not a pressing item on the national agenda.

Church-state relations only became a major topic of political discussion in the 1940s, when the United States Supreme Court began to reinterpret the First Amendment's language on religion. During a period of reappraisal that stretched from the mid-1940s to approximately the mid-1970s, the Court provided a new legal framework that, although under serious challenge today, has since governed American practice about church-state relations.

During this era of judicial ferment, the Supreme Court departed from previous church-state doctrine in three important respects. First, it abandoned the traditional distinction between national and state action toward churches. Whatever the First Amendment forbade or required the national government to do about religion, it was now held by the Court, also applied to the state and local levels of government. Second, the Court attempted to extend the boundary between church and state by broadening the list of government actions that constituted an impermissible establishment of religion. Formerly understood to forbid only actions that treated religious groups unequally, establishment was now seen to encompass many activities that appeared to favor religion in general. Last, the Court became much more sensitive to claims that government rules and regulations unconstitutionally interfered with the free exercise of religion. Before this period, the justices had tended to strike down only those practices that seemed to force individuals to endorse religious beliefs that might be contrary to their own. Now, however, they began to identify a wide range of actions that produced the same effect and either prohibited their enforcement or required government to exempt persons from certain practices on grounds of conscience.

As noted above, the First Amendment says only that *Congress* is forbidden to make laws about religious establishment or otherwise restrict religious exercise. In practice, the courts had interpreted that language as binding all agencies of the national government, those of the judicial and executive branches included, but leaving states free to support religion through their own constitutions. Many did, maintaining customs and practices that gave religion a favored legal standing. The different treatment of religion by nation and state was first rejected in principle in a 1940 Supreme Court decision; eight years later, a policy developed by an Illinois school board became the first state or local regulation actually struck down by the Supreme Court as being in conflict with the establishment clause. The Court has since applied its doctrine of church-state separation uniformly to all levels of government. In doing so, the Supreme Court did nothing to the religion clauses of the First Amendment that it had not previously done to the rest of the Bill of Rights. By restricting states in the same way as the federal government, the new interpretation treated religion as part and parcel of a national list of rights that all governmental institutions must respect.

The extension of the First Amendment to the states became so important because the Court had widened its definition of what the word *establishment* covered. Most of the important cases in which this concern arose had to do with actions affecting public elementary and secondary schools. Because children are thought to be especially open to influence, Americans have been most sensitive to government's treatment of religion insofar as it affects the youngest members of society. That concern has been magnified because children are required by law to attend school and most of them do so in educational institutions paid for by tax revenues. In such politically delicate circumstances, any apparent favoritism toward a religious faith can appear to constitute government endorsement of religion. Because attendance at institutions of higher learning represents a voluntary choice by more mature individuals who often bear a substantial part of the costs of schooling, the courts in general have allowed much greater latitude for proposals to assist religiously affiliated colleges and universities.

The progress of the Supreme Court's ideas was uneven, and the new doctrine about establishment did not unfold clearly from one case to the next. A pattern of fits and starts is common when the Court changes direction; it was especially marked in the "boundary" cases because the Court itself underwent changes in composition and because the problems of interpretation in the area were so difficult.

In 1947 the Court decided a case that was to herald a flood of litigation about the modern meaning of First Amendment prohibitions "respecting an establishment of religion."[9] In *Everson* v. *Board of Education,* the justices ruled that New Jersey could constitutionally compensate the parents of all children, including those attending religious schools, for expenses incurred in bus transportation to and from school. Defraying the cost that parents incurred for sending their children to religious schools, the Court held, did not involve an excessive degree of state support for religion. Even though this ruling appeared on the surface as a victory for advocates of governmental aid to religious education, the language of the majority opinion made it clear that breaches of the wall of separation would be tolerated only under the narrowest of circumstances. Consistent with that warning, in *McCollum* v. *Board of Education* (1948) the Court said that the school board in Champaign, Illinois, could not allow students in public schools to receive religious instruction on the premises even though attendance at such classes was voluntary and paid for privately. Opening up the school buildings to religious training while other classes were in session struck the Court as virtual endorsement of religion by the local government, an action that fell within the meaning of the establishment clause. But suppose that instead of inviting religious teachers to offer voluntary instruction in the school building, the state simply allowed students to travel off-campus for that purpose during the school day? In a 1952 decision, *Zorach* v. *Clauson*, the justices ruled that a New York City law releasing students from normal classes to attend religious classes somewhere else did not offend the establishment clause. This pattern of ruling first to permit some action, then to deny others, has continued to the present day.

Rulings about how far the state could go in helping students receive religious training did not settle the issue of what the public schools could do about religious ideas. The two decisions that spoke clearly to that issue rank among the most unpopular rulings in the history of the Supreme Court. The 1962 case of *Engel* v. *Vitale* raised a challenge to the prayer that New York State required teachers to read at the beginning of the day. Because an agency of government composed the prayer and insisted that it be read as part of the daily routine, six justices declared that the New York practice illustrated precisely the type of action that the First Amendment forbids as an establishment of religion. A year later, in *Abington Township School District* v. *Schempp,* the Court extended the ban on state-mandated religious ceremonies to cover a Pennsylvania law requiring the reading of Bible verses and recitation of the Lord's Prayer over the loudspeaker at the beginning of the school day. By these two decisions, the Court seemed to say that "establishment" included any celebration of religion conducted by an agency of the government.[10] Such actions have since been routinely struck down by courts across the land.

Once that precedent had been established, the focus of debate over the church-state boundary in education shifted back to government actions vis-à-vis religious schools. In a 1968 case, *Board of Education* v. *Allen,* the Court decided that New York State could constitutionally loan parochial school students the same textbooks provided free of charge to students in the public schools. The *Allen* decision, which appeared to open the door to several different types of state support for church-related schools, inspired legislatures throughout the country to funnel various forms of aid to parochial schools. As these laws were challenged and the cases eventually made their way through the appeals process to the Supreme Court, it became clear that the justices viewed the provision of textbooks, like reimbursement for bus transportation, as one of very few ways that government could legitimately assist schools that taught religious faith. In a string of cases decided during the 1970s, the Court ruled that the boundary was violated if states contributed to the salaries of parochial school teachers to cover their "nonreligious" responsibilities (*Lemon* v. *Kurtzman,* 1971), allowed church schools to finance the upkeep of their buildings with tax money (*Committee for Public Education* v. *Nyquist,* 1973), reimbursed parents for the costs of private school tuition (same case), paid religious schools for the cost of educational testing required by state law (*Levitt* v. *Committee for Public Education,* 1973), or loaned instructional materials other than textbooks to schools supported by religious institutions (*Meek* v. *Pittenger,* 1975). The justices appeared to relent a bit when, in *Wolman* v. *Walter* (1977), they held that the state of Ohio was allowed to defray parochial school expenses incurred in conducting diagnostic and therapeutic services and in purchasing textbooks and some standardized test material. But the Court invalidated those parts of the law authorizing the state to help pay church-related schools for field trips, some instructional materials, and equipment.

For a judicial system that puts a high value on clarity, consistency, and tradition, the record in the establishment cases does not reveal many of those qualities. Part of the difficulty in this regard stemmed from the division of the Court into factions with different interpretations of the meaning of the First Amendment's language (Pritchett 1984, 158). Because these groupings were fluid and relatively evenly balanced, changes in circumstances from one case to another could swing enough votes to produce apparent contradictions between decisions. Over time, however, the Court moved closer to a common set of standards for determining if certain activities undermined the Constitution by establishing religion. Stated most fully by Chief Justice Warren Burger in the 1971 *Lemon* decision (cited in Pfeffer 1977, 30), the Court's standard required that a law pass three tests before it could be deemed compatible with the anti-establishment language of the First Amendment: a primarily secular purpose, primarily secular consequences, and no excessive entanglement of church and state.

To pass the first test, a law's major purpose must be to further some secular mission of government. Though it may touch on religion in so doing, that cannot be its principal intention. Thus, compensation for bus transportation was valid because New Jersey wanted *primarily* to get all children safely to and from school—a perfectly reasonable state policy not connected to religion. Because of this legitimate secular purpose, the law was acceptable even though it indirectly helped religious schools by marginally reducing the transportation costs parents would otherwise have had to bear. In contrast, an Arkansas law that prohibited the teaching of evolution in public schools had no discernible purpose except to give legal support to a tenet of the religious faith predominant in the state, and hence was voided by the Court (*Epperson* v. *Arkansas,* 1968).

The second test set up by the Court applies the same standard of secularity to primary *effects*. Because loaning textbooks to all students, in private and public schools alike, would principally expand knowledge in secular subjects, New York was authorized to keep its law on distribution. As long as the undeniable benefit to religion was not the principal outcome of the legislation, the law fell within the Supreme Court's view of legitimate public policy. But the New York law that permitted parents to receive tax credits for private school tuition had the primary effect of supporting instruction for religious purposes. Children would certainly benefit from attending schools with greater resources, but that was not deemed to be the primary consequence of the state law. Hence, the tuition tax credit was rejected for breaching the boundary.

Even if a law is deemed principally nonreligious in purpose and result, it must still satisfy the requirement that it does not "excessively entangle" the church and government. That means that a law should neither bring the government too deeply into the affairs of religion nor encourage religious groups to enter the political process as religious groups.[11] The first type of entanglement was cited when the Court ruled that paying parochial school teachers for secular instruction imposed on government a responsibility to see that the teachers did not let their religious values intrude upon that portion of their work supported by tax revenues. To enforce such a provision, the justices decided, the government would have to monitor teaching in church schools and so involve itself deeply in matters best left free from state action. The other entanglement the Court wanted to avoid was the encouragement of continuous political activism by churches as corporate bodies. If local school boards had the discretion to give certain types of assistance to private religious schools, the justices thought, school board elections would inevitably become transformed into conflicts between churches and candidates would be judged primarily by their religious affiliations.[12] Acknowledging that church members could and should get involved in politics as individuals, the Court sought to discourage the evolution of churches into political parties.

What kind of state action could survive scrutiny on this entanglement rule? The Court pointed with approval to a New York law that exempted churches and church-related institutions from the property tax. In *Walz* v. *Tax Commission of New York* (1971), it upheld the state's decision to keep religious property and the holdings of other nonprofit institutions off the tax rolls. Reasoning that taxation of churches would require local governments to assign a monetary value to church property and might even lead the state to put liens on the property or foreclose if taxes were not paid, the Court preferred exemption as much the lesser evil. Once certified as a nonprofit institution, exempt from the taxing authority of government, the church would be relatively free from the excessive entanglement that threatened the wall of separation. For that reason, among others, the Court's majority sustained tax exemption for property held by religious bodies. So, "entanglement" prohibited programs which might enable the church to draw on the resources of the government, as in the case of salary supplements for parochial school teachers, or policies of taxation which gave government potential power to interfere with the mission of religious bodies. Whatever the effect, too much intermingling of church and state made government action unconstitutional.

Under the Court's three-part rule, statutes involving religion were presumed to violate the establishment clause unless they could be shown to meet all three requirements. Challengers had to demonstrate only one failing for the law to be declared invalid. With such a demanding set of conditions, it is hardly surprising that the advocates of a high wall of separation won most of the critical Supreme Court cases and generally succeeded in church-state litigation when cases were decided by lower courts (see Sorauf 1976). If the Court nonetheless appeared indecisive in accepting some actions and rejecting others, that probably reflected the inherent difficulty of applying general rules to specific cases. Critics have argued that the Court could have avoided the problem altogether by either leaving alone the tradition that granted states substantial freedom in promoting religion or, failing that, accepting the judgment of democratically elected legislatures about what "establishment" means to modern public opinion. To supporters of the courts' understanding of the "wall of separation," however, the states had brought the problems on themselves by failing to heed clear signals to restrict their support for religion.

EXTENDING FREE EXERCISE CLAIMS

Even as it was broadening the meaning of "establishment" and thus restricting the scope of state action to encourage religion, the Court was growing markedly more receptive to individuals who challenged governmental actions as barriers to the practice of their faith. The same justices who demonstrated a concern to protect individuals from unwanted religious influences emanating from the government also showed a willingness to defend worship and other forms of religious activity from interference on the part of public authorities. The Court's concern was particularly likely to surface in cases in which the faith involved was unconventional and the restrictive government regulation may have reflected hostility to the minority religion by better-established religious groups.

The Court's initial concern in this regard was to ensure that religious groups enjoyed full freedom to practice their faith and to undertake activities related to it. For religions outside the mainstream, such as the Jehovah's Witnesses and Seventh-Day Adventists, the practice of religion involved public activities that might run afoul of local and state ordinances regulating access to public facilities or limiting door-to-door soliciting. Given its propensity to support speech and other forms of public expression about political ideas, the Court had little difficulty offering the same support to religious ideas.

As Pritchett has noted (1984, 133–34), many of the critical decisions in this area asserted that religious minorities should enjoy the same basic freedoms extended to unpopular political movements and causes. As early as 1938, the Court cited freedom of the press in allowing Jehovah's Witnesses to sell literature door-to-door without first having to obtain a municipal permit. The same rationale was cited in a 1943 ruling that exempted Jehovah's Witnesses from a Pennsylvania municipal license fee required of all door-to-door commercial solicitors. The free speech clause of the First Amendment provided the basis for a 1948 decision upholding the right of a preacher from the same sect to broadcast his sermons in a public park. In a Maryland case decided in 1951, the justices overturned the conviction of some Witnesses who had preached in a public park in defiance of municipal ordinances prohibiting such activity. Noting that the ordinance was enforced against the Witnesses but had not been used when mainstream religious groups held prayer services in the same location, the Court decided that the law was enforced unequally—a violation of the Fourteenth Amendment's requirement that all must enjoy the equal protection of the laws.

The Supreme Court also moved to defend religious freedom by explicit reference to the free exercise clause. The majority opinion in *Cantwell* v. *Connecticut* (1940) was the first to enshrine the principle of free exercise on its own terms and became a powerful precedent. The case arose when three ministers of the Jehovah's Witnesses were convicted of several offenses against municipal ordinances in New Haven, Connecticut. The key conviction of soliciting without a license was overturned on the ground that the law unconstitutionally allowed the state government to determine if the ministers' actions were motivated by genuinely religious convictions. For the government to screen religions in this manner, Justice Robert Jackson wrote, would "lay a forbidden burden upon the exercise of [religious] liberty protected by the Constitution" (cited in Pfeffer 1977, 137). In subsequent cases, the Court struck down a number of laws, regulations, ordinances, and administrative practices for interfering with religious exercise or preaching. In recent years, the free exercise principle has been used to prohibit government from interfering with the use of peyote, an otherwise illegal substance, in Navajo religious ceremonies. Similarly, prison authorities have been required to extend a number of privileges to inmates who practice Muslim, Buddhist, and Native American religions.

Worship and preaching clearly fall under the scope of free exercise. But what happens when the exercise of religion appears to be inconsistent with an obligation that government imposes upon citizens? In dealing with this difficult question, the Court has distinguished between government-mandated expressions of political sentiment, which have usually been invalidated, and government-mandated actions, which generally have been judged acceptable under the Constitution.

At first, the Court sided with the state in compelling certain expressions of political sentiment even when they violated religious beliefs. In *Minersville School District* v. *Gobitis* (1940), a controversial decision that unleashed violence in several states, the Supreme Court backed a Pennsylvania school board that had expelled two young members of the Jehovah's Witnesses for refusing to salute the flag in a public school ceremony (Manwaring 1962). In its opinion, the Supreme Court recognized that the children were sincere in their belief that saluting the flag was akin to worshiping a "graven image," a practice apparently forbidden by a literal reading of some passages in the Book of Exodus (20: 4–5). Yet, the majority argued, government had an overriding interest in promoting patriotism and national unity, for liberty was not possible without a strong sense of national community. As the flag symbolized the nation, government could legitimately insist that it be honored by schoolchildren.

Just three years later, in what must be close to a record turnaround, the Supreme Court overturned the *Gobitis* decision. Inspired by the ruling on behalf of Pennsylvania and by the wartime atmosphere of intense patriotic sentiment, West Virginia's Board of Education had demanded that public school students salute the American flag or face punishment for insubordination. Members of the Jehovah's Witnesses had sued on the grounds that salutes conflicted with the biblical injunction. In terms of issues and combatants, therefore, the case of *West Virginia State Board of Education* v. *Barnette* was identical to *Gobitis*. This time, however, the Supreme Court sided with the Witnesses against the state, arguing that the regulation unconstitutionally enforced belief rather than conduct. The flag was a symbol of state, comparable to the banner of a fraternal organization or the cross of a church, and the salute nothing more than a gesture of respect. As such, it was an expression of opinion that could not be forced upon a person who was unwilling, for any reason, to endorse the sentiment. As the majority opinion stated, the constitutional provision that "guards the individual's right to speak his own mind" did not give government the authority "to compel him to utter what is not in his mind" (cited in Pfeffer 1977, 130). Ever since that landmark decision, the courts have generally supported religious minorities seeking the protection of the First Amendment against different types of required patriotic expression, such as reciting the "Pledge of Allegiance" or standing during the National Anthem. In 1977, to take one of the most recent cases of this type, the Court supported New Hampshire residents who had taped over the "Live Free or Die" slogan on their license plates as inconsistent with their faith.

The Court has been slower to free religious groups from laws alleged to impose behavior repugnant to religious scruples. Even though the Court has not sided consistently with such claims, it has moved away from the traditional presumption that the needs or purposes of government must take precedence over conscience. Under that presumption, for example, the Supreme Court ruled in the 1934 case of *Hamilton* v. *Regents of the University of California* that a state was entitled to require military training for able-bodied male students enrolled at state universities. In that case, the paramount need for military preparedness was seen as taking precedence over religiously grounded objections to participation in military activity. In time this presumption was relaxed, if not discarded, as the Court insisted that government must have a very strong reason to force people to act against religious conscience. Unless the government could show that exemption would do severe damage to some important national or state function, the Court insisted that "free exercise" of conscience had priority. In the words of a 1972 opinion, assigning a "preferred position" to the First Amendment rights meant that "only those interests of the highest order not otherwise served can overbalance legitimate claims to the free exercise of religion" (Pfeffer 1977, 35).

In decisions handed down in several cases involving national security and loyalty, the Court explicitly recognized religious motives as a basis for principled dissent and limited forms of disobedience. In 1943 a Seventh-Day Adventist from Canada was refused American citizenship because he said religious beliefs would prevent him from taking up arms to defend the United States. Like other members of his faith who had served as noncombatants in the military and contributed in nonviolent ways to the war effort, the applicant was willing to support the nation by other means. Hence, Justice William O. Douglas argued for the majority in *Girouard* v. *United States* (1946), any attempt to demand the willingness to fight as a condition for citizenship contravened religious scruples for no good purpose. The right to seek noncombatant status, which Congress had granted to persons with religious scruples, was upheld when the Court ordered a draft board to grant conscientious objector status to a member of Jehovah's Witnesses (*Sicurella* v. *U.S.*, 1955). The types of religious scruples protected under the free exercise clause were enlarged by the Court's 1965 decision in *United States* v. *Seeger*. In this and related cases, it ordered local draft boards to treat applications for conscientious objector status with the same respect whether the individual cited nontraditional forms of belief in a Supreme Being or orthodox ideas of God as the basis for exemption.

Considering that the Court recognized the primacy of faith in so sensitive an area as national security, it is not surprising that rules conflicting with faith were challenged successfully in several other areas. In *Wisconsin* v. *Yoder* (1972), the Court upheld the right of Amish parents to keep their children out of public school after the age of fourteen. As the state could not convince the justices that an additional year or two of schooling was critical for any social purpose, the Court was more impressed by Amish fears that exposure to additional secular instruction might undermine the children's commitment to their community's values. Similar rulings upheld religious belief as a warrant for refusing jury duty and prohibited state governments from denying unemployment benefits to persons whose religious beliefs against work on Saturday kept them out of a job. As recently as 1981, the Court demanded that Indiana pay unemployment compensation to a member of Jehovah's Witnesses who quit a job rather than take an assignment to work on gun turrets for tanks (*Thomas* v. *Review Board*). By decisions such as these, free exercise has been extended to support mandatory exemption from a variety of obligations imposed on American citizens.

Despite this general trend toward expanding the list of state actions that unconstitutionally interfere with the free exercise of religion, the Court from time to time has permitted some limitations. Recognizing the state's interest in protecting public health and safety, the Court has approved compulsory vaccination and other medical procedures, especially those involving children, and permitted government to ban religious practices that might endanger the participants. (Such precedents suggest that the Faith Assembly members in the Indiana cases mentioned earlier would not find the Court very receptive to their pleas.) The Supreme Court has also upheld the constitutionality of the so-called blue laws, state statutes that compel businesses to close on Sunday. Originally passed as part of the Protestant campaign to give legal support to the Sabbath—clearly a religious purpose—they were upheld by the Court because they had become a species of welfare legislation, serving the interests of public safety and employee health by stopping business activity on one day of the week. Over the protests of some orthodox Jewish merchants, for whom the law meant another day of shutdown after the Jewish Sabbath, the Court adjudged the laws reasonable and saw no alternative way to achieve a valid public purpose.

Over time, the Supreme Court has developed a two-part test to evaluate free exercise claims that resembles the standard it has used in judging cases involving the establishment clause. When confronted with charges that a secular law or custom unconstitutionally limits the right of free exercise, the Supreme Court first asks if the policy places a burden on the exercise of religion by individuals or groups. If so, the government must demonstrate that it has a compelling interest in the law or policy and that its goal cannot be achieved without hindering religious observance. The spirit of this standard was illustrated in a recent lower court ruling in a free exercise case. On safety grounds, a local school board prohibited an Orthodox Jewish student from wearing a skull cap while playing basketball for his school. The Court accepted the student's argument that forcing him to remove the yarmulke during games constituted interference with the right of free exercise. Yet it also acknowledged the school board claim that that the skull cap might be dislodged during play, potentially causing another player to slip and fall. Rather than side with the government, however, the Court asked if player safety could not be achieved by allowing the student to affix the skull cap firmly to his head with an elastic band that would fasten under the chin. The presumption of this test normally places a burden of proof upon the government, which must demonstrate that it cannot find an acceptable alternative that leaves persons free to exercise their faith.

The Court's tendency to support religious objections to secular law has inspired a substantial growth in the filing of such cases and a dramatic increase in the success of such suits. A recent study by Way and Burt (1983) illustrated the magnitude of the trend away from the presumption favoring government. During the first decade covered by their study, 1946–56, the state and federal courts decided thirty-four cases in which minority religions—groups outside the Protestant, Catholic, and Jewish families—claimed free exercise rights. Although the courts sustained the claims in only 20 percent of the cases, the significance of the decisions apparently stimulated more litigation. Between 1970 and 1980, the number of such cases more than quadrupled, to 145. Over that period, "marginal" religious groups won slightly more than half of the cases they brought; in contrast, victories resulted in only about one-third of the lawsuits involving mainstream religions. The minority religious groups were most likely to succeed in legal challenges to laws or practices that limited efforts to spread the faith and in suits brought to extend rights of practice to prisoners. They broke even in cases related to employment and taxation and lost most attempts to gain exemptions from secular laws governing schools or to refuse medical care for minors.

Thanks to almost forty years of intense judicial activity, both the free exercise and establishment clause of the First Amendment have taken on new and broader meanings. In the process, the actions of the courts raised new issues and fueled compelling debates about the place of religion in American society.

THE POLITICS OF CHURCH-STATE RELATIONSHIPS

In the majesty of their surroundings and the dignity of their procedures, the courts often appear isolated from the normal processes of political conflict. Despite the exalted image of the judiciary, its behavior is permeated by the same types of political influences that affect other arenas of government. Any discussion of church-state relationships must, therefore, take account of the larger political context in which judicial decisions are taken. An investigation of the politics of church-state interaction is necessary to understand why the issue became so important when it did, how the religious community reacted to crucial court decisions, and whether or not a restoration of the prewar legal framework is likely.

The Supreme Court's radical transformation of church-state doctrine from the 1940s through the 1970s did not occur in isolation. As noted above, one source of revision was the general tendency of the justices to extend the First Amendment to cover the actions of state and local governments. In that sense, the new limitations on government action toward religion were by-products of a broader tendency to "nationalize" the Bill of Rights. But beyond this general shift in constitutional interpretation, another factor was involved in the Court's specific rulings about religion. As is often the case in political and legal change, the consciousness of the Court was shaped by intensive grass-roots political activity that raised the church-state issue to a high place on the national agenda (Morgan 1980; Sorauf 1976). Throughout the era of judicial activism on the church-state question, the churches, allied groups of laypeople, and interfaith organizations functioned much like classic interest groups—designing legislation, raising public support in well-orchestrated campaigns for public opinion, lobbying legislatures and courts, bringing and defending lawsuits. This description fits both the coalition that supported state aid to religious schools and those who sought to defend Jefferson's "wall of separation" from state aid to church-affiliated education.

Many of the state aid laws the Supreme Court evaluated in the decades after World War II were inspired by religious groups as a means of supporting church-affiliated schools, whose financial health had been seriously impaired by a combination of social changes. As most of these schools were Roman Catholic, the principal groups defending aid to parochial schools were Catholic organizations, such as the Education Division of the United States Catholic Conference, the National Catholic Educational Association, the Catholic League for Religious and Civil Rights, and the Knights of Columbus. They were joined by several organizations representing non-Catholic private schools: Citizens for Educational Freedom, the National Association for Hebrew Day Schools, the National Jewish Commission on Law and Public Affairs, and others. Ranged on the other side were liberal Protestant groups in the National Council of Churches, those conservative Christian denominations that feared state aid as the opening wedge in a government drive to take over the schools (e.g., the Baptist Joint Committee on Public Affairs), secular groups such as the American Civil Liberties Union and the American Association of Humanists, and the major umbrella organizations for the American Jewish community. As should be evident from the diverse nature of these coalitions, the conflicts involved cannot be reduced simply to proreligion versus antireligion or to a simple Christian versus anti-Christian dimension. While some of the opponents of state aid were motivated by hostility to Catholicism in particular or to religion in general, the debate also split many religious communities internally.

Even though most of the constitutional battles were won by groups that opposed state aid, the Court's decisions limiting government support and restricting religious observance in the schools inspired much discontent. Public opinion polls have consistently revealed that a clear majority of Americans—possibly as much as two-thirds of the population—favors some sort of organized prayers in the public schools. The apparent public support for restoration of school prayer has made it politically appealing to challenge the *Engel* and *Schempp* rulings. When Court rulings strike an exposed nerve, those most affected will sometimes attempt to get around them by interpreting the decisions narrowly, by evading them, or, those options having failed, by trying to override the Court by changing the Constitution. In the case of the school prayer decision, critics of the Court ruling tried each of these strategies.

As an example of the first strategy, the courts were besieged with new state laws attempting to alter this or that feature of a school prayer policy that had previously been struck down. The hope—which had been rewarded in some other types of cases—was that the courts might relent, allowing some variant of state-supported prayer to stand as law. However, the Court consistently ruled against the constitutionality of governmental efforts to celebrate religion in public schools. Undaunted, supporters of religious observance then tried to undermine the prayer decisions with "silent meditation" laws. Passed by more than half of the states, these statutes typically provided for a moment of silence or meditation during the school day. Challenges to these procedures as attempts to sneak in organized prayer by the back door were sustained by some lower courts but dismissed by others. The Supreme Court subsequently ended most doubts about the constitutionality of this newest form of school prayer law when it struck down Alabama's silent meditation statute in *Wallace* v. *Jaffree* (1985).

Rather than petition the courts for an allowable
organized prayer, some authorities attempted to evac
cause control over school religious practices effective
sands of local school districts and tens of thousands of
the prayer and Bible-reading decisions offered great
portunities for noncompliance. In a study of Tennes
Court's prohibition of Bible reading, Robert Birkby (1966) discovered
that all but one school district had allowed the forbidden practice to
continue. At the advice of the state superintendent of education, most
districts simply revised their policies to leave the question of religious
ceremonies in the classroom to the discretion of the teacher. Even though
the Court had ruled that voluntary religious activity was no more constitutional than was coerced worship, local school boards adopted it unless
they were faced with legal challenges. Similar patterns of widespread
local evasion were apparent following the *Schempp* decision on Bible
reading, as well as earlier Supreme Court decisions restricting religion in
the public schools (Patric 1957; Katz 1965; Sorauf 1959).

The widespread adoption of the teacher discretion policy throughout the United States did not prevent a substantial decline in formal
religious observance in the classroom. A nationwide survey of public
school teachers during the 1964–65 school year found that the incidence
of morning prayers declined from 60 percent before the *Engel* decision to
28 percent after, and that Bible reading, a regular practice in the class-
rooms of 48 percent of the teachers before *Schempp,* survived in only 22
percent after the case was decided (Way 1968, 191; see also Dierenfeld
1967). Reported compliance was lowest in the southern states, where
nearly three-fifths of the teachers continued reading the Bible and just
under two-thirds maintained the practice of morning prayers. Twenty
years later, noncomplicance was still widespread in those parts of the
country where evangelical Protestantism is strongest (Rosenbaum 1984).
Studies of compliance patterns in local communities by Muir (1967),
Johnson (1967), and Dolbeare and Hammond (1977) have suggested that
the degree of conformity to the Court's will depended on a variety of
factors—the religious composition of the area, the prestige of the Supreme Court, the willingness of individuals to demand implementation,
and the position taken by political elites. Depending on the mix of circumstances in the local environment, the Court decisions were either
implemented in full, accepted in a half-hearted manner, or treated as a
dead letter.

Other critics have mounted frontal attacks on the Court's rulings,
without much success. The favorite instrument, a constitutional amendment to overturn *Engel* and *Schempp,* has failed repeatedly to obtain the
required two-thirds majority in the House and Senate. (Unless they receive that extraordinary majority in both houses of Congress, amend-

ents cannot be submitted to the states for approval.) In 1984, President Ronald Reagan supported an amendment to permit vocal prayer by individuals or groups in public institutions, schools included (Tolchin 1984a). Although the amendment was supported by fifty-six senators, it still fell eleven votes short of the sixty-seven needed for further action. The diversity of both the support for and the opposition against the proposal underlines how such church-state issues split normal coalitions in American politics. Supporters of the proposed amendment included liberals and conservatives (e.g., Senator William Proxmire of Wisconsin and Jesse Helms of North Carolina), Jews and Mormons (Senator Edward Zorinsky of Nebraska and Orrin Hatch of Utah), and representatives of both the mainline and evangelical wings of Protestantism. The forty-four Senate opponents of organized school prayer included some of the most conservative members of that body (Barry Goldwater of Arizona), its only clergyman (John Danforth of Missouri, an ordained Episcopal priest), and one of its most prominent evangelical spokesmen (Mark Hatfield of Oregon). With the subsequent replacement of several supporters of the prayer amendment by opponents of the measure, the prospects for amending the Constitution to overturn the prayer decisions now seem remote.[13]

The failure to capitalize on such a strong public mood favoring the return of school prayer has been ascribed to several factors. Although the polls have indicated support for overturning the Court decisions, the level of support may not have been intense enough to prompt legislative action. Unless legislators judge that public sentiment is deeply engaged over an issue, they may not respond even when polls show majority approval. The advocates of school prayer have been put at a further disadvantage by the fact that citizens who support such legislation have tended to be less educated and less affluent than supporters of the current policy (Elifson and Hadaway 1985). Accordingly, those seeking to overturn the restrictive policy on religious observance in the schools must rely on a constituency that has relatively few political resources. Moreover, the church organizations that might be expected to lead the effort have divided over the wisdom of challenging school prayer restrictions.

Although efforts to bring organized prayer back into the classroom have not gained much ground, Congress did give tangible support to religious observance by its passage in 1984 of what was called an "equal access" law (Tolchin 1984b). Under its provisions, high schools that allow extracurricular student groups to meet on campus before or after classes must extend the same privileges to students who want to form religious associations. This apparent concession to the advocates of school prayer, passed shortly after the Reagan prayer amendment was defeated, was qualified in several respects. For one thing, it applies only to high school students, whereas many prayer advocates regard elementary school students as especially in need of moral guidance. Also, in recognition of the Court's insistence on governmental neutrality, the law stipulates that no teachers or other school personnel may participate actively or supervise worship. Even more significantly, the equal access law appears to give administrators several openings for evasion. By prohibiting the government from denying or withholding education funds from noncomplying school districts, Congress reduced the incentive for compliance. Furthermore, the requirement that religious groups enjoy the same access to facilities as other extracurricular groups may have undermined the law's intent (Reid 1984). The Boulder school board has already announced that it will withdraw meeting privileges from all student groups not directly related to the curriculum. The courts will have to decide if these strategies of compliance with the letter but not the spirit of equal access are legitimate; and the same institution will probably be called upon to judge the constitutionality of the statute that authorizes religious activity. On technical grounds, the Supreme Court passed up an opportunity to rule on the issue during its 1985–86 session. Only a constitutional amendment could remove this issue from the jurisdiction of the courts.

A CONSTITUTIONAL COUNTERREVOLUTION?

The most likely path for a return to the prewar interpretation of the First Amendment's religious clauses is through a change of mind by the United States Supreme Court. Should that happen (a prospect considered below), the grounds for reversion will have been prepared by a steady barrage of legal criticism against the Court's rulings. Scholars sympathetic to a more accommodating government position regarding religion have mounted a searching intellectual challenge to postwar doctrines of separation and free exercise (Cord 1982; Goldberg 1984; Howe 1965; Morgan 1984). To these critics, the landmark decisions establishing the new legal framework for church-state relationships were simply bad law.

Such critics have contended that the Court disregarded both the intentions of the founders and the predominant body of constitutional interpretation by interfering with state actions and broadening the meaning of "establishment." Some have even accused the more activist judges of cynically distorting the framers' words and ideas in an effort to disguise their real intention: writing their own preferences into the Constitution. Court decisions—especially those limiting state aid to parochial schools—have also been denounced for their allegedly adverse policy consequences. The self-defeating nature of Court decisions, critics have argued, is evident in the fact that "isolation" of the churches behind a wall of separation prevents the state from cooperating with institutions that could advance the quality of national education and achieve other valid public purposes (Berger and Neuhaus 1977). If the state suffers by reducing national capacity to confront public problems, the Court also inflicts a wound upon itself. By issuing decisions that fly in the face of public support for religion, it has been claimed, the Court diminishes public esteem for the rule of law and reduces the likelihood of compliance with its rulings. (Note that these are precisely the consequences that Madison cited to argue against establishment.)

These arguments might have been dismissed as inconsequential had they not received strong support from the Reagan administration. During President Reagan's second term in office, key members of his administration put a high priority on a return to traditional—that is, pre–World War II—constitutional interpretation. The campaign was led by Attorney General Edwin Meese III, who attacked the general pattern of Supreme Court decisions in many areas as fundamentally inconsistent with the intentions of the founders of the country. The decision to liberalize abortion policy by invalidating restrictive state laws was condemned by Meese as an intrusion upon the legislative prerogative of the states. He also called upon the Court to respect what he believed to be the wishes of the founders regarding religion, arguing that "neutrality between religion and irreligion would have struck the founding generation as bizarre" (see Blumenthal 1985).

Defenders of the Supreme Court's postwar church-state rulings have offered several responses, ranging from an insistence that the Court has correctly read the Constitution to the argument that the interpretation of ambiguous phrases such as "establishment" and "free exercise" must be allowed to evolve with changing social conditions and religious diversity (Fey 1963; Gordon 1963; Pfeffer 1967). The Court's defenders have also made use of public opinion polls to undercut the claim that religious rulings have undercut public support for the judiciary. Although studies have revealed some public displeasure with Court decisions about religious observance in the schools, on balance they have suggested only modest spillover to the general image of the Court (Kessel 1966; Dolbeare 1967). The most useful information was uncovered in a 1966 poll of voting-age American citizens (Murphy, Tanenhaus, and Kastner 1973). Of nearly 1300 persons surveyed in the study, only about 500 made any response when asked if there was something they liked or disliked about the recent work of the Supreme Court. If less than 40 percent of the sample felt the need to volunteer any praise or condemnation of the Court just four years after the first decision on school observance, the salience of the issue for the general public must be questioned. It is not clear what to make of the further finding that the school prayer and Bible-reading decisions were the source of 30 percent of the actions that displeased respondents. On the one hand, the fact that no other set of decisions accounted for more criticism suggests that the issue was relatively important. On the other, different issues were the subjects of 70 percent of the critical remarks. It should also be kept in mind that unhappiness with the Court's religious rulings may have been part and parcel of more general displeasure with the Court's liberal orientation on questions of civil rights, prisoner rights, reapportionment, and other policy areas. To the extent that public opinion polls can gauge such matters, the broadening of the establishment clause was not the object of widespread enthusiasm, particularly insofar as it prohibited religious observance as an official part of the school day; but the hostility it engendered should not be overstated, either.

With changes in the composition of the Supreme Court and the onset of a more conservative political climate, what are the chances that the Supreme Court will heed the criticism and reconsider some of the postwar decisions? Although not yet producing the counterrevolution that some have hoped for (Goldberg 1984) and others have feared (Redlich 1984), recent Supreme Court decisions have substantially qualified some of the pioneering doctrines first advanced in the 1940s and 1950s. The Court now seems disposed to permit more state action on behalf of religions and to give less support to individuals who cite conscience as the basis for exemption from secular law. Several important decisions seemingly have heralded a Court movement away from an insistence on state neutrality vis-à-vis religion and toward what has been described as "detente," or accommodation. In *Donnelly* v. *Lynch,* decided in 1984 on a 5–4 vote, the Court ruled that the city of Pawtucket, Rhode Island, could put a Christmas nativity display on public property without violating the establishment clause. The same clause was held to allow the Nebraska legislature to pay a chaplain with state funds (*Chambers* v. *Marsh,* 1983). Both decisions suggested that the Court was prepared to give governments more leeway in recognizing the strength of religious convictions in their official actions. In 1983 the Court pleased the advocates of state support for religious education by upholding a Minnesota law that gave state tax deductions for the expenses of sending children to private sectarian schools. That decision, in *Mueller* v. *Allen,* suggested that many different forms of direct financial support for the nonreligious functions of sectarian schools might eventually command majority support from the Court.

Finally, in an important series of decisions the justices have appeared to narrow the application of free exercise claims. In *Trans World Airlines* v. *Hardison* (1973), a majority of the justices decided that private employers could dismiss an employee whose religion forbade him from working on a day the company deemed essential. A 1983 decision, in *Bob Jones University* v. *United States,* maintained that tax-exempt status could legitimately be withheld from church schools that claimed a theological basis for treating students according to race. Together with the decision handed down in *Heffron* v. *International Society for Krishna Conscious-ness* (1981), in which the Court upheld a Minnesota regulation that con-fined religious solicitation to fixed locations in a state fair, the *Jones* ruling seemed to signal a less sympathetic attitude toward religious claims for exemptions than the Court had previously displayed.

These decisions, however, fell far short of overturning the landmark rulings reviewed in previous sections. For one thing, most of the recent decisions cited turned upon particular circumstances that do not seem to challenge the basic principles established over the preceding thirty years. In the *Donnelly* case, the Court permitted a nativity scene on municipal land because it regarded the creche as a cultural rather than a religious symbol—a designation that outraged some observers. Nebraska's legisla-tive chaplains were justified on the grounds of historical practice, a fairly narrow basis that would not apply to most other kinds of state religious action. In the Minnesota tax case, the justices were favorably impressed because the deduction covered all parental educational expenses, not just those incurred for parochial school tuition. In upholding TWA, the Court merely reiterated an established principle that individuals may legiti-mately be required to incur some financial cost for acting on religiously inspired principles. It remains to be seen whether these decisions will be applied more broadly to challenge the church-state framework that emerged from the postwar Court.

Furthermore, the same Court that issued these decisions has in other cases upheld the logic of some important postwar decisions. On establish-ment grounds, the Court recently struck down state practices of posting the Ten Commandments on classroom walls (*Stone* v. *Graham,* 1980), printing a "motorists' prayer" on state maps (*Bradshaw* v. *Hall,* 1981), and extend-ing veto power over liquor licenses to churches that are close to the site of the application (*Larkin* v. *Grendel's Den,* 1982). On the issue of religious observance in the public schools, the Court sustained lower-court decisions prohibiting voluntary organized prayer (*Treen* v. *Karen B.,* 1982) and ban-ning religious activities on school premises before or after the school day (*Lubbock Independent School District* v. *Lubbock Civil Liberties Union,* 1983). And if the Court has slackened in its support for marginal religions, in 1981 it did rule on behalf of a Jehovah's Witness who was fired for refusing to work on a gun turret.

Observers who had hoped for a more accommodationist and less separationist Supreme Court suffered a major setback during the Court's 1984–85 term. In three major decisions having to do with the establish-ment clause, the Court adhered to the strongly separationist posture of most major church-state rulings since World War II. The most publi-cized case was a long-awaited decision about the constitutionality of "silent moment" laws passed by many states. On the grounds that Ala-bama had no purpose beyond promoting prayer in mandating a moment of silence during the school day, the Court struck down that state's statute by a 6–3 vote (*Wallace* v. *Jaffree,* 1985). In *Aguilar* v. *Felton* and *Grand Rapids* v. *Ball,* two related cases decided in 1985, the Supreme Court also ruled that states could not send public school teachers into church schools to provide remedial assistance to needy and deprived students, on the grounds that such programs would be construed by students as state support for religion. In the third establishment decision, the justices refused to exempt private religious organizations from minimum wage laws in their commercial enterprises. Taken together, the three cases seemed to reflect a strong endorsement of the high wall of church-state separation.[14]

The two free exercise cases decided in 1985 suggested further movement away from postwar trends favoring exemption from burdens hindering religious observance. In *Thornton* v. *Caldor,* the Supreme Court was asked to consider a Connecticut law that required private-sector employers to give religiously observant workers a day off on whichever day of the week they recognized as the Sabbath. The Court decided that it would impose an intolerable burden on employers and other employees if the special claims of each individual worker had absolute priority. Although the judges were sympathetic to employees who wanted to honor the Sabbath by abstaining from work, they saw the Connecticut law as an excessive remedy that gave unconstitutional preference to religious over nonreligious motivations. The Court also failed to decide in favor of a Nebraska woman who wanted a driver's license but refused on religious grounds to have the required photograph affixed to it. While the Court's 4–4 tie vote upheld a lower-court ruling on the woman's behalf, it did not establish a precedent that would have settled the question definitively.

In 1986, by the narrowest possible margin of 5 to 4, the Court sided with the U.S. Air Force and against an orthodox Jewish officer who sought exemption for uniform regulations so he could wear the skullcap required by his faith. In the face of such a fluid pattern of decision-making, it would be hazardous to generalize about future Supreme Court trends. Many of the decisions were reached on very close votes that may have turned upon the particular facts of the case. Nonetheless, there has been little evidence that the Court has become strongly disposed to return to the pre–World War II tradition in interpreting the religion clauses of the First Amendment. In view of the limited nature of recent rulings and the Court's general tendency to uphold the postwar precedents, predictions about the imminent reversal of earlier decisions affecting church–state relations in the United States seem to have been premature.

*   *   *   *   *

As the litany of Supreme Court cases has demonstrated, conflict between church and state may arise under a wide variety of circumstances. My clipping file of local and regional newspaper stories reports many incidents that will probably never make it to a high appellate court: debates about the legal status of information disclosed to clergy during counseling sessions, a church's request for exemption from a proposed historical preservation district, the conviction of two fundamentalist Christian families for educating their children at home, malpractice suits against clergy alleging incompetent counseling, cases involving the rights of preachers on public property, and the dismissal of an elementary school principal for illegally teaching religion in a public school. As argued above, conflict and interaction of this type is inevitable, because the two institutions involved, church and state, each claim authority to regulate human behavior.

When faced with such competing claims, some political systems have given supreme authority to the church and others have subordinated the religious institutions to the state. Characteristically, the playing out of this issue in the United States has taken place in the middle ground. As commonly understood today, the Constitution prevents the government from granting its authority to any particular church or from routinely using that authority to restrict religious liberty. As the detailed examination of Supreme Court decisions demonstrated, deciding just how to implement these principles can be a daunting and confusing task. In an effort to maintain neutrality toward religion, the government may act in ways that appear to imperil the free exercise rights of majority religions. Thus, the Court decisions prohibiting organized prayer sessions in the classroom on establishment grounds have been attacked by some religious people as interference with their First Amendment rights. Yet by accommodating religious sentiment, as when the Court permitted Amish children to leave school early, the government may be granting favors to a religion in direct violation of the "no establishment" requirement. Even people committed to reason and good will may find it difficult to strike the proper balance.

Despite the emphasis in this chapter on church-state conflict and tension, it is worth remarking that the American compromise seems to have worked quite well. As a rule, the churches have remained relatively independent of government and the latter appears to have recognized the rights of persons of diverse faith. The current balance of power does not make everyone happy, but it appears to have helped to prevent the widespread religious and political violence that has plagued other societies.

The relative independence of religion from the government has left the churches and religious people free to pursue political ends. In some cases, as this chapter outlined, this power has been used to secure the immediate interests of the religious group. But churches and religious coalitions have also been involved in a wide range of public controversies that raised questions of belief and morality outside the narrow bounds of issues like public prayer or state aid to religious schools. The next chapter examines the role of religion in the formation and execution of public policy.

NOTES

[1] I did not realize quite how much the facts can be scrambled in discussion of this subject until I came across a recent "Dear Abby" column. The columnist answered a letter from a woman who was unhappy about her daughter's decision to raise her child outside the family faith. According to the columnist, the constitutional guarantee of freedom of religion meant that the letter writer had no right to criticize her daughter's choice in religion. Although the free exercise clause of the Constitution does prohibit interference with an adult's choice of faith, it does not compel tolerance.

[2] The major difference was that King did not seek to escape punishment for his behavior; indeed, he hoped that the conscience of the nation would be so moved by the example of unjust suffering that the law in question would subsequently lose credibility and be repealed. From the newspaper accounts of the incident in Indiana, it seems that the accused parents denied that their behavior constitutes a breach of the law.

[3] Like corporate entities, churches may also be held liable for damages or enjoined from engaging in certain behavior. In fact, churches have increasingly been sued for damages by parishioners alleging such things as malpractice in clergy counseling. Several members of the Southern Baptist Convention have filed suits against church authorities for procedural irregularities involving political resolutions submitted to the annual meeting.

[4] In attempting to reconcile the claims of church and state, other societies have experimented with a variety of policies. Some, such as contemporary Iran, have melded the two institutions so closely that they constitute what is known as a theocracy. Motivated by pronounced hostility to religious influences, the government of Mexico has strictly separated religion from the protection of the state and severely limited its permissible activities. Similarly hostile to a force that it identifies with counterrevolutionary activity, the Soviet Union has attempted to reduce the church to the status of a government department that can be carefully regulated to prevent excessive authority. For information about these policies, see Bellah and Hammond (1980); Kramer (1980); Fireside (1971); and Sawatsky (1977).

[5] Unless otherwise indicated, the quotations from early political leaders have been taken from Cousins (1958).

[6] Malbin has argued that when behavior collides with secular law, there is no justification for exempting people who claim religious motivation. He thus applied his interpretation to limit free exercise claims rather than to uphold a strong separationist position. As indicated in the paragraph above, I find that the distinc-

tion between belief and behavior supports a strong interpretation of the establishment clause.

[7]Material on the Sunday mail issue is available in Blakeley's compilation (1970).

[8]The reports of the committees also stressed uncertainty that Congress had the right under the First Amendment to legislate on what was a religious matter. Despite this uncertainty, the reports denounced the proposals as unwise even if Congress could rule in their favor.

[9]The full text of the Supreme Court decisions referred to in this chapter can be found in either the *United States Reports* or in the privately published *Digest of U.S. Supreme Court Reports*. Useful compilations of the most important decisions include Tussman (1962), Pfeffer (1977), and Miller and Flowers (1982).

[10]The critical issue appeared to be the role of governmental authorities—specifically, teachers and other school personnel—in leading religious ceremonies. When officials take the initiative in leading prayers or reading from the Bible, the state appears to be endorsing a particular doctrine. Inflamed rhetoric about "banning God from the schools" notwithstanding, the rulings do not prohibit prayer by individual students. The circumstances of individual prayer may be regulated so that it does not disrupt educational activities, but voluntary prayer is permissible if the student can find an opportunity for it.

[11]For particularly pointed criticism of this standard, see Weber (1984).

[12]That appears to have been precisely the case in Great Britain during the period 1870–1902, when that nation experimented with elective school boards (see Cruickshank 1963).

[13]In 1985 the Senate overwhelmingly rejected a bill that would have withdrawn the issue of school prayer from the jurisdiction of the federal courts. This approach to restoring the pre-1960s situation was defeated so handily (by a 62–36 vote) both because of its dubious constitutionality and because of a reluctance to give states such wide latitude to restore prayer to the classroom.

[14]In a case that appeared to contradict this trend, the Court ordered local officials in a New York suburb to allow a Christmas display in a public park. However, the decision came on a 4–4 vote that might have changed if Justice Lewis Powell had not been prevented by illness from casting the deciding vote.

REFERENCES

Associated Press. 1984a. "Faith Healers Convicted of Homicide and Child Neglect in Daughter's Death." *Gainesville Sun.* September 12: 4A.

Associated Press. 1984b. "Faith-Healing Couple Sentenced to Five Years in Death of Infant." *Gainesville Sun.* September 25: 6B.

Associated Press. 1984c. "Girl's Mom Belittles School Decision to Forbid Cards." *Gainesville Sun.* December 21: 4A.

Bellah, Robert N., and Phillip E. Hammond. 1980. *Varieties of Civil Religion.* San Francisco: Harper and Row.

Berger, Peter L., and Richard John Neuhaus. 1977. *To Empower People: The Role of Mediating Structures in Public Policy.* Washington, DC: American Enterprise Institute.

Birkby, Robert H. 1966. "The Supreme Court and the Bible Belt: Tennessee Reactions to the 'Schempp' Decision." *Midwest Journal of Political Science.* 10: 304–319.

Blakeley, William Addison, compiler. 1970. *American State Papers Bearing on Sunday Religion.* Revised and enlarged edition. New York: Da Capo Press. Reprint of 1911 edition.

Blumenthal, Sidney. 1985. "They May Be Meese's Founding Fathers but They're Not Mine." *Washington Post Weekly Edition.* November 18: 23–24.

Committee on Post Offices and Post Roads. 1830. *Report No. 271.* 21st Congress, First Session: House of Representatives.

Cord, Robert L. 1982. *Separation of Church and State: Historical Fact and Current Fiction.* New York: Lambeth Press.

Cousins, Norman, editor. 1958. *In God We Trust: The Religious Beliefs and Ideas of the American Founding Fathers.* New York: Harper and Brothers.

Cruickshank, Marjorie. 1963. *Church and State in English Education.* New York: St. Martin's Press.

Curry, Thomas J. 1986. *The First Freedoms: Church and State in America to the Passage of the First Amendment.* New York: Oxford University Press.

Dierenfeld, R.B. 1967. "The Impact of the Supreme Court Decisions on Religion in the Public Schools." *Religious Education.* 62: 445–451.

Diggins, John P. 1984. *The Lost Soul of American Politics.* New York: Basic Books.

Dolbeare, Kenneth. 1967. "The Public Views the Supreme Court." In *Law, Politics, and the Federal Courts,* ed. Herbert Jacob. Boston, MA: Little, Brown, 194–212.

Dolbeare, Kenneth, and Phillip Hammond. 1977. *The School Prayer Decisions: From Court Policy to Local Practices.* Chicago, IL: University of Chicago Press.

Dunn, Charles W., editor. 1984. *American Political Theology.* New York: Praeger.

Elifson, Kirk W., and C. Kirk Hadaway. 1985. "Prayer in Public Schools: When Church and State Collide." *Public Opinion Quarterly.* 49: 317–329.

Fey, Harold E. 1963. "A Protestant View: An Argument for Separation." In *The Wall Between Church and State,* ed. Dallin H. Oaks. Chicago, IL: University of Chicago Press, 26–40.

Fireside, Harvey. 1971. *Icon and Swastika: The Russian Orthodox Church Under Nazi and Soviet Control.* Cambridge, MA: Harvard University Press.

Goldberg, George. 1984. *Reconsecrating America.* Grand Rapids, MI: William B. Eerdman's.

Gordon, Murray A. 1963. "The Unconstitutionality of Public Aid to Parochial Schools." In *The Wall Between Church and State,* ed. Dallin H. Oaks. Chicago, IL: University of Chicago Press, 73–94.

Greenhouse, Linda. 1984. "High Court Gets Views on Days Off for Sabbath." *New York Times.* November 8: 19.

Howe, Mark DeWolfe. 1965. *The Garden and the Wilderness: Religion and Government in American Constitutional History.* Chicago, IL: University of Chicago Press.

Johnson, Richard M. 1967. *The Dynamics of Compliance: Supreme Court Decision-Making from a New Perspective.* Evanston, IL: Northwestern University Press.

Katz, Ellis. 1965. "Patterns of Compliance with the Schempp Decision." *Journal of Public Law.* 14: 396–408.

Kessel, John H. 1966. "Public Perceptions of the Supreme Court." *Midwest Journal of Political Science.* 10: 167–191.

Kirby, James C., Jr. 1977. *"Everson* to *Meek* and *Roemer:* From Separation to Detente in Church-State Relations." *North Carolina Law Review.* 55: 563–575.

Kirwin, Harry W., editor. 1959. *The Search for Democracy.* Garden City, NY: Doubleday-Christendom.

Kramer, Martin. 1980. *Political Islam.* Beverly Hills, CA: Sage Publications. "The Washington Papers," Volume 8, Number 73.

Malbin, Michael J. 1978. *Religion and Politics: The Intentions of the Authors of the First Amendment.* Washington, DC: American Enterprise Institute.

Manwaring, David R. 1962. *Render unto Caesar: The Flag Salute Controversy.* Chicago, IL: University of Chicago Press.

Marty, Martin E. 1984. *Pilgrims in Their Own Land.* Boston, MA: Little, Brown.

Miles, Steven. 1984. "Freedom from Religion." *Independent Florida Alligator.* November 19: 6.

Miller, Robert T., and Ronald B. Flowers. 1982. *Toward Benevolent Neutrality: Church, State, and the Supreme Court.* Revised edition. Waco, TX: Baylor University Press.

Morgan, Richard E. 1984. *Disabling America.* New York: Basic Books.

Morgan, Richard E. 1980. *The Politics of Religious Conflict.* Second edition. Lanham, MD: University Press of America.

Muir, William K., Jr. 1967. *Prayer in the Public Schools: Law and Attitude Change.* Chicago, IL: University of Chicago Press.

Murphy, Walter F., Joseph Tanenhaus, and Daniel L. Kastner. 1973. *Public Evaluations of Constitutional Courts: Alternative Explanations.* Beverly Hills, CA: Sage Publications. "Sage Professional Papers in Comparative Politics," Volume 4, Series 01-045.

Patric, Gordon. 1957. "The Impact of a Court Decision: Aftermath of the McCollum Case." *Journal of Public Law.* 6: 455–464.

Pfeffer, Leo. 1977. *Religious Freedom.* Skokie, IL: National Textbook Company.

Pfeffer, Leo. 1967. *Church, State, and Freedom.* Revised edition. Boston, MA: Beacon Press.

Pritchett, C. Herman. 1984. *Constitutional Civil Liberties.* Englewood Cliffs, NJ: Prentice-Hall.

Redlich, Norman. 1984. "Religious Liberty." In *Our Endangered Rights,* ed. Norman Dorsen. New York: Pantheon Books, 259–280.

Reid, T. R. 1984. "Boulder's Equal Non-Access Rule." *Washington Post Weekly Edition.* December 31: 33.

Rosenbaum, David E. 1984. "Prayer in Many Schoolrooms Continues Despite '62 Ruling." *New York Times.* March 11: 1, 32.

Sawatsky, Walter. 1977. "Religious Administration and Modernization." In *Religion and Modernization in the Soviet Union,* ed. Dennis J. Dunn. Boulder, CO: Westview Press, 60–104.

Schaeffer, Francis. 1984. "A Christian Manifesto." In *American Political Theology,* ed. Charles W. Dunn. New York: Praeger, 127–141.

Schappes, Morriss U., editor. 1971. *A Documentary History of the Jews in the United States.* Third edition. New York: Schocken Books.

Sorauf, Frank J. 1976. *The Wall of Separation: The Constitutional Politics of Church and State.* Princeton, NJ: Princeton University Press.

Sorauf, Frank J. 1959. *"Zorach v. Clauson:* The Impact of a Supreme Court Decision." *American Political Science Review.* 53: 777–791.

Tocqueville, Alexis de. 1945. *Democracy in America*. New York: Vintage.

Tolchin, Martin. 1984a. "Amendment Drive on School Prayer Loses Senate Vote." *New York Times*. March 21: 1, 15.

Tolchin, Martin. 1984b. "Prayer Meetings in Public Schools Cleared by House." *New York Times*. July 26: 1.

Tussman, Joseph, editor. 1962. *The Supreme Court on Church and State*. New York: Oxford University Press.

Way, Frank, and Barbara J. Burt. 1983. "Religious Marginality and the Free Exercise Clause." *American Political Science Review*. 77: 652–665.

Way, H. Frank, Jr. 1968. "Survey Research on Judicial Decisions: The Prayer and Bible-Reading Cases." *Western Political Quarterly*. 21: 189–205.

Weber, Paul J. 1984. "A Wavering First Amendment Standard." *Review of Politics*. 46: 483–501.

Weber, Paul J. 1982. "James Madison and Religious Equality: The Perfect Separation." *Review of Politics*. 44: 163–186.

Wilhelm, Kathy. 1985. "Synod-Splitting Rift Causes Lutherans 'Enormous Pain.' " *Gainesville Sun*. January 5: 1B.

Zlatos, Bill. 1984. "When Faith Lets Children Die." *Washington Post Weekly Edition*. October 15: 31–32.

6

Religion and American Public Policy

Despite a strong public preference for churches to remain neutral in political controversies, American religious institutions have repeatedly been drawn into the thick of the political process. On some occasions, as the previous chapter recounted, churches have entered the public realm because they felt that their spiritual mission had been endangered by some action of government or of another secular institution. Yet the churches have also become important participants in public decision-making about issues that do not appear to touch on their immediate interests. Religious institutions have taken public stands on issues as narrow as the zoning decisions of local planning boards and as broad as the state of the national economy. The focus of recent political activity by American religious bodies has ranged from government policy on the morality of personal conduct to global problems of hunger and war.

Whatever the basis for political involvement—be it a policy affecting the capacity of churches to perform religious activities, an issue that addresses the social concerns of church members, or a government action that is seen to challenge church doctrine—religion is a potentially significant factor in the policy-making process. Religion's contribution to some other dimensions of political life having been examined, it is time to turn to the role of religion in forming public policy about major issues and problems. In the first part of the chapter, "religion" appears as a political actor in the guise of churches and church-related interest groups. In exploring the day-to-day political activity of religious groups, the chapter describes the methods by which they attempt to influence government decision-making, along with other avenues through which religious and moral considerations may bear on public issues. The remainder of the chapter is devoted to the vastly more difficult task of estimating the impact of religious forces in resolving certain policy disputes. Is religious influence most apparent on well-focused issues about personal behavior, a domain in which churches have traditionally taken strong stands? And on larger issues involving many participants, are religious institutions equipped with sufficient resources to compete effectively for influence with major secular actors and institutions? The answers to such questions will help to illuminate the significance of the churches relative to other agencies that participate in public decision-making.

INTEREST-GROUP ACTIVITIES

The techniques used by religious groups in attempts to shape public policy are conditioned by the nature of the political process in the United States. Like other participants in the policy-making process, religious groups confront a system of extraordinary complexity. Partly as a legacy of the Puritan distrust of human nature described in Chapter 3, political decision-making takes place in three different spheres of authority—the legislative, judicial, and executive branches of government. Overlaying this division of power among relatively equal branches is a further division of political authority among local, state, and national levels of government. To further complicate the matter, many areas of public life are left altogether outside the scope of government action, reserved instead for private associations such as business corporations. The diverse political strategies of "religion"—a term that encompasses individuals, congregations, denominations, church-affiliated groups, and interchurch organizations—are dictated by this fragmentation of political influence in the American system.

For any group that wants to influence public life, the complexity of the political structure creates a multitude of opportunities and access points. Churches may try to pursue political goals through statutes, administrative procedures, and/or court cases. Along with a choice of arenas, they can decide to concentrate on influencing local, state, or national authorities or to apply pressure on nongovernmental organizations. The options for involvement also extend to the various stages of the policy process: churches and religious groups can specialize in raising awareness of problems, shaping policy alternatives, trying to influence the content of policies, or monitoring the implementation of government action. Like all interest groups, religious groups can employ strategies that fall into four major categories: direct public action, lobbying the government, campaign-related activities, and what I choose to call "infiltration." Although the strategies differ in levels of risk and likelihood of success, each has at one time or another been adopted by groups and individuals motivated by religious concern.

The strategy of *direct action* may entail activities as diverse as peaceful demonstrations, public relations campaigns, civil disobedience, and in extreme cases, violence. These techniques, utilized extensively by persons on both sides of the civil-rights and Vietnam controversies, have been widely adopted by various religious groups.

Peaceful demonstrations have been particularly attractive to groups motivated by intense and deeply felt commitments but lacking in resources such as money, political experience, and organization. For example, in a last-ditch effort to maintain the distribution of Bibles in the public schools—a practice clearly inconsistent with Supreme Court rulings—an ad hoc religious coalition in an eastern Kentucky county tried to exert pressure by packing the public gallery at monthly school board meetings (Rainey 1981). By holding prayer services in public, religiously motivated demonstrators have tried to add moral weight to the force of their argument. Where I live, open air services have been conducted both outside the walls of the state prison, to protest capital punishment, and on the sidewalk outside a medical clinic, in protest against abortions performed there. Rather than concentrate on sporadic demonstrations, other religious groups have organized boycotts against institutions that offended their religious principles. Over the past twenty years or so, many clergy have participated in nationwide boycotts of certain agricultural products as a way to force growers to bargain collectively with their workers. The boycott was the weapon favored by an interfaith coalition that successfully persuaded international corporations to change their practice of marketing potentially dangerous infant feeding products in poor countries (Ermann and Clements 1984). Along the same lines, an evangelical minister from Mississippi has tried to put pressure on the television networks by urging viewers to avoid patronizing companies that sponsor what the minister perceives as immoral programming. That effort has been extended to a direct boycott of corporations charged with purveying pornography (see Swatos 1985).

In an attempt to gain public sympathy for their efforts, religious groups may reach out to a larger audience by using various public relations techniques. The Church of Scientology borrowed a page from corporations by advertising regularly in the pages of the *Washington Post*. Facing several indictments by the federal government, the church placed the full-page ads hoping to recruit public support against the government. Subscribers to national newspapers and magazines should be familiar with other religiously sponsored advertisements, addressing issues such as abortion, school prayer, and foreign policy. Lacking the resources to purchase expensive newspaper advertisements, yet other religiously affiliated groups have sought free publicity by writing letters to the editor or issuing public letters and press releases that receive news coverage. In this way, the groups have sought to create a favorable climate of opinion for their causes.

Peaceful demonstrations, boycotts, and public relations campaigns are types of public action that normally fall within the letter of the law. Sometimes, though, frustrated by the failure of more conventional efforts to influence policy, religiously oriented persons have purposely taken actions that violated the law. Religion has inspired many campaigns of civil disobedience, in which protesters have intentionally challenged laws that conflicted with their religious values. One such campaign now in progress is the Sanctuary movement, an effort to provide asylum in the United States for refugees from civil strife in Central America (Murphy 1984; Taylor 1985b; Van Dyke 1985). Defying a national policy of tight limits on immigration from Central America, Sanctuary workers have smuggled refugees into the United States and harbored them in churches, religious houses, and private homes.[1] Despite the alleged illegality of the actions, the program has been endorsed by national organizations affiliated with a wide range of churches: the American Friends (Quakers), the Conservative wing of Judaism, United Presbyterians, United Methodists, and the northern wing of the Baptists. More than 150 local congregations, including Roman Catholics, Unitarians, and ecumenical groups as well as the denominations mentioned above, have supported the movement financially and indicated a willingness to offer places of refuge. Considering that much of the leadership of the movement consists of clergy and other devout believers, it is not surprising that the illegal actions taken have been defended in the name of moral and ethical premises derived from religious teaching. Under the same claim of conscience, groups morally opposed to nuclear armaments have committed symbolic acts of sabotage and withheld income tax payments.

The most extreme form of public action, calculated acts of violence, has occasionally been undertaken by people who claimed to hear God's command. No modern moral issue can match abortion as a focus of religiously connected violent protest. The Supreme Court justice who wrote the majority opinion in *Roe* v. *Wade* (1973), in which the Court removed many restrictions on the availability of the controversial medical procedure, apparently was the target of an assassination attempt. And in 1983 and 1984 alone, the U.S. Justice Department recorded nearly 200 attacks, incidents ranging from minor vandalism to arson and lethal bombings, on medical clinics that performed abortions (Barron 1984). Although violence has been denounced by virtually all leaders of the antiabortion movement, some of the persons convicted of major assaults have cited religious convictions in their defense.[2] The ambivalent attitude of some religious leaders toward antiabortion violence was symbolized by the Baptist minister who hailed as "heros" the four young people accused of bombing two facilities in a Florida city (Kaczor 1985). There is nothing particularly new about the use of violence to further moral causes. The antislavery movement of the nineteenth century, thoroughly infused by religious passion, decried the "martyrdom" of John Brown, who had killed unarmed civilians in assaults upon proslavery settlements and government facilities. Like some of today's antiabortion zealots, Brown portrayed himself as the instrument of God's will, wreaking vengeance in the name of higher law. Those who have associated the "holy war" mentality only with fanatical sects in the Middle East should be reminded that intense religious commitment has occasionally prompted the systematic use of violence in this nation, too.

Efforts to influence the law by *lobbying* may accompany or supplant direct action by religious groups (O'Neil 1970). Like other interest groups, church-related organizations can attempt to influence public officials by communicating their point of view,[3] an activity that encompasses a variety of specific methods. The American tradition of letter-writing campaigns to public officials has been followed by many religious organizations engaged in matters of public controversy. When, for example, President Gerald Ford proposed to sell several sophisticated intelligence-gathering airplanes to Saudi Arabia, several Jewish groups fought the proposal as a threat to the national security of Israel. In a coordinated campaign to defeat the sale, members of the Jewish community in some cities were sent preprinted postcards addressed to congressional representatives. By flooding Capitol Hill mailbags with messages opposing the sale, the Jewish groups hoped (unsuccessfully) that Congress would overturn the president's decision. The same strategies have been aimed at the other organs of national government. Because of the importance of the president in the process of policy-making, the White House is the favorite target of lobbying campaigns organized by religious groups. By spearheading the sending of telegrams, letters, postcards, petitions, and telephone calls, a religiously affiliated organization may attempt to enlist the executive branch on one side or another of a policy controversy. Even though direct communication with members of the Supreme Court is not deemed appropriate in the American political system, the justices can be lobbied through so-called "friend of the court" briefs. Under this procedure, groups may present written arguments that pertain to the issues of a case under Supreme Court consideration. In the important case in which the Court first evaluated the constitutionality of affirmative action for disadvantaged minority groups, the flood of briefs sent to the justices included submissions from the National Council of Churches, the Young Women's Christian Association, and the Anti-Defamation League of B'nai B'rith.

Religious groups may also opt for more direct contact with public officials. Shortly before a 1985 vote to authorize the building of MX missiles, U.S. senators were visited by members of the clergy on both sides of the issue. Even the presidents occasionally have been subjected to similar treatment during well-publicized White House conferences with religious leaders. Further, some presidents have encouraged clergymen to provide them with spiritual guidance—another avenue for religious influence on the policy process. Of course, this avenue can run both ways, in that public officials may ask religious groups to support their programs. Presidents frequently have spoken to meetings of religious organizations or invited religious leaders to "public affairs" briefings at the White House, using those forums to enlist the membership in efforts to persuade Congress and the public opinion of the benefits of certain policies.

Whatever the method of lobbying, its goal is to advance the theological, institutional, or communal interests of a religious group. Consider the report of the official lobbyist for the Florida Catholic Conference for one week in 1985 (Florida Catholic Conference 1985), which highlighted three bills under consideration by the state legislature. The church opposed on theological grounds one bill that permitted withdrawal of intravenous food and fluids from terminally ill patients. Because food and water are necessities of life rather than forms of medical treatment, the official testified, their withdrawal would constitute a type of euthanasia, which church doctrine condemned. A concern for the institutional strength of the church was evident in the lobbyist's support for a bill to grant privileged status to communication between clergy and church members in cases involving child and adult abuse. Without the protection of the law, it was argued, the church's counseling programs might be threatened. Finally, the lobbyist expressed grave concern about a bill on the state senate floor to repeal all state and local tax exemptions, including those for the religious, educational, and charitable activities sponsored by churches. Even though the repeal was merely a device designed to permit the legislature to reconsider each category of tax exemption on the books, the church opposed the bill because it threatened "the freedom of religion, the separation of church and state, and the orderly planning for . . . institutions which provide basic necessary services." It should be pointed out that the Catholic church was not the only participant in lobbying on these bills, and that its lobbying was not successful in two of the three cases. Even more important, although each bill touched a particular facet of the Catholic religion, it would be foolish to claim that one particular motivation was paramount in any one issue. The churches, like other interested actors, may intervene for a variety of religious and secular reasons.

Lobbying is likely to be especially powerful if the person on the receiving end thinks that the lobbyist can affect his or her chances for retaining public office. Hence, religious groups have become involved in various phases of *political campaigning* at all levels of the government. For some religiously affiliated groups, campaign involvement may take the form of merely questioning candidates about issues in which the church takes an interest. That familiar mixture of theological, institutional, and social concern was very much in evidence in the questions sent to the 1984 presidential nominees by the St. Augustine (Florida) diocese of the Roman Catholic church (Catholic Diocese of St. Augustine 1984). The candidates were asked if they supported or opposed a constitutional ban on abortion, elimination of capital punishment, cutbacks in the deployment of nuclear weapons, income tax credits for private school tuition, and major new federal programs to combat hunger and increase housing opportunities. In addition to indicating their orientations on human life issues (abortion and capital punishment), state legislative candidates were asked their views on welfare funding, the provision of services to nonpublic schools, ratification of the Equal Rights Amendment, and the broadcasting of "indecent" material on cable television. Having defined each of these concerns as moral issues, the church encouraged its members to consider the candidates' responses before casting their ballots. Forbidden from endorsing candidates or parties as a condition for maintaining tax-exempt status, the churches can nonetheless use such interrogations to inform members as to which candidate is most in line with the church's preferred position on the issue.

The prohibition on formal endorsement by churches as churches does not prevent the clergy from attempting to influence the votes of church members or from participating as private citizens in political campaigns. By extolling the moral virtues of one candidate and pointedly refraining from comment about the competition, a minister can clearly indicate a preference without actually recommending a vote from the pulpit. Even that fine line can be breached when ministers make explicit endorsements of candidates from a platform outside the church. Does ministerial support pay off at the polls? When asked where they turn for political advice and guidance, Americans do not frequently mention the church. That finding may indicate only that Americans feel it is improper for churches to take sides in elections—not that they are unaffected by clergy influence. In the black community, where the clergy have long been recognized as an important source of political authority, voters certainly seem to respond to cues from the pulpit (Vedlitz, Alston, and Pinkele 1980).

In an age of weak political parties and generally low rates of political participation, the support of religious groups usually is seen as a valuable asset in a political campaign. Through several mechanisms, religiously involved people can supply resources to help favored candidates or, conversely, defeat candidates they find unacceptable. Simply providing the candidate a forum from which to address the membership gives free publicity and the opportunity to spread a message among attentive audiences. As organizations possessing membership lists and other resources, the churches may even be pressed into action as the core of a candidate's campaign effort. In his bid for the Democratic presidential nomination in 1984, the Reverend Jesse Jackson relied heavily on the black churches for leadership, funding, electoral support, and campaign workers (Boyd 1984). The model provided by the black community has recently been imitated by other groups favoring different causes. Throughout the United States, pastors and evangelical congregations have flocked into political campaigns on behalf of conservative candidates. Since 1978, antiabortion activists in New York have supported the Right-to-Life party, which as of 1984 had more than 17,000 enrolled members. Though not formally tied to any church, the leaders and members of the party appear to have been recruited mainly from denominations that favor conservative theology and positions on public issues (Spitzer 1984).

Finally, there is the option labeled *infiltration*. Reasoning that the most reliable kind of official is the one who shares the group's values, a religious organization may seek to place one of its members in office. If the office is filled by public election, members of a religious group may organize to win the seat for a fellow member. Although the Constitution forbids the government to impose "religious tests" for holding office, it does not restrict citizens from supporting candidates out of religious loyalty.

Judging by their determined efforts to publicize religious affiliation and church membership, candidates seem to have recognized the electoral power of religious affiliation. In 1982 a candidate with the decidedly non-Jewish name of Larry Smith wanted to indicate his Jewish identity to voters in a Florida congressional district. Concerned that his name would be a handicap in a race against other Jewish candidates in a district with a predominantly Jewish electorate, Smith had his wife introduced to district residents by her maiden name, Sheila Cohen, and distributed campaign literature with pictures of his son's Bar Mitzvah ceremony (Ehrenhalt 1983, 333). Also, in a packet of material sent out to influential leaders and community groups, the candidate called attention to his active membership in a local synagogue and reminded readers that he had helped found a chapter of B'nai B'rith and had been named "Man of the Year" by the local chapter of the Jewish National Fund. Consistent with the tactics that eventually brought victory in the election, Smith's 1984 campaign biography called attention to his membership in the congressional Caucus for Soviet Jewry and an award received for zeal in promoting the sale of Israeli bonds. Quite the opposite problem faced Marc Holtzmann, a Jewish candidate for a Pennsylvania congressional seat with a majority of Roman Catholic voters (Taylor 1985a). To offset the potential disadvantage of a Jewish-sounding name, Holtzmann asked the American ambassador to the Vatican to arrange a meeting with Pope John Paul II. Pictures of the meeting between the candidate and the spiritual leader of the Catholic church were widely distributed throughout the district.

Do voters actually respond positively to such appeals to vote for "their own kind" of people? Although complex motivations cannot be attributed to any single factor, a candidate's religious affiliation clearly can play a role in voter decision-making. The most persuasive evidence leading to this conclusion has been obtained in experiments simulating the electoral process. In a classic study by the psychologist Leon Festinger (1947), a group of female college students was asked to listen to speeches by candidates for the presidency of a college club. On contrived grounds, the first vote (in which the names and religious identities of the candidates were not revealed) was voided. After a suitable interval, during which the participants learned the candidates' religious affiliation, a second ballot was conducted. Festinger interpreted the changes in preference between ballots as evidence that knowledge of a candidate's religious identity inflated support among members of the candidate's religious family. That conclusion has been sustained by studies in which voters have been asked to choose between hypothetical candidates for public office. In these studies the ethnic identity of the candidate, a quality frequently associated with religious affiliation, apparently brought in additional support from members of the same ethnic group (Kamin 1958; Lorinskas, Hawkins, and Edwards 1969—see Pomper 1966 for actual election data). Studies of Catholic voting patterns in 1956 and 1960 showed that Catholic candidates running for national offices against candidates from other faiths earned substantially more support from their coreligionists than party ties alone could have explained (Campbell et al. 1960, 319–21; Converse 1966).

All other things being equal—and they rarely are in electoral politics—voters usually favor a candidate of their own religion.[4] Religious affiliation is only one element in the voters' image of the candidate, which is, in turn, only one of the three factors that strongly sway electoral choice. The other two factors—partisanship and the issues—may limit or offset the impact of religious affiliation. In two studies that examined the impact of candidates' ethnic and religious traits under partisan conditions, the effect was clearest when the normal party cues were absent (Kamin 1958; Pomper 1966). When a voter has to cross party lines to support a candidate with the same ethnic or religious identity, the religious factor has a much smaller impact. The candidate's stands upon the issues may also deter members of his or her religious community from giving additional support. As has been shown by studies of predominantly Jewish districts, Jewish candidates whose political views differed from those of most of his coreligionists have lost badly to non-Jewish candidates whose policies were more closely attuned to public opinion (Leventman and Leventman 1976). These studies have suggested that voters do not attribute quite as much significance to a candidate's personal religious affiliation as candidates seem to imagine.

The religious factor has also played a role in the politics of appointments. When President Ronald Reagan filled an important position in the

U.S. Department of Education with an official from the conservative religious group Moral Majority and named a leader of the antiabortion movement to the post of surgeon general, he reenacted the familiar American ritual of awarding patronage to a group that had supported his election (Shuster 1981). Moral Majority undoubtedly welcomed the appointment as providing a way to safeguard its growing private school movement and to interject its moral concerns into the decision-making process on education policy. If that case illustrates how religious groups may take the initiative to receive appointments, it is worth remembering that public officials may seek out religious leaders for positions on public bodies. As respected community leaders with considerable prestige, members of the clergy may seem to be perfectly positioned to lend credibility to policies that would otherwise inspire political controversy. It was no coincidence that a committee appointed by a Florida school superintendent to review a program of stress control for students included ministers as well as parents, teachers, and professional educators (Leisner 1985). Similarly, before the U.S. government abolished the military draft, local boards charged with classifying individuals of draft age often included members of the clergy.

Given the central role of judges in the policy process, it should not be surprising that judicial appointments have also been the subject of intense religious group activity. At congressional hearings on the appointment of federal judges, representatives of church groups have testified in favor of or against nominees because of preferences on policy issues. Antiabortion groups persuaded the Republican conventions of 1980 and 1984 to pledge support for restricting federal judicial nominations to persons who "respected the sanctity of human life." What might sound like routine political rhetoric struck many observers as a commitment to make opposition to abortion a requirement for judicial appointment. Studies of the judicial appointment process in the Reagan administration have suggested that the platform pledge has been carried out (Kurtz 1985b). In 1984 the Reagan administration withdrew support from its own nominee for a seat on the District of Columbia Court of Appeals, in part because of conservative complaints that he belonged to the National Abortion Rights Action League and Planned Parenthood. In a questionnaire sent by three Republican senators, a nominee for a federal judgeship in New Jersey was asked seven questions about the legalization of abortion and about such religiously based issues as school prayer, the death penalty, the Equal Rights amendment, and public financing for private schools. And when the administration was considering the appointment of an outspoken evangelical to chair the Justice Department committee in charge of judicial selection, fears of religious tests for the judiciary inspired fierce, and ultimately successful, opposition (Kurtz 1985a).

Churches resemble secular interest groups in their ability to use several or all of the methods of political action. Few religious groups have

used as many different techniques as the Unification church, a religious
and political movement founded by the Reverend Sun Myung Moon, a
South Korean businessman (Horowitz 1978; Isikoff 1984; Boyer and
Alem 1985a,b). A fervent if unorthodox Christian, Moon has propagated
a world view in which international communism is seen as a representative of the anti-Christ and the church exists as "the instrument to be used
by God" in his unceasing battle against Marxism (Isikoff 1984, 8). Financed by several profitable international business ventures (as well as by
the smaller-scale soliciting so familiar to airport travelers), the Unification church has deployed a vast array of devices in its anticommunist
crusade. To influence American public opinion directly, the church pub-
lishes daily newspapers in Washington and New York, as well as a nationally distributed Spanish-language daily. Aiming to win over opinion
leaders and, through them, the mass public, the church has also established a "think tank" in Washington and underwritten seminars and conferences throughout the nation. In addition, it has transported journalists,
scholars, congressional staff members, black ministers, and other influential citizens to national and international meetings. The Unification
church also has been involved in direct lobbying in Washington, D.C. It
has contributed to an alliance of conservative groups that lobby Congress
on behalf of anticommunist measures and has paid for Central American
trips by some congressional staff assistants. Church officials have been
linked to the alleged effort by the Korean government to influence congressional and executive branch officials through a coordinated campaign
in the 1970s (Horowitz 1978, chaps. 8, 10, 11; Isikoff 1984, 7). Church
leaders were strong supporters of President Richard Nixon, and their
Spanish-language newspaper endorsed Ronald Reagan in his 1980 campaign for the Republican nomination. One church leader apparently met
with President Reagan, and several key officials in the administration, the
president included, have granted exclusive interviews to the *Washington
Times,* the newspaper financed by the Unification church. Finally, a congressional committee recently investigated charges that the church fun-
neled aid to anticommunist troops in Nicaragua at the behest of the
Reagan administration (Chardy 1985). These claims about Unification
church activities, some of which have not been documented, are cited as
examples of the wide range of actions that religious groups can take in the
service of political goals.

ORGANIZING FOR POLITICAL ACTION

Rather than rely solely on informal pressure or the actions of individual congregations, religious groups have also created specialized organizations to advocate their views on public issues. Although problems

of definition make it difficult to come up with an accurate tally of these "social action" organizations or religious interest groups, they clearly have been active in political conflict from the local to the national arena and have also gotten involved with international organizations (Adams 1970; Dexter 1938; Malicky 1968; Cohen 1985; Pratt 1962). In surveying seventy-five such groups that maintained offices in the nation's capital in 1981, Paul Weber (1982) was particularly struck by the diversity of the groups on a number of dimensions. In terms of denominational orientation, there were groups representing the views of Catholics, Jews, mainline and evangelical Protestants, black Christians, and secularists with a strong interest in church-state relations. Some groups represented single denominations, others broad coalitions with common interests. As organizations, some relied on dues-paying individual members, whereas others were subsidized departments of national church organizations whose very existence might not be known by the church members who supported them financially. The social issues pursued by the groups were in some cases identified by an elaborate system of consultation reaching down to member churches and, in others left to the discretion of centrally based leaders of the church organization. Politically, the groups ranged from narrowly conceived single-issue movements that worked alone to organizations with a broad range of concerns that were willing to coalesce with secular groups if that would advance their preferred policies.

Beyond a common commitment to monitor government actions and report back to the membership, the religious interest groups also differed in strategy. Some went beyond that baseline activity to lobby government officials and testify in public hearings, and some even worked to develop specific pieces of legislation. In carrying out these actions, the groups relied on very unequal resource bases. Budgets ranged from less than $100,000 to more than $1 million, and the full-time staffs varied from fewer than ten to more than thirty.

Some of these figures may sound impressive in the abstract, but it should be kept in mind that even the most well-endowed of the religious lobbies was nowhere near as well-financed as were many secular interest groups. In recent years the General Electric Corporation, a major manufacturer of military hardware, medical technology, and nuclear power plants, has maintained a staff of 120 in Washington offices that cost over $1 million annually for rent alone (Edsall 1985). Resources alone do not guarantee success, but they probably correlate with scope of influence. However, religious interest groups can compensate for this comparative disadvantage by intelligent use of their limited resources (Weber and Stanley 1984). This means, among other things, focusing on a limited set of issues, attempting to influence the early stages of legislation through contacts with key officials, and developing expertise and effective communication skills. With their highly positive images and substantial social prestige, the religious lobbies often have enjoyed success, particularly in securing religious liberty.

In choosing to enter the political fray, religious groups do not always take the initiative; at times, they are drawn into controversies at the urging of secular political forces. In the debate over revisions of the federal tax code, for example, political leaders structured their proposals in terms designed to bring certain religious groups into the conflict. To enlist conservative evangelical Protestants on behalf of President Reagan's plan, the administration put a great deal of rhetorical emphasis on the proposed doubling of the personal exemption. The proposal was offered to "profamily" groups on the grounds that it would relieve large families of extra financial burdens; presumably, that would reduce incentives for women to enter the labor force and, by making another child less expensive, discourage elective abortion for economic reasons. The proponents of the plan hoped that these features would appeal to the socially conservative values of the evangelical lobby, bringing in additional congressional support for a plan that covered many sections of the federal tax code (Mayer 1985; Mayer and Murray 1985).

Not all religious denominations support social action campaigns. Among those who do, aspects of a denomination's religious tradition, and particularly its preferred form of organization, may shape the process by which it develops a position on a public issue and attempts to persuade policymakers to adopt it. For purposes of comparison, the Catholic and Jewish communities provide an excellent contrast (Fisher and Polish 1980). Catholicism is organized on a hierarchical basis with centralized decision-making; Judaism, in this respect resembling many of the Protestant denominations in the United States, accords individual congregations a very high degree of autonomy.

The American Jewish community is divided into three major theological camps that support a wide range of organizations for both religious and secular purposes. Many organizations function at the local level to secure the immediate interests of the Jewish community. In addition to these local organizations, there are a number of national groups and federations of congregations. Furthermore, the spiritual leaders of Judaism, the rabbis, have traditionally enjoyed wide latitude in making social pronouncements as individuals or as members of rabbinic associations. Each of these groups may take public positions on issues of national and international concern, leading to a chorus of voices singing in different keys. Attempt at coordination can be made through the National Jewish Community Relations Advisory Council, described as "an umbrella body consisting of all national Jewish organizations and 106 local Jewish Community Relations Councils drawn from almost every community in the country containing an organized Jewish community" (Brickner 1980, 9). However, the NJCRAC is merely an advisory body that lacks the authority to issue binding pronouncements on questions of public policy. When an authoritative Jewish voice is sought out by the media—as it was, for instance, when President Reagan announced plans to visit a German cemetery containing the graves of Nazi Stormtroopers—there is no single "obvious" place to go.

In the Catholic church, in which the lines of authority are much more clearly drawn, political decision-making reflects a hierarchical pattern.[5] As the apex of the authority pyramid, the pope may issue binding statements about Catholic policy on social issues. These statements of church policy may not persuade all Catholics, but the pope wields enough disciplinary power to enforce some compliance. Thus, Pope John Paul II has ordered priests and nuns to avoid public office, forcing the resignation of a U.S. congressman, and has threatened expulsion from religious orders for clergy who publicly challenge the papal policy toward abortion. Within the United States, the Catholic church addresses public issues through the Catholic Conference, an organization of bishops from the dioceses who meet periodically and issue various types of statements on questions of public policy. The head of the conference, elected by the bishops, is widely recognized as the authoritative spokesman for the church and may even become a major public figure.

The Jewish and Catholic policy-making procedures clearly reflect differing ideas about organization and authority, but they do not necessarily differ in effectiveness. Depending upon the circumstances, both approaches can yield political cohesiveness or contribute to disarray. Thus, despite its organizational fragmentation, the American Jewish community rallied with extraordinary unity to the defense of Israel when it was attacked by Egypt during the fall of 1973 (Elazar 1976, appendix A). Under the threat of an external enemy, the local and national Jewish organizations cooperated in a fund-raising drive aimed at the collection of almost $1 billion in emergency aid. The organizations also exhibited efficiency in coordinating volunteers for service in Israel and in local fund drives. In terms of direct political action, the heads of major Jewish organizations lobbied the administration and Congress to provide assistance to Israel and worked to enlist American public opinion on behalf of that country. By all accounts, these efforts at mobilization contributed to subsequent Israeli success. An apparently equivalent success in group mobilization followed the 1984 issuance by the Catholic bishops of a pastoral letter on nuclear policy. In the document, which was supposed to be studied by Catholics and discussed from the pulpit during worship services, the bishops generally called for restraint in the use of force to solve world conflicts. The content of the letter marked a sharp reversal of the church's traditional endorsement of aggressive action against communism and apparently was responsible for a massive reduction in Catholic support for military spending (Greeley 1985).

These examples of successful group mobilization can be countered by stories illustrating the limits of organized political activity by religious groups. The American Jewish community, united behind Israel under the impetus of the Egyptian invasion, split into competing camps once the immediate threat abated. Even as American Jews have continued to strongly support Israel, they have differed over some Israeli policies. Likewise, American Catholics have not been of one mind about how to implement their church's formal condemnation of abortion. Proponents of restrictive policies have argued over the best mechanism to achieve their goal, and opponents have insisted that Catholics have no obligation to follow church doctrine. In a telling comment on the limits of church authority, scholars have reported that the contraceptive practices and abortion attitudes of American Catholics do not differ significantly from those followed by persons from other churches (Greeley 1977, 141–51, 245–47; Westoff and Bumpass 1973; Westoff and Ryder 1970; Jaffe, Lindheim, and Lee 1981, 106). Religious groups, like other politically organized interests, cannot simply command their members to toe the line.

PATHS OF INFLUENCE

Up to now, religious groups have been viewed as supplicants for power, outsiders trying to influence the decisions of insiders. This is consistent with the image of the policy process as a struggle for influence in which the government simply bends to the will of outside pressure brought upon it. But in fact, religion may also influence policy more directly, through its impact on the views and preferences of policymakers.

Religion can become the foundation for public policies in several ways. When laws are decided through public referenda, religious groups may simply vote their preferences into law. As Morgan and Meier (1980) demonstrated in a study of Oklahoma referendum voting on propositions affecting alcohol and gambling, religious groups often vote cohesively when the issue involved touches on questions of personal morality and the churches have taken a clear stand. Considering their historical record of opposition to "loose behavior," evangelical Protestants not surprisingly ranked among the strongest opponents of liberalizing drinking and gambling policy in the Oklahoma referenda. The same conclusion has been reached in studies focused on other policy areas. Howard Hamilton (1970) noted a peculiar pattern in the relationship between religion and support for "open housing" laws in three referenda conducted during the early 1960s. In two of the contests, persons with no religious preference gave greater support to the proposals than did members of Christian churches—a finding consistent with survey data, cited in Chapter 4, on the greater racial liberalism of the "no preference" respondents in comparison with white church-affiliated Protestants and Catholics. But in a similar referendum in Toledo, Ohio, all groups of churchgoers were more likely than nonmembers to endorse antidiscrimination housing legislation. Hamilton explained this deviation by noting that the Toledo churches had taken a strong and active role on behalf of the fair housing ordinance (Hamilton 1970, 719), apparently exposing churchgoers to positive information and mobilizing them to vote in favor of the proposal. Religious values can influence public policy through the mechanism of direct legislation when the church provides unambiguous clues for its membership (see Richardson 1984).

Most laws are enacted not by a public vote, but by the concerted action of elected officials. Religion can play a role in this process by influencing the values of officeholders. Particularly when they are chosen by public election, government officials are likely to share the dominant religious values of the community. Even if the officials come from another religious tradition, a dependence upon public approval for reelection should motivate them to express the preferences of their constituents. In either case, government officials can play a crucial role in translating religious sentiment into public law.

It is important to recognize the limits of the hypothesis that the behavior of political elites can be shaped by their personal religious orientations. Political scientists continue to debate the relative weight to assign the many factors that influence the behavior of public officials. In deciding how to cast a roll call vote, for example, members of Congress are subject to the pull of party loyalty, regional culture, judgments about constituency preferences, the influence of the president, the flow of national public opinion, staff recommendations, the lobbying efforts of myriad groups, and personality characteristics. Although the sources of influence might be different, officials in the executive and judicial spheres are similarly buffeted by forces that could override any single personal characteristic. Religion is just one of the factors that might account for an official's decision to favor or oppose a particular course of action on a public problem.

Considering the clear importance of religion in mass voting, it is remarkable to discover how little attention has been devoted to the study of the religious factor in congressional behavior. Most systematic research has simply attempted to establish if members of Congress vote as religious blocs on issues decided by roll call votes. Even with this limited focus on basic denominational differences, the studies have not reached consensus. John Fenton (1960) compared the behavior of Catholic and Protestant members of the House and Senate during the 1959–60 session of Congress. Fenton found that for the most part, when compared with members from the same party and region, Catholics and Protestants did not differ much in their support for civil rights legislation, foreign aid, or bills affecting organized labor. In contrast, Leroy Rieselbach (1966) showed consistent differences between Catholic and Protestant representatives on foreign aid votes in five Congresses from 1934 to 1964. In most cases, Catholics were more supportive of foreign aid appropriations than were their fellow partisans, whether Democratic or Republican, or representatives from urban districts. This difference did not extend, however, to the realm of foreign trade issues, the other dimension in Rieselbach's study. Using roll call votes on those social welfare issues that had elicited policy statements from mainstream Protestant denominations, John Warner, Jr. (1968), also observed significant differences among Catholic, Protestant, and Jewish members of the 89th Congress. Like other observers, Warner found Protestants to be the most conservative and Jews to be the most liberal, but he also found no significant policy differences between mainstream and evangelical Protestant legislators once party affiliation had been taken into account.

Denominational affiliation might prove to exert a significant impact on legislative voting only when the issue under consideration has been the subject of intense religious controversy. The abortion issue, which has long engaged the attention of many churches, would seem to offer a good test case for this proposition. Two studies of voting on abortion laws in the American West have indeed revealed clear differences in legislative behavior by different religious groups.[6] In a study of legislators from an unnamed state, Richardson and Wightman (1972) sought evidence for the impact of religious affiliation in votes on bills to liberalize abortion policy. Taking into account the urbanization levels of the districts and the legislators' age and party—factors likely to influence votes on moral issues—they found support for more liberal access to abortion among the Protestant and Jewish members of the lower house, and opposition to the proposals from the Catholic representatives. The Mormon legislators, who had favored a more liberal policy in the first of the two votes, switched to the opposition side after their church issued clear statements about the incompatibility of liberalized abortion with Mormon doctrine. Observing a similar battle in another western state, O'Neil (1973) found essentially the same pattern of conflict in the Senate committee that killed a proposal for liberalized abortion. The ill-fated bill was supported by all liberal Protestants and Jewish members of the committee and opposed by every Roman Catholic and conservative Protestant.

The principal weakness of these studies was their failure to sort out systematically the impact of personal religion from either district composition or the other sources of influence on congressional voting. That problem has been addressed in three other published studies. In the first, which examined roll call voting records for approximately one-fourth of House members in the 95th Congress (Page, Shapiro, Gronke, and Rosenberg 1984), the legislators were ranked according to their attitudes toward social welfare spending, race relations, women's rights, law and order, and finally, abortion. Using a powerful statistical technique, the researchers then attempted to assess the influence on this ranking of the demographic characteristics of the district, its collective opinions on public issues, the representative's party affiliation, and his or her personal traits (including religious affiliation). On most issues, the investigators found little significance in personal traits. Abortion was an exception: even taking into account the impact of district characteristics, the religious affiliation of the representatives exerted a significant impact by prompting Catholic members to support restrictive measures on abortion. The same conclusion emerged from a study of three votes on abortion taken by the House of Representatives in 1976 (Vinovskis 1979). Through a complex statistical analysis, this study found legislators' personal religious affiliation to be one of the most powerful predictors of a vote on a motion to prohibit the use of federal funds for abortions. Even after the application of controls for personal traits, partisanship, liberalism, and several district characteristics, Catholics gave disproportionate support to the amendment, Protestants gave a lower level of support, and Jewish representatives were strongly opposed to it. Finally, when the Senate voted in 1985 to reject a constitutional amendment that would have overturned the *Roe* v. *Wade* decision, Catholic legislators were more likely to support the amendment than were non-Catholics (Granberg 1985b). The impact of Catholicism in this case withstood controls for region, party, state economic standing, and votes on school prayer amendments.

As valuable as they are, these statistical investigations of denominational differences in legislative behavior only scratch the surface of possible religious effects on political elites. Much additional light has been shed by a pair of studies that transcended simple denominational classifications by interviewing legislators to learn their religious values. Based on her interviews with twenty-five Catholics serving in the United States Congress in 1973–74, Mary Hanna (1979) concluded that Catholics did not form a separate bloc and, with a few exceptions on issues such as abortion, were not strongly influenced by their Catholic constituents or the lobbying efforts of the church. Rather, Hanna found, the principal contribution of faith to Catholic legislators' political identity was its influence on their basic political attitudes. Two different streams of Catholicism guided their values: "A religious formation that emphasized strict codes of conduct, rules and guidelines, a rather rigid, puritannical devotion to duty and order; and one which stressed Christian love, compassion, and concern for one's fellowman, especially the poor, the helpless, and the unfortunate" (Hanna 1979, 99). Not surprisingly, adherents of the first tradition were conservative Republicans and legislators who drew on the social reform stream were liberal Democrats.

A similar distinction between different types of religion was noted by Peter L. Benson and Dorothy L. Williams (1982), who interviewed eighty members of the House of Representatives from a wide range of denominations. Politically conservative and liberal representatives were found in each major American denomination, but members of the two camps tended to stress different aspects of belief. The conservatives conceived of religion as something for the individual, a force that gave them comfort in times of distress, strength of convictions, self-discipline, and the promise of eternal reward. In contrast, political liberals put a great deal of emphasis on the communal aspect of religion. Where conservatives saw religion as a one-to-one relationship between individuals and God, the theology of liberalism stressed the oneness of humanity and the need for social transformation on earth if God's will is to be recognized adequately. These differences in ultimate value showed up in voting on specific types of legislation. "Individualism-preserving" religion was correlated with support for free enterprise, private ownership, and military expenditures and with opposition to government spending on social programs. Its opposite, what Benson and Williams labeled "community-building" religion, encouraged support for programs of foreign aid, hunger relief, civil liberties, and liberalized abortion. These differences in religious style appeared much stronger than the group differences normally observed when legislators are divided into broad families, such as Protestant, Catholic, and Jew, or classified according to denomination. This finding suggests that studies using denominational affiliation may underestimate the connection between religious values and legislative behavior.

THE JUDICIARY AND THE BUREAUCRACY

If legislators may be influenced by religious backgrounds, the same force could in principle affect the decisions of judges. Some scholars have argued that in the American political system, in which judges are given broad discretion to interpret the laws, a complete understanding of judicial decisions requires the use of information about personal and social background. Although this point by no means has been universally accepted by judicial scholars, it has inspired several careful studies that have traced patterns of judicial behavior to the traits of individual judges. The need to be cautious in ascribing religious motives to public acts once again must be recognized. A judge's decision is likely to reflect certain "norms" of the legal profession—a respect for precedent, the quality of advocacy, views about the proper scope for judicial discretion, and, of course, the facts surrounding any particular case. If religion fits into the equation, it does so merely as one factor among many.

Systematic analysis of religion has been as scarce in research on judicial behavior as in studies of legislative behavior. Probably the best evidence for a religious effect can be found in Sorauf's (1976, chap. 9) analysis of denominational differences in voting on church-state issues by judges on high appellate courts. In analyzing nonunanimous decisions during the 1950s and 1960s, he found that more than 80 percent of Jewish judges favored a strict "separationist" policy that limited government's ability to recognize religion, whereas Roman Catholic judges, by an equally lopsided margin, voted to endorse policies and practices which accommodated religious interests. Protestants, who made up by far the bulk of the judges hearing the church-state issues, split roughly in half between the separationist and accommodationist camps. The historic tension between Protestants and Catholics in the United States was apparent in the tendency of Protestant judges to become more accommodationist when Catholics were not a party to a lawsuit and for Catholics to become decidedly more separationist when non-Catholic groups were involved in the case (Sorauf 1976, 225). As Sorauf realized, this set of cases was particularly conducive to the operation of a denominational effect because "the religious affiliation of the judge relates in the judicial decision to the direct and immediate interests of his religious group as well as to the social values derived from the religious tradition and its belief system" (Sorauf 1976, 222). In cases in which the interests of specific denominations are not so self-evident, religious affiliation should play a lesser role.

That conclusion can be supported by a review of existing research. Analyzing the decisions issued by state and federal supreme court justices in 1955, Stuart Nagel (1962) found statistically significant differences between Protestants and Catholics in four out of fifteen categories of cases. In three of the types which fall on a conservative-liberal spectrum, the Catholic judges were more liberal: they were more likely than their Protestant colleagues to rule on behalf of convicted criminals appealing a verdict, government agencies engaged in regulating business practices, and employees seeking compensation for injuries. In divorce cases, however, the Catholic judges exhibited a much higher tendency to rule in favor of the wife—perhaps a reflection of the tradition of Catholic conservatism in family matters. Most of the difference between Catholics and Protestants was associated with partisanship rather than religion, however (Nagel 1961). Skepticism about a religious effect on judicial decisions was supported by Goldman's (1966, 1975) studies of decisions issued by the federal courts of appeal during the 1960s. In only two of the ten issue areas examined by Goldman did significant Protestant/non-Protestant differences surface, and most of the apparently greater conservatism of Protestant judges could be explained by the high proportion of southerners in the Protestant category. S. Sidney Ulmer (1973) extended this type of social background analysis to the U.S. Supreme Court in examining voting patterns on criminal cases from 1947–56. He concluded that Protestants were more likely than non-Protestants to support the government side against appeals by convicted criminals, although his method and results have been challenged (Payne and Dyer 1975).

Rather than investigate a range of issues, some scholars have concentrated on one particular area of judicial activity—race relations. The courts were the catalysts for racial change in the southern states, and some observers have thought that religious values could have accounted for the willingness of federal judges to challenge the deeply entrenched system of segregation in the South. The guiding hypothesis has been that those judges who were least immersed in the southern culture of segregation, including those who were not affiliated with the numerically dominant evangelical Protestant churches, would be most inclined to rule on behalf of another out-group. Kenneth Vines (1964), the first to check out this expectation with social scientific methods, examined judicial rulings in nearly 300 civil rights cases decided in southern circuits from 1954 through 1962. On the basis of decisional patterns, thirty-seven federal district judges were classified as segregationist, moderate, or integrationist. As one might expect, there was a demonstrable difference in rulings associated with religious affiliation. The "orthodox Protestants," a term Vines used for denominations defined here as evangelicals, were principally found in either the segregationist (45 percent) or moderate (36 percent) camps, leaving less than 20% for the integrationist. At the other extreme, the two Catholic judges were classified as integrationists. That left the middle position for judges who were presumed to be mainline Protestants. They were less likely to be integrationist than Catholics (45 percent) but also less likely to issue rulings in favor of segregation (21 percent). Despite its conformity to prediction, the Vines study suffered from weaknesses of technique. By using religion without any controls for possibly related factors, he exposed himself to a charge of spurious correlation. Furthermore, because the cases differed from circuit to circuit, he may have, in effect, compared apples with oranges. To remedy those defects and to update the findings, Giles and Walker (1975) examined the problem anew. Rather than use dissimilar cases, they used the same measure in each circuit—racial imbalance in public schools. Because all schools were under court order to implement antisegregation policies, Giles and Walker contended, the measure of racial imbalance remaining in 1970 indicated "the district judge's policy decision in implementing the [desegregation] mandate at the local level" (Giles and Walker 1975, 924). Trying to capture the religious factor, the analysis compared judges from what the authors labeled as fundamentalist Protestantism with members of all other religious affiliations. Religion, included as a social background factor in an equation that also contained a measure of the racial climate, the judge's connection to the community, and several characteristics of the school district, was not found to exert a substantial influence on the racial imbalance permitted in the district. Whether these conflicting findings can be laid to different techniques or to a real change cannot be determined; on balance, however, the systematic studies examined in this section do not strongly support the notion of a religious effect in judicial decisions.

If analysis of religion in Congress were similarly dependent solely on statistical studies, negative conclusions about religious effects in that branch might also have been reached. A fuller understanding of the legislative arena was possible because members of Congress were available for interviews that could elicit religious beliefs beyond mere denominational affiliation. Because judges rarely submit to such interviews, it has been difficult to find out if more sensitive measures of religious values might account for behavioral differences. Some judicial biographies have speculated about possible religious influences on particular decisions or even judicial style. Late in 1981, when the Equal Rights Amendment (ERA) to the U.S. Constitution was in the waning days of its unsuccessful ratification period, a federal judge from Idaho issued an adverse ruling that further reduced the amendment's slim chances for passage. Because the judge held a position of authority in the Mormon church, which vehemently opposed the ERA, several critics charged that his ruling improperly reflected his religious values. Then, too, in a psychologically oriented analysis of the great Supreme Court justice Felix Frankfurter, H.N. Hirsch (1981) argued that religion influenced the judge's highly combative and aggressive style. Though the point is too complex to summarize easily, Hirsch argued that Frankfurter, the child of Jewish immigrants from Austria, was caught between the attractiveness of the Protestant establishment that dominated the legal profession and his standing as a conspicuous outsider who was reminded powerfully that he did not fit in. Consequently, he developed a personality and style highly conducive to the role of the outsider. That kind of linkage cannot as yet be subjected to systematic testing, but at least it suggests how religion may contribute to judicial behavior by an indirect path.

Because laws are not self-executing, the administrative agencies of government play an important part in public policy-making. Yet as little as is known about religion in the legislative and judicial branches, even less seems clear about the executive wing. For the political appointees and career civil servants who staff the executive branch and its agencies only fragmentary evidence about religious values is available.

As the official head of the executive branch and the principal focus of American government, the president has a unique opportunity to affect both the substance and tone of public policy. In this area, as in the others examined in the chapter, scholars have disagreed about the importance of social background factors relative to the many competing influences brought to bear on presidential decision-making. The specific influence of religion has been even harder to assess, because almost all recent presidents have come from the mainline Protestant tradition. Nonetheless, there is at least suggestive evidence that religious background may affect a president's approach to politics, if not the specific policies of a chief executive. This can best be demonstrated by comparing the two most recent occupants of the White House.

To a degree that had not been common in the twentieth century, Jimmy Carter brought questions of religious values and character to the center of his political campaigns. A devout Southern Baptist, churchgoer, and "reborn Christian" who apparently was familiar with the work of modern theologians and experienced in missionary work, Carter was a novel factor in the 1976 presidential campaign (Kucharsky 1976; Miller 1978, Pippert 1978). His candidacy appeared to hearten evangelical Protestants (though they certainly did not unanimously vote for him) and worry many mainline Protestants, Catholics, Jews, and nonaffiliates. Partly because of unfamiliarity with the Southern Baptist tradition and partly because of the presumed association of evangelical Christianity with social conservatism and intolerance, many worried that a deeply religious president would try to enforce his "narrow" moral preferences on the nation or, fortified by a belief in a personal relationship with God, would reject compromise and negotiation with those who did not see the world in the same way. Throughout the campaign, Carter attempted to assure voters that he did not see God's hand in every policy proposed in his platform and that he would not use the law to enforce narrow standards of moral rectitude. Rather than prompting an unshakable faith in the rightness of his own preferences, he argued, his religious values had taught him the need to recognize his own fallibility. And to those who expressed concern about the Baptist social agenda, Carter emphasized the Social Gospel tradition of religion as a force for economic and political reform.

In practice, few observers were able to link Carter's major political tendencies to his personal religiosity. On church-state issues, for example, he adhered to the traditional Baptist insistence on a sharp wall of separation, even refusing to hold worship services in the White House (Flowers 1983). His religious background showed up in several ways that might not have been apparent to most observers, however. According to one analysis, Carter's personal style—marked by enormous self-discipline, a commitment to hard work, orderliness, and fiscal conservatism—bore the unmistakable traces of the Puritanism from which his faith had descended (Mazlish and Diamond 1979, 253). In his insistence that other nations be held to high standards of behavior, as in the crusade for international human rights, Carter might have been exhibiting a "typical" evangelical's missionary tendency. A fellow Southern Baptist (Baker 1977) suggested another carryover of Carter's religion into his politics. One of Carter's first and most controversial acts as president was to issue a pardon to draft evaders—not an amnesty, which declares that a person did no wrong, but a pardon, which forgives a wrongdoer. In that distinction, Baker argued, lay evidence of the biblical spirit of grace that offers love and forgiveness to the sinner. Carter's major triumph, bringing the leaders of Egypt and Israel together on a framework for peace in the Middle East, has also been attributed to a religious trait. Only a person of sublime self-confidence, a faith in himself born of religious certainty, and one who was more than usually committed to bringing peace to the Holy Land would have had the audacity to undertake such a challenging mission or the stamina to succeed in it.

Unfortunately, the validity of this analysis is anything but certain. The only other Southern Baptist to hold the presidency, Harry Truman, exhibited few traits in common with his coreligionist. And some presidents from different religious traditions acted in ways similar to Carter. John Kennedy spoke in missionary terms about the nation's world role. Gerald Ford issued an even more controversial pardon (of ex-president Richard Nixon). Few presidents in history could match Lyndon Johnson's skill as a negotiator and persuasive advocate. Because each of these men was far removed from Carter's religious background, it is clearly dangerous to draw too firm a conclusion about the impact of theology on politics.

Carter's successor, Ronald Reagan, also described himself as a born-again Christian and argued strongly for the relevance of religion to public policy. But unlike Carter, whose theology treated politics as a calling to establish social justice, Reagan's view has been that active government intervention will usually create problems rather than solve them. In one sense, Reagan's political theology is close to that of the Puritan founders, with whom he shares a dismal assessment of humanity's natural impulses. Like the founders, Reagan has tended to regard human beings as creatures of impulse who need the hand of government "to restrain the darker impulses of human nature" (Reagan 1981). In this light, the only legitimate role of government is negative: to maintain order so that humanity's goodness and creativity can flourish in the social and economic realms. This view of government recalls the emphasis of the American founders on politics as a barrier to the worst excesses of sinful people—and nothing more. Such a perspective may explain why Reagan has foreseen dramatic improvements in the quality of life with a reduction in the level of government activity (Thomas 1984).

By his penchant for quoting Bible verses to support certain policies (Reagan 1985, 130) and his references to the Soviet Union as the "focus of evil" in the modern world, Reagan has certainly encouraged observers to analyze his political preferences in terms of explicit theological values. During the 1984 campaign, critics expressed concern about the influence of what has been called "Armageddon theology" on Reagan's attitude toward the use of force in world politics (Herbers 1984; Goodman 1984; Castelli 1985). The phrase refers to an interpretation of the Bible that foresees a time of worldwide turbulence, including the possibility of a nuclear war in the Middle East, on the eve of the second coming of Jesus. A president who subscribed to that apocalyptic view of the world, it has been argued by some theologians, would have less incentive to strive for peace or nuclear arms control and might be tempted to ignore the long-run cost of social policies. (That theological issue cropped up in the confirmation hearings for James Watt, Reagan's first secretary of the interior, who was reported to have expressed the view that Jesus' imminent return meant that preservationist environmental policies could be relaxed.) To counter this interpretation, Reagan declared during a televised debate with Mondale that his interest in prophecies would not inhibit his efforts to secure peace.

RELIGIOUS VALUES AND GOVERNMENT ACTIVITIES

Whatever types of influence religious groups may attempt to wield, is the political system responsive to religious values and appeals? Although it is very difficult to sort out the relative importance of all the factors that influence government decisions in any policy area, there is much evidence linking general patterns of public policy to religious factors.

Because American churches have traditionally given major priority to questions of personal conduct, it should not be at all surprising to find a strong link between religious affiliation and government "morality" policies, as has been demonstrated in a series of studies tracing policy differences between the states to variations in religious composition. David Fairbanks discovered a strong correlation in the American states between the proportion of the population belonging to Protestant churches and the restrictiveness of state statutes affecting gambling and liquor (Fairbanks 1977). Because the evangelical churches have usually regarded these activities as inconsistent with Christian orthodoxy, it seems reasonable to conclude that state laws have reflected community values. Similarly, the clearly expressed resistance of the Catholic church to artificial birth control and divorce probably explains why in the various states, as in many economically developed countries (Field 1979; Wasserman 1983), the strictness of contraception and marriage laws has varied directly with the proportion of Catholics in the population (Fairbanks 1979). Because these relationships have survived the application of several environmental factors that might be supposed to underly them, it appears that the moral values of a state's dominant religious group are somehow conveyed to lawmakers.

In abortion, a policy area heavily laden with moral issues, religious groups also appear to have played a decisive role in determining how the Supreme Court's decision was implemented. Jon R. Bond and Charles A. Johnson (1982) surveyed a national random sample of hospitals in 1979, six years after the Supreme Court struck down legal restrictions on a woman's right to terminate a pregnancy. They found that despite a national policy of permitting abortions without restrictions during the first six months of pregnancy, only about one-fifth of the hospitals surveyed provided abortion services to the full limit allowed by the *Roe* v. *Wade* decision. A substantial percentage allowed abortion only during the first three months (39 percent) or under specified conditions (13 percent). Of those that did not allow abortions to be performed, the policy ranged from facilitating abortion by providing referrals to other facilities to discouraging it by counseling on the medical and moral issues of abortion. In trying to explain differences among hospitals, the authors hypothesized that community preference would be a critical influence; accordingly, they tested the permissiveness of the policy against hospital administrators' perceptions of community and elite-group opinion about abortion, the level of interest-group activity on the issue, and a measure of the level of church membership in the community. Two of the three measures of community preference (interest-group activity was the exception) were found to exert a significant influence on hospital abortion policy. The more supportive the personal attitudes of the community and elites and the lower the level of church membership, the more permissive the abortion policy. In that public opinion on the issue has been shown to be strongly related to religious affiliation and activity, it seems appropriate to attribute the religious characteristics of a community with substantial influence on the availability of facilities for abortion.

That conclusion was supported by Susan B. Hansen's (1980) study of state-level differences in 1976 abortion rates. If all states were operating under the same Supreme Court ruling, why did New York and California report approximately 40 abortions per 1,000 women of child-bearing age whereas the comparable rate was only about 3 per 1,000 in Mississippi and West Virginia? Like Bond and Johnson, Hansen observed that the major direct influence on the performance rate was the availability of hospitals willing to offer abortion services. The restrictiveness of hospital policy, in turn, depended upon a number of factors, including the state's religious composition. The percentage of Mormons in the population had a negative impact on community tolerance for abortion and direct depressive effect upon the rate of abortion.[7] Similarly, the greater the Catholic share of the state population, the lower the community support for abortion and the more restricted the availability of facilities offering abortion.[8]

Given that churches have often spoken out forcefully on matters of personal conduct, it should not be surprising to discover a correlation between legal restrictions on unorthodox activities and religious geography. But studies of the American states have supplied much evidence that religious composition is related to policy patterns that do not have such an obvious link to theological values. Most such studies have built upon the hypothesis that religion contributes in a major degree to the assumptions, values, and habits that may define policy preferences over a wide range of public issues.

In the area of race relations, for example, Fenton and Vines (1967) argued that the level of voter registration of Louisiana blacks depended largely upon the religious values of the politically dominant whites in the community. More than a decade after the Supreme Court struck down state laws excluding blacks from voting in public elections, local communities had found ways to keep more than two-thirds of black adults off the electoral registers. As a rule, the level of black registration in Louisiana was much higher in the predominantly Catholic parishes (counties) of the southern area of the state than in the northern area, where Protestant groups predominated. Finding that this difference held up in the face of checks for the influence of various nonreligious social, political, and cultural factors, the investigators pointed to differences in social attitudes between Catholics and Protestants.

> Permissive attitudes toward Negro registration in French-Catholic parishes seem expressive of the basic value that the Negro is spiritually equal in a Catholic society. Such a view of man's relation to man, a scheme of elementary justice implicit in a Catholic society, some Catholics maintain, is sustained by traditional Catholic theology and actively promoted by the Church in Louisiana. There is little evidence in the Protestant parishes of cultural values assigning the Negro a spiritually equal place in the community or of activity by the church itself toward these values. (Fenton and Vines 1967, 176)

In addition to a doctrinal basis for racial tolerance, the Catholic church also had institutional and social reasons to discourage ill treatment of blacks. As a universal church that crosses racial and ethnic boundaries, Catholicism would be threatened if all the faithful were not treated on equal terms. Moreover, because the Catholic church was one of the few integrated institutions in the South, its members were given the opportunity to dispell their prejudices and stereotypes by the experience of interracial contact. In contrast, the segregated white Protestant churches of northern Louisiana catered to the segregationist values of their members and did little to promote the contact between races that might have fostered mutual tolerance.

Religion may affect an even broader range of policies through its influence on attitudes toward the role of government in society. In Chapter 3, I noted that one way religion might shape American political behavior is by its general effect on the national political culture. Along the same lines, a leading authority on American federalism has suggested that the religious and ethnic groups that settled the various American states were the carriers of particular cultural values that have left a mark upon contemporary state politics and policy. According to Daniel Elazar (1970, 476), different migrating groups subscribed to different views about the nature and purpose of government, the role of politics in society, and other politically relevant beliefs. For example, he noted the emphasis in Puritan thought on using the power of the state to create a holy commonwealth on earth. In the parts of the country settled by Puritans, their successors, and immigrants with similar religious traditions, this conception of politics as a calling has survived in a highly moralistic approach to politics.

> Politics, to the moralistic political culture, is considered one of the great activities of humanity in its search for the good society—a struggle for power, it is true, but also an effort to exercise power for the betterment of the commonwealth. Consequently, in the moralistic political culture both the general public and politicians conceive of politics as a public activity centered on some notion of the public good and properly devoted to the advancement of the public interest. Good government, then, is measured by the degree to which it promotes the public good and in terms of the honesty, selflessness, and commitment to the public welfare of those who govern. (Elazar 1984, 117)

This approach, like those of the individualistic and traditionalistic cultures elsewhere, dictates a particular configuration of values that should affect the scope, nature, and style of political practice. Citing the fact that religious groups with such distinctive political conceptions clustered in different parts of the country, Elazar predicted a correlation between state policy orientations and ethnoreligious settlement patterns.

Although it was developed principally to account for contemporary policy differences, Elazar's theory has been strikingly confirmed by studies of political conflict in the nineteenth-century United States (Hammond 1979; Kleppner 1979). Movements for abolition of slavery, Prohibition, and a host of other social reforms were fired by the enthusiasm and crusading mentality that characterizes a moralistic culture and resisted in terms of values that sound remarkably like Elazar's description of the traditionalist culture. What is more, according to the influential "ethnocultural" school of American history, the basic groupings of voters were defined largely by the type of religious values that Elazar identified as the core of differing political cultures. Whatever its historical value, Elazar's assertion about the policy impact of religiously based value systems has inspired several research projects on contemporary state-level variations in public policy. Although specific predictions have not always been confirmed (Schiltz and Rainey 1978), several scholars have detected affinities between the concentration of certain religious groups and particular sets of policies enacted by the states.

Based on statistics of church membership, Hutcheson and Taylor (1973) classified American states in terms of the proportion of the population affiliated with fundamentalist denominations—defined in the study as religious groups who believe in the Bible as the literal word of God. The groups in Hutcheson and Taylor's "fundamentalist" category—essentially the same denominations classified as evangelical Protestants in Chapter 3—have been identified by Elazar (1984, 130–31) as carriers of the "traditionalistic" political culture. Precisely as would be expected from a culture that wants government to play a "conservative and custodial" role (Elazar 1984, 119), the fundamentalist share of the population was associated with a high teacher-pupil ratio in public schools and a low level of state taxation. Using a similar technique, Johnson (1976) reported that the concentration of religious groups with a moralistic orientation correlated strongly with high levels of spending for social welfare programs but that the proportion of traditionalistic denominations depressed governmental efforts in that area. In a more recent study, Klingman and Lammers (1984) confirmed that conclusion with a different approach. The states were ranked on a scale of "general policy liberalism" in which high scores identified a willingness to utilize government power on behalf of disadvantaged groups. The scale included such diverse components as state efforts to combat racial discrimination, spending for child welfare and social services, ratification of the Equal Rights Amendment, and level of consumer protection efforts. Although no direct measure of religious concentration was included in the long list of factors tested as possible influences on policy liberalism, the analysis did rank each state by the moralism of its political culture. As it happens, the measure of state political culture turned out to be one of the two strongest predictors of a state's ranking on the policy liberalism dimension. The states with the most moralistic political cultures were the most likely to adopt innovative policies designed to improve the status of disadvantaged groups.

In one of the most imaginative studies of its kind, Michael Johnston (1983) managed to demonstrate a connection between religious geography and a moral approach to politics. As an expert on political corruption, he wanted to test an explanation for what appears to be very different levels of toleration for illegal acts by public officials. In some communities, official misconduct is accepted as a fact of life, something as inevitable and irresistible as bad weather; other communities react to governmental malfeasance with shock and horror, deploying the full resources of the law to combat it.

On the assumption that communities with high concentrations of moralistic denominations would be especially averse to such misconduct, he included religious affiliation in a model explaining the rate of conviction for public officials. As it did in the other studies conducted in Elazar's framework, the variable that tapped the moralism of political culture exerted a strong influence in the predicted manner. The higher the concentration of denominations that Elazar identified as carriers of a moralistic outlook on politics, the greater the number of successful prosecutions for official lawbreaking.

On the basis of this evidence, it appears that political culture—which Elazar traced specifically to the beliefs and historical experience of religious denominations—affects not only the content of state policy, but its style as well. This conclusion could be subjected to the same criticism about spurious relationships that was raised in the discussion of religion as mass political behavior. Surely, a state's level of spending, its social programs, and its record of prosecution for corruption and other actions depend, for the most part, on its governmental capacity and level of economic development. In each of the studies cited above, that possibility was taken into account by the inclusion of variables representing the social and economic status of the areas under comparison. Although the precise measures differed somewhat, the application of controls for economic development did not eliminate the linkage between religious groups and policy patterns. Religion, which according to the previous chapters has left its mark upon American political values, mass political behavior, and the law, apparently has also contributed to the different configurations of public policy pursued by the states.

LIMITATIONS ON RELIGIOUS INFLUENCE

The influence of a particular religious group in a particular policy area represents only one force in the struggle to shape government action. Because of the complexity of public policy-making in the United States, it is important to appreciate how religion and moral influences compete with other factors for an impact on decisions. The need for a balanced appraisal can best be conveyed through a case study of American policy in the Middle East. Though frequently cited to illustrate the potential impact of religious considerations, this case also points to conditions that limit religious influence on public policy.

In the nearly forty years since the state of Israel was founded, the United States has consistently supported it with vigorous diplomatic action, military aid, and significant amounts of economic assistance. That support has frequently been attributed to a pair of "religious" factors—namely, the actions of the "Jewish lobby" in the United States and the moralistic strain in American foreign policy. American Jews have used their considerable political resources—voting strength, organizational ties, campaign contributions, access to decision-makers, media influence—to mount an energetic campaign on behalf of Israeli interests. The campaign has succeeded because a pro-Israeli position fits in well with the moralistic style of American foreign policy. Formed in the shadow of the Holocaust, besieged by hostile neighbors, holding steadfastly to the same political values as the United States, Israel can draw on a powerful current of good will in American opinion. As Lyndon Johnson is said to have told the Soviet leader who asked why America was pledged to Israel, "We think it's right" (Glick 1982, 106). Taken together, the political strength of American Jews and the moralistic tendency of American foreign policy seem to explain the content of American policy in the Middle East and to illustrate the importance of religious influence.

Yet before too much influence is conceded to religion, it is crucial to put U.S. policy toward Israel into a broader context. According to scholars who have studied foreign policy-making, the critical element in American support for Israel has been a perception of national self-interest rather than Jewish lobbying or attachments of sentiment. After a careful reconstruction of the events that led President Truman to make the initial commitment to Israel, Ganin (1979) concluded that the chief motivations were fear of disorder and bloodshed in Palestine, competition with the Soviet Union for Middle East influence, and Truman's desire to assert his primacy over the U.S. State Department. The American commitment to Israel has been maintained and expanded by successive administrations because it has continued to serve their overriding foreign policy objectives (Spiegel 1985). The Carter administration, preoccupied with maintaining American access to Middle East oil supplies, valued Israel because of its location near the crucial transportation lanes for petroleum exports. Concerned above all else to counter alleged Soviet expansionism, the Reagan administration has seen great benefits in cooperating with a nation that has the military might to deter Soviet action in the Middle East. Hence, although religious factors help to explain the pro-Israeli thrust of U.S. Middle East policy, most authorities have given precedence to the overriding strategic objectives and perceptions of American foreign policy decision-makers.

To the extent that religion has facilitated a pro-Israeli policy, that issue illustrates how many factors must fall into place before religion assumes an important role. There are several unique aspects to the origins of U.S. policy toward Israel. To begin with, the religious group in question, the American Jewish community, was overwhelmingly united behind a common goal that it considered extraordinarily important. Jewish support for Israel arises from the combination of institutional self-interest, social concerns, and theology. Israel represents a chance for the survival of Judaism as a religion and the Jewish people as a distinct community—and no institutional interest could be more basic than self-preservation. The fate of Israel also touches the social aspirations of Jews, who have been a minority, and often a despised one, throughout their history. Israel's success thus serves to provide "psychological, ethnic, and religious pride" for American Jews (Glick 1982, 126). An additional basis for American Jewish support of Israel can be found in the theological call for a return to Zion and the opportunity it provides for realizing Jewish social values. The combination of these factors raised Israel to the forefront of the political consciousness of many American Jews. It certainly has helped the Israeli cause that no opposing religious groups have been able to match the American Jewish community in political sophistication and strength of purpose.

As to the nature of the issue, an important factor was that Israel's moral claim for support was compatible both with the U.S. government's secular interest and with religious values almost universally shared by Americans. As few other political causes have done, Zionism appealed to a broad spectrum of American Christianity. Israel earned sympathy from the politically liberal segments of American religion because of its social and ethical values. At the other extreme, the most politically conservative wing of Protestantism could find support for the restoration of a Jewish state in Bible prophecy.[9] In such a supportive environment, the moral justification for Israel's existence was not challenged.

These conditions, which are highly conducive to religious impact, have not been common in other areas of policy-making. To begin with, few political issues are as salient and unifying to members of a religious group as the cause of Israel was for American Jews. The abortion issue, which has become the basis of political mobilization for some Catholics, has actually divided church members and reduced political unity. As a political issue becomes further removed from a religious group's self-interest or traditional level of concern, cohesion becomes even harder to maintain. Without a common front, a religious group has a lesser chance of influencing public policy. Furthermore, because of differing institutional interests, social status, and theological traditions, religious groups usually have not made common cause on most issues of public policy. Whether the issue has been something as basic to religious interests as prayer in public schools or as global as the policy to freeze production of nuclear weapons, denominations have rarely spoken with a single voice. Divisions within the religious community have further retarded the impact of moral concern on public policy.

The nature of the Middle East policy-making process, unusual in several respects, also contributed to the apparent influence of religious factors. Religious pressure could be brought to bear effectively because the decision-making process was relatively centralized, involving only a handful of officials. The authority to extend diplomatic recognition and to cooperate militarily belonged to the president alone. When military and economic assistance was proposed, Congress entered the process. Because of the nature of the policy, neither the courts nor state and local government agencies played a role. With the decision-makers reduced to a select few, each possessing clear authority, lobbying efforts could be concentrated for maximum effectiveness and opposing forces had fewer avenues for delay and appeal. In addition to the elite nature of the decision, the Israeli case was unusual because the fundamental issues were presented in fairly straightforward terms and embodied in a series of concrete decisions: Should the United States extend diplomatic recognition to Israel? How much U.S. economic and military aid should Israel receive? Should the United States provide Israel with military intelligence and emergency supplies in armed conflict with the Arab states? Because these questions were often posed in what amounted to life-or-death situations, there was an opportunity for decisive action with relatively clear understanding of the implications of each potential course of action.

In most policy areas, religious influence is inhibited from bearing heavily on decision-making. In the typical policy debate, power and authority are widely diffused among many actors, making it unclear who, if anyone, has the decisive role. With fragmented authority, a victory at any level has less long-term significance. Even more fundamentally, the typical government policy is rarely so clear-cut as it was in the Middle East case. As many authorities have concluded, policy-making is a process rather than an event. When issues enter the process, they are often subdivided into components and acted upon by different authorities rather than treated as a single problem. A decision reached in one sector is not binding upon another; a victory in one arena can be reversed in another. In any case, the consequences for a particular course of action are likely to be uncertain.

For these reasons, policymakers usually stress the difficulty of applying moral insights to items on the public agenda. According to Senator Paul Simon of Illinois (1984, 131), "Practical dilemmas that real-life politicians face do not fit into easily wrapped packages to which moral labels can be attached." As an example, Simon cited a 1977 congressional debate on a bill to renew a federal program that sent American agricultural products to countries facing food shortages (1984, 22–23). When a representative introduced an amendment to prohibit the purchase of tobacco for export under the program, Simon faced a moral dilemma. Because tobacco was a significant crop in nearly 100 House districts, the amendment might endanger support for the program, resulting possibly in the "clearly immoral" denial of food to starving people. Yet without the amendment, the government would spend money that could buy food for 900,000 hungry people on a product with lethal consequences for public health. As Simon asked rhetorically, "What could be a clearer moral issue?" The testimony of other legislators and administrators amplified Simon's conclusion that policymakers normally confront choices between conflicting moral norms, rather than simply between good and evil (Anderson 1970; Haughey 1979).

*   *   *   *   *

From the evidence presented in this chapter, it seems clear that religious influence can be brought to bear on political decision-making, particularly when issues are narrow in scope, but that it is rarely the decisive factor in the outcome of a complex policy. Aside from competing interests, the major limits on religious impact are divisions of opinion within and between religious groups and the inherent confusion of the policy-making process.

The decision to enter the political arena, whether taken by a religious group on its own volition or virtually imposed upon it by external authorities, may impose a significant cost. Political conflict is characterized by disagreement, strife, and competition. In associating itself with such a process—or being seen as part of it—the church may lose its reputation as a place of refuge from the sordid reality of life. Yet paradoxically, abstention from politics may also diminish the church's stature. If members of the community perceive religious values as relevant to a political issue or under threat from some external actor, they may lose faith in a church that stands idly by. Because religious values are so all-encompassing, and couched in a universal language, it is difficult to defend indifference as a political strategy.

Throughout the chapter, it was largely taken for granted that religious groups declare positions on public issues in order to focus on how such positions are advocated in the public realm. Left open was the vital issue of what different religious groups actually stand for and how they have come to favor certain political options. Because shifting patterns of religious group politics have undermined many comfortable images inherited from the past, such as the stereotypes of conservative Catholicism or apolitical evangelicalism, the next topic of inquiry is the emerging pattern of political identity among the major denominational families in the United States.

NOTES

[1]Sanctuary workers have been tried and convicted on federal charges of harboring illegal immigrants. The courts trying the cases have generally refused to accept defenses rooted in free exercise claims, treating the acts as they would any violations of immigration law.

[2]They also claim that their attacks on abortion facilities represent a measured response to the much greater level of violence used against the aborted fetus.

[3]Under federal law, a nonprofit organization can maintain tax-exempt status so long as less than 20 percent of its budget is used to influence the decisions of public authorities.

[4]Before jumping to the conclusion that voters are bigoted and irrational in favoring a candidate of the same religion just because of the common tie of church membership, consider another possibility. Because religion is an important element in influencing the social system, persons from the same religious community may share similar experiences and develop similar views about the issues of the day. These features, not the mere fact of common religious affiliation, can make a candidate attractive to a voter. It is worth keeping in mind that the studies cited on this subject (except for Pomper) used hypothetical candidates in fictitious races; hence, there were few cues other than ethnicity or religion to guide electoral choice. As Donald Granberg (1985a) demonstrated with both survey and experimental data, voters who lack information about a candidate's position upon an issue—particularly an issue with religious implications—may infer a position by using religious affiliation as a cue.

[5]Using the issue of the Equal Rights Amendment, White (1984) has shown how the Mormon system for reaching judgments on public issues also follows a very centralized pattern.

[6]On such a sensitive issue as abortion, participants in legislative struggles may be unwilling to confide in academic researchers. To alleviate fears that their comments may become public knowledge, researchers have sometimes had to disguise the state in which the study was conducted.

[7]Lacking any direct measure of community support for abortion, she used a surrogate measure indicating the proportion of a state's congressional delegation supporting federal abortion funding in several 1977 votes.

[8]The finding that a concentration of antiabortion religious groups diminishes the availability of abortion facilities may well explain why Borders and Cutright (1979) failed to find a significant Catholic effect on abortion rates in metropolitan areas. Once the level of services enters the analysis, it masks the impact of religious composition—suggesting the need for a two-step analysis such as that performed by Hansen.

[9]For those Christians who were not moved by either appeal, it might not have escaped notice that the probable alternative to a Jewish state was further migration of Jewish refugees to the United States.

REFERENCES

Adams, James L. 1970. *The Growing Church Lobby in Washington.* Grand Rapids, MI: William B. Eerdman's.

Anderson, John B., editor. 1970. *Congress and Conscience.* Philadelphia, PA: J. B. Lippincott.

Baker, James T. 1977. *A Southern Baptist in the White House.* Philadelphia, PA: Westminster Press.

Barron, James. 1984. "Abortion Issue Takes a Violent Turn." *New York Times.* November 25: 2E.

Benson, Peter L., and Dorothy L. Williams. 1982. *Religion on Capitol Hill: Myths and Realities.* San Francisco, CA: Harper and Row.

Bond, Jon R., and Charles A. Johnson. 1982. "Implementing a Permissive Policy: Hospital Abortion Services After *Roe v. Wade.*" *American Journal of Political Science.* 26: 1–24.

Borders, Jeff A., and Phillips Cutright. 1979. "Community Determinants of U.S. Legal Abortion Rates." *Family Planning Perspectives.* 11: 227–233.

Boyd, Gerald M. 1984. "Black Churches Play Big Role in Jesse Jackson's Campaign." *Gainesville Sun.* February 18: 1B.

Boyer, Jean-Francois, and Alegandro Alem. 1985a. "Moon in Latin America: Building the Bases of a World Organization." *Manchester Guardian Weekly.* March 3: 12–14.

Boyer, Jean-Francois, and Alegandro Alem. 1985b. "The Moonies: A Power in the Service of Anticommunism." *Manchester Guardian Weekly.* February 24: 12–13.

Brickner, Balfour, 1980. "Social Policy-Making Structures of the Jewish Community." In *The Formation of Social Policy in the Catholic and Jewish Traditions,* ed. Eugene J. Fisher and Daniel F. Polish. Notre Dame, IN: University of Notre Dame Press, 5–14.

Campbell, Angus, Phillip E. Converse, Warren E. Miller, and Donald Stokes. 1960. *The American Voter.* New York: John Wiley.

Castelli, Jim. 1985. "Reagan Looks Down on 'Blessed are the Peacemakers.' " *Gainesville Sun.* April 23: 11A.

Catholic Diocese of St. Augustine. 1984. "Candidates' Poll, General Election 1984." *Gainesville Sun.* October 28: 10G.

Chardy, Alfonso, 1985. "Did Moon Give Aid to Contras?" *Miami Herald.* January 30: 1A, 12A.

Cohen, Richard E. 1985. "Getting Religion." *National Journal.* September 14: 2080–2084.

Converse, Philip E. 1966. "Religion and Politics: The 1960 Election." In *Religion and the Political Order,* ed. Angus Campell, Philip E. Converse, Warren E. Miller, and Donald Stokes. New York: John Wiley, 96–124.

Dexter, Lewis Anthony. 1938. "Administration of the Social Gospel." *Public Opinion Quarterly.* 2: 294–299.

Edsall, Thomas B. 1985. "The GE Lobby." *Washington Post National Weekly Edition.* 6–7.

Ehrenhalt, Alan, editor. 1983. *Politics in America 1984.* Washington, DC: Congressional Quarterly Press.

Elazar, Daniel J. 1984. *American Federalism: A View from the States.* Third edition. New York: Harper and Row.

Elazar, Daniel J. 1976. *Community and Polity: The Organizational Dynamics of American Jewry.* Philadelphia, PA: Jewish Publication Society of America.

Elazar, Daniel J. 1970. *Cities of the Prairie.* New York: Basic Books.

Ermann, M. David, and William H. Clements, II. 1984. "The Interfaith Center on Corporate Responsibility and Its Campaign Against Marketing Infant Formula in the Third World." *Social Problems.* 32: 185–196.

Fairbanks, David. 1979. "Politics, Economics, and the Public Morality: Why Some States are More 'Moral' Than Others." *Policy Studies Journal.* 7: 714–720.

Fairbanks, David. 1977. "Religious Forces and 'Morality' Policies in the American States." *Western Political Quarterly.* 30: 411–417.

Fenton, John H. 1960. *The Catholic Vote.* New Orleans, LA: Hauser Press.
Fenton, John H., and Kenneth N. Vines. 1967. "Negro Registration in Louisiana." In *Negro Politics in America,* ed. Harry A. Bailey, Jr. Columbus, OH: Charles E. Merrill, 166–177.
Festinger, Leon. 1947. "The Role of Group Belongingness in a Voting Situation." *Human Relations.* 1: 154–180.
Field, Marilyn. 1979. "Determinants of Abortion Policy in the Developed Nations." *Policy Studies Journal.* 7: 771–781.
Fisher, Eugene J., and Daniel F. Polish, editors. 1980. *The Formation of Social Policy in the Catholic and Jewish Traditions.* Notre Dame, IN: University of Notre Dame Press.
Florida Catholic Conference. 1985. "Lawmakers Debate Three Critical Issues." *Gainesville Sun.* April 21: 13G.
Flowers, Ronald B. 1983. "President Jimmy Carter, Evangelicalism, Church-State Relations, and Civil Religion." *Journal of Church and State.* 25: 113–132.
Ganin, Zvi. 1979. *Truman, American Jewry, and Israel, 1945–1948.* New York: Holmes and Meier.
Giles, Micheal W., and Thomas G. Walker. 1975. "Judicial Policy-Making and Southern School Desegregation." *Journal of Politics.* 37: 917–936.
Glick, Edward Bernard. 1982. *The Triangular Connection: America, Israel, and American Jews.* London: George Allen and Unwin.
Goldman, Sheldon. 1975. "Voting Behavior on the U.S. Court of Appeals Revisited." *American Political Science Review.* 79: 491–506.
Goldman, Sheldon. 1966. "Voting Behavior on the United States Courts of Appeal, 1961–64." *American Political Science Review.* 60: 374–383.
Goodman, Walter. 1984. "Religious Debate Fueled by Politics." *New York Times.* October 28: 31.
Granberg, Donald. 1985a. "An Anomaly in Political Perception." *Public Opinion Quarterly.* 49: 504–516.
Granberg, Donald. 1985b. "The United States Senate Votes to Uphold *Roe v. Wade.*" *Population Research and Policy Review.* 42: 115–131.
Greeley, Andrew. 1985. "Why the Peace Pastoral Did Not Bomb." *National Catholic Reporter.* April 12: 11.
Greeley, Andrew. 1977. *The American Catholic: A Social Portrait.* New York: Basic Books.
Hamilton, Howard D. 1970. "Voting in Open Housing Referenda." *Social Science Quarterly.* 51: 715–729.
Hammond, John L. 1979. *The Politics of Benevolence: Revival Religion and American Voting Behavior.* Norwood, NJ: Ablex Publishing.
Hanna, Mary. 1979. *Catholics and American Politics.* Cambridge, MA: Harvard University Press.
Hansen, Susan B. 1980. "State Implementation of Supreme Court Decisions: Abortion Rates Since *Roe v. Wade.*" *Journal of Politics.* 42: 372–395.
Haughey, John C., editor. 1979. *Personal Values in Public Policy.* New York: Paulist Press.
Herbers, John. 1984. "Armageddon View Prompts a Debate." *New York Times.* October 24: 1, 13.
Hirsch, H.N. 1981. *The Enigma of Felix Frankfurter.* New York: Basic Books.
Horowitz, Irving L., editor. 1978. *Science, Sin, and Scholarship: The Politics of Reverend Moon and the Unification Church.* Boston, MA: MIT Press.
Hutcheson, John D., and George A. Taylor. 1973. "Religious Variables, Political

System Characteristics, and Policy Outputs in the American States." *American Journal of Political Science.* 17: 414–421.

Isikoff, Michael. 1984. "What the Moon Church Wants for Its Millions." *Washington Post National Weekly Edition.* December 10: 7–8.

Jaffe, Frederick S., Barbara Lindheim, and Philip R. Lee. 1981. *Abortion Politics: Private Morality and Public Policy.* New York: McGraw-Hill.

Johnson, Charles A. 1976. "Political Culture in American States: Elazar's Formulation Examined." *American Journal of Political Science.* 20: 491–509.

Johnston, Michael. 1983. "Corruption and Political Culture in America: An Empirical Perspective." *Publius.* 13: 19–39.

Kaczor, Bill. 1985. "Defense Fund Set Up for Bombing Suspects." *Gainesville Sun.* March 19: 11A.

Kamin, Leon J. 1958. "Ethnic and Party Affiliations of Candidates as Determinants of Voting." *Canadian Journal of Psychology.* 12: 205–212.

Kleppner, Paul. 1979. *The Third Electoral System, 1853–1892.* Chapel Hill, NC: University of North Carolina Press.

Klingman, David, and William W. Lammers. 1984. "The 'General Policy Liberalism' Factor in American State Politics." *American Journal of Political Science.* 28: 598–610.

Kucharsky, David. 1976. *The Man From Plains.* New York: Harper and Row.

Kurtz, Howard. 1985a. "Opposition to Reagan's Choice for Legal Policy Job Is Mounting." *Washington Post Weekly Edition.* August 5: 34.

Kurtz, Howard, 1985b. "The Ideology of Federal Judgeships." *Washington Post National Weekly Edition.* April 15: 9–10.

Leisner, Pat. 1985. "School Children's 'Stress Control' Program Upsets Some Parents." *Gainesville Sun.* March 18: 1B.

Leventman, Paula Goldman, and Seymour Leventman. 1976. "Congressman Drinan, S.J., and His Jewish Constituents." *American Jewish Historical Quarterly.* 66: 215–248.

Lorinskas, Robert A., Brett W. Hawkins, and Stephen D. Edwards. 1969. "The Persistence of Ethnic Voting in Urban and Rural Areas: Results from the Controlled Elections Method." *Social Science Quarterly.* 49: 891–899.

Malicky, Neal. 1968. "Religious Groups at the United Nations: A Study of Certain Religious Non-Governmental Organizations at the United Nations." Ph.D. thesis, Columbia University.

Mayer, Jane. 1985. "Ways and Means Panel's Tax-Overhaul Proposal Brings 'Family' Strife to Conservative Coalition." *Wall Street Journal.* November 27: 52.

Mayer, Jane, and Alan Murray. 1985. "Substance, Tactics of Tax Revision Cause Conflict Among Administrative Hard-Liners, Pragmatists." *Wall Street Journal.* October 8: 64.

Mazlish, Bruce, and Edwin Diamond. 1979. *Jimmy Carter: A Character Portrait.* New York: Simon and Schuster.

Miller, William Lee. 1978. *Yankee from Georgia: The Emergence of Jimmy Carter.* New York: Times Books.

Morgan, David R., and Kenneth J. Meier. 1980. "Politics and Morality: The Effect of Religion on Referenda Voting." *Social Science Quarterly.* 61: 144–148.

Murphy, Caryle. 1984. "Sanctuary: How Churches Defy Immigration Law." *Washington Post National Weekly Edition.* September 17: 8–9.

Nagel, Stuart S. 1962. "Ethnic Affiliations and Judicial Propensities." *Journal of Politics.* 24: 92–110.

Nagel, Stuart S. 1961. "Political Party Affiliation and Judge's Decisions." *American Political Science Review*. 55: 843–850.

O'Neil, Daniel J. 1970. *Church Lobbying in A Western State: A Case Study on Abortion Legislation*. Tucson, AZ: University of Arizona Press. "Arizona Government Studies," #7.

Page, Benjamin I., Robert Y. Shapiro, Paul W. Gronke, and Robert M. Rosenberg. 1984. "Constituency, Party, and Representation in Congress." *Public Opinion Quarterly*. 48: 741–756.

Payne, James L., and James A. Dyer. 1975. "Betting After the Race Is Over: The Perils of Post Hoc Hypothesizing." *American Journal of Political Science*. 19: 559–564.

Pippert, Wesley G., compiler. 1978. *The Spiritual Journey of Jimmy Carter*. New York: Macmillan.

Pomper, Gerald A. 1966. "Ethnic and Group Voting in Non-Partisan Municipal Elections." *Public Opinion Quarterly*. 30: 79–99.

Pratt, Henry Johnson. 1962. "The Protestant Council of the City of New York as a Political Interest Group." Ph.D. thesis, Columbia University.

Rainey, Jane G. 1981. " 'Stand Up for Jesus': A Case Study of Confrontation and Cultural Encounter in the Educational Politics of the Christian Right." Paper presented at the annual meeting of the Southern Political Science Association, Memphis, TN.

Reagan, Ronald. 1985. "Remarks at the Annual Convention of the National Religious Broadcasters Association." *Weekly Compilation of Presidential Documents*. 21: 129–131.

Reagan, Ronald. 1981. "Remarks at the Annual Meeting of the International Association of Chiefs of Police." *Weekly Compilation of Presidential Documents*. 17: 1039–1046.

Richardson, James T. 1984. "The 'Old Right' in Action: Mormon and Catholic Involvement in an Equal Rights Amendment Referendum." In *New Christian Politics*, ed. David G. Bromley and Anson Shupe. Macon, GA: Mercer University Press, 213–234.

Richardson, James T., and Sandie Wightman Fox. 1972. "Religious Affiliation as a Predictor of Voting Behavior on Abortion Reform Legislation." *Journal for the Scientific Study of Religion*. 11: 347–359.

Rieselbach, Leroy N. 1966. *The Roots of Isolationism: Congressional Voting and Presidential Leadership in Foreign Policy*. Indianapolis, IN: Bobbs-Merrill.

Schiltz, Timothy D., and R. Lee Rainey. 1978. "The Geographic Distribution of Elazar's Political Subcultures Among the Mass Population: A Research Note." *Western Political Quarterly*. 31: 410–415.

Shuster, William G. 1981. "Appointments." *Christianity Today*. March 13: 58.

Simon, Paul. 1984. *The Glass House: Politics and Morality in the Nation's Capital*. New York: Continuum Publishing Company.

Sorauf, Frank J. 1976. *The Wall of Separation: The Constitutional Politics of Church and State*. Princeton, NJ: Princeton University Press.

Spiegel, Stephen. 1985. *The Other Arab-Israeli Conflict*. Chicago, IL: University of Chicago Press.

Spitzer, Robert J. 1984. "The Right to Life Movement as Partisan Activity." Paper presented at the annual meeting of the American Political Science Association, Washington, DC.

Swatos, William H., Jr. 1985. "Morality and Middlecore: Picketing Satan at 7-Eleven." Paper delivered to the annual meeting of the Religious Research Association, Savannah, GA.

Taylor, Paul. 1985a. "He Went Out for Pizza and Came Back the Definitive Campaigner." *Washington Post Weekly Edition.* September 30: 12.
Taylor, Paul. 1985b. "The Road to Sanctuary." *Washington Post National Weekly Edition.* March 11: 6–7.
Thomas, J. Mark. 1984. "Reagan in the State of Nature." *Christianity and Crisis.* September 17: 321–325.
Ulmer, S. Sidney. 1973. "Social Background as an Indicator to the Votes of Supreme Court Justices in Criminal Cases: 1947–56 Terms." *American Journal of Political Science.* 17: 622–630.
Van Dyke, Tana. 1985. "Sanctuary." *Gainesville Sun.* February 2: 1–2B.
Vedlitz, Arnold, Jon P. Alston, and Carl Pinkele. 1980. "Politics and the Black Church in a Southern Community." *Journal of Black Studies.* 10: 367–375.
Vines, Kenneth. 1964. "Federal District Judges and Race Relations Cases in the South." *Journal of Politics.* 26: 337–357.
Vinovkis, Maris A. 1979. "The Politics of Abortion in the House of Representatives in 1976." *Michigan Law Review.* 77: 1790–1827.
Warner, John B., Jr. 1968. "Religious Affiliation as a Factor in the Voting Records of Members of the 89th Congress." Ph.D thesis in Religion, Boston University.
Wasserman, Ira M. 1983. "A Cross-National Comparison of Contraception and Abortion Laws." *Social Indicators Research.* 13: 281–310.
Weber, Paul J. 1982. "Examining the Religious Lobbies." *This World.* 1: 97–107.
Weber, Paul J., and T. L. Stanley, 1984. "The Power and Performance of Religious Interest Groups." *Quarterly Review.* 4: 28–43.
Westoff, Charles F., and Larry Bumpass. 1973. "Revolution in Birth Control Practices of United States Roman Catholics." *Science.* 179: 41–44.
Westoff, Charles F., and Norman R. Ryder. 1970. "Conception Control Among American Catholics." In *Catholics/U.S.A.*, ed. William T. Liv and Nathaniel J. Pallone. New York: John Wiley, 257–268.
White, O. Kendall, Jr. 1984. "Overt and Covert Politics: The Mormon Church's Anti-ERA Campaign in Virginia." *Virginia Social Science Journal.* 19: 11–16.

7

The Political Mobilization of Evangelical Protestants

Like other fields of study, political science responds to events in the world. During the 1970s, an apparent revival in the fortunes of traditional religion and the simultaneous eruption of religious controversy renewed scholarly interest in the relationship between religion and American politics. No other single factor contributed as much to that trend or received as much attention as the political awakening of evangelical Protestants. Commenting on the spectacular growth rates of theologically conservative churches, one journalist commented that the striving for personal fulfillment of the "me" decade had quickly given way to the spiritual emphasis of the "thee" decade. Like all important social developments, the renewed religious consciousness was bound to influence the tenor of American politics.

This chapter examines recent expression of political activity by theologically conservative Christians. What do evangelical Protestants think about contemporary political issues? What caused the upsurge in political action by conservative Christians? Has the attempt to mobilize them altered the pattern of American political life? These questions will guide the analysis of a new political force that some observers have denounced as dangerous to the political system and others have heralded as a movement to revitalize American politics.

THE POLITICAL BACKGROUND

Of all the shifts and surprises in contemporary political life, perhaps none was so wholly unexpected as the political resurgence of evangelical Protestantism in the 1970s. Modernization theory had led many observers to treat traditional religion as a spent force in the United States and to discount its influence in the realm of national politics. Like other predictions associated with modernization theory, this assessment was rudely challenged by evidence that evangelical Christianity had achieved new strength and was ready to assert that power in political activity. The nomination of Jimmy Carter in 1976, the rise to national notice of organizations such as Moral Majority, the restoration of spirited public debate about certain "moral" issues—all these signs of evangelical political awakening marked the return to national prominence of a force that knowledgeable observers had long ago written off.

Until the 1920s, evangelical Protestantism was an animating force in American political life.[1] It had contributed greatly to the growth of antislavery sentiment in the Northern states during the period leading up to the Civil War and, paradoxically, reinforced the commitment of Southerners to the maintenance of the slave economy. In the decades following that great conflict, evangelicals generally sided with a variety of movements designed to purify American politics of various corrupting influences. In the twenty years before World War I, when it was embodied in the national arena by William Jennings Bryan, the evangelical impulse was a driving force behind such disparate movements as currency reform, women's suffrage, regulation of corporate abuses, arbitration of international conflicts, and adoption of "direct democracy" through the initiative, referendum, and recall election (Levine 1975). These reforms of the Progressive Era were advanced as means to defend the economic interests and social values of traditional Protestantism. Their widespread adoption before World War I attested to the central place of evangelicalism in American culture.

In the period following World War I, evangelical Protestantism was displaced from its perch as a major cultural force by a series of major social developments that culminated in a virtual social revolution. It is important to recognize the shattering impact of these trends.

> The disintegration of traditional American values—so sharply recorded by novelists and artists—was reflected in a change in manners and morals that shook American society to its depths. The growing secularization of the country greatly weakened religious sanctions. People lost their fear of Hell and at the same time had less interest in Heaven; they made more demands for material fulfillment on Earth. . . . Most important, the authority of the family, gradually eroded over several centuries, had been sharply lessened by the rise of the city. "Never in recent generations," wrote Freda Kirchwey, "have human beings so floundered about outside the ropes of social and religious sanctions." (Leuchtenburg 1958, 158)

Under the impact of rapid urbanization, the spread of science and technology, and skyrocketing birth rates in the predominantly non-Protestant immigrant communities, the conditions that had once favored traditional Protestant religion began to lose hold. The weakening of the social values associated with evangelicalism was apparent in such disparate trends as the growth in women's employment, the loosening of restraints on sexuality, the rising prestige of science, and a general tendency to exalt hedonism and materialist values. Whether these developments were ever as widespread as imagined is really beside the point. Accurately or not, evangelicals thought they were confronted with threats to orthodox Christianity, and they reacted with furious defensive activity. Attempting to resist the encroachments of secularism in the political realm, they concentrated in the 1920s on a pair of causes—the campaigns to restrict the sale of intoxicating liquor and to prohibit the teaching of evolution in the public schools. Both movements attained temporary success, but in the end, neither could withstand the shift of political power to the burgeoning cities, where evangelicalism was weak and a new set of issues commanded public interest.

The fate of evangelicalism was tied to "a receding and beleaguered small-town culture" (Burner 1967, 4). As many predominantly northern denominations embraced modernity and expressed a willingness to apply scientific insight to religious belief, the center of gravity in evangelicalism shifted to the rural South. There were significant political implications in the increasing southern orientation of traditional Protestantism. Unlike northern evangelicals, who had argued that salvation depended both upon faith and works, the southern variety of Protestant Christianity stopped short of demanding social transformation as a condition for salvation. To most southern theological conservatives,

> salvation was an act, a transaction between God and the individual that was separable from the life that followed. Those who had been born again were expected to practice Christian morality, to behave rightly in their own lives, and to work and pray for the conversion of others. Yet these expectations were never connected with any imperative to transform their culture in the name of Christ. They did not deprecate the world about them; they simply saw religious life as something to be carried on in a separate compartment (Kleppner 1979, 187).

From its new southern base, evangelicalism thus chose to remain outside the political arena—a withdrawal broken only by participation in sporadic rearguard actions through fringe movements and extremist crusades (Clabaugh 1974; Grupp and Newman 1973; Jorstad 1970; Orum and McCrane 1970; Ribuffo 1983).

The apparent links between evangelicalism and regressive political movements fixed traditional religion in the public mind as narrow-minded, bigoted, and backward-looking—an image that obscured earlier associations between the same religious community and progressive political causes (Warner 1979). Observers relied on social and theological factors to explain the political quiescence of traditional Protestantism after World War I. The social and economic deprivation that typified evangelicals denied them the time, energy, and skill to carry on sustained political participation and isolated them from experiences that would have promoted tolerance, compromise, and other democratic values. Lesser educational opportunities were said to afflict evangelicals with cognitive rigidity, an inflexibility of mind that kept them at a disadvantage in genuinely democratic political competition (Lipset 1960, 100). Furthermore, the otherworldly orientation of southern religion, the divorce between religion and social conditions, discouraged participation in the earthly process of political action. Many observers who associated evangelicalism with reactionary and violent movements such as the Ku Klux Klan shared an unspoken assumption that political abstinence by evangelicals contributed to the stability of the political system.

To the extent that evangelicals participated in conventional political life after Bryan's eclipse, their sympathies seem to have been with the Democratic party.[2] The alliance between theological conservatives and the more liberal of the national parties can be explained largely in regional and class terms. The force of tradition kept white Southern Baptists, the largest evangelical denomination, firmly attached to the party that had reestablished white political dominance in the late nineteenth century. The linkage was further cemented in the 1930s by the popularity of New Deal social welfare programs that attacked poverty and agricultural distress in the region. The first academic studies of public opinion and party allegiance, published in the 1940s and 1950s, confirmed what southern election returns had suggested—that white Southern Baptists were disproportionately attached to the Democratic party and much more prone than other groups to support government programs of economic security (Allinsmith and Allinsmith 1948; Pope 1953). Though the "states' rights" revolt at the 1948 Democratic national convention had demonstrated the capacity of the civil rights issue to draw southern whites away from a Democratic allegiance, the partisan impact of the controversy was checked by the similarity of the Democratic and Republican positions until the 1960s.

The first stirrings of change in the pattern of evangelical politics were visible in the presidential elections of the 1960s. When the Democratic party nominated a Catholic for president in 1960, large numbers of white, churchgoing southern Protestants defected to the Republican candidate (Converse 1966; Pool, Abelson, and Popkin 1965, 115–22; Dawidowicz and Goldstein 1974, 41–48). Four years later, the same parts of the country that had given William Jennings Bryan his greatest margins of support responded favorably to the candidacy of Barry Goldwater, a Republican who had cultivated their favor by emphasizing conservative social values (Burnham 1968). Goldwater's candidacy appeared to galvanize many evangelicals who had previously stayed outside the political arena. In 1968, George Wallace's independent presidential candidacy carried five southern states, apparently on the strength of an appeal to whites belonging to theologically conservative denominations (Crespi

1971; Oldendick and Bennett 1978). By the end of the decade, the level of psychological attachment to the Democratic party and voting support for its presidential candidates had eroded considerably among white southerners (Knoke 1976, 23; Ladd 1975, 229).

These trends did not wholly prepare observers for the subsequent attempts to turn evangelical Protestants to the political right. The changing voting patterns in the South were not interpreted principally in terms of a revolt by theological conservatives, but rather in racial and economic terms.[3] The Republican surge in 1960 was attributed directly to anti-Catholic sentiment, but most observers perceived it in the context of a steady postwar erosion of Democratic support in the region, occasioned by the increasing liberalism of the national Democratic party on race and social welfare issues and the corresponding move to the right by the Republican leadership. Unaware that this partisan reaction was especially pronounced among persons deeply committed to orthodox Protestantism, most influential commentators on Southern politics did not dwell on the role of religious values in stimulating voter transitions.

The rise of Jimmy Carter to national power both focused public attention on the growing political significance of evangelical Protestantism and further undermined the stereotype of rabid extremism (Jorstad 1981). A well-educated and scientifically trained person, comfortable with contemporary culture and familiar with modern theology, Carter advocated moderate to liberal policies without the excited appeals to emotion that had been the hallmark of evangelical politics. In the face of publicly expressed doubts by Catholic, Jewish, and black leaders who associated Southern evangelicals with religious and racial bigotry, Carter's moderation seemed to promise a welcome break with that unpleasant historical tradition. In the election of 1976, he carried Catholic and Jewish voters by the same or greater margins as had most other postwar Democratic presidential candidates and, like Lyndon Johnson and Hubert Humphrey, received virtually unanimous support from blacks (Miller, Miller, and Schneider 1980, 332). That Carter could appeal so strongly to liberal social groups and carry most of the Southern states suggested the end of evangelical political distinctiveness. That impression might not have been so widely accepted if more people had realized that Carter actually lost a majority of his fellow white Southerners to the Republican candidate (*Public Opinion* 1985).

THE "NEW CHRISTIAN RIGHT"

The return of evangelicals to organized political action, manifested in what has been labeled the New Christian Right or the New Religious Right, was facilitated by a number of local movements that developed during the social ferment and upheaval of the 1970s. Alan Crawford (1980), a conservative journalist who looks with disfavor upon the evangelical influence in politics, has argued that the ground for national organizations such as Moral Majority was prepared by three grass-roots campaigns that unexpectedly caught fire: a textbook controversy in West Virginia, a gay rights referendum in Dade County (Miami), Florida, and a spirited campaign to defeat the proposed Equal Rights Amendment to the Constitution. In each case, evangelical Protestants rallied strongly to the defense of traditional cultural and social values.

In the mid-1970s, protesters in a mining valley of West Virginia challenged some of the English textbooks that the Kanawha County Board of Education had approved for use in public schools. Led by the wife of a fundamentalist minister, who denounced most of the books as "disrespectful of authority and religion, destructive of social and cultural values, obscene, pornographic, unpatriotic, or in violation of individual and familial rights of privacy" (Jenkinson 1979, 18), the campaign ignited a massive boycott of the schools by the parents of most students, sympathetic wildcat strikes by coal miners, mass picketing all across the county, a teachers' strike, temporary closure of the schools, and several violent assaults on people and property. Although all of the books were eventually approved for classroom use, the controversy led to the resignation of the school superintendent and a new textbook adoption procedure that made it easier for parents to screen out "offensive" books. The apparent success of the parent groups in the Kanawha County "Battle of the Books" inspired similar challenges around the country (Goff 1977; Richburg 1986).

The seeds of the New Christian Right were also planted by the 1977 Dade County, Florida, referendum on a gay rights ordinance. As part of a nationwide campaign to gain legal protection for their lifestyle, homosexuals had persuaded the Dade County Commission to pass an ordinance prohibiting discrimination on the basis of sexual preference in housing, employment, and public accommodations. The ordinance prompted formation of a new organization, called Save Our Children, which claimed that the law would require private and religious schools to employ homosexuals as teachers (Bryant 1977). After a petition drive led by the singer Anita Bryant and many religious leaders, the ordinance was submitted to a popular referendum and voted down by more than a 2–1 margin. Similar ordinances were subsequently repealed in several other cities across the United States.

The potential clout of religious conservatism was also on display in the remarkable campaign that defeated the proposed Equal Rights Amendment to the Constitution (Boles 1979). Approved by Congress early in 1972, an amendment prohibiting sexual discrimination by the states and the federal government quickly sailed through ratification votes in twenty-two state legislatures, leaving it only sixteen states short of formal adoption. The seemingly inevitable path to constitutional status was interrupted by the formation of "Stop-ERA," under the leadership of Phyllis Schlafly, a longtime activist in conservative political causes. In the face of determined lobbying by Schlafly's organization and allied groups, the rate of ratification dropped sharply and the amendment ultimately died three states short of the thirty-eight needed. To underline the religious dimension of the conflict, most of the states that failed to ratify had substantial concentrations of Mormons (Utah, Nevada, Arizona) or evangelical Protestants (all the southern states except Texas and Tennessee), and conservative churches supplied the recruitment base for most of the antiratification leaders and activists (Arrington and Kyle 1978; Brady and Tedin 1976; Conover and Gray 1983; Mueller and Dimieri 1982; Tedin 1978; Tedin et al. 1977).

Although motivated by different issues, these three campaigns were tied together by a common dissatisfaction with what the participants saw as a godless society that had replaced firm moral standards with a system of relativism (Phillips 1982, chap. 14). The campaigns against "obscene" schoolbooks, the gay rights ordinance, and the ERA attracted a variety of supporters but appealed most strongly to evangelical Protestants, who saw each movement as a crusade in defense of traditional Christian values and institutions. The particular value presumed under attack ranged from respect for social conventions in West Virginia to heterosexual marriage in Miami to the maintenance of traditional social roles for women in the struggle over the ERA. Underlying these challenges to orthodox Christian values, it was argued by some leaders of the movement, was a doctrine called secular humanism. Although definitions of that concept varied from one critic to another, social conservatives generally agreed that at its core lay a belief in the supremacy of humanity rather than of God. According to the advocates of traditional social values, the doctrine of secular humanism had become entrenched in the government, schools, media, and other institutions that molded public perceptions. Through state and local campaigns against particular outcroppings of what they saw as a pernicious idea, conservative religious activists began to forge organizational links and a common view about the source of major social problems.

The political success of grass-roots evangelical actions did not go unnoticed by "secular" conservative activists who were seeking popular support for a broad agenda encompassing social, economic, defense, and foreign policy issues. Evangelical activities drew particular attention from four conservative activists who had no background in the evangelical community: Howard Phillips of the Conservative Caucus; John "Terry" Dolan of the National Conservative Political Action Committee; Paul Weyrich of the National Committee for the Survival of a Free Congress;

and Richard Vigurie, a major fund-raiser for conservative causes. Spurred on by the availability of a large pool of potential allies, Phillips and his colleagues offered assistance to the emerging leaders of the Christian conservative movement and urged the most vocal leaders of the evangelical community to make common cause with other single-issue groups. The basis for coalition would be a frontal attack on "big government" as a threat to traditional religious and economic values. With that theme, they hoped to harness evangelicals to a comprehensive conservative program, including opposition to liberal policies on gun control, the treaty relinquishing American control over the Panama Canal, nonrestrictive abortion laws, compulsory unionization, and defense cutbacks. Using their contacts and ample political resources—in particular, a capacity to raise money through mailing lists—the secular conservatives helped build up several national organizations designed to appeal to evangelical Protestants and other theological conservatives.[4]

The most prominent of the new organizations, Moral Majority, has almost become synonymous with the entire religious right. Properly speaking, Moral Majority is a lobbying organization founded in 1979 by television evangelist Jerry Falwell, the minister of the nation's largest independent Baptist church, in Lynchburg, Virginia. Falwell, who had assisted Anita Bryant in the Dade County repeal campaign, used the mailing list for his *Old Time Gospel Hour* television program to recruit supporters and financial contributions. Concentrated mostly in the southeastern states, Moral Majority has drawn most of its membership from independent Baptist churches and virtually all of its leadership from pastors of that confession. Organized in state chapters, it has concentrated on lobbying public officials and encouraging church members to register as voters. In response to alleged misrepresentation of the organization by the media, Moral Majority recently was merged into an umbrella organization organized by Falwell under the name of the Liberty Federation.

To reach into the Southern Baptist Convention, the largest association of evangelical Protestants, as well as other conservative denominations, a retired Memphis sales executive named Ed McAteer founded the Religious Roundtable. Unlike Moral Majority, which aimed at building a mass movement of evangelicals, the Roundtable was intended primarily to provide a common meeting ground where theologically conservative pastors could learn the fine arts of political mobilization on behalf of various conservative causes. This was accomplished by periodic mass meetings, or "public affairs briefings," featuring conservative speakers and workshops on various aspects of political action. Christian Voice, the oldest national organization in the New Christian Right, grew out of an unsuccessful attempt by California evangelicals to pass a state law prohibiting the employment of homosexuals or advocates of homosexuality in publicly supported teaching positions. Similar in many respects to Moral

Majority, it has a western and southwestern base and a particular appeal to members of the Assemblies of God. More so than the other two organizations, Christian Voice has concentrated its efforting on election-eering—compiling information on candidates, offering lists of favored and opposed candidates, and raising funds to support independent campaigns for favored candidates.

Although the existence of three separate organizations reflects some of the diversity in the evangelical community and a degree of rivalry among the prominent television ministers, the different groups frequently have shared members, staff, support services, funding sources, and office space (Hill and Owen 1982, 56). The principal leaders form something of an interlocking directorate, holding seats on the boards of one another's organizations and leadership positions in the secular conservative groups with whom they are allied. All the organizations established at the end of the 1970s have also drawn upon the experience and expertise of earlier movements designed to spur evangelicals into political action, including some that had ties to the unsuccessful attempt by Ronald Reagan to win the 1976 Republican nomination for president (Pierard 1983b; Blumenthal 1984).

Most important, Moral Majority, Christian Voice, and the Roundtable have capitalized on essentially the same set of issues to rally evangelicals to political action (Shriver 1981). Described by the Christian Right as the "profamily" program, the same specific proposals have shown up in the literature of all three organizations. Reverend Falwell's "Christian Bill of Rights" stresses opposition to abortion, support for voluntary prayer and Bible reading in public schools, the responsibility of government to encourage the "traditional family unit," the maintenance of tax exemption for churches, and noninterference by the authorities with Christian schools. The ten "amendments" from an advertisement by the Moral Majority are as follows:

Christian Bill of Rights

Amendment I   We believe that, from the time of conception within the womb, every human being has a scriptural right to life upon this earth. (Ex. 20:13; Psa. 139-13-16)

Amendment II   We believe that every person has the right to pursue any and all scriptural goals that he or she feels are God-directed during that life upon this earth. (Prov. 3:5–6)

Amendment III   We believe that, apart from justified capital punishment, no medical or judicial process should be introduced that would allow the termination of life before its natural or accidental completion. (Psa. 31:15)

Amendment IV   We believe that no traitorous verbal or written attack upon the beloved nation advocating overthrow by force be permitted by any citizen or alien living within this country. (Rom. 13:1–7)

Amendment V   We believe that all students enrolled in public schools should have the right to voluntary prayer and Bible reading. (Josh. 24:15)

Amendment VI   We believe in the right and responsibility to establish and administer private Christian schools without harassment from local, state, or federal government. (Deut. 11:18–21)

Amendment VII   We believe in the right to influence secular professions, including the fields of politics, business, legal, medical, in establishing and maintaining moral principles of Scripture. (Prov. 14:34)

Amendment VIII   We believe in the right to expect our national leaders to keep this country morally and militarily strong so that the religious freedom and Gospel preaching might continue unhindered. (I Pet. 2:13–17)

Amendment IX   We believe in the right to receive moral support from all local, state, and federal agencies concerning the traditional family unit, a concept that enjoys both scriptural and historical precedence. (Gen. 2:18–25)

Amendment X   We believe in the right of legally-approved religious organizations to maintain their tax-exempt status, this right being based upon the historical and scriptural concept of church and state separation. (Matt. 22:17–21)

In an effort to explain the need for mobilizing evangelicals, Christian Voice has expanded the list of social evils to include the teaching of evolution, pornography, the alleged celebration of "immoral" behavior on television, and liquor and drug abuse. The same topics were stressed in Roundtable briefings and embodied in the Family Protection Act, a composite piece of legislation introduced by Senator Paul Laxalt of Nevada.

While assigning preeminence to issues affecting church and personal conduct—the profamily agenda—the leaders of these movements have not ignored the issues that concern "secular" conservatives, including increased defense spending, support of anticommunist movements around the globe, antiinflationary policies, efforts against street crime, and calls for a balanced budget. In each case, conservative positions on these issues have been advocated with a religious rationale. Thus, increased defense spending has been justified as a way of keeping the nation free for the continued preaching of the Gospel and support for the governments of Taiwan and South Africa have been defended as necessary to protect Christian allies from the "Godless forces of anti-Christ Communism." Similarly, Jerry Falwell has asserted a scriptural basis for low inflation, flat-rate taxation, and a balanced federal budget. Such diffuse policies have usually been offered as a package designed to counteract the influence of secular humanism.

In attempting to discover if the majority of Americans actually subscribe to the New Christian Right definition of public morality, scholars have conducted a multitude of opinion surveys based on local, state, and national samples. With an unusual degree of accord, these surveys have challenged the most enthusiastic claims about the extent of broad public support for the profamily agenda. In fact, support for the core items making up the "profamily" agenda has been limited to a minority of the population and apparently has declined over the course of the 1970s and 1980s (Mueller 1983; Smith 1982; Yinger and Cutler 1982—but see Simpson 1983). In the face of New Right efforts to the contrary, the public apparently has become more liberal on issues like abortion, tolerance for homosexuality, and women's rights.

The profamily agenda and the organizations that have propagated it have struck the most responsive chord precisely where they might have been expected to make a strong appeal—in persons deeply attached to evangelical Protestant denominations. As many studies have suggested, involvement in theologically conservative churches seems to breed a strong attachment to traditional moral values and support for the efforts of clergy and church members to enshrine these values in public policy.[5] But as noted in Chapter 4, even among the core constituency of evangelical Protestants, support for conservative social policies has been far from unanimous. The degree of political variation within the evangelical community emerged quite clearly from analysis of a unique set of interviews conducted in 1983 with approximately 600 white Protestants (Rothenburg and Newport 1984; Kellstedt 1985). The members of the sample were registered voters who had passed a two-part test of theological convictions designed to identify commitment to evangelicalism. Majorities of the sample approved school prayer, American support for Israel, and tuition tax credits—all items on the New Christian Right agenda. Yet substantial majorities also took positions diametrically opposed to the leadership of the conservative Christian organizations. In supporting the distribution of birth control information in the schools, favoring passage of the Equal Rights Amendment, and rejecting the notion that acquired immune deficiency syndrome (AIDS) is a form of divine retribution for homosexuality, the evangelicals broke ranks with some of their spokesmen. On other issues on which the New Christian Right has conveyed clear preferences—supporting increases in defense spending, opposing a nuclear freeze, calling for restrictive abortion policy—evangelical opinion was split, with no single option clearly preferred over the alternatives. Perhaps the most striking indication of evangelical diversity was the finding that the Reverend Falwell was actually less popular among respondents than was the National Organization for Women, a feminist organization that New Christian Right literature has labeled antifamily.

If the evangelical community as a whole has displayed considerable political diversity, however, certain subgroups have shown higher-than-average support for the New Christian Right. In the interviews with evangelicals described in the previous paragraph, agreement with the Falwell platform was most pronounced among the older, less educated, and lower-income members of the sample. Women who were not employed outside the house and residents of the South also exhibited a stronger-than-average commitment to the issue positions endorsed by the New Christian Right. In a pattern consistent with modernization theory, those evangelicals least exposed to institutions that promote a modernizing outlook proved to be the most receptive to the traditional values of orthodox Christianity.

These findings should serve as a caution against attributing a single, unified political perspective to what is a diverse community of evangelical Protestants. In terms of the attitudes of both their "natural" supporters and the population outside the evangelical tradition, the organization of the New Christian Right clearly have a long way to go before they can legitimately claim to represent majority opinion in the United States. The same can be said for nearly all interest groups that compete for influence in the American system.

EVANGELICAL POLITICAL ACTION IN THE 1980s

The groups of the New Christian Right first gained widespread national attention during the presidential campaign of 1980, when they coalesced, formally or informally, around the candidacy of Ronald Reagan. Divorced, an intermittent churchgoer from a mainline denomination, the father of children who have pursued unconventional lives, and a veteran of show business, Reagan seemed a most unlikely object of support for the devout—doubly so in a race with two other evangelical Protestants, Jimmy Carter and John Anderson. But as Reagan alone endorsed the political efforts of the conservative evangelical leaders and pledged to work for enactment of the profamily agenda, he increasingly drew the New Christian Right into his camp. Christian Voice was the first and most enthusiastic supporter, creating a political action committee called Christians for Reagan to raise funds and propagandize on behalf of the Reagan campaign. The Roundtable brought Reagan to speak at its major public affairs briefing in Dallas during the summer of 1980, an event that gave him direct access to more than 15,000 clergymen and brought national attention to the movement. Moral Majority refrained from formal endorsement but conveyed its enthusiasm in every possible way short of outright recommendation. All the groups encouraged pastors to sign up evangelicals on the voter rolls and impress upon churchgoers the necessity of expressing their religious convictions in the polling booths. These efforts led to a substantial evangelical presence in political party activities during the 1980 campaign (see Chapters 5–7 in Baker, Steed, and Moreland 1983). Only twenty years earlier, John Kennedy had traveled to Houston in a well-publicized effort to reassure Protestant clergy that he would not attempt to impose Catholic doctrine on the nation. As recently as 1976, Jimmy Carter had felt it necessary to emphasize his intention to respect the separation between personal religious values and public policy. By 1980, the circle had come full turn, and the joining of the religious and political wings of conservatism was epitomized by a bumper sticker bearing the word "vote" with the *t* in the shape of a cross.

Despite criticism of the administration's failure to push hard enough on the profamily agenda, the leaders of the New Christian Right lined up even more enthusiastically behind the Reagan reelection effort in 1984. In states such as Minnesota, where Republicanism had been a weak force, members of the religious right virtually took over the party apparatus (Pressman 1984, 2317–18). In July 1984, 300 conservative Christian ministers, including most of the prominent television evangelists, met at the White House with the president, the vice-president, and two cabinet members (Clendinen 1984). Shortly before the Republican national convention began in August, the campaign chairman solicited the support of Christian leaders in a letter sent to 45,000 ministers. Plans to include a copy of the New Testament in the welcoming kit prepared for delegates to the Dallas convention were only dropped at the last moment (Bergstrom and Saperstein 1984).

The 1984 Republican convention opened with a prayer by the Reverend James Robison, a Texas evangelist who had been vice-president of the Roundtable, and closed with a benediction from the Moral Majority president, Jerry Falwell, who referred to the Republican presidential and vice-presidential nominees as "God's instruments in rebuilding America" (Dickenson 1984). The platform committee, liberally staffed with legislators who had been strong supporters of the New Christian Right in Congress, produced a document that called for a constitutional amendment to restrict abortion, legalization of prayer and religious meetings in public schools, a ban on abortion, and no pledge of support for the Equal Rights Amendment. In language that spoke directly to the concerns that had prompted formation of the evangelical political movement, the platform accused the Democrats of "assaulting our basic values": "They attacked the integrity of the family and parental rights. They ignored traditional morality. And they still do" (Dickenson 1984). To hammer home the point about the differing stands taken by the two major parties, speakers referred constantly to their opponents as "the San Francisco Democrats," linking the freewheeling city where the Democrats had met for their convention with the policies pursued by the party. And on the morning of his renomination, President Reagan brought religion even more firmly into the campaign by giving a speech at a prayer breakfast that had been organized by the convention host committee (Reagan 1984).

The same techniques that had been used in 1980 were tried again in 1984. As in 1980, Moral Majority and Christian Voice appealed to their members on a profamily basis. (The Roundtable was less in evidence, as its president, Ed McAteer, ran an unsuccessful independent campaign for a U.S. Senate seat from Tennessee.) Under the leadership of the American Coalition for Traditional Values (ACTV), an umbrella group whose board included Falwell and Robison but whose director and key staff members came from Christian Voice, $1.5 million was budgeted to mount voter registration drives in evangelical churches. The organization was structured as a pyramid, with the ACTV national field director supervising the work of 350 field directors, who, in turn, oversaw the work of "church captains" in individual congregations.

As with almost every activity associated with the religious right, there has been disagreement over the effectiveness of these efforts, with estimates of the number of new registered voters placed as low as 200,000 and as high as 3 million (Spring 1984; Harwood 1985b; Associated Press 1984). In order to maintain its tax-deductible status, ACTV could not endorse any candidate. However, its literature made it clear to the new voters that the organization's preferred moral stands were fully represented in the Republican platform, and it distributed a leadership manual for which President Reagan had written an introduction (Spring 1984).

CIVILITY AND CONSENSUS

Before the effects of this activity are considered, it is worth examining the representativeness of the New Christian Right, both in terms of the historical pattern of evangelical politics in the United States and the attitudes of evangelicals today. In a few cases, experience has confirmed the fears of some observers that the application of religious fervor to politics would heighten tensions in both spheres. When religion motivates political action, there is always the danger that people will assume that their positions are ordained by God and will regard their opponents as sinful. A development that some took as evidence of that intolerance was the issuance of "moral report cards" by several of the New Christian Right organizations during the 1980 and 1984 campaigns (*New York Times* 1980; *Congressional Quarterly* 1980; United Press International 1984). Like other interest groups that rate elected officials by their support for favored causes, the evangelical lobbies identified a key set of roll call votes and ranked candidates by their fidelity to the position endorsed by the group. The issues were identified as moral questions, and representatives who "failed" the test were targeted for defeat in literature distributed to churchgoers.

This action received substantial criticism from persons who could not discern a moral dimension in voting to cut spending on behavioral research from the budget of the National Science Foundation, to abolish the Department of Education, to require a balanced federal budget, or to prohibit school busing—to cite just a few of the issues that made up the various report cards, or profamily voting indexes. Others resented the claim that there was only one "moral" position on such complicated issues as abortion and school prayer or denied that a representative's underlying attitude could accurately be discerned from just a single vote. Ironically, the "moral voting" test was failed by several of the most widely respected representatives in Congress, as well as most of the ordained clergy in the legislative branch. Even though the literature distributed to churchgoers did not expressly declare that officials who voted "wrong" were necessarily immoral in their own lives, the inference could easily be drawn from the accompanying claim that the nation's decline had stemmed from the failure of government leaders to adhere to the "Godly principles" of the nation's founders. In some local areas, candidates who had flunked the Christian Voice test claimed that they were being accused of immorality or "unchristian" voting (*Congressional Quarterly* 1980, 2624; Simon 1984, 89–90). (The flavor of the conflict is reflected in a Christian Voice flyer distributed in 1984, reproduced here as a table.) All in all, the ratings left hard feelings in the Congress and may have contributed to the rough going that the New Right platform encountered after the election. The resentment was only partially redeemed when it became known that the highest-scoring group of congressmen included a representative who was caught on videotape accepting a bribe, another who was convicted of tax evasion, and two who confessed to sexual misconduct.

The responsibility for raising the temperature of the political atmosphere with strident appeals did not rest exclusively with the evangelical action groups. The opponents of the New Christian Right were not reluctant to indulge in some of the same tactics they condemned in the conservative movement. While thoughtful and reasoned critiques were presented, careful examination of the literature of groups such as People for the American Way or well-established organizations like the American Civil Liberties Union reveals examples of self-righteousness, distortion, oversimplification and attempts to "monopolize the symbols of legitimacy" (Hunter 1983, 162) by staking exclusive claim to the flag, national traditions, and common American values. As Hunter has pointed out, members of the evangelical movements are expressing their dissatisfaction with important changes in American society. If the methods and

REPORT CARD:
Reagan vs. Mondale vs. Hart

Take the issues test. The following are the Presidential candidates' positions on issues important to Christian voters. Match your position with the candidates'.

Issue	Ronald Reagan	Walter Mondale	Gary Hart	Your Position yes/no
Prayer in School	yes	no	no	
Taxpayer Funded Abortion	no	yes	yes	
Gay Rights Amendment	no	yes	yes	
Equal Rights Amendment	no	yes	yes	
Unverifiable U.S.-Soviet Arms Agreement	no	yes	yes	
Excessive Government Spending	no	yes	yes	

SOURCE: Christian Voice Moral Government Fund, Washington, DC: 1984.

language of advocacy have not always been moderate, it is also true that the claim has not always been treated with the respect and civility it deserves.

If the New Religious Right was reminiscent of past evangelical political involvement in some respects, it differed markedly in others. Largely absent have been the attacks on racial and religious minorities that had disfigured evangelical political crusades of the past. Moral Majority, in particular, reached out directly to Catholics, Jews, and blacks by describing itself as a political rather than a religious movement, by opening up membership to all persons, and by stressing issues that might build alliances across religious lines. Support for Israel has been a constant theme in Moral Majority literature, and Falwell repeatedly has referred to the Judeo-Christian basis of the nation's heritage. In 1984 the Minnesota chapter of Moral Majority actually endorsed the reelection effort of a Jewish senator (Pressman 1984, 2317). The abortion issue, on which the New Christian Right has been as adamant and unyielding as any group in America, offered a potential bridge to Catholics, and the interpretation of abortion as a civil rights issue for the unborn represented an oblique appeal to blacks. Even feminists, who recoiled from the New Christian Right because of its opposition to the Equal Rights Amendment and general support for male authority in the family, were offered support in their fight against pornography (Duggan 1985). Occasional public expressions of anti-Semitism and anti-Catholicism from movement activists put some dents in this image of respectability and breadth of vision, however.

In claiming to speak for evangelical Protestants, its core constituency, the New Christian Right encountered significant opposition. Some leaders of the fundamentalist wing adamantly refused to depart from the position that the only task of the churches was to win souls for Christ, an attitude Falwell himself had expressed with great force in condemning clergy involvement with civil rights in the mid-1960s. Charging that involvement in political action would divert the churches from their paramount responsibility, the Reverend Bob Jones denounced Falwell as "the most dangerous man in America" (D'Souza 1984). Adhering to a strong separationist position, Jones condemned Falwell for working in concert with people who did not agree with fundamentalist religious doctrine. From the other wing of evangelicalism, Social Gospel advocates such as the Sojourners, who shared Falwell's opposition to abortion, condemned him for joining that sentiment to a host of what they called "antilife" causes—military spending, capital punishment, and the like. And, motivated by the same belief in biblical authority that characterizes the conservative evangelicals, supporters of the evangelical left have marched in Washington, D.C., to call for an end to the nuclear arms buildup, American military activity in Central America, apartheid in South Africa, Soviet involvement in Afghanistan, the death penalty, and abortion (Monroe 1985). Finally, evangelical theologians have offered some of the most thoughtful and penetrating criticisms of the theology undergirding the New Christian Right (Fackre 1982).

The New Christian Right has also enjoyed a less than overwhelming endorsement from the recognized leadership of the evangelical community. As Robert Booth Fowler (1982) has so clearly documented, the most influential leaders of evangelical Protestantism had been moving toward a more moderate political position throughout the 1960s. An organization called Evangelicals for Social Action was formed to capitalize on the growing willingness of theological conservatives to support social reform. The most widely recognized spokesman for evangelical concerns in the United States today, the Reverend Billy Graham, is a case in point (Pierard 1983a). At the beginning of his career, Graham exhibited some of the political and social tendencies that were typical of fundamentalist Protestants. But over the course of the years, Graham moved toward the center of the political system by integrating his crusades, speaking out in favor of civil rights legislation, and, most recently, advocating strenuous efforts to improve relations with the Soviet Union and diminish the nuclear arms race. Graham has repeatedly warned that any attempt to identify a particular political agenda with Christianity is likely to bring discredit on religion and interfere with evangelization.

The strengths and weaknesses of the New Christian Right appeal to evangelicals can be seen clearly in attempts to convert the Southern Baptist Convention, the single largest element in evangelical Christianity (Blumenthal 1984, 23). Believers in a strong wall of separation between church and state, church delegates to the annual convention had endorsed abortion as a right just two years before the Supreme Court decision of

Roe v. *Wade* and had repeatedly passed resolutions commending the Supreme Court for rulings that prohibited organized prayer in public schools. Through its Baptist Joint Committee and Christian Life Commission, the church had lobbied for the types of welfare policies consistent with a Social Gospel approach to Christianity. A survey of church pastors conducted shortly after the 1980 election showed that it was grossly inaccurate to portray them as a right-wing bloc (Guth 1983a,b). Nearly half of the pastors surveyed expressed disapproval of Moral Majority and defined themselves as sympathetic to the Democratic party. As theological and political conservatives organized to combat these tendencies, they succeeded in electing their own candidates to the presidency of the Southern Baptist Convention and in reversing previous commitments to more liberal stands on school prayer and abortion. In a 1984 follow-up survey Guth (1985) found evidence of a shift to Republican identification and conservative policy preferences among SBC clergy. The experience of the Southern Baptists demonstrates that this critical group of evangelicals, although far from unanimous in its conversion to right-wing political action, has moved rapidly away from its traditional patterns of political support. Similar battles have raged in other Protestant denominations.

POLITICAL AND RELIGIOUS RAMIFICATIONS

As an electoral movement, the New Christian Right adopted two major goals—to get evangelical Protestants to participate in politics and to support candidates who endorsed conservative programs and policies. How realistic was this strategy and to what extent has it succeeded?

If it could counteract the powerful historical traditions of evangelical political passivity and Democratic partisanship, it was widely thought, the religious right might actually tip the scales in national elections. In discussing the possible impact of the New Christian Right's electoral bloc, commentators have tended to refer interchangeably to evangelicals, fundamentalists, born-again Christians, and conservative Protestants. Given the invocation of such diverse and poorly defined groups, it is not surprising that estimates of the potential constituency have differed widely. Depending upon who was doing the estimating, the potential target for the New Christian Right has been said to range from 30 million to 130 million Americans of voting age. The lowest figure represents an estimate of the church membership in the major evangelical denominations, whereas the higher figure includes "morally conservative" members of other Protestant denominations and sympathizers from the Mormon, Catholic, and Jewish communities, as well as all persons within listening range of television evangelists.

To pin down the figure more precisely than is possible with church membership statistics, several investigators have attempted to identify potential New Right voters by their personal religious beliefs. Because labels such as "evangelical," "fundamentalist," and "born again" have no fixed legal meaning, scholars have debated how best to distinguish members of this bloc from other religious groups (Kellstedt and Smidt 1985). The most widely used definition of evangelicalism in polling is a three-part scale developed by the Gallup organization (Gallup 1981). In order to qualify as an evangelical under Gallup's formula, a person must respond to a series of questions by affirming they (1) have had a "born-again" experience or call themselves born-again Christians, (2) have encouraged other people to believe in Jesus Christ, and (3) believe in a literal interpretation of the Bible. The Gallup definition has gained support both because it appears to identify the essential elements of evangelical religious belief and because it makes room for fundamentalists such as Bob Jones and Jerry Falwell, moderates like Billy Graham, and more liberal groups such as the Sojourners. When applied to national survey data, this formula identifies about 20 percent of the voting-age population, or about 35 million potential voters, as evangelicals. This is a substantially smaller proportion than has been obtained through the use of single questions—such as the "born-again" question, which was the sole criteria in some early studies—and a larger pool than those obtained with more demanding definitions (Kellstedt 1984).

Even though the Gallup formula represents a major improvement over estimates based on denominational membership or single questions from surveys, it probably exaggerates both the size of the evangelical community in the United States and the population available for political mobilization on a profamily platform. Specifically, there is evidence suggesting that the first and third criteria, self-description as born-again and acceptance of a literal view of the Bible, draw agreement from people who are not necessarily committed to evangelical theology. In one study of adults from Memphis, Tennessee, people who said they had been born again were asked to describe what the experience had actually meant to them. Even with due allowance for the difficulty of expressing a complex theological idea, it was clear that many persons applied the term to themselves without intending to signify any distinctive religious orientation. About one-fifth of the the respondents merely restated the phrase with no evidence of understanding. Almost one-quarter defined born-again status in terms of the Golden Rule or living a good life. Roughly one-third referred to increased churchgoing or strengthening of faith. That left only about one-fifth of the sample who described the experience in a theologically sophisticated fashion or spoke about it in mystical or spiritual terms. For many of these respondents, the phrase "born-again" seemed to tap a vague approval of faith that was not even necessarily related to Jesus.[6]

Similarly, it is not always clear how to reliably measure a person's belief about the infallibility of the Bible. To judge by a national survey sample that presented different options to respondents, a significantly higher percentage of people are likely to accept Gallup's measure of literalism, "The Bible is God's Word and all it says is true," than a more demanding statement such as "The Bible is the actual Word of God and is to be taken literally, word for word" (Davis 1984). The difference in agreement between parallel national samples—46 percent endorsing the Gallup measure versus 38 percent accepting the more demanding option—suggests that the measurement of a "literal belief in the Bible" is no more reliable than the attempt to ask people to define themselves as born-again.

Given the flabbiness of the questions, it seems that the pool of "evangelicals" derived from the standard survey-based definition includes many people who do not fit the image of the typical supporter of the New Christian Right. In fact, about one-fourth of the persons designated by their answers to pollsters as evangelicals are black and another 10–15 percent are Catholic. Since, as noted in Chapter 4, black Protestants and Catholics are decidedly more liberal on most issues than are white Protestants from the mainline and evangelical camps, a substantial share of the population that fits the three-part Gallup formula would be unlikely to support the New Christian Right's political agenda. When Catholics and blacks are removed, the ranks of the evangelicals falls to around 15 percent of the population—principally southerners who belong to the Baptist or Methodist churches or to one of the smaller groups, such as Church of Christ, Assemblies of God, or Church of God. This is not to say that the appeal of the New Christian Right is necessarily limited to this group, but rather to recognize that the latter represents the core constituency to whose concerns mobilization has mainly been directed.

In trying to overcome the evangelical tradition of low political involvement, the New Right groups have devoted considerable energy to persuading members of conservative Protestant churches that political action is consistent with both the U.S. Constitution and scriptural admonitions. Based on comparisons between 1976 and 1980, this effort appears to have paid off. Using a variant of the Gallup definition, Corwin Smidt (1983) reported that white evangelicals, who had formerly lagged behind nonevangelicals in conventional political participation, showed up at the polls in greater numbers, percentage-wise, than did nonevangelicals in 1980. The growth was most pronounced among the southern evangelicals, who probably had the weakest tradition of participation before 1980. The increase in participation was all the more remarkable because voter turnout among most other social groups actually declined between 1976 and 1980.

Getting evangelicals to the polls was only the first step. In order for the Christian Right to achieve its goals, both newly mobilized and traditional voters must endorse the candidates favored by the organizations. In that regard, the religious right can report mixed success. The best available evidence of evangelical voting patterns in presidential elections indicates that the evangelical vote split 60–40 in favor of Gerald Ford in 1976 (Menendez 1977, 197) and 61–34 in favor of Ronald Reagan in 1980. (Schneider 1984, 2132). These figures disclose that evangelicals were more likely than the nation as a whole to vote for the Republican presidential candidate, even when his opponent was a fellow evangelical, and that their preference for the Republican candidate increased across two elections. Closer inspection, however, reveals the need for qualification on a number of points.

First, the Republican preference was established *before* the New Christian Right organizations began their mobilizing efforts. The groups thus appear to have capitalized upon an underlying transformation rather than to have created it. Second, if the evangelicals' Republican vote increased between 1976 and 1980, so did everyone else's, largely in response to dissatisfaction with President Carter's leadership (Himmelstein and McRae 1984; Hibbs 1982). In both 1976 and 1980, the evangelicals were about 10 percent more supportive of the Republican candidate than the entire electorate. Third, and perhaps most tellingly, the evangelicals who entered the electorate for the first time in 1980 were actually *more* likely to support the Democratic presidential candidate than were nonevangelicals or evangelicals who had voted before (Smidt 1983, table 8). When combined with evidence that a sizable portion of the evangelicals who supported Reagan in 1980 moved back into the Democratic column in the 1982 midterm elections (Rothenberg and Newport 1984, 86), it appears that the New Religious Right has a substantial distance to go before it attains its goal of enlisting orthodox Protestants in a grand conservative coalition.

Why, in spite of the strenuous efforts of the New Christian Right, haven't evangelicals closed ranks to support a resurgent conservatism? As noted in Chapter 4 and continued in studies cited earlier in this chapter, evangelical Protestants may be more conservative than other groups on the social issues that form the basis of the profamily agenda, but these are not the only issues affecting the presidential vote of most citizens. When the focus shifts to other political issues—economic policy, foreign relations, the environment—the evangelicals are not nearly so cohesive, nor do they diverge so much from the attitude patterns of other religious groups.

The explanation for this phenomenon is fairly simple. As emphasized in previous chapters, evangelical churches have traditionally stressed conservative social values on questions of personal conduct, giving their members clear direction about preferred policy in areas such as abortion, homosexual rights, sex roles, drug and alcohol use, and similar controversies. But other social characteristics of evangelical Protestants might be more relevant than religious belief to public issues on which their churches have not traditionally taken official positions. Hence, evangelicals tend to divide along lines of class, region, gender and the like when the issue does not relate to the profamily issue, and sometimes even when it does (Auerbach and Hutcheson 1982; Hohmann 1980; Wald and Lupfer 1983).

This conclusion gains force from an analysis of voting patterns in 1984. According to exit polls (*New York Times*-CBS News 1984a), white evangelicals favored Ronald Reagan by the massive ratio of 80–20, making them approximately 20 percent more Republican than the rest of the electorate. Before concluding that this finding marks the decisive shift to conservatism that the New Religious Right has hoped for, it is important to recognize how many conditions in 1984 favored a Republican trend among theological conservatives. The economic and foreign policy issues that might normally have drawn evangelicals toward the Democrats ran strongly in favor of Republicans in 1984. With no compelling reason to favor the Democrats on issues that traditionally divided the parties, the social issues took on a greater importance for evangelicals (Clymer 1984). In 1984 the Republican platform was clearly much closer to evangelical values on questions like abortion, school prayer, and other issues related to traditional moral values. In addition to issues, the Republicans benefited from public evaluations of candidates. President Reagan strongly emphasized the profamily themes likely to attract evangelicals, whereas Walter Mondale argued strenuously for keeping contentious moral issues off the national agenda (Mondale 1984). To the factors enhancing Republican appeal among white evangelical Protestants in 1984 must be added the Democratic decision to nominate a liberal, northeastern, Catholic woman for the vice-presidency. These factors are not likely to play the same role on the next occasion when voters are asked to choose a president.[7]

Given the magnitude of Ronald Reagan's national victories in both 1980 and 1984, the New Christian Right could not plausibly be credited with a deciding role in the presidential election. Similarly, several voting analysts have refuted claims that the groups were responsible for the defeat of several Democratic senators in 1980 (Lipset and Raab 1981; Zwier 1984). Because small, well-organized groups often enjoy their best opportunities for impact in primary elections with low rates of voter participation, there is some credibility to the claim that evangelicals newly registered by Moral Majority were crucial in the primary defeat of a moderate Republican congressman from Alabama in 1980 (*Congressional Quarterly* 1980). The other election in which evangelical mobilization played an important role, the 1984 contest for the U.S. Senate in North Carolina between incumbent Jesse Helms and challenger Jim Hunt, was probably decided by the massive effort to register white voters from conservative churches. In the Senate, Helms had been one of the strongest and most vociferous advocates of the policies favored by the New Christian Right, earning Falwell's designation as "a national treasure." Countering Democratic efforts to place more blacks on the voter roles, the Helms campaign relied on an organization headed by a Moral Majority state chairman, a minister, to eke out a narrow victory (Johnson and Edsall 1984; Luebke 1985–86). In this contest, as in others in which the religious right may have played a role, it is difficult to sort out the relative contribution of the churches from those of the many other secular interest groups who contributed money and manpower to the conservative candidate.

Against these possible successes, the New Christian Right has suffered some significant defeats. For many Americans, who interpret the concept of church-state separation to mean that ministers should stay out of electoral politics, the public efforts of mobilizing support with religious appeals have been disturbing. These efforts reached a crescendo in 1984 with the well-publicized political activity of black churches, white evangelical groups, and the Catholic bishops. In reaction, the polls registered opposition from the electorate to the entanglement of religion and politics (*New York Times*-CBS News 1984b; *Savannah Evening Press* 1984).

Amid this general recoil from the church-state interaction, the evangelical right drew especially hostile reactions. National polls have revealed Reverend Falwell to be one of the least popular figures on the national political scene and the Moral Majority to suffer from a very negative public image (Miller and Wattenberg 1984, 304; Lipset 1985, 30). As part of a major survey of the electorate conducted during each presidential campaigns, a large sample of Americans is asked to rank a variety of groups on a scale from zero, representing coldness and hostility, to 100, signifying complete approval. In both 1980 and 1984, respondents put "evangelical groups, like the Moral Majority" near the bottom of the list (Perkins 1985). News that Falwell supported the Republican nominee for governor of Virginia was reported to be the "kiss of death" for that candidate (MacPherson 1984, 9). More generally, according to polls in his home state, Falwell's endorsement does more harm than good for statewide candidates (Clendinen 1985). In other states, some recipients of Moral Majority support have tried to keep their distance from the organization, because of its negative image among important segments of the electorate.

In strategic terms, the emergence of the evangelical conservatives presents a danger for the Republicans and a challenge to the Democrats. As noted earlier, evangelical Protestants are particularly responsive to candidates who stress conservative social values, or what has been tagged profamily issues. To get evangelicals firmly into the Republican camp will require a consistent emphasis on these themes, rather than on the issues which divide evangelicals. Yet if the Republicans are to make good on their goal of replacing Democrats as the majority party at all levels of government, they will also have to appeal to the nonevangelical voters, who increasingly seem to be combining social liberalism with economic conservatism (Ladd 1982, chap. 3; Miller and Levitin 1976; Maddox and Lilie 1984).

Young voters and the well-educated members of the post–World War II "baby boom" generation —the critical elements in any contemporary realignment of parties—have been particularly responsive to the conservative economic programs offered by Republicans but decidedly liberal on the social issues (Harwood 1985a). For voters such as these, an emphasis on New Right concerns is likely to be counterproductive (Broder 1984). As the 1984 election illustrated, the Republicans can avoid the dilemma when a strong economy rallies the affluent nonevangelicals and leaves their presidential candidate free to emphasize social issues. But the conflict is likely to come out in full force when the business cycle is less kind to the GOP.

Because all this electoral activity has been aimed at influencing public policy, it is appropriate to examine the success of Christian political action at that level. For the most part, the record has been one of failure. Despite the prodding of the evangelical groups, lobbying by church members, the support of President Reagan, and fear of electoral retribution, the major programs advocated by groups like Moral Majority have not been enacted. The *Roe* v. *Wade* decision on abortion remains in place and has in fact been reaffirmed by the Supreme Court. The Senate voted down a constitutional amendment permitting organized school prayer and has not enacted the tuition tax credit requested by supporters of religious schools.

The symbolic nature of most of the New Christian Right's victories is exemplified by a 1985 Education Department regulation prohibiting local school districts from using certain federal funds to support courses in "secular humanism." As noted above, that term has come to symbolize the philosophy that many evangelical spokesmen regard as the root of American problems—that is, a belief in humanity as the supreme force in the universe. Because secular humanism has been identified as the foundation of such topics as biological evolution, prohibitions on prayer in public schools, and any number of other practices (Eidsmoe 1984, chap. 15), the ruling might seem to have been an important victory. However, the regulation left the concept undefined, and any attempt to specify it would almost certainly fail to pass judicial scrutiny (Barringer 1985). From "victories" such as this, the members of the religious right may have learned, as have other change-oriented persons before them, that the American political system has a genius for resisting external pressure.

Still, evangelical groups have affected national politics in many ways short of changing public policy. As Matthew C. Moen (1985) has argued, the New Christian Right has succeeded in obtaining passage of national legislation offering partial redress of its grievances. In place of organized school prayer, it has received "equal access" for religious group meetings in class. Abortion has not been prohibited, but federal funds no longer support it. The Equal Rights Amendment was defeated once and has a long way to go before it again approaches passage. The failure of the conservative religious groups to get all they want may even have fueled the drive for a new national constitutional convention. At the state and local level, where they are often the best organized groups, local chapters of New Christian Right organizations have carried some of their proposals into law (Pierard and Wright 1984).

Moen also noted that efforts to challenge national policy on social issues has kept those controversies from falling off the national agenda. Finally, the emphasis in New Christian Right rhetoric on traditional values has encouraged politicians of all stripes to discuss those values in the public realm. As illustrated by Governor Mario Cuomo's keynote address to the 1984 Democratic National Convention, both parties have come to believe that there is a political advantage in appeals to moral concerns. These successes were not the kind of outcomes envisioned by the advocates of the profamily agenda, but they did mark progress that should not be disregarded.

THEORIES OF EVANGELICAL MOBILIZATION

Describing the origins and development of the New Christian Right is much easier than explaining it. The emergence of the movement contradicted social science research about the secularization of political conflict and the social and doctrinal basis for evangelical political apathy. Initially caught off guard by the upsurge in evangelical political action, scholars soon began to analyze the new coalition according to theories and concepts that have been applied to similar social movements of the past. Because no single factor is sufficient to explain such an unexpected social development, the responsibility for the New Religious Right must be apportioned among the three facets of religion previously shown to have political relevance: social group, institution, and values.

As a social group, the evangelicals have achieved dramatic gains in socioeconomic status since the end of the World War II (compare McKinney and Roof 1982 with Pope 1953; Lazerwitz 1961; Bogue 1959, 697–709). From the late 1940s through the mid-1950s, white Southern Baptists averaged just under eight years of formal education, and roughly two-thirds did not complete high school. By the 1970s, the average years of school completed by the same group had risen to almost eleven, and the proportion with less than a high school degree declined to substantially less than half. These gains in education signaled the growing presence of evangelicals in urban areas, higher income brackets, and white-collar occupations. Although evangelicals continued to lag behind the rest of the white population on most measures of socioeconomic achievement, the younger members of the community came to resemble mainstream American groups. The development of an evangelical middle class was symbolized by the replacement of modest, ramshackle churches with lavish and well-appointed centers of worship.

This objective gain in economic standing probably helped undercut the evangelical traditions of political apathy and Democratic partisanship. As evangelicals moved into the middle class, they were likely to gain such valuable political resources as increased free time and energy, organizational skills, access to social and communication networks, contacts with government officials, and greater exposure to information. Such resources facilitate the learning of democratic norms and thus encourage political participation (Wolfinger and Rosenstone 1980). With increasing economic standing, evangelicals also tended to acquire more of an interest in the policies of low taxation and limited government unceasingly advocated by the Republican party. As a result of this social transformation, evangelicals emerged in the 1970s with a greater capacity and disposition for political action.

But to explain why evangelicals were mobilized principally on the basis of traditional moral and social values, rather than economic appeals, reference to changes in objective economic achievement do not suffice. For most observers, the critical factor in preparing the ground for the New Christian Right was change in subjective social status. According to the "status politics" model that has been used to explain different types of right-wing political action, moral crusades such as that mounted by the religious right represent a symbolic response by groups to declines in their social prestige (Lipset and Raab 1970, 1981). Joseph Gusfield (1963, 4–5) described the process of status politics in the following terms.

> As his own claim to social respect and honor are diminished, the . . . citizen seeks for public acts through which he may reaffirm the dominance and prestige of his style of life. Converting the sinner to virtue is one way; law is another. Even if the law is not enforced or enforceable, the symbolic import of its passage is important to the reformer. It settles the controversies between those who represent clashing cultures. The public support of one conception of morality at the expense of another enhances the prestige and self-esteem of the victors and degrades the culture of the losers.

The evangelicals, it has been argued, watched with dismay as society turned away from the values represented by traditional morality and opinion leaders appeared to give priority to the interests and aspirations of groups, such as blacks, who had long ranked below them in social esteem. Under this interpretation, resentment of changes in the respect that society paid to devout members of the evangelical community prompted the development and support of movements that pledged "to reestablish, through formal political processes, the social support that the group's values once commanded" (Crawford 1980, 149).

Challenging the assumption that evangelicals were necessarily losing social prestige, some observers have adopted a "symbolic politics" explanation in place of the status politics framework. In this view such movements as the New Christian Right, rather than trying to recapture lost prestige or social honor, have attempted to defend the values, customs, and habits that form the basis of their lifestyle (Conover 1983; Lorentzen 1980; Page and Clelland 1978). Through early training and later participation in group life, evangelicals are exposed to a culture that emphasizes "adherence to traditional norms, respect for family and religious authority, asceticism and control of impulse" (Wood and Hughes 1984, 89). When social policies appeared to challenge this frame of reference by endorsing attacks on religion or encouraging self-indulgence and alternatives to the traditional family, it has been argued, evangelicals fought back by supporting policies more in tune with their cultural values.

Although it is not readily apparent how the distinction between the status politics and symbolic politics frameworks can be assessed in practice, both explanations assert that the roots of evangelical political mobilization can be found in perceived social group interests. To explain why this process did not emerge until the late 1970s, it is necessary to go back to the earlier finding about the movement of evangelicals from a position of deprivation and isolation to the socioeconomic mainstream. Increasing educational levels gave evangelicals the political skills necessary to assert their claims in the public sphere, while urbanization increased the possibility that they would encounter cultural values that challenged their inherited beliefs. The objective and subjective social forces thus interacted to foster the New Christian Right.

The role of religious institutions was also important in this regard. The social transformation of evangelicals produced a major emphasis on what was called church planting. The so-called "super churches," such as Jerry Falwell's Thomas Road Baptist Church, took on a wide range of functions and developed into religious equivalents of major corporations (Fitzgerald 1981). Less ambitious local churches also began to provide a wide array of services for their members. As the ministry became more professional, the seminaries produced clerical leaders who managed church entry into such fields as education, day-care, and counseling. The evolution of the churches from places of worship to social service centers brought them under the authority of government regulations affecting zoning, educational practices (curriculum content, teacher certification, desegregation mandates, tax-exempt status), day care facilities, minimum wage laws, and working conditions. The result was a series of classic confrontations between the state's interest in regulating the private provision of social services and the church's claims of immunity under the free exercise clause. With such substantial investments, the churches could no longer afford a policy of political disengagement.

The rapid expansion of the "electronic church" was another manifestation of evangelical growth that stimulated political involvement (Hadden and Swann 1981). According to recent figures (Hadden 1984, 162–63; Rifkin 1979, 99–108), more than 1,000 radio stations and sixty-five television stations currently are devoted exclusively to religious broadcasting. Three "Christian" television networks now broadcast around the clock, and several others offer similar programming for parts of the day; together, these networks reach an audience estimated at 25 million people. Still more such activity can be expected with the growth of cable television coverage and the proliferation of low-power television stations. Because the airwaves are regulated by the Federal Communications Commission, religious broadcasters have a natural interest in government decision-making.

The growth of evangelical institutions affected not only the interests but also the political capacity of the religious right. Social movements depend on access to potential supporters and to resources that can be pressed into the services of movement goals. Potentially powerful political forces in their own environment, local evangelical churches are also aligned with central organizations that can coordinate nationwide political action. Part of Moral Majority's strength has lain its direct access to local preachers through the network of churches affiliated with the Baptist Bible Fellowship (Liebman 1983). Television evangelists have direct access to viewers and the capacity to tap into mailing lists with millions of names. Not surprisingly in view of these resources, the major political movements targeting evangelicals were initiated by pastors with access to vast broadcasting empires. Jerry Falwell of Moral Majority has his *Old Time Gospel Hour,* the Christian Voice was connected to the Reverend Pat Robertson's Christian Broadcasting Network, and the Roundtable's leading spokesman, James Robison, had a nationally syndicated program.

Of course, reliance on broadcasting and national church alliances cannot guarantee success in political life. As some of the liberal clergy had already discovered, an evangelist who preaches politics instead of the Gospel may lose those in the audience who want religion to address their spiritual concerns. Moreover, constant demands for funds may produce decreasing returns from a weary audience. The local churches that serve as the base of operations for the New Religious Right, finally, may fiercely resist attempts at central coordination, fragmenting the energy of the group and giving unwanted publicity to loose cannons such as the

Moral Majority chapter head from California who publicly advocated the execution of homosexuals (Clendenen 1984; Perry 1981).

The third aspect of religion, theology and values, has also played a part in stimulating the New Christian Right. The new willingness of evangelicals to apply their religious values to public policy has been especially puzzling to the social theorists who used to explain evangelical abstention from politics by citing religious values. How could a theology that once emphasized otherworldliness and personal salvation now become a basis for political activism? Of course, as the case of the Reverend Bob Jones demonstrated, not all evangelicals have approved of the new political activism; enough have embraced it, however, to lend urgency to the problem.

Robert Wuthnow (1983) has suggested that in engaging in politics, the evangelicals were responding to changes in society that encouraged the application of religious values to public policy. At the national level, several trends blurred the traditional view of "morality" as a matter largely for individual behavior, and thus raised new public concern about the ethical standards of public institutions. As evidence of the growing trend to approach public policy from an ethical viewpoint, Wuthnow cited "criticism of the Vietnam war as an act of public immorality, the various legislative actions taken in the aftermath of Watergate to institutionalize morality as a matter of official concern, and major Supreme Court decisions symbolically linking government with morality" (1983, 176). Ironically, Jimmy Carter helped point the way for evangelicals when he hinged his 1976 campaign on the need to restore trust, honesty, and morality to American public life. All these developments reflected growing recognition that government should not be totally independent of moral considerations and paved the way for morally based criticism of national policy.

Few groups were as receptive to this approach as the evangelicals. Contrary to their historical image, evangelicals have a long tradition of fighting back against perceived assaults by public authority on their favored social values. In the past, this tendency had surfaced mostly in local conflicts over issues such as liquor licensing, sex education, and pornography. In the 1970s, however, the challenge appeared to emanate from a national government that seemingly had loosened restraints in hundreds of ways. Faced with a Supreme Court that reduced limits on public expressions of sexuality and an administration that allowed homosexuals to meet with a presidential assistant, evangelicals felt their values under siege in the national arena.

The actions of secular authority not only offended traditional moral values—which was reason enough to act—but also seemed to threaten the ability of evangelicals to protect themselves and their families from corrupting influences. Encouraged by the politicizing of morality exhibited in reaction to civil rights, Vietnam, and Watergate, theological conservatives sought to apply the same moral outrage to social policy questions. And to prosecute the crusade, they could call upon an increasingly affluent constituency through several organizational channels.

*   *   *   *   *

With the New Christian Right, as with other political movements, things are not always as they seem to be. Its magnitude and impact have not been so immense as supporters have claimed nor so insignificant as opponents would like to believe. In terms of origins the movement may be new, but it draws upon well-established traditions of American life. Some observers have even interpreted the new Christian conservatism as an attempt to revitalize the civil religion discussed in Chapter 3. The idea of the United States as a redeemer nation and its people as "chosen" to lead humankind took a severe beating from the traumas of the 1960s and 1970s. These developments may have accelerated an ongoing shift in cultural values that undermined the moral consensus in American society (Anthony and Robbins 1983). Hence, in a 1975 book describing the status of civil religion, Robert Bellah referred to the "broken covenant." By insisting on official support of traditional moral values and of the view of the United States as a nation under divine judgment, the leaders of the New Christian Right have sounded themes with a strong civil religious orientation. As I argued when the concept of civil religion first came up in Chapter 3, that tradition has both noble and seamy aspects.

Looking toward the next decade, the New Christian Right appears well placed to maintain a major role in American political life. The alliance between organized religious conservatives and the Republican party has remained intact for about a decade. In the assessment of *Washington Post* reporter Thomas Edsall (1985, 8), "The muscle of the Christian right in the GOP is roughly parallel to the power of the AFL-CIO or the NEA within the Democratic Party." If it seems excessive to equate the power of the conservative evangelicals to that of traditional Democratic power brokers, Edsall reported estimates from Republican officials that members of the Christian right may claim one in five seats at the party's 1988 national convention. The organizational skills that have enabled the Christian conservatives to defeat moderates in many state parties are precisely those required for success in the complex process of delegate selection to national conventions. Hence the prediction by some Republicans that the New Christian Right will have a determining voice in the identity of the 1988 nominee and the shape of the party's platform.

As the newest players in the game of national politics, the evangelical Protestants have attracted most of the attention of trend spotters. But the evangelicals have not been the only religious group to reassess traditional political loyalties. As the next chapter will make clear, Catholics also have undergone a profound political transition, at the same time that mainline Protestant churches have appeared to lose enthusiasm for constant political engagement. Only black Protestants and Jews seem to have resisted pressures for political change.

NOTES

[1]It is worth emphasizing that "evangelicalism" is used here to identify a particular orientation to religion rather than a specific set of denominations. Over time, the evangelical impulse was accentuated by some denominations and lost influence in others.

[2]It is very difficult to find information about the political behavior of northern evangelicals after the 1920s. John Hammond's (1979) study of the revivalist ethos in Ohio and New York suggested that northern evangelicals remained politically distinctive in their support for restrictive social policies and high level of Republicanism.

[3]Unpublished studies by Damaske (1970), Freeman (1962), George (1971), and Reinhardt (1974) did document the political conservatism of evangelicals, but their findings do not seem to have made their way into the mainstream of electoral analysis.

[4]There are also a large number of groups that attempt to apply a Christian perspective in particular policy areas such as education or defense. The efforts of these specialized groups may well feed into the comprehensive organizations or be coordinated by them.

[5]See the studies by Barrett and Harris 1982; Buell and Sigelman 1985; Baker, Epstein, and Furth 1981; Patel, Pilant, and Rose 1982, 1985; Penfield and Davis 1981; Tamney and Johnson 1983; Wilcox 1983; Yinger and Cutler 1982; Shupe and Stacey 1983; Wald and Lupfer 1983.

[6]These findings are from an unpublished study that I conducted with Michael Lupfer.

[7]In the most comprehensive account of evangelical voting patterns in 1984, Corwin Smidt (1985) also found mixed evidence about trends toward Republicanism. Although he detected some movement toward the GOP among young evangelicals, he found little change among southerners and a decline in participation among evangelicals from that region.

REFERENCES

Allinsmith, Wesley, and Beverly Allinsmith. 1948. "Religious Affiliation and Politico-Economic Attitude: A Study of Eight Major U.S. Religious Groups." *Public Opinion Quarterly.* 12: 377–389.

Anthony, Dick, and Thomas Robbins. 1983. "Spiritual Innovation and the Crisis of American Civil Religion." In *Religion and America,* ed. Mary Douglas and Steven M. Tipton. Boston, MA: Beacon Press, 229–248.

Arrington, Theodore S., and Patricia A. Kyle. 1978. "Equal Rights Amendment Activists in North Carolina." *Signs.* 3: 666–680.

Associated Press. 1984. "Falwell: Moral Majority Was Crucial to Reagan's Landslide." *Gainesville Sun.* November 9: 10B.

Auerbach, Jill L., and John D. Hutcheson, Jr. 1982. "Issue Constraint and the Religious New Right." Paper prepared for the Citadel Conference on Southern Politics, Charleston, SC.

Baker, Ross K., Laurily K. Epstein, and Rodney D. Furth. 1981. "Matters of Life and Death: Social, Political, and Religious Correlates of Attitudes on Abortion." *American Politics Quarterly.* 9: 89–102.

Baker, Tod A., Robert P. Steed, and Laurence W. Moreland, editors. 1983. *Religion and Politics in the South: Mass and Elite Perspectives.* New York: Praeger.

Barrett, Sharon W., and Richard J. Harris. 1982. "Recent Changes in Predictors of Abortion Attitudes." *Sociology and Social Research.* 66: 320–334.

Barringer, Felicity. 1985. "A Ban on Teaching 'Secular Humanism.' " *Washington Post National Weekly Edition.* January 28: 32.

Bergstrom, Charles V., and David Saperstein. 1984. "God and Politics." *Washington Post National Weekly Edition.* September 10: 28.

Blumenthal, Sidney. 1984. "The Righteous Empire." *New Republic.* 191: 18–24.

Bogue, Donald J. 1959. *The Population of the United States.* New York: Free Press of Glencoe.

Boles, Janet K. 1979. *The Politics of the Equal Rights Amendment.* New York: Longman.

Brady, David W., and Kent L. Tedin. 1976. "Ladies in Pink: Religious and Political Ideology in the Anti-ERA Movement." *Social Science Quarterly.* 56: 564–575.

Broder, David S. 1984. "In Oregon, Voting for President Means Choosing the Lesser Evil." *Washington Post National Weekly Edition.* September 24: 12.

Bryant, Anita. 1977. *The Anita Bryant Story.* Old Tappan, NJ: Fleming H. Revell Company.

Buell, Emett H., and Lee Sigelman. 1985. "An Army That Meets Every Sunday? Popular Support for the Moral Majority in 1980." *Social Science Quarterly.* 66: 426–434.

Burner, David. 1967. *The Democratic Party in Transition.* New York: W.W. Norton.

Burnham, Walter Dean. 1968. "American Voting Behavior and the 1964 Election." *Midwest Journal of Political Science.* 12: 1–40.

Clabaugh, Gary K. 1974. *Thunder on the Right: The Protestant Fundamentalists.* Chicago, IL: Nelson-Hall.

Clendinen, Dudley. 1985. "Virginia Polls and Politicians Indicate Falwell Is Slipping in His Home State." *New York Times.* November 24: 1.

Clendinen, Dudley. 1984. "Spurred by White House Parley, TV Evangelists Spread Political Word." *New York Times.* September 10: 1.

Clymer, Adam. 1984. "Religion and Politics Mix Poorly for Democrats." *Gainesville Sun.* November 25: 5B.

Congressional Quarterly. 1980. "Lobbying for Christ." *Congressional Quarterly Weekly Report.* September 6: 2627–2634.

Conover, Pamela Johnston. 1983. "The Mobilization of the New Right: A Test of Various Explanations." *Western Political Quarterly.* 36: 632–649.

Conover, Pamela Johnston, and Virginia Gray. 1983. *Feminism and the New Right: Conflict over the Family.* New York: Praeger.

Converse, Philip E. 1966. "Religion and Politics: The 1960 Election." In *Elections and the Political Order,* ed. Angus Campbell, Philip E. Converse, Warren E. Miller, and Donald Stokes. New York: John Wiley, 96–124.

Crawford, Alan. 1980. *Thunder on the Right.* New York: Pantheon.

Crespi, Irving. 1971. "Structural Sources of the George Wallace Candidacy." *Social Science Quarterly.* 52: 115–132.

D'Souza, Dinesh. 1984. "Will the Christian Right Help Reagan?" *Washington Post.* August 19: 1, 4B.

Damaske, Frederick Hans. 1970. "Sects and Politics: The Political Attitudes and Behavior of Conservative-Evangelical and Neo-Fundamentalist Protestants." Ph.D. thesis, Department of Political Science, University of Minnesota.

Davis, James A. 1984. *General Social Surveys, 1972–1984: Cumulative Codebook.* Chicago, IL: National Opinion Research Center.

Dawidowicz, Lucy S., and Leon J. Goldstein. 1974. *Politics in a Pluralist Democracy: Studies of Voting in the 1960 Election.* Westport, CT: Greenwood Press. Reprint of 1963 edition.

Dickenson, James R. 1984. "Religion Is Powerful GOP Theme." *Washington Post.* August 24: 8A.

Duggan, Lisa. 1985. "The War on Pornography Makes Strange Bedfellows." *Washington Post Weekly Edition.* September 16: 24–25.

Edsall, Thomas B. 1985. "Pulpit Power: Converting the GOP. *Washington Post National Weekly Edition.* July 8: 8–9.

Eidsmoe, John. 1984. *God and Caesar.* Westchester, IL: Crossway Books.

Fackre, Gabriel. 1982. *The Religious Right and Christian Faith.* Grand Rapids, MI: William B. Eerdmans.

Fitzgerald, Frances. 1981. "A Disciplined, Charging Army." *New Yorker.* 57: 53–141.

Fowler, Robert Booth. 1982. *A New Engagement: Evangelical Political Thought, 1966–1976.* Grand Rapids, MI: William B. Eerdmans.

Freeman, Donald M. 1962. "Religion and Southern Politics: A Study of the Political Behavior of Southern White Protestants." Ph.D. thesis, Department of Political Science, University of North Carolina.

Gallup, George, Jr. 1981. "Divining the Devout: The Polls and Religious Belief." *Public Opinion.* 4: 20, 41.

George, John H. 1971. "The Collegiate Silent Majority: Social Class, Religion, and Politics." Ph.D. thesis, Department of Political Science, University of Oklahoma.

Goff, Robert O. 1977. "The Washington County Schoolbook Controversy: The Political Implications of a Social and Religious Conflict." Ph.D. thesis, Catholic University of America.

Grupp, Fred W., and William M. Newman. 1973. "Political Ideology and Religious Preference: The John Birch Society and the Americans for Democratic Action." *Journal for the Scientific Study of Religion.* 4: 401–413.

Gusfield, Joseph. 1963. *Symbolic Crusade: Status Politics and the American Temperance Movement.* Urbana, IL: University of Illinois Press.

Guth, James. 1985. "The Christian Right Revisited: Partisan Realignment Among Southern Baptist Ministers." Paper presented to the annual meeting of the Midwest Political Science Association, Chicago, IL.

Guth, James. 1983a. "Preachers and Politics: Varieties of Activism Among Southern Baptist Ministers." In *Religion and Politics in the South,* ed. Tod A. Baker, Robert P. Steed, and Laurence W. Moreland. New York: Praeger, 161–183.

Guth, James. 1983b. "Southern Baptist Clergy: Vanguard of the Christian Right?" In *The New Christian Right,* ed. Robert C. Liebman and Robert Wuthnow. New York: Aldine, 117–130.

Hadden, Jeffrey. 1984. "Televangelism and the Future of American Politics." In *New Christian Politics,* ed. David G. Bromley and Anson Shupe. Macon, GA: Mercer University Press, 151–165.

Hadden, Jeffrey K., and Charles Swann. 1981. *Prime Time Preachers.* Reading, MA: Addison-Wesley.

Hammond, John L. 1979. *The Politics of Benevolence: Revival Religion and American Voting Behavior.* Norwood, NJ: Ablex.

Harwood, John. 1985a. "Religious Right, GOP Sometimes Spar." *St. Petersburg Times.* January 28: 8A.

Harwood, John. 1985b. "The 'Arrival' of Jerry Falwell." *St. Petersburg Times.* January 28: 1, 8A.

Hibbs, Douglas A., Jr. 1982. "President Reagan's Mandate from the 1980 Elections: A Shift to the Right?" *American Political Quarterly.* 10: 387–420.

Hill, Samuel S., and Dennis E. Owen. 1982. *The New Religious Political Right in America.* Nashville, TN: Abingdon.

Himmelstein, Jerome L., and James A. McRae, Jr. 1984. "Social Conservatism, New Republicans, and the 1980 Election." *Public Opinion Quarterly.* 48: 592–605.

Hohmann, Ann A. 1980. "Political Conservatism and Fundamentalist Christianity: A Reexamination." Paper presented to the annual meeting of the Midwest Political Science Association, Chicago, IL.

Hunter, James Davison. 1983. "The Liberal Reaction." In *The New Christian Right,* ed. Robert C. Liebman and Robert Wuthnow. New York: Aldine, 150–167.

Jenkinson, Edward B. 1979. *Censors in the Classroom: The Mind Benders.* New York: Avon Books.

Johnson, Haynes, and Thomas B. Edsall. 1984. "North Carolina's Three Rs: Race, Religion, and Registration." *Washington Post National Weekly Edition.* October 15: 12–13.

Jorstad, Erling. 1981. *Evangelicals in the White House: The Cultural Maturation of Born-Again Christianity, 1960–1981.* New York: Edwin Meller Press.

Jorstad, Erling. 1970. *The Politics of Doomsday.* Nashville, TN: Abingdon.

Kellstedt, Lyman A. 1985. "The Falwell 'Platform': An Analysis of Its Causes and Consequences." Paper presented to the annual meeting of the Society for the Scientific Study of Religion, Savannah, GA.

Kellstedt, Lyman A. 1984. "Religion and Politics: The Measurement of Evangelicalism." Paper presented to the annual meeting of the American Political Science Association, Washington, DC.

Kellstedt, Lyman A., and Corwin Smidt. 1985. "Defining and Measuring Fundamentalism: An Analysis of Different Conceptual and Operational Strategies." Paper delivered to the annual meeting of the American Political Science Association, New Orleans, LA.

Kleppner, Paul. 1979. *The Third Electoral System, 1853–1892.* Chapel Hill, NC: University of North Carolina Press.

Knoke, David. 1976. *Change and Continuity in American Politics: The Social Bases of Political Parties.* Baltimore, MD: Johns Hopkins University Press.

Ladd, Everett Carll. 1982. *Where Have All the Voters Gone?* Second edition. New York: W. W. Norton.

Ladd, Everett Carll, Jr., with Charles D. Hadley. 1975. *Transformations of the American Party System.* New York: W. W. Norton.

Lazerwitz, Bernard. 1961. "A Comparison of Major United States Religious Groups." *Journal of the American Statistical Association.* 56: 568–579.
Leuchtenburg, William E. 1958. *The Perils of Prosperity, 1914–1932.* Chicago, IL: University of Chicago Press.
Levine, Lawrence W. 1975. *Defender of the Faith: William Jennings Bryan—The Last Decade, 1915–1925.* New York: Oxford University Press.
Liebman, Robert C. 1983. "Mobilizing the Moral Majority." In *The New Christian Right,* ed. Robert C. Liebman and Robert Wuthnow. New York: Aldine, 50–73.
Lipset, Seymour Martin. 1985. "The Elections, the Economy, and Public Opinion: 1984." *PS.* 18: 28–38.
Lipset, Seymour Martin. 1960. *Political Man.* Garden City, NY: Doubleday-Anchor.
Lipset, Seymour Martin, and Earl Raab. 1981. "The Election and the Evangelicals." *Commentary.* 71: 25–31.
Lipset, Seymour Martin, and Earl Raab. 1970. *The Politics of Unreason.* New York: Harper and Row.
Lorentzen, Louise J. 1980. "Evangelical Life-Style Concerns Expressed in Political Action." *Sociological Analysis.* 41: 144–154.
Luebke, Paul. 1985–86. "Grass-Roots Organizing: The Hidden Side of the 1984 Helms Campaign." *Election Politics.* 3: 30–33.
MacPherson, Myra. 1984. "Jerry Falwell: The Teflon Preacher." *Washington Post National Weekly Edition.* October 15: 8–9.
Maddox, William S., and Stuart A. Lilie. 1984. *Beyond Liberal and Conservative: Reassessing the Political Spectrum.* Washington, DC: Cato Institute.
McKinney, William, and Wade Clark Roof. 1982. "A Social Profile of American Religious Groups." In *Yearbook of American and Canadian Churches 1982,* ed. Constant H. Jacquet, Jr. Nashville, TN: Abingdon, 267–273.
Menendez, Albert J. 1977. *Religion at the Polls.* Philadelphia, PA: Westminster Press.
Miller, Arthur H., and Martin P. Wattenberg. 1984. "Politics from the Pulpit: Religiosity and the 1980 Elections." *Public Opinion Quarterly.* 48: 301–317.
Miller, Warren E., and Teresa E. Levitin. 1976. *Leadership and Change: Presidential Elections from 1952 to 1976.* Cambridge, MA: Winthrop.
Miller, Warren E., Arthur H. Miller, and Edward J. Schneider. 1980. *American National Election Studies Data Sourcebook, 1952–1978.* Cambridge, MA: Harvard University Press.
Moen, Matthew C. 1985. "Religion and the Congressional Agenda." *Extensions.* Spring: 7–8.
Mondale, Walter. 1984. "Religion Is a Private Matter." *Church and State.* 37: 12–14.
Monroe, Ann. 1985. "Devout Dissidents." *Wall Street Journal.* May 24: 1, 16.
Mueller, Carol. 1983. "In Search of a Constituency for the 'New Religious Right.' " *Public Opinion Quarterly.* 47: 213–229.
Mueller, Carol, and Thomas Dimieri. 1982. "The Structure of Belief Systems Among Contending ERA Activists." *Social Forces.* 60: 657–675.
New York Times. 1980. "Evangelical Group Disagrees with 276 in Congress." *New York Times.* November 2: 34.
New York Times and CBS News. 1984a. "Portrait of the Electorate." *New York Times.* November 8: 11.
New York Times and CBS News. 1984b. "Voters Found Uneasy over Religion as Issue." *New York Times.* September 19: 13.

Oldendick, Robert, and Stephen E. Bennett. 1978. "The Wallace Factor: Constancy and Cooptation." *American Politics Quarterly.* 6: 469–484.

Orum, Anthony M., and Edward W. McCrane. 1970. "Class, Tradition, and Partisan Alignments in a Southern Urban Electorate." *Journal of Politics.* 32: 156–176.

Page, Ann, and Donald Clelland. 1978. "The Kanawha County Textbook Controversy: A Study in Alienation and Lifestyle Concern." *Social Forces.* 57: 265–281.

Patel, Kant, Denny Pilant, and Gary L. Rose. 1985. "Christian Conservatism: A Study in Alienation and Life Style Concerns." *Journal of Political Studies.* 12: 17–30.

Patel, Kant, Denny Pilant, and Gary L. Rose. 1982. "Born-Again Christians in the Bible Belt." *American Politics Quarterly.* 10: 255–272.

Penfield, Irvin H., and Natalie Davis. 1981. "The Religious Right: A Southern Phenomenon?" Paper presented to the annual meeting of the Southern Political Science Association, Memphis, TN.

Perkins, Jerry. 1985. "The Moral Majority as a Political Reference in the 1980 and 1984 Elections." Paper presented to the annual meeting of the Society for the Scientific Study of Religion, Savannah, GA.

Perry, James M. 1981. "The Moral Majority Finds Its Own Units May Need Guidance." *Wall Street Journal.* February 12: 1, 17.

Phillips, Kevin P. 1982. *Post-Conservative America.* New York: Vintage Books.

Pierard, Richard V. 1983a. "From Evangelical Exclusiveness to Ecumenical Openness: Billy Graham and Socio-Political Issues." *Journal of Ecumenical Studies.* 20: 425–446.

Pierard, Richard V. 1983b. "Reagan and the Evangelicals: The Making of a Love Affair." *Christian Century.* 100: 1182–1185.

Pierard, Richard V., and James L. Wright. 1984. "No Hoosier Hospitality for Humanism: The Moral Majority in Indiana." In *New Christian Politics,* ed. David G. Bromley and Anson Shupe. Macon, GA: Mercer University Press, 195–212.

Pool, Ithiel de Sola, Robert P. Abelson, and Samuel Popkin. 1965. *Candidates, Issues, and Strategies.* Cambridge, MA: MIT Press.

Pope, Liston. 1953. "Religion and the Class Structure." In *Class, Status, and Power,* ed. Reinhard Bendix and Seymour Martin Lipset. New York: Free Press of Glencoe, 316–323.

Pressman, Steven. 1984. "Religious Right: Trying to Link Poll Power and Lobby Muscle." *Congressional Quarterly Weekly Report.* September 22: 2315–2319.

Public Opinion. 1985. "Southern Whites: The Great Conversion." *Public Opinion.* 7: 34.

Reagan, Ronald. 1984. "Religion and Politics Are Necessarily Related." *Church and State.* 37: 9–11.

Reinhardt, Robert Melvin. 1975. "The Political Behavior of West Virginia Protestant Fundamentalist Sectarians." Ph.D. thesis, Department of Political Science, West Virginia University.

Ribuffo, Leo. 1983. *The Old Christian Right.* Philadelphia, PA: Temple University Press.

Richburg, Keith R. 1986. "Public Schools and the Politics of Curriculum." *Washington Post Weekly Edition.* January 20: 14–15.

Rifkin, Jeremy, with Ted Howard. 1979. *The Emerging Order.* New York: Ballantine.

Rothenberg, Stuart, and Frank Newport. 1984. *The Evangelical Voter.* Washington, DC: Free Congress Research and Education Foundation.

Savannah Evening Press. 1984. "Do Politics and Religion Mix?" *Savannah Evening Press.* November 2: 26.

Schneider, William. 1984. "An Uncertain Consensus." *National Journal.* November 10: 2130–2132.

Shriver, Peggy. 1981. *The Bible Vote.* New York: Pilgrim Press.

Shupe, Anson, and William Stacey. 1983. "The Moral Majority Constituency." In *The New Christian Right,* ed. Robert C. Liebman and Robert Wuthnow. New York: Aldine, 104–117.

Simon, Paul. 1984. *The Glass House: Politics and Morality in the Nation's Capital.* New York: Continuum.

Simpson, John H. 1983. "Moral Issues and Status Politics." In *The New Christian Right,* ed. Robert C. Liebman and Robert Wuthnow. New York: Aldine, 188–207.

Smidt, Corwin. 1985. "Evangelicals and the 1984 Election: Continuity or Change?" Paper presented to the annual meeting of the Society for the Scientific Study of Religion, Savannah, GA.

Smidt, Corwin. 1983. "Born-Again Politics: The Political Behavior of Evangelical Christians in the South and Non-South." In *Religion and Politics in the South,* ed. Tod A. Baker, Robert P. Steed, and Laurence W. Moreland. New York: Praeger, 27–56.

Smith, Tom W. 1982. "General Liberalism and Social Change in Post–World War II America: A Summary of Trends." *Social Indicators Research.* 10: 1–28.

Spring, Beth. 1984. "Some Christian Leaders Want Further Political Activism." *Christianity Today.* 28: 46–49.

Tamney, Joseph, and Stephen D. Johnson. 1983. "The Moral Majority in Middletown." *Journal for the Scientific Study of Religion.* 22: 145–157.

Tedin, Kent L. 1978. "Religious Preference and Pro/Anti Activism on the Equal Rights Amendment Issue." *Pacific Sociological Review.* 21: 55–66.

Tedin, Kent L., and others. 1977. "Social Background and Political Differences Between Pro- and Anti-ERA Activists." *American Politics Quarterly.* 5: 395–408.

United Press International. 1984. "Moral Scorecard." *Washington Post.* August 18: 13A.

Wald, Kenneth D., and Michael B. Lupfer. 1983. "Religion and Politics in the Urban South." In *Religion and Politics in the South: Mass and Elite Perspectives,* ed. Tod A. Baker, Robert P. Steed, and Laurence W. Moreland. New York: Praeger, 84–102.

Warner, R. Stephen. 1979. "Theoretical Barriers to the Understanding of Evangelical Christianity." *Sociological Analysis.* 40: 1–9.

Wilcox, Clyde. 1983. "The New Christian Right: Patterns of Political Belief." Paper presented to the annual meeting of the Midwest Political Science Association, Chicago, IL.

Wolfinger, Raymond E., and Steven J. Rosenstone. 1980. *Who Votes?* New Haven, CT: Yale University Press.

Wood, Michael, and Michael Hughes. 1984. "The Moral Basis of Moral Reform: Status Discontent vs. Cultural Socialization as Explanations of Anti-Pornography Social Movement Adherence." *American Sociological Review.* 49: 86–99.

Wuthnow, Robert. 1983. "The Political Rebirth of American Evangelicals." In

The New Christian Right, ed. Robert C. Liebman and Robert Wuthnow. New York: Aldine, 168–187.

Yinger, J. Milton, and Stephen J. Cutler. 1982. "The Moral Majority Viewed Sociologically." *Sociological Focus.* 15: 289–306.

Zwier, Robert. 1984. "The New Christian Right and the 1980 Elections." In *New Christian Politics,* ed. David G. Bromley and Anson Shupe. Macon, GA: Mercer University Press, 173–174.

8

Continuity and Change Outside the Evangelical Camp

The last few years have been marked by great ferment in the relationship between religion and American political life. As previous chapters have demonstrated, religious issues and controversies have assumed much greater importance in politcal debate than they had commanded previously. With public attention so concentrated on attempts to forge the evangelical Protestants into a cohesive voting bloc, it has been easy to lose sight of the constant pressures for political change that were also faced by the majority of Americans affiliated with nonevangelical churches. Like the evangelicals, the other major religious groups in America have also been encouraged to modify various aspects of their traditional political patterns and to increase their level of involvement in public affairs. The response of the various nonevangelical groups to a changing political environment is the subject of this chapter.

After a period of dramatic internal change, the Catholic church has shed its predictable conservatism, especially on foreign and military policy, to adopt a new role as gadfly and activist on a wide range of issues. Although Catholic thought has moved generally to the left, the church fathers have also maintained a staunchly conservative outlook on the issue of abortion. In the process, members of the Catholic clergy have largely replaced the ministers from mainline Protestantism as the leading political activists among the clergy. The mainline denominations in American Protestantism, once the driving force for many social reform campaigns, seem to have pulled back somewhat from active engagement in the political realm. The patterns of black politics have shifted the least, with Protestant clergy continuing to play a leading role as spokesmen for the minority community. And Jews, though still a mainstay of left-wing thought, have experienced occasionally strained relationships with other members of the liberal coalition.

In examining the new political tendencies of American religious groups, I will put great emphasis on the role of religious leaders. In many religious communities, the clergy take the lead in defining institutional interests and applying theology to public issues. If social change alters the perspective of church members, the impact will usually register first with the ministry. Hence, my discussion of general trends in the political behavior of religious groups would be incomplete without close attention to the trends exhibited by members of the clergy. At the same time, it is important to recognize that religious leaders do not control the political perspectives of church members. Rather, in their attempt to shape the political outlook of coreligionists, ministers compete for influence with secular politicians, the media, and many other organized groups. The political attitudes of congregants are also shaped by personal experiences and the perspectives derived from living in a variety of social contexts that cannot be manipulated by the church. In each religious group under study here, even the most centralized and hierarchical, some discrepancy between the attitudes of the religious elite and the views from the pews is inevitable.

CATHOLICISM: THE CONSERVATIVE POLITICAL HERITAGE

For persons whose impression of Catholic politics has been formed by the recent pastoral letters on nuclear war and the economy issued by the American bishops or by the antiwar activities of the radical Jesuit priests the Berrigan brothers, it may be hard to imagine just how radically the situation has changed in a short time. For most of the twentieth century, the Catholic church in the United States was closly associated with conservative political causes. Although that political tradition has not been extinguished—as testified to by the national prominence of Catholic conservatives like Richard Vigurie, Terry Dolan, Phyllis Schlafly, William F. Buckley, and Henry Hyde—it must compete for Catholic allegiance with a liberal tradition represented by Mario Cuomo, Geraldine Ferraro, Edward Kennedy, and Thomas P. "Tip" O'Neill. As we saw in Chapter 4, Catholic attitudes on most issues now cluster around the middle of the American political spectrum. This leftward shift among Catholics has been every bit as substantial as the more publicized right-wing movement of the Protestant evangelicals.

The traditional pattern of Catholic politics in the United States was epitomized by the career of Francis Cardinal Spellman, from 1939 to 1967 the archbishop of New York. As head of the major Catholic center in the United States and a person of considerable persuasive ability, he imposed a distinctly conservative tilt to the church's effort to influence the public realm. Intensely anticommunist, suspicious of the civil rights and labor

movements, and a strong advocate of government efforts to prohibit public displays of "immorality," Spellman forged strong links between the
church and leaders of secular-conservative movements. Under his influences, a biographer has reported (Cooney 1984), the Catholic hierarchy
enthusiastically endorsed the active involvement of the United States in
military conflicts wherever communism was thought to be a threat. From
Spain in the 1930s through Vietnam in the 1960s, Spellman consistently
favored a policy that has been satirized by the phrase "Praise the Lord
and pass the ammunition."

Although it is difficult to sort out cause and effect, an exhaustive
review of polling data by Seymour Martin Lipset (1964) concluded that
Spellman's views on world affairs were echoed by rank-and-file members
of the church. Two major ultranationalistic mass movements of the twentieth century, the Couglinite and McCarthy crusades, were led by Catholics and drew somewhat more support from Roman Catholics than from
other religious groups.[1] The John Birch Society, a right-wing organization
that gained notoriety in the 1960s, also appears to have drawn greater
backing from Catholics than from the population at large.[2] Because all
these movements enjoyed substantial support from Protestants and were
opposed by some Catholics, their special appeal to Catholics should not
be exaggerated (Crosby 1978). Nonetheless, when compared to the rest
of the population, Catholics exhibited greater readiness to support
American military involvement around the globe.

The same militaristic tendency was apparent among the young Catholic college students who participated in a number of studies about attitudes toward the use of force in international politics. In a 1952 survey of
almost 3,000 students on eleven university campuses, Peter Blau (1953)
found that devout Catholics scored higher than other religious groups on
a scale measuring emphasis upon power (rather than cooperation) in
world affairs. When a similar study was conducted in 1967 by Connors
and associates (1968), the same pattern was noted. Among approximately
1,000 students from four eastern colleges, Catholics exhibited the most
warlike attitudes. In both studies, which controlled for social characteristics associated with religion, the disposition to support the use of force
was greatest among Catholics who were most deeply attached to the
church and exposed to Catholic institutions (but see Starr, [1975] for
evidence that religious involvement was not important).

The strong conservatism evinced by American Catholics during the
time of Spellman's reign as the "American pope" can be explained in terms
of group interests, social standing, and theology. In many of the countries
where communism seemed about to gain power, the Catholic church had
been a dominant social force and often a political factor of immense significance. As such, communism represented not just a set of economic arrangements, but also a fundamental threat to the established power of Catholic
institutions. The outspokenly antireligious opinions of communist leaders

and the active persecution of the church wherever communism had come to power further inflamed Catholic opinion, thus giving Catholics a tangible reason to oppose the expansion of communist influence.

In a controversial hypothesis that has never been fully tested, the appeal of anticommunism has also been traced to the insecure social status of Catholic immigrants and their families. As the historian Richard Hofstadter (1965) speculated in an essay first published during the 1950s, immigration can create status problems that can be resolved by expressing love of country in extreme ways. During the period of immigration, militant native-stock citizens, mainly Protestants, had impugned the "Americanism" of Catholic immigrants, leaving the victims with a strong desire to prove their worthiness. Even immigrants who embraced their new country with full and unconditional loyalty might also have been "troubled by the thought that since their forebears have already abandoned one country, one allegiance, their own national allegiance might be considered fickle" (Hofstadter 1965, 59). To reassure themselves and others that this reputation for disloyalty was not warranted, Hofstadter suggested, Catholic immigrants and their descendants flocked to patriotic societies and veterans' groups, eager to display extreme vigilance through acts of superpatriotism. From this viewpoint the fervent anticommunism of Catholics represented an opportunity to assert their oneness with American values. Like other theories which attribute deeply felt political attitudes to personal insecurities, this application of the status politics framework has been controversial.

The conservatism of American Catholics has also been attributed to theology. Although it differs radically on matters of church organization, Catholicism shares with Protestantism a creed that stresses human sinfulness. Unlike Protestantism, however, Catholicism traditionally trusted to faith, rather than to political action, the cure for social evil. Frustrated by the indifference of Catholic leaders to the poverty of an industrial city, a socialist pioneer in early twentieth-century Great Britain decried the otherworldly basis of Catholic social doctrine (McMillan 1927, 88):

> Rome never forgot the individual and was sensitive to every change in his condition or prospects. But she took little account of this perishing life, and her regard for the human body was very much that of the mediaeval ascetic or Jesuit priest. The soul alone persists and endures. The salvation of the soul is, then, the great end of life and all saviours. Nothing else matters. The people's children suffered and had suffered more cruelly during this century and the last, than ever before. No matter. The stake and the rack have a place in the scheme of salvation. The insanitary area may also cure heretics, may discipline fruitfully even the children of Mother Church.

According to this perspective, otherworldliness was responsible for a basic indifference to questions of social reform, be it domestic or international, and diminished the attractiveness of left-wing ideologies to Catholics.[3]

On the basis of such explanations, Catholics acquired a reputation for political conservatism that has been hard to shake—even in the face of evidence like that presented in Chapter 4. That reputation was never entirely warranted, even in the heyday of anticommunism during the 1950s. Catholic politicians like Alfred E. Smith and Robert F. Wagner, who served as New York's governor and senator, respectively, helped lay the foundations for the welfare system in the United States (O'Brien 1968). During the period that Cardinal Spellman tried to steer Catholics in the New York diocese to conservative causes, a Catholic woman named Dorothy Day founded the Catholic Worker movement in an attempt to steer the church toward progressive views on issues such as poverty, labor, social justice, civil liberties, and international disarmament (Piehl 1982). Catholic theologians, too, were steadily moving away from traditional beliefs about the rigid separation between heaven and earth, forging a new concern with social ethics (Curran 1982).

Even if they dismissed the signs of liberalization as unrepresentative of mainstream Catholic thought, political analysts could not overlook hard evidence of Catholic support for the Democratic party. Yet rather than acknowledge that this partisan tradition indicated the potential for Catholic liberalism, most scholars attempted to explain away the Democratic affiliation with the same economic self-interest argument used to account for the Democratic affiliation of southern evangelicals. By addressing the economic problems of the working class, they argued, Franklin D. Roosevelt had safeguarded the immediate interests of most American Catholics. One of gratitude for his policies and for his appointments of Catholics to public office, Roosevelt and his immediate successors enjoyed continuing electoral support from the Catholic voter. But as the memory of the New Deal eroded and issues of foreign policy and civil rights replaced economic security on the Catholic political agenda, the "natural" conservatism of American Catholics once again came into play. During the late 1960s, when conservative political activists hoped to replace the New Deal coalition with a right-wing majority more to their liking, Catholics were perceived as the most likely converts and became the target of special appeals. Despite these efforts, the subsequent political movement of Catholics has not been toward a wholehearted embrace of conservatism but, at least among the clergy, toward a more liberal posture on most major national issues.

THE TRANSFORMATION OF CATHOLIC ATTITUDES

If the conservatism of traditional Catholic politics had been due to communal isolation and immigrant culture, the social transformation of Catholic life was bound to produce new departures in political action.

Indeed, during the decades after World War II, Catholics in America experienced dramatic upward mobility. Even when allowance is given for the enormous variation among individual Catholics, the community as a whole enjoyed substantial increases in economic status, social acceptance, and the acquisition of politically relevant skills and resources.[4] Having "left the ghetto" (Hanna 1979, 22) economically and psychologically, Catholics were primed to assume a larger role in national political life. The direction of that new energy was principally determined by events in Rome.

What changed the Catholic church in America—or what gave official approval to trends that might have been developing independently—was a meeting of the world's bishops called in 1962 by Pope John XXIII. Known as Vatican II or the Ecumenical Council, this historic meeting of church fathers revolutionized church liturgy and ritual. Most important from a political standpoint was that the leaders of the Catholic church called upon the members to apply their Christian values to the problems of the world. In documents condemning the sinfulness of poverty, war, injustice, and other social ills, the church put its authority squarely behind the worldwide movement for social change. This profound shift of mood, coinciding with the assumption of the presidency by an energetic and vigorous Catholic, prompted an enthusiastic response from the American Catholic community (Hanna 1979, chap. 2). In developments that did not always meet with the approval of the older and more conservative bishops or of many Catholic laypeople, many young priests and nuns enrolled in the civil rights and antipoverty movements.

The enthusiasm for political change among Catholic leaders might not have survived into the 1980s without a corresponding transformation in the organization of the American church (Hanna 1985; Kennedy 1985). Under the impact of Vatican II, the American bishops established the United States Catholic Conference to speak with one voice about public issues. Absorbing several older institutions, the newly established organization developed departments specializing in domestic antipoverty efforts, campaigns for Third World economic development, and the promotion of world peace and social justice. This action-oriented church bureaucracy was increasingly staffed by professionals with substantial secular training and a commitment to broad-ranging social reform. As Mary Hanna (1985, 15) notes, the reform impulse has persisted to the present day because it was embodied in new institutions that "push the Church as a whole and the bishops toward action on social and political questions." A new breed of bishops, large in number because a mandatory retirement age produced more openings than normal in the hierarchy, has proven highly receptive to the Vatican II outlook. While the differences between the current and pre-Council bishops can easily be overstated (see the data in Kennedy 1985, chap.

2), the contemporary leadership of the Catholic church, like the parishioners, experienced a much more cosmopolitan upbringing than their predecessors. Young enough to have absorbed the liberalism of the 1960s and more familiar with secular environments, they have imparted a much more liberal cast to Catholic social and political thought.

The liberalization of Catholic attitudes did not occur overnight, nor was it always clear that the church was moving in that direction. The most dramatic evidence of the new mood came in Catholic reactions to the war in Vietnam. As it did for so many other Americans, the Vietnam War eventually prompted many Catholics to rethink their traditional support for American military involvement around the globe. At the extreme wing of the antiwar movement, a Catholic was the first young man to be imprisoned for publicly destroying a draft card, and a pair of Jesuit priests, Daniel and Phillip Berrigan, became leaders of a campaign of civil disobedience launched to protest American military action in Vietman (Meconis 1979). Among the young men who fled to Canada rather than serve as conscientious objectors, Catholics were apparently represented to a disproportionate degree (Surrey 1982). Despite these passionate expressions of antiwar feeling, most Catholics did not abandon their strong support for military action during the early years of the war. In Gallup polls taken between 1965 and 1967, Catholics were more supportive than Protestants of American military participation by about 10 percent (calculated from data in Mueller 1973, 143). Whereas many Protestant and Jewish spokesman condemned American participation in the war, the Catholic bishops issued a statement that concluded "it is reasonable to argue that our presence in Vietnam is justified" (reprinted in Drinan 1970, 192). Cardinal Spellman was perhaps the most enthusiastic supporter of military action in American religious circles.

But as the war dragged on into the late 1960s, Catholic support gradually eroded. In 1968 the bishops issued a new pastoral letter that was notably less enthusiastic than its 1966 predecessor (Drinan 1970, 195). While raising more questions than answers, the new statement called on Catholics to judge the legitimacy of American participation in Vietnam by the "just war" principle—a doctrine that deems military action appropriate only if all other methods have failed to achieve an equitable settlement and if the use of force is proportional to the goal of the war. Recognizing that Catholics differed among themselves over whether the Vietnam conflict passed the test of a just war, the bishops pointedly refrained from reaching a judgment. One Catholic clergyman who decided that Vietnam violated the standard set by just war doctrine, Father Robert Drinan of Boston, ran for a seat in the U.S. Congress on an antiwar platform and became the first priest elected to the House in many years. By 1971 the bishops moved explicitly into the antiwar camp passing a resolution calling for an immediate halt to American military participation in Southeast Asia. Consistent with this new "dovish" emphasis, they also took a strong position in favor of amnesty for draft evaders and war resisters and expressed opposition to the use of conscription outside the context of a genuine national emergency. As the hierarchy moved toward positions taken up earlier by the religious leadership of mainline Protestantism and Judaism, the Catholic lay population also developed attitudes toward the Vietnam War that were indistinguishable from the rest of the American public (Mueller 1973, 143).

Since those watershed years, the American bishops have consistently called for conciliation and negotiation in preference to military action in world affairs. In Latin America, for example, the Catholic church has spearheaded opposition to U.S. financial and military assistance to governments threatened by leftist insurgents. As noted earlier, Catholics have played a key role in providing illegal sanctuary for refugees from the strife in Central America. Through acts of civil disobedience ranging from nonpayment of income taxes to assaults on military property, individual Catholics, including members of the clergy, have protested efforts by the U.S. government to take the side of conservative forces in that region. In addition, missionaries from the Maryknoll order have worked throughout Latin America to promote social change through programs of land reform, social welfare benefits, and the like (Briggs 1984a).

In 1983, when the bishops issued a well-publicized letter on nuclear weapons, the American hierarchy bid what has been seen as a final farewell to the Spellman era.[5] Entitled "The Challenge of Peace: God's Promise and Our Response," the lengthy letter was intended to educate Catholics about church doctrine on war and violence in world affairs. The letter expanded upon many of the themes that first appeared in the Vietnam-era statements, emphasizing the relevance of the "just war" standard and the need for the individual Catholics to reach their own, independent judgments rather than to accept governmental decisions as inherently worthy of support. Catholics were also told that although military service was a worthy endeavor when motivated by a generous love of country, the church fathers supported persons whose conscience prompted them to refuse to bear arms or to otherwise defend themselves with tools of violence. On the issue of nuclear weapons, the major focus of the statement, the bishops declared that the idea of deterring war by matching the weaponry of an opponent—a cornerstone of American nuclear strategy—was an inadequate basis for longterm peace on earth. Noting that nuclear weapons could almost never be used in a manner that satisfied Catholic standards for a just war, they called on governments to accelerate efforts to achieve disarmament.

As abstract expressions, these statements could be endorsed in principle by nearly all public officials, even those identified as conservative on the issue of nuclear policy. But the letter provoked controversy because it challenged the Reagan administration policy on several counts. Specifically, the bishops called upon the U.S. government to undertake exploratory, independent initiatives for weapons reduction; to set up a regular schedule of summit meetings with the leaders of adversary governments; to tighten controls on the export of nuclear materials with potential military uses; and, in an effort to promote research and teaching on the peaceful resolution of conflicts, to establish a national Peace Academy. Each of these actions had previously been rejected by administration policymakers. Morever, the bishops condemned as "morally reprehensible in its hypocrisy" Reagan's policy of supporting repressive governments when he thought that the likely alternative would be even less desirable (18–19). By noting that the United States shared responsibility for the conditions that generated world tension and had not always behaved honorably in global affairs, the bishops further took on the president, who had publicly attributed global disorder to the evil empire of the Soviet Union. For the first time in American history, the Catholic hierarchy had lined up against a president on questions of fundamental military policy.

Did the hierarchy carry the parishioners with them? Although some conservative Catholics denounced the letter as naive or inappropriate, it apparently stimulated the Catholic rank and file to reconsider their positions on questions of peace and war. As Andrew Greeley first pointed out, Catholic opinion on military spending underwent a dramatic shift after the issuance of the pastoral letter in 1983. As Table 8.1 shows, the 1983 Protestant and Catholic attitude distributions on the level of U.S. military spending were very similar.[6] Although Catholics were even then more likely than Protestants to believe that the United States was overspending for military purposes, the group differences were small enough to be attributable to chance. But in 1984, Catholics shifted dramatically into the "too much" category and opened up substantial differences between themselves and Protestants. By comparison with both their 1983 attitudes and the 1984 Protestant preferences, Catholics in 1984 had moved significantly toward the view that the United States was devoting too many resources to military purposes. Coupled with evidence that Catholic attitudes on other issues had not changed much or moved further away from Protestant opinion, this finding made a strong case for attributing the transformation to the bishops' pastoral letter on nuclear weapons. To further bolster that interpretation, a study in one midwestern city found that Catholics were substantially more likely than Protestants to know of their church's position on nuclear weapons and that knowledge of the hierarchy's position produced greater approval for a "freeze" on the further construction and deployment of nuclear warheads (Tamney and Johnson 1985) (see Figure 8.1).

Figure 8.1 Catholic Versus Protestant Attitudes to Defense Spending, 1983 and 1984

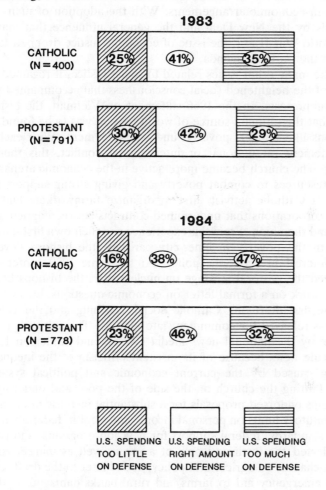

1983

CATHOLIC
(N = 400) 25% 41% 35%

PROTESTANT
(N = 791) 30% 42% 29%

1984

CATHOLIC
(N = 405) 16% 38% 47%

PROTESTANT
(N = 778) 23% 46% 32%

U.S. SPENDING TOO LITTLE ON DEFENSE   U.S. SPENDING RIGHT AMOUNT ON DEFENSE   U.S. SPENDING TOO MUCH ON DEFENSE

Source: General Social Surveys, 1983 & 1984

This leftward shift on international politics was accompanied by a growing concern among Catholic clergy about questions of economic policy. Rather than speak of this concern as a break with tradition, it is more accurate to describe it as renewed emphasis upon a traditional theme in Catholic social thought. In its modern statements on economic questions, the papacy had never given wholehearted endorsement to the doctrine of capitalism and had criticized the system for its undue emphasis upon competition and individualism. Reflecting that skepticism about the merits of unrestricted market economies, the American bishops had in 1919 issued a "Program of Social Reconstruction" that called for major changes in economic arrangements. With the adoption of many of these proposals by the New Deal and the general affluence that marked the post–World War II era, the issue of economic justice dropped to a lower place on the Catholic agenda.

Like many other issues related to social justice, it regained primacy as part of the heightened social consciousness that accompanied the Vietnam War protests. In the 1966 statement on Vietman, the bishops had hinted that the ultimate source of world tension was to be found in social conditions like hunger, poverty, and unemployment. With each successive statement on national or international conflict, this theme grew stronger. The church became more active in the economic arena, concentrating resources to combat poverty and giving strong support to Cesar Chavez, a Catholic activist, first to organize farmworkers and then to boycott corporations that undermined contracts between agricultural producers and the union. From this experience and their own firsthand experience with the poverty in inner-city parishes, the bishops developed a strong interest in economic policy. At the same 1980 conference that authorized the pastoral message on nuclear war, the bishops began preliminary work on a formal letter on economic questions.

The first draft on "Catholic Social Teaching and the U.S. Economy" was released for commment late in 1984. The subject of intensive coverage by the national news media (Weber and Anderson 1985), the letter made news because of its insistent criticism of the inequality and suffering caused by the current economic and political system (Silk 1984a). Putting the church on the side of the poor and underprivileged, the bishops endorsed proposals for a substantial increase in the minimum wage, statutory limits on personal income and wealth, federally mandated welfare standards, federal support for new job programs, and pay scales that reflected the intrinsic worth of a job as well as market considerations. A chapter on agricultural policy, added later to the draft, called for massive emergency aid to farms and rural banks damaged by defaulted loans (Furlow 1985). Many of the specific proposals embedded in the report had already been rejected by the Reagan administration. Even though the draft was not released until after the 1984 presidential election so that it would not be taken as a criticism of President Reagan's policies, its recommendations collided with the administration's announced commitment to reduce governmental involvement in the domestic economy.[7]

Although no systematic data are yet available, the bishops apparently will face considerable difficulty in swinging Catholic opinion to their side on this issue (Williams 1984). A group of conservative Catholics, including business leaders, public officials, and scholars, drafted a letter of their own that beat the bishops' pastoral letter into print (Briggs

1984b). Described by one reporter (Silk 1984b) as "a strong celebration of the capitalist system and the individual entrepreneur, not the government, as the true benefactors of the poor and jobless," the letter from the "Lay Commission on Catholic Social Teaching and the U.S. Economy" argued that the political freedom accompanying free enterprise economies promotes the living standards of all citizens. Just as the bishops' draft can too easily be treated as an endorsement of socialist economics, the unofficial response can unfairly be caricatured as a brief for laissez-faire policies. In fact, the commission praised labor unions and recognized that the profit motive is not sufficient to care for the entire interests of humanity and may introduce significant evils that call for government response. Still, the issuance of such a missive indicated that influential Catholics were not unanimously favorable to the bishops' economic proposals, and other impressionistic reports have suggested that the official statement will be greeted unenthusiastically by the rank and file.

The American bishops are poised to confront yet another contentious issue, the role of women in the church. Polling data suggest that support for traditional sexual distinctions had dropped substantially among American Catholics (New York Times News Service 1985). Slightly more than half of the Catholic respondents in national polls now favors the ordination of women as priests; on other issues having to do with the maintenance of traditional sex roles, the dissent from offical church teachings is even more dramatic. Large majorities support the elimination of mandatory celibacy among the priesthood and call for more permissive policies on divorce, artificial conception, and abortion. These ideas are particularly widespread among younger Catholics. Except for abortion, where their attitudes do conform to official doctrine, the American bishops are thought to be sympathetic to their parishioners on these issues. While stopping short of outright endorsement of the particular solutions advocated by the laity, the Bishops Conference has urged the Vatican to make stronger efforts to admit women to leadership roles in the church. In 1983 the bishops authorized work on a pastoral letter about women in Catholicism, a project that is expected to take five years and is likely to put even greater distance between the American church and its traditional social conservatism (Greer 1985; Hawk 1985a).

ABORTION: A CATHOLIC ISSUE?

During the same period that Catholics were rethinking their traditional positions on a wide range of political issues, the church gained public attention as a major force resisting the liberalization of abortion laws in the United States.[8] That stance was derived from Catholic doctrine defining the fetus as a form of human life that should enjoy a nearly absolute right to existence. From that perspective, abortion along with any other deliberate interference with the gestation of a fertilized human egg, constitutes the moral equivalent of murder (Callahan 1970, chap. 12).

Although the abortion debate reached the national agenda only in 1973, when the U.S. Supreme Court handed down its momentous decision striking down most existing state laws, the lines of the conflict had been drawn much earlier.[9] Responding to a worldwide liberalization of abortion laws, Pope Paul VI had reiterated Catholic opposition to any termination of pregnancy in his 1968 encyclical, *Humanae Vitae*.[10] When church law was revised in 1971, abortion was added to the list of crimes that mandated excommunication from Catholicism. As the states began to loosen restrictions on abortion in the 1960s, often at the urging of physicians and lawyers, Catholics took the lead in the so-called Right to Life organizations formed to oppose the new trends. Late in 1972, the American bishops created a committee to publicize the church's position and to coordinate its antiabortion activities. Armed with a record of public opposition to what the advocates of liberalization called abortion reform and a network to organize parishioners, the Catholic church was well placed to provide leadership when the *Roe* v. *Wade* decision brought the issue to national prominence.

The attack on liberalized abortion laws was waged on several fronts. Shortly after the decision was announced, the bishops created a lobbying organization, the National Committee for a Human Life Amendment, whose goal was to reverse the Supreme Court decision by passage of a constitutional amendment. When the Senate Judiciary Committee held hearings on proposed antiabortion amendments in 1974, four Catholic bishops appeared among the many clergy who testified on the issue. When the Senate Judiciary Committee deadlocked over the issue, failing to send any of the nearly sixty proposed amendments to a vote on the Senate floor, abortion opponents decided to press the attack through a variety of interim measures. While keeping as their ultimate objective a constitutional amendment prohibiting abortion, antiabortion forces focused on the more immediate goal of limiting the availability of abortion by restricting funding at the state and national levels and by adopting administrative regulations to deter women from using abortion facilities.

Like other groups who seek to wield influence in the legislative process, the opponents of abortion have attempted to accumulate power through the development of grass-roots electoral organizations. Although they have intervened in presidential politics, even to the extent of sponsoring a symbolic campaign for the Democratic presidential nomination, their major focus has been on electing prolife candidates to state and congressional office. The full extent of church involvement in these actions was spelled out in the highly detailed *Pastoral Plan for Pro-Life Activities* issued in 1975 by the bishops. The bishops' plan called for "the development in each congressional district of an identifiable, tightly knit and well-organized pro-life unit" (Jaffe et al. 1981, 75) that would provide financial assistance, campaign workers, and publicity to antiabortion candidates. The plan envisioned close ties between secular "right-to-life" organizations and Catholic parishes. In practice, the church has supplied the movement with physical, financial, and human resources, leading some critics to the conclusion that the right-to-life movement is largely an expression of the Catholic hierarchy (Merton 1981; Jaffe et al. 1981, 76–83; Paige 1983). Although academic researchers have expressed skepticism about the electoral impact of abortion in national elections (Traugott and Vinovskis 1980; Granberg and Burlison 1983; Vinovskis 1979), the antiabortion movement has gained a reputation for political clout that has prompted many lawmakers to pay it careful heed (Margolis and Neary 1980). And as the prospect of amending the Constitution has faded, the opponents of abortion have capitalized on their electoral reputation to gain passage of restrictive laws. In several states and localities, legislative bodies have tried to qualify the Court's ruling by imposing preconditions on women seeking abortions—permission of the spouse or parents, mandatory waiting periods—or by setting medical requirements intended to make the operation impractical. Some localities have adopted zoning regulations designed to prevent the operation of abortion facilities and have required that physicians warn prospective patients to expect serious physical and psychological aftereffects. The Supreme Court has struck down most of these restrictive features as religiously motivated laws with no overriding secular purpose (Friedman 1983).

Other laws and regulations have received Court approval, however. Most important, the Court upheld the legality of a ban on the use of Medicaid funds for abortion under most circumstances and permitted publicly funded hospitals to refuse to perform elective abortions. Given the green light in the Medicaid decision, Congress has put similar antiabortion restrictions on military benefits, District of Columbia appropriations, federal employee health insurance, and the foreign assistance program (Cohodas 1983, 1692). In addition, thirty states have prohibited their health care contributions from being used to support elective abortion, and others are being forced to consider the issue through ballot initiatives supported by petition (Matthews 1985). Consistent with President Reagan's vocal condemnation of elective abortion (Reagan 1984), the administration has championed most of these efforts and recently extended them to the international sphere. Late in 1985, the Agency for International Development, which channels American funds to global programs of family planning, decided to withhold grants from any institution that directly or indirectly encouraged any "artificial" method of contraception or abortion (Barker 1985a, 1985b). On the domestic front, the administration joined the efforts of antiabortion groups to eliminate federal support for birth control activities that had proceeded under Title X of the Public Health Act. Despite these attempts to raise the cost of abortions beyond the ability to pay, specialized clinics have emerged to perform a mounting number of abortions annually. As a result, critics of liberalized policies still hope for a constitutional amendment or a change of heart by the Supreme Court.[11] Perhaps the frustration caused by the slow progress of the antiabortion crusade explains the rising tide of harassment and violence that has been directed against medical facilities that perform the operation.

Although the fact has often been overlooked in public commentary, the antiabortion movement has not gained the unanimous endorsement of the Catholic community. In the most active disagreement, some Catholic women have utilized the freedom of *Roe* v. *Wade* to obtain legal elective abortions.[12] Less dramatically, as demonstrated by the public opinion data given in Chapter 4, Catholics have split over the question of abortion policy, with sizable minorities favoring a liberalized policy in cases of rape, probable birth defects, or serious threat to maternal health. Even during the 1984 presidential campaign, when the hierarchy communicated church doctrine with great emphasis, less than a majority of churchgoing parishioners approved a total ban on abortion and only about one-fifth of nonpracticing Catholics supported such a constitutional amendment (New York Times 1984). The poll data described in Chapter 4 showed that Catholics were not even the most intransigent opponents of abortion; that status fell to the evangelical Protestants, white and black alike. Even though the church's position on the issue has not provoked the same level of dissent as its policy against artificial contraceptives, visible signs of disagreement within the Catholic community have cropped up. One small group, Catholics for Free Choice, has publicly argued that church teaching is in fact compatible with the public availability of abortion (Herbers 1984b; Kissling 1985). As evidence of the hierarchy's sensitivity on the issue, however, the clergy who signed a public advertisement promoting a prochoice perspective claims to have been subjected to major pressure (Hawk 1985b).

If opposition to abortion is not a Catholic monopoly nor a position accepted by all members of the church, neither is support for *Roe* vs. *Wade* a wholly secular phenomenon. While public leadership of the prochoice movement has been associated with feminist organizations like the National Organization of Women and the family planning advocate, Planned Parenthood, several Protestant and Jewish groups have worked to resist restrictive abortion policy (Rainey 1985). The Religious Council for Abortion Rights (RCAR), a Washington-based umbrella group with more than thirty institutional members, has gained a reputation for effective lobbying in Congress. It has recently branched out to monitor abortion-related activity in the administrative agencies and has tried to raise public support for the principle of free choice in reproductive decisions. RCAR does not take a theological position on the abortion issue but rather emphasizes the diversity among American faiths over the status of the fetus as a human being. With such divergent views, the organization argues, extending legal protection to the fetus amounts to enshrining one theological view—the Catholic doctrine—as law. The alleged Catholic basis for antiabortion legislation is then cited as a violation of the anti-establishment clause of the First Amendment. From this legal perspective, which has yet to gain constitutional standing by a Supreme Court decision, *Roe* vs. *Wade* is treated as a positive contribution to the level of religious freedom in America.

While abortion cannot be reduced to an exclusive Catholic issue, the most active opponents of liberalization have indeed been recruited from the Catholic community. Several studies of the prolife movement have identified the typical activist (outside the South) as a Catholic housewife of limited education, much of it obtained in church-affiliated schools. Deeply devout and a regular churchgoer, she was likely to come from a large family and to be the mother of several children (Granberg 1981a, 1982a, 1982b; Luker 1984). According to a study of California right-to-lifers conducted by sociologist Kristin Luker (1984), these women overcame a background of political inactivity out of anger at a Supreme Court decision that seemed to strike directly at their fundamental values about motherhood, the role of women, and the purpose of sex. Assuming that men and women differ in nature, the former best suited for the role of public work and the latter for raising children, the women chose to forgo opportunities for attaining professional skills in favor of stressing their role as caregivers to children and husband. Luker pointed out that a policy of liberalized abortion undermines that set of values in three respects:

> First, it is intrinsically wrong because it takes a human life and what makes women special is their ability to nourish life. Second, it is wrong because *by giving women control over their fertility,* it breaks up an intricate set of social relationships between men and women that has traditionally surrounded (and in the ideal case protected) women and children. Third and finally, abortion is wrong because it fosters and supports a world view that deemphasizes (and therefore *downgrades)* the traditional role of men and women. Because these roles have been satisfying ones for pro-life people and because they believe this emotional and social division of labor is both "appropriate and natural," the act of abortion is wrong because it plays havoc with this arrangement of the world (1984, 161–62).

The supporters of liberalized abortion have proven to be almost the complete opposite of these traditionalist Catholics in social condition and outlook. On the evidence available from this type of intensive interview and from sample surveys, the apparent Catholic versus non-Catholic di-

mension to the abortion debate is part of a broader conflict over the place
of traditional values and sexual norms in society (Jelen 1984; Wagenaar
and Bartos 1977; Legge 1985). Liberalized abortion is particularly abhor-
rent to persons enmeshed in traditional social settings and imbued with
conservative norms—many but not all of whom are Catholic—and acceptable to persons who have been part of modernizing institutions. The
conflict is less a denominational fight or a battle between religion and
irreligion than a dispute between differing styles of religious belief.

Since abortion touches upon such fundamental differences in how
some people view the world and their own place in it, it should not be
surprising that the debate has unleashed so much passionate energy. The
tension has been particularly acute for Catholics in public office. Traditionalist Catholics, whose views were formed in the pre–Vatican II era,
have tended to justify opposition to abortion in terms of a universal
doctrine of the sanctity of life that need not be restricted to Catholics.
But other Catholic officials, including those sympathetic to liberalized
abortion on social grounds and representatives of constituencies with
mixed attitudes, have not found it easy to stake out an acceptable position. If they were to honor their Catholic background by opposing the
free availability of abortion, they could be criticized for representing
Catholic interests—a charge that historically has handicapped Catholics
seeking public office in the United States. Yet coming down upon the
side of liberalized abortion would endanger their ability to draw Catholic
electoral support.

The Catholic officials who have supported liberalization have justified their position by claiming that their primary responsibility as public
officials is to uphold decisions legitimately promulgated by the Supreme
Court. Just how fiercely church officials have reacted to this claim was
illustrated in 1984, when Representative Geraldine Ferraro, a devout
Catholic, received the Democratic nomination for vice-president. Though
personally opposed to abortion, she had voted against curbs on the use of
federal funds to prohibit elective abortion and indicated that her votes on
abortion policy would not be influenced by her private faith. This position
drew a rebuke from the head of the U.S. Catholic Conference, Bishop
John Malone of Youngstown, Ohio, who criticized attempts by candidates to distinguish between private and public morality (Furlow 1984).
More pointedly, the newly installed archbishop of New York, John Cardinal O'Connor, wondered aloud during a television interview how Catholics could vote in good conscience for a candidate who did not pledge to
support restrictive abortion policies. The steady drumbeat of criticism
directed at Ferraro and the appearance of several bishops at Reagan
campaign rallies came close to an endorsement of the Republican ticket
(Dickenson 1984; Herbers 1984a). Recognizing an opportunity to make
inroads on the traditional allegiance of Catholics to the Democratic party,

Republican spokesmen called attention to the bishops' criticism of pro-choice Catholics and emphasized that the GOP platform more closely mirrored the church's teachings on abortion.

By seeming to endorse a candidate in a partisan election, the church hierarchy came in for its own share of criticism from political leaders (Califano 1984). While endorsing the church's right to speak out on issues with a moral dimension, leading Catholic Democrats asserted that the clergy had overstepped the proper "wall of separation" between church and state. Senator Edward Kennedy (1984) publicly asserted the impropriety of church attempts to impose a restrictive abortion policy on the nation:

> Where decisions are inherently individual ones or in cases where we are deeply divided about whether they are, people of faith should not invoke the power of the state to decide what everyone can believe or think or read or do. In such cases—cases like abortion or prayer or prohibition or sexual identity—the proper role of religion is to appeal to the free conscience of each person, not the coercive rule of secular law.

In his defense of Ferraro and other Catholic politicians who opposed restrictive abortion policies, New York Governor Mario Cuomo revived the notion of "civil peace" first enunciated in the 1950s by the Catholic theologian John Courtney Murray. In a religiously diverse society like the United States, Murray had argued, attempts by one religious group to prohibit what it regards as evil practices might endanger the harmony of the social order. Hence, it is better to tolerate such evil rather than undermine a society that has permitted such a wide degree of freedom to Catholics and other religious minorities (Wolf 1968, chap. 1). By insisting on the need for an abortion policy that did not enjoy national consensus, Cuomo (1984) argued, the Catholic church might well encourage other religious groups to press for policies that endangered religious liberty.

> The Catholic public official lives the political truth most Catholics through most of American history have accepted and insisted on: the truth that to assure our freedom we must allow others the same freedom, even if occasionally it produces conduct by them which we would hold to be sinful. We know that the price of seeking to force our beliefs on others is that they might someday force theirs on us.

Thus, according to Cuomo, Catholics should not threaten the peace of society and the freedom accorded to religion by using the state to impose policies deeply offensive to many people. He conceded that the church had every right to condemn abortion and to work for conditions that would eliminate its necessity but, echoing Senator Kennedy, he believed that it should attempt to implement its views by appealing to the consciences of individuals.

As the campaign progressed, the church leadership appeared to draw back from the implied attack on Ferraro and other Catholic politicians who had supported *Roe* v. *Wade*. In a statement issued on behalf of his fellow members of the U.S. Catholic Conference, Bishop James Malone (1984) emphasized that the church had no intention of supporting candidates for office and insisted that abortion was one issue among many that Catholics should use to judge potential officeholders. In the end, nearly 60 percent of Catholic voters supported the Republican ticket in 1984, and the defections from the Democratic party appeared to have been highest among those Catholics the most deeply involved in parish life. That the Democratic ticket fared so poorly among Catholics, even with a Catholic on the ballot, indicated the potential of abortion to disrupt traditional alliances.[13]

Despite Bishop Malone's attempt to defuse tension, the 1984 debate revealed a church leadership deeply divided over tactics. For some bishops, abortion is still the paramount moral issue of the day and a candidate's position on that single issue remains a litmus test of acceptability (O'Connor 1984). The other camp, represented by Bishop Malone, has taken the position that abortion should be part of a "seamless garment" of issues, including nuclear war, human rights, capital punishment, and poverty, that constitute the basis for a prolife platform. The latter position seems most consistent with Pope John Paul II's current emphasis on social justice and the maintenance of traditional sexual morality. While reaffirming Catholic teaching on abortion, birth control, and premarital sex, the pope has also condemned the sinfulness of unemployment, excessive concern for business profits, and the denial of liberty to trade unions (Costelloe 1985).

Despite this apparent support from the pope, those who subscribe to the "seamless garment" approach face an uphill battle to restructure Catholic opinion along new lines. As research has revealed (Granberg 1981b; Granberg and Granberg 1981; Sawyer 1982), abortion opponents have not been noted for their opposition to capital punishment, military spending, and the use of force in world affairs—all positions that the bishops have treated as expressions of the prolife ethic. Despite the prolife implications of those issues, antiabortionists have not differed from supporters of liberalization levels of support for increased spending on health, gun control laws, or the mandatory use of seat belts.[14] What distinguishes the prolife activists—aside from resistance to abortion, euthanasia, and suicide—is conservative preferences on social issues relating to traditional sex roles.

The potential and limits of the prolife theme are illustrated by the information given in Figure 8.2. As in the first table of the chapter, the data compare Catholic attitudes on defense spending in 1983 and 1984—this time, in order to examine the relationship between attitudes on military spending and preferences about abortion policy. These have been the two public issues on which the bishops have attempted to forge a common prolife outlook. In the table, Catholics have been divided into two groups—those who are unwilling to accept abortion even in cases of birth defects, rape, and danger to maternal health and those who approve of abortion for all of those reasons.[15] Because a substantial majority of Catholics accept abortion in all these circumstances, those who reject it in any one of them must be counted as strong opponents of liberalization.

Figure 8.2 Relationship Between Catholic Attitudes on Abortion and Defense Spending, 1983 and 1984

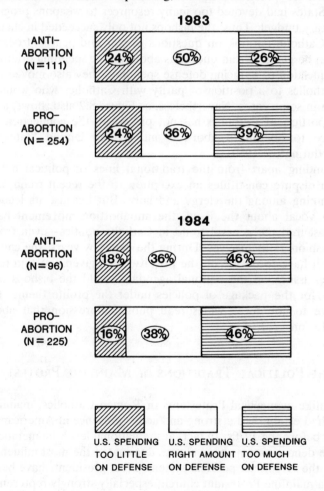

1983

ANTI-
ABORTION
(N = 111)
24%   50%   26%

PRO-
ABORTION
(N = 254)
24%   36%   39%

1984

ANTI-
ABORTION
(N = 96)
18%   36%   46%

PRO-
ABORTION
(N = 225)
16%   38%   46%

U.S. SPENDING   U.S. SPENDING   U.S. SPENDING
TOO LITTLE   RIGHT AMOUNT   TOO MUCH
ON DEFENSE   ON DEFENSE   ON DEFENSE

Source: General Social Surveys, 1983 & 1984

In 1983, before the church position on military spending was widely recognized, only about one-fourth of antiabortion Catholics thought the United States was spending too much on defense. A majority of Catholics in that category actually approved of the currrent level of military spending. The Catholics who were willing to accept abortion because of medical circumstances came closer to the bishops' position on military spending. As shown in Figure 8.2, a plurality picked the "too much" option to describe the American level of expenditure on armaments. Before the pastoral letter, then, there was some truth to the claim that antiabortion Catholics limited their prolife orientation to that issue alone.

But by 1984, the difference had disappeared. Precisely the same proportion of prochoice and antiabortion Catholics agreed that the United States had devoted too many resources to weapons programs and the military budget. Thus, the bishops not only succeeded in changing the overall Catholic outlook on questions of war and peace—to extent that these can be gauged from questions about public spending prioities—but, on the question of reducing defense spending, they also moved antiabortion Catholics to a position of parity with Catholics who would permit abortion in some cases. Nevertheless, as Figure 8.2 also shows, a substantial proportion of Catholics has not picked up the connection between resistance to liberalized abortion and to the United States military buildup during the 1980s.

Standing apart from the traditional lines of political debate, the abortion dispute constitutes an exception to the recent trend of liberalized thinking among the clergy and laity. But because its leaders have been so vocal about the issue, the antiabortion movement has sometimes obscured the general trend in Catholic politics—even from Catholic parishioners themselves. During the next few years, the church hierarchy will have to decide on the priority to be given abortion relative to the other issues on the national agenda. Should the bishops opt unreservedly for the package of policies under the prolife theme, they will still have to counter a widespread public impression that abortion is their sole concern.

THE POLITICAL TRADITIONS OF MAINLINE PROTESTANTS

Unlike evangelical Protestants or Roman Catholics, mainline Protestants had established a strong and active presence in American political life well before the 1970s. In fact, at the national level the members of the mainline denominations have always dominated the most influential positions in the American political system. Most presidents have been members of a mainline Protestant church; especially strongly represented have been Episcopalians and Presbyterians (Kane 1974, 325). For most of the twentieth century, Catholics and Protestants from an evangelical background were rarely considered serious canidates for the nation's highest elective position. Although Congress has been more accessible to members of other religious groups, the churches associated with "liberal Protestantism" have also claimed a far greater share of the membership in that body than size alone would warrant (Gaustad 1968, 125–28; Menendez 1977, 219–20).[16]

The political predominance of mainline Protestants has largely stemmed from their high socioeconomic status. Although any large religious community inevitably contains persons of diverse social background, taken as a group, the members of mainline churches have enjoyed a higher socioeconomic standing than have members of the other major religious families in the United States. As a result, they have tended to support the social system from which they have derived substantial benefits. In the twentieth century, when national political conflict has been organized around the issue of governmental responsibility for social welfare and regulation of economic activity, individuals affiliated with the mainline denominations have for the most part sided with conservative political forces. As noted in Chapter 4, members of this religious tradition have evinced the highest levels of Republican support and the most conservative outlook on economic policy questions.

Never has the conservative orientation of the membership enjoyed unanimous support from church leaders. Indeed, the mainline Protestant denominations have periodically given birth to movements that cast a skeptical eye on prevailing social and economic arrangements. Known as the "Social Gospel" movement, the distinctive feature of reform sentiment has been a belief that God is revealed in the world. Rather than treating the deity solely in supernatural terms, as a force hovering sublimely in the heavens, aloof to human social patterns, the liberal theological tradition has insisted that God is "immanent" in human life. Consequently, love of one's neighbor should replace personal holiness as the principal ethical concern of Christianity (Gilkey 1968). According to this perspective, the will of God is associated with particular schemes for social reform so it falls to the Christian, as a religious duty, to strive to bring about change in human social conditions. Clergymen have usually been the most active carriers of this particular vision (Garrett 1973).

At the beginning of the twentieth century, when the Social Gospel movement was particularly strong, it contributed to the split in American Christianity between the mainline denominations and their evangelical and fundamentalist adversaries. Although the conflict was rooted in a number of sources, the traditionalists who appropriated the evangelical label objected to the tendency among modernist theologians to equate Christianity with support for social reform. Though the evangelicals were not indifferent to social problems, they emphasized the priority of spiritual communion between God and individuals. Hence, they interpreted social problems as the outgrowth of individual moral failings and supported solutions such as conversion or spiritual rebirth. As pointed out in the last chapter, the evangelical wing eventually found itself cast in the role of defending traditional social values against the onslaught of modern forces and largely retreated from the national political arena after repeated defeats during the 1920s.

Even though members of what became known as the mainline wing were divided internally over the proper definition of Christianity, much of the clergy moved into the Social Gospel camp. Their enthusiasm for social reform waxed and waned with national political circumstances (Carter 1954; May 1963; Meyer 1961). It was high in the period before World War I, low in the decade after, and high again during the presidency of Franklin Delano Roosevelt. Interest in social problems dropped to the bottom of the church agenda during the prosperous years of the post-World War II era, when many churches concentrated their energies on building new facilities for their suburban congregants. By the late 1950s, the Protestant churches from the mainline denominations were the target of strong attacks for their supposed indifference to social problems.

Few of the critics could have imagined just how sharply the situation would change in a short time. During the 1960s, social reform moved back to the top of the Protestant agenda. In the churches, a "new breed" of social action-oriented clergy jumped enthusiastically into a variety of progressive causes (Cox 1968). Members of the new breed were found leading rent strikes, organizing pickets around city hall, serving in community action organizations, financing low-cost housing projects, helping welfare recipients form unions to better press their claims upon reluctant government bureaucracies. At the same time that such actions flourished in isolated communities, national attention was drawn to the Protestant clergys' participation in civil rights demonstrations and their leadership role in organizations that opposed American involvement in the Vietnam War.

In a 1968 survey of parish ministers in California, taken when political activism was at its height, political scientist Harold Quinley (1974) reported on the extent of clergy involvement in three social movements—a campaign to defend California's "fair housing" ordinance from a repeal effort, support for efforts to unionize migrant farm workers, and opposition to the Vietnam War. Among the 1,580 clergy who responded to Quinley's survey, the rate of activism was pronounced—though uneven—across the three issue areas. On the fair housing campaign, a civil rights issue that attracted the highest level of activism, a clear majority of the Protestant ministers took public action in the form of sermons, petitions, or other public statements conveying support for maintenance of the ordinance. For Methodist, Congregationalist, Episcopalian, and Presbyterian clergy, who most enthusiastically endorsed the social reform ministry, antirepeal activity also included prayers about the issue, organization of study or advocacy groups in the church, service on public committees, and the writing of letters to public officials. Roughly one-fourth of the ministers took similar high-profile stances on the Vietnam War, including a substantial number who attended protest meetings, belonged to antiwar organizations, or participated in public marches. The plight of farmworkers drew somewhat lower rates of involvement but still gained attention and support from a sizable share of the sample.

The impression of a united bloc of liberal clergy was further reinforced by their high visibility in some of the most dramatic protests of the era. In a number of southern communities where conflict over desegration of public schools raised social tension to a fever pitch, clergymen played a key role on the front lines, frequently exposing themselves to intimidation and violent assaults from segregationists (Campbell and Pettigrew 1959, 3–4). Shortly before the 1965 Selma-to-Montgomery march to secure voting rights, the civil rights movement gained another martyr in the Reverend James Reeb of Boston. A Unitarian minister who had answered the Reverend Martin Luther King, Jr.'s call for ministerial involvement, Reeb died from a savage beating inflicted by opponents of the planned march. Other ministers similarly risked their lives in boarding buses bound for the South during the "Freedom Summer" campaigns. In expressing their opposition to racial segregation and, later, to American policy in Vietnam, some clergy departed from conventional political activity to perform acts of civil disobedience or even violence. The nation grew accustomed to pictures of clergymen being led off to jail for participation in illegal sit-ins or other such activities.

It is important to keep in mind that a great many ministers did not conform to this description of social action. In their study of the Little Rock (Arkansas) school desegregation crisis of 1957–58, Campbell and Pettigrew (1959) stressed that most ministers from the mainline churches, while not supporting school segregation, kept their distance from the controversy engulfing their community. Similarly, if Quinley's study of California ministers held true nationwide, many clergy apparently kept their Sunday sermons free of any sustained commentary on the divisive political and social issues of the 1960s (Stark et al. 1971, chap. 5). Neither would it be accurate to conclude that the politically active mainline clergy uniformly supported the liberal side on these issues; some members of Quinley's sample reported undertaking activities in favor of repealing the housing ordinance, defending American military involvement in Southeast Asia, or resisting the unionization campaign on the farms. Similarly, several community surveys revealed that substantial numbers of mainline ministers continued to preach the traditional Protestant perspective, emphasizing personal piety as the best response to social problems (Koller and Retzer 1980; Nelsen 1975). Such conservative activism was rare, however. Quinley and others (Tygart 1977) noted two strong trends in the data: first, the level of clergy activism was highest among the theological liberals; and second, the bulk of activists did in fact work on what was defined as the liberal side on the three issues.

In attempting to account for the different levels of political activism among mainline clergy, scholars have stressed both individual and structural factors. As individuals, the activist clergy were more likely than their inactive counterparts to have received advanced education from secular institutions and to have been raised in urban areas (Ammerman, 1981). These traits reflected exposure to agents of modernization that probably undermined the traditional conception of religion and encouraged clergy to view their task in much broader terms. Indeed, according to the research of sociologist Hart Nelsen (1975; Nelsen, Yokley, and Madron 1973), activists and nonactivists exhibited very different understandings about the role of religion in society and adjusted their ministerial priorities accordingly. Using postal surveys, Nelsen discovered that clergymen who regarded themselves principally as spiritual leaders, personal counselors, church administrators, or educators tended to embrace conservative political ideas and to preach the traditional moral concerns about individual rectitude. The activists were recruited from the ranks of clergy who defined their principal responsibility as community problem-solving. With a belief that they were meant to address a wide range of problems that could not necessarily be solved by personal piety, clergy were more likely to sermonize on social problems and to favor direct political involvement as a solution.

These differences in role orientation were reinforced by participation in supportive social networks. Protestant parish ministers were more likely to engage in civil rights activity—even in the face of congregational resistance—when they belonged to national denominations that issued clear directives in support of the civil rights movement (Wood 1981). It was equally important for activists to find a local haven to sustain their liberal activities. In her study of civil rights involvement among Protestant ministers in Tuscaloosa, Alabama, Nancy Ammerman (1981) found that geographical proximity to a university campus and a perception of pro-civil rights attitudes in the local community were important factors drawing clergymen into public activism. Ministers could apparently draw emotional and intellectual support from these sources to offset the hostility their actions might arouse among parishioners and fellow ministers.

MAINLINE ACTIVISM: SOURCES AND REACTIONS

To understand why the "new breed" clergy emerged when it did, it is important to consider the social, creedal, and institutional aspects of mainline Protestantism. I noted earlier that changes in the national political climate drew both evangelicals and Catholics more fully into the political arena. The same factors had some influence on the mainline Protestants. The political issues that engaged clergy during the activist era—civil rights, Vietnam, social justice—touched on profound moral values at the core of Christian thought. As Quinley (1970, 3) put it, "The churches could hardly preach Christian brotherhood and love for one's fellow man and at the same time remain silent on such issues as civil rights and the war in Vietnam." But the explanatory power of this theological explanation is limited by the awareness that Protestant clergy had historically kept silent in the face of social conflicts no less harmful to the spirit of brotherhood and love for one's fellow man and that many ministers did refrain from speaking out publicly even in the turbulent 1960s. Another explanation of the clergy's decision to speak out points to a perceived need to preserve the institutional strength of the church and the social influence of the ministry. According to this theory, the liberal Protestant churches saw an emphasis on social action as a bridge to the well-educated and modernized members of their parishes. The demand for relevance was particularly urgent at a time of radical challenge to Christian orthodoxy, when a scientific world view had undermined some traditional elements of belief and Americans seemed disposed to experiment with Eastern religions. Unless the churches could seem relevant to contemporary social problems, in other words, they would lose their appeal to young people and progressive thinkers. For the clergy, who had been criticized earlier for silence on pressing moral matters, participation in social movements may have presented an opportunity to maintain a leadership role in society, through aggressive championing of liberal causes. This interpretation of the clergy's motivation amounts to yet another application of the "status politics" framework.[17]

If the causes of activism among the clergy were debatable, the immediate effect was clear-cut. In church after church, the activist clergy ran headlong into the status quo sentiments of more conservative congregants (Quinley 1970, 1974; Hadden 1969). In what one author described as a "gathering storm," the clergy encountered substantial resistance to their attempts to speak for the church on controversial public issues. By majorities ranging from 55 percent on the farm worker issue to 83 percent on the fair housing referendum, the clergy in the California sample reported encountering opposition from at least some members of their congregation. On the race relations campaign, about one-third indicated conflict with the church board, and one in ten said their position had produced efforts to remove them from the pulpit. The Vietnam issue and the farm worker dispute incited conflicts of similar intensity, although with lower rates of opposition.

Faced with this resistance from congregations who apparently preferred a priority on worship and spirituality, many clergy sought safe havens in appointments outside the local parish. Accordingly, the liberal ministers took refuge in campus ministries, denominational "social action" bureaucracies, the seminaries, and other environments that were more supportive of political activity by church leaders. Freed from accountability to a conservative constituency, ministers in these positions supplied a disproportionate share of the activist clergy (Hadden and Rymph 1971). To this day, nonparish environments continue to harbor a large number of politically liberal clergymen who would probably find it difficult to coexit with typical members of their denominations (IEA/ Roper Organization 1982). Other reform-minded clergymen and seminary students, weary of the constant battles within the church, simply opted to leave the ministry for opportunities in secular agencies.

The problems faced by the clergy stemmed in large measure from the social perspectives of church members. As Wade C. Roof (1978) has demonstrated in his study of North Carolina Episcopalians, the social basis of contemporary Christianity has shifted because of the declining plausibility of religious doctrine to persons most deeply affected by modernization. Traditional religious teachings have the greatest appeal for persons with limited exposure to education, urbanization, and impersonal bureaucracies. Such persons who are deeply anchored in their local communities tend to exhibit a narrow perspective on the world and to defend vigorously those traditional social values that have lost favor among the progressive clergy. As a consequence, even liberal denominations with many new breed clergymen draw their church members and activists disproportionately from theological and political conservatives. It is *not* the case, as Roof stressed, that theological conservatism causes traditional attitudes on social and political issues. Rather, he contended, traditional religious values are the most plausible to persons whose limited exposure to the outside world had safeguarded them from the challenge of modern social thought.

In a religious marketplace in which churches compete for membership, the individual Protestant faces a wide choice of potential churches with which to affiliate. From the late 1960s through the current period, membership trends have run against the mainline denominations and in favor of the evangelical confessions. Some observers have interpreted the erosion of mainline membership in terms of parishioner resistance to the social activism characteristic of liberal Protestantism. What people want from their churches, declared Dean Kelley (1977) of the National Council of Churches, is comfort rather than challenge. When the liberal ministers nonetheless insisted upon social reform as the first priority, Kelley and others maintained, the members voted with their feet, deserting in favor of evangelical churches that spoke to the personal needs and fears of Christians. The mainline clergy seem to have ended up with the worst of both worlds: too action-oriented to suit the preferences of many congregants, new breed ministers were also too conventional to maintain the faith of their young, affluent, well-educated constituents.

PATTERNS OF RETRENCHMENT

Faced with pressure from parishioners and church boards, the mainline churches have adopted a lower profile and curtailed some of their social and political activites. Much conservative criticism had come to focus on the National Council of Churches (NCC), an ecumenical organization of mainline denominations that spearheaded church social action during the 1960s (Pratt 1972). In response to declines in membership and complaints about the appropriateness and representativeness of NCC activity, affiliated churches began to reduce their contributions to NCC and other interfaith organizations. The organizations, in turn, cut back on staff and social action (Briggs 1976). More recently, the general secretary of the Council announced plans to increase the voice of member churches in the decision-making process and to give greater emphasis to worship and spiritual matters (Fox 1985). While the Council has not stopped issuing statements critical of prevailing social arrangements, it has given more attention to traditional religious issues such as the extent of sex and violence in popular media (Associated Press, 1985). These steps have not eliminated suspicion of the NCC among many parishioners from member denominations.

Within the individual churches themselves, similar patterns have been evident. In response to the eroding membership base, churches have given renewed attention to worship and other traditional activities. To make more effective use of limited resources, smaller denominations have joined together in merged confessions. Already, various branches of Lutherans and Presbyterians have joined in new churches, and nine other denominations, with more than 20 million members, have been considering a new union (Marty 1984). Because endorsement of controversial social and political policies might threaten the harmony of these new unions, the denominations have been reluctant to tread too deeply into the realm of public action. In contrast to their previous willingness to enter the political arena, the mainline churches have been conspicuously silent during the last few presidential elections.

As both a symbol and source of the political retreat, eighteen clergymen issued "An Appeal for Theological Affirmation" at the conclusion of a meeting in Hartford, Connecticut, in January 1975. Although the signers included Catholics and evangelicals, most were from mainline churches and the instigators had strong liberal credentials as civil rights activists and leaders of organizations that had opposed American involvement in Vietnam. Widely interpreted as call for withdrawal from the social activism of the 1960s, the "Hartford Appeal" condemned a number of fashionable doctrines as "false and debilitating to the Church's life and work." The signers insisted that the essence of Christianity could not be reduced to modern movements for social reform, whether left- or right-wing, and reaffirmed traditional beliefs about the primacy of God and the need for individual redemption (Berger and Neuhaus 1976).

In all facets of the mainline church, then, the past decade has been marked by political retrenchment. The new breed, who never represented more than a minority force within a largely conservative tradition, succeeded for a time in altering the image of liberal Protestantism but eventually succumbed to pressures for a lower profile. Though individuals continue to press for liberal political causes, the family of mainline Protestants has let the leading role go by default to the newly energized evangelicals and Roman Catholics.

Black Protestants: The Perpetuation of Liberalism

To a greater or lesser degree, the discussion of political trends among evangelical Protestants, Roman Catholics, and liberal Protestants has emphasized change—from inaction to mobilization for the first two groups, and a shift in the opposite direction for the mainline Protestants. But for the two remaining religious groups, Jews and black Protestants, the operative word has been stability. Although neither group was unmoved by the events of the 1970s, they have remained the most reliable pillars of national support for liberal candidates and causes.

That blacks have stayed on the political left is hardly surprising. As an identifiable minority group still clustered in particular areas, subject to the highest rates of unemployment and the lowest levels of economic security, the black community has remained overwhelmingly in favor of an activist government. In the 1980s, Republican attacks on many programs and policies that blacks have ardently supported have cemented blacks' ties to the Democratic party. In polls from the 1984 national elections, about 90 percent of black voters said that they supported the Democratic presidential candidate and House nominees from the same party; and approximately 80 percent described themselves as Democrats—the highest level of commitment from any group in the electorate ("Opinion Roundup" 1985, 35).

More surprising has been the continued presence of members of the black clergy in political leadership roles. Through the Southern Christian Leadership Conference (SCLC) and local ministerial alliances, the Reverend Martin Luther King, Jr., and like-minded black clergymen provided vital organizational resources and strategy for the civil rights movement in the late 1950s and early 1960s. In a fascinating reconstruction of the early days of the civil rights campaign, Aldon Morris (1981, 1984) has demonstrated the critical role of black ministers and churches in training and recruiting volunteers, communicating with supporters, and providing havens for the early sit-ins, boycotts, and mass marches. Even those southern blacks who were outside the centers of organized resistance to segregation recognized ministers as the natural leaders of political activism (Mattews and Prothro 1966, 180–185). The same pattern held in the early 1970s, according to a national survey of black adults conducted by political scientist Hanes Walton (1985, 47–49). When asked to identify the major influences on their thinking, respondents identified the "black church" and the "black minister" more frequently than any other institution or organization.

But with time and changes in the political and social situation of blacks, the political leadership of ministers came to be challenged by new elites. The first signs of competition for leadership emerged when the civil rights movement entered what was described as its black power phase. Disappointed with the limited consequences of the civil rights legislation passed into law in 1964 and 1965, younger activists from outside the churches called on blacks to pursue more aggressive action to achieve social, economic, and political progress. As part of their appeal to black nationalist sentiment, the more militant leaders frequently denounced the clergy of the major black denominations for a supposed unwillingness to challenge the white power structure. To the extent that the black power movement was church-related, its center of gravity was located in nontraditional religious faith rather than in the mainstream black churches. The religious group most critical of Christianity, the Black Muslims, called for a complete separation of blacks from the white community and developed a theology that identified the white man as the incarnation of the devil. Although these non-Christians have never come close to displacing the traditional denominations, the assassination of Martin Luther King, Jr., robbed the civil rights movement of the most prominent leader with a distinctly Christian orientation to political action.

The black power revolt represented dissatisfaction with the limited progress of the civil rights movement under the leadership of the mainline clergy. Ironically, however, the very successes of the movement also produced a rival set of claimants for community leadership. With some relaxation of segregation and expanded educational opportunities, limited numbers of blacks were able to move into formerly white-dominated voluntary associations specializing in policy areas such as health, employment, education, and social welfare. With professional training, administrative skills, and political sophistication, such experts assumed some of the political and social responsibilities previously monopolized by the ministers (Wilson 1965, 297–300). The growing corps of blacks in government positions—another consequence of the civil rights movement—

further accentuated the transition away from clergy domination. Today, the typical black candidate for public office, be the position elective, appointive, or administrative, is most likely to emerge not from the clergy but from the sector of black professionals trained in law, business, public administration, or another field outside the church (Cole 1976, 43; Smith 1981, 210). Unlike the leadership of the black power revolt, however, the black professionals and public officials have remained closely tied to the mainstream churches (Salamon 1973, 628–29; Fenno 1978, 113–24).

Despite the emergence of a secular leadership class, the clergy have continued to provide major political leaders of the black community. In Congress, the Reverend Walter Fauntroy of Washington, D.C., has been one of the leading spokesmen for the concerns of the black community. A Philadelphia preacher, the Reverend William Gray, was elected in 1984 to chair the House Budget Committee—a signal honor for a representative in only his third congressional term and probably the single most influential position yet attained by a black in the House.[18] Andrew Young, a minister who was King's assistant in the SCLC, resigned a House seat to accept the cabinet-level position of ambassador to the United Nations during the Carter administration. In social action, too, black ministers have continued to provide the lead. As of 1982, the three top officials in the National Association for the Advancement of Colored People, the oldest civil rights organization in the United States, were Protestant ministers ("The Black Church" 1982, 5), as were the founders and leaders of the urban job-training organizations such as the Chicago-based "People United to Save Humanity" (PUSH) and the Opportunities Industrialization Commission (OIC) in Philadelphia. The founder of OIC, Reverend Leon Sullivan, has also been instrumental in forging American opposition to the white minority regime in South Africa. At the local level, too, ministers have continued to play an important political role even with the advent of the new black leadership class (Hadley 1985).

Black ministers have been able to play such a strategic role because they command the resources of the strongest institution in black life. The roots of the church run deep enough to make it the natural focus of organized activity in the black community and to enable it to withstand competition from secular organizations. As a typical example, the minister of the Shiloh Baptist Church in the nation's capital presides over a community outreach program that provides more than ninety separate services to neighborhood residents and over 5,000 parishioners (Noble 1984). The church has hosted most of the leading lights of the civil rights movement and has been visited in the recent past by such major national political leaders as Senator Edward Kennedy and President Ronald Reagan. In other urban centers, there have been church-based organizations such as the East Brooklyn Churches (EBC), described by an observer as "a powerful, politically independent, dues-paying organization that can turn out 7,000 people for a rally, register 10,000 new voters in a year and persuade politicians to put up new street signs [and] inspect local grocery stores" (Hornblower 1985). The EBC was instrumental in the building of low-cost housing that has restored to viability parts of Brooklyn that were once written off as terminally blighted.

From the perspective of organizational theory, leaders of the church enjoy (1) regular opportunities to communicate their views on issues to members of the community, (2) immense prestige and credibility, and (3) control over a network of social agencies that meet human needs. Such resources can easily be turned to political advantage. When black politics was restricted by law and custom, the black church could still provide a basis for some, limited bargaining with the white political elite. In Chicago during the turn of the century, a bishop of the local African Methodist Episcopal church used his pulpit, personal influence, and administrative control over an extensive system of welfare activities to mold blacks into a cohesive voting bloc. In exchange for supporting a victorious white mayoral candidate, the clergyman was able to obtain new public facilities in the black community and some patronage positions in municipal government for congregants (Katznelson 1976, 92–93).

To judge by the role of black churches in more recent Chicago elections, the stakes may have changed but the methods have not. With the prospect of electing a black to the mayor's office, the churches played a crucial role in a dramatic voter registration drive late in 1982 (Kleppner 1985, 145–50). One prominent black priest bluntly told his parishioners that nonregistrants were not welcome in the congregation. A voter registration card was the price of access to the free food distributed by one of the major Baptist churches in the black community. Under the slogan "Praise the Lord and Register," the black churches committed themselves wholeheartedly to serving as registration centers. Because of the massive increase in black voter enrollment and high turnout among the newly registered, the black candidate, Harold Washington, won the Chicago mayoral election in 1983. The churches have provided similar support for successful black mayoral candidates in Philadelphia and Birmingham.

When public office-holding came to be a realistic possibility, the political options of black clergymen expanded well beyond the limits of the segregation era. In fact, securing public office has frequently come to be viewed as an extension of the pastoral role. As one black minister with congressional experience told another who was considering running for office, "Congress will not be difficult. It is essentially pastoring, ministering to the folks in your district" (Hall 1985, 13). Combined with a gospel of social action, these institutional and social forces have provided a powerful impetus to organized political action.

While the black churches themselves may recently have pulled back somewhat from political action (Washington 1978), the clergy have remained the most recognized public symbol of black politics. The 1984 presidential campaign of the Reverend Jesse Jackson reinforced the trend by providing the clergy-activist with a national platform. An associate of the Reverend Martin Luther King, Jr., Jackson had concentrated on black economic development during the 1970s. In Chicago, he founded the PUSH organization (People United to Save Humanity), which eventually spread throughout the United States. The PUSH philosophy encourages blacks to cultivate conservative social values (self-help, strong discipline, drug avoidance) in the pursuit of what most conservative whites must surely regard as radical social, economic, and political objectives. True to his background in the civil rights movement, Jackson has not shied away from the use of boycotts, demonstrations, and sit-ins to protest alleged discrimination. Although he failed to win the 1984 Democratic presidential nomination, he succeeded in mobilizing impressive political support within the churches.

There is every reason to believe that the church will continue as the vanguard of political action for black Protestants. This does not mean that all black clergy should be expected to play a leadership role in political life. Like its white Protestant counterpart, the black religious community contains ministers who firmly believe that political mobilization ought to be a secondary concern lest it detract the church from the paramount task of saving souls. Even in the heyday of the civil rights movement, the SCLC was regarded with suspicion by some leaders of major black confessions and many preachers refrained from taking aggressive or challenging political stances (Hamilton 1972, chap. 5; Paris 1978).

In terms of social traits such as youthfulness and extensive educational experience, the most politically active ministers of the black church closely resemble their white counterparts in the new breed clergy of the mainline Protestants (Berenson, Elifson, and Tollerson, 1976). But because the laity of the largest and most active black churches recognizes a need for an activist government to promote social change, black clergymen face much less resistance to social and political activism. As scholars continue to debate whether the impact of clerical leadership and religious themes has helped or hindered the development of black political consciousness (Marx 1967, chap. 4; Hunt and Hunt 1977; Nelsen, Madron, and Yokley 1975), there can be little doubt that the black religious tradition will continue to shape the form of modern black political action.

JEWS AND AMERICAN POLITICAL TRENDS

Since the 1960s, some observers have predicted that urban unrest, affirmative action, and concern for the fate of Israel would eventually drive Jews out of the Democratic coalition and into alliance with conservative forces. But as noted in Chapter 4, if the bonds of Jewish political solidarity have loosened somewhat, Jews have continued to stand out from the rest of the public by a strong commitment to liberalism on a wide range of domestic issues. A yearly survey of political attitudes since 1981 has similarly testified that Jews have largely resisted the apparent conservative trends in American political life (Cohen 1984). In 1982, they voted for Democratic congressional candidates by a ratio of 3:1 ("Opinion Roundup" 1983, 36). In 1984, exit polls suggested a Jewish vote division of approximately two-thirds for Walter Mondale to only one-third for Ronald Reagan, and an even more lopsided Jewish Democratic preference in Congressional contests ("Opinion Roundup" 1985, 32; Schneider 1985). That made Jews one of only two groups in the electorate to move away from Ronald Reagan between 1980 and 1984.[19]

The erosion of Jewish liberalism was predicted in response to an upsurge in conflict between Jews and blacks. Before the black power movement, when the civil rights campaign concentrated principally on attacking formal barriers to equality, Jews were the single more ardent supporters of the movement in the white community. Aside from membership and leadership roles in interracial civil rights organizations, Jews made up a massively disproportionate share of the young white students who went South as volunteers for desegregation (Liebman 1979, 68). White politicians who developed a reputation as civil rights activists enjoyed nearly unanimous electoral support from Jewish voters; those who became symbols of white resistance, such as George Wallace of Alabama, looked elsewhere for support.

Once the civil rights movement moved to northern cities and came to focus upon *de facto* expressions of racism, however, the two communities began to divide.[20] Tensions arose over demands by the advocates of black power for "community control" of ghetto life. As the immigrant group that had preceded blacks to the city, Jews still occupied an important place in private businesses and public institutions in the central city. Hence, though directed at whites in general, demands for black ownership of businesses, black-only leadership in civil rights groups, and increased black representation in pubic employment challenged Jews in particular. The bitter expressions of hostility from some protagonists on both sides conveyed the impression of a fundamental estrangement rooted in a rising tide of black anti-Semitism and Jewish racism.

In New York, the city with the largest concentration of American Jews, these clashes became particularly intense. Attacks on Jewish-owned businesses during ghetto riots and conflicts between blacks and Jews in the public schools brought national publicity. Relationships eventually deteriorated to the point that a Brooklyn rabbi, Meier Kahane, formed a "Jewish Defense League" (JDL) to patrol inner-city neighborhoods with sizable concentrations of Jews. By offering armed protection to Jews who felt threatened by crime and anti-Semitic attacks, the JDL bore a strong resemblance to the most militant black organizations in the ghetto. Condemned by many Jewish leaders as a thinly disguised appeal to racist sentiment, the JDL nonetheless played upon fears of racial violence widespread in the Jewish community.[21]

On a more general level, tensions arose over the development of "affirmative action" programs in public employment, graduate and professional school admission, and other important sectors. The principle of affirmative action is that past discrimination against blacks or any other group can most effectively and justly be overcome by giving temporary preference to black applicants in competition for channels to upward mobility. The legitimacy of the principle and its application to concrete situations have generated considerable conflict within the liberal community. The doctrine goes well beyond the traditional understanding of "equality" into realms that have been described by unfriendly observers as "reverse discrimination" or "affirmative discrimination." Some of the most trenchant criticisms of the new policy came from Jews who regarded the programs as tantamount to setting up governmentally approved "quotas" for access to social advancement. Since such quotas had once been used to exclude Jews from careers in prestigious and remunerative occupations, their proposed introduction for purposes of spurring black advancement called forth strong opposition from much of the Jewish community. When the Supreme Court considered cases about the constitutionality of specific affirmative action programs, the major Jewish organizations that had once joined black plaintiffs in discrimination cases usually weighed in on the side challenging the new schemes.

Once the closest of allies, the two groups began to trade charges of racism and anti-Semitism. Blacks attributed the deteriorating relationship to Jewish unwillingness to admit their legitimate claims for jobs, housing, and political power, whereas Jews tended to blame racial agitation and black envy of Jewish achievement. In retrospect, the clash seems to have been a predictable outcome of the process of ethnic succession in American cities, more intense but otherwise quite like the earlier battles between white ethnic groups on the urban frontier. Even at the height of the conflict in New York, a specially commissioned public opinion poll revealed an underlying harmony between blacks and Jews (Harris and Swanson 1970, chap. 2). According to the poll, Jews were more likely than white Catholics and no less likely than white Protestants to acknowledge that blacks suffered discrimination, and only blacks shared the Jewish perspective that the latter were still victims of discrimination in the city.

The Jewish commitment to liberalism was thought to have been further undermined by the issue of Israel. As noted earlier, the Jewish community was galvanized by the outbreak of the 1967 Middle East war, which immeasurably strengthened the commitment of American Jews to the Zionist cause. As American Jews increased their support for the Jewish "homeland" in the Middle East, many self-identified liberals moved the other way by showing greater sympathy for the claims of Palestinian nationalists. Jews who had once championed the United Nations and given verbal support to some national liberation movements watched with dismay as the General Assembly declared Zionism to be a form of racism and equated Israelis with white South Africans as colonial oppressors.

During the administration of President Carter, the Israeli issue fused with concern over black attitudes to the Jewish community (Feuerlicht 1983, chap. 6; for an earlier tie, see Carson 1984). At the United Nations, Ambassador Andrew Young had forged strong ties with some of the Third World representatives who had been the most vociferous critics of American support for Israel. In August 1979, it was revealed that Young had held a meeting with a representative of the Palestine Liberation Organization (PLO), the umbrella group of Palestinian nationalism. Since the United States had an official policy to boycott the PLO until it granted recognition to Israel, Young's meeting was condemned by Israel and by leaders of American Jewish organizations. Under pressure from the State Department, Young eventually resigned. Blacks were angry about the apparent Jewish attack on their most influential advocate in the administration and felt that Young had been singled out for retribution. The Jews were outraged at the sympathy that blacks had shown to an organization that advocated violence in order to achieve Palestinian aims. In 1980, Jewish voters appeared to repay the Carter administration for its alleged pro-Arab tilt by giving President Carter less than a clear majority of their vote in his reelection bid. Although Israel was not the only reason for the decline in Jewish support for the Democratic ticket, it surely contributed in a major way.

These various tensions prompted a small group of Jewish intellectuals to argue that it was time for a change in alliance. In journals like *Commentary* and *Public Interest,* "neoconservatives" like Irving Kristol urged Jews to reconsider their traditional attachment to liberalism.[22] Jewish interests, it was argued, were most likely to be served by the conservative policies of the Republican administration that took office in 1981. In national defense, for example, Jews were told that Israel would benefit from the massive rearmament undertaken by the Defense Department. The administration's hostility to "affirmative action" programs fell well within the Jewish opposition to the use of quotas to increase black representation in the public sector and other places. Similarly, the neoconservatives encouraged Jews to vote their pocketbooks by supporting the antiinflation and tax–cutting programs that were launched by the Reagan White House.

The attempt to move Jews out of the Democratic camp received an unexpected push from the 1984 presidential campaign of the Reverend Jesse Jackson. During a public appearance, Jackson was overheard to refer to Jews as "Hymies" and New York City as "Hymietown." Although Jackson apologized for his offensive language, bad feelings were revived as the public learned more about his ties with Minister Louis Farrakhan, the head of a Black Muslim sect known as the Nation of Islam (Cohen 1984). By meeting with Libyan leader Moammar Khadafy and referring to Judaism as either a "gutter" or "dirty" religion, Farrakhan revived all the Jewish fears about the growth of black anti-Semitism. Jackson's insistence on condemning Farrakhan's remarks but not the man himself further exacerbated Jewish anger.[23] In spite of attempts at unity during the Democratic convention, many commentators expected Jews to react by shunning the Democratic ticket in November (Madison 1984).[24] As they did with the conflict of Geraldine Ferraro and the Catholic bishops, the Republicans emphasized these incidents and condemned the Democrats for failing to denounce anti-Semitism in their platform.

All told, the signs looked good for a historic shift in Jewish voting patterns in 1984. When that did not happen, most observers concluded that Jewish voters were more worried about the new political prominence of the evangelical Protestants than about the conflicts with black leaders. In support of this interpretation, a *Los Angeles Times* poll revealed that Jewish voters were actually more hostile to the Reverend Jerry Falwell, who had actually courted them on behalf of the Reagan campaign, than to Jesse Jackson (Schneider 1985, 58). And while 58 percent of Falwell's Jewish critics supported Walter Mondale, a whopping 78 percent of the anti–Jackson Jews stayed with the Democratic ticket on election day. Why did Jews react so much more negatively to a white Protestant preacher who supported Israel unreservedly than to a black Protestant preacher who flirted with the Arab cause? According to political scientist Seymour Martin Lipset (1985, 23), "The answer would seem to lie in the millennia-old history of European Jewry as a minority, persecuted and discriminated against by conservative religious and secular establishments." The evangelical Protestants are associated in the Jewish mind both with the policies of "Christian government" and with skepticism about the value of government support for welfare. Neither association endeared Jews to the Republican ticket in 1984 (Schindler 1984).

*   *   *   *   *

The most recent trends in political thought and action among the major religious families in the United States clearly indicate strong ties bind religion and politics in the 1980s. Yet it has also been demonstrated in this and the previous chapter that religious groups have reacted quite differently to national political trends. They have not all responded to the same issues nor responded similarly to common developments. While some of the uniqueness reflects group tradition and the pull of traditional loyalty, equal weight must be given to factors rooted in creedal, social, and institutional traits.

The larger consequences of the relationship between religion and politics—the important question of whether religious involvement is good or bad for the political system—will be taken up in the concluding chapter.

NOTES

[1] Charles E. Coughlin was a Detroit priest who had become a national celebrity with his radio broadcasts in the 1920s. During the 1930s, his broadcasts combined economic radicalism with attacks on Jews, communists, and the "New Deal" of Franklin D. Roosevelt. A U.S. senator from Wisconsin, Joseph McCarthy drew fame for his attacks on alleged communist penetration of the United States government in the late 1940s and early 1950s.

[2] According to Lipset, Catholics became more favorable to the John Birch Society only after the impact of partisanship was controlled. For other evidence, see Grupp and Newman 1973.

[3] Some commentators have speculated that American Catholics drew their fatalism from the peasant culture of the Italian and Irish countrysides. If urbanized and cosmopolitan European Catholics had predominated among American immigrants, the story of Catholic social values would probably have read very differently.

[4] This was true mostly for Catholic natives who were at least the third generation of their family in America. For more recent immigrants, especially Hispanic Catholics from Mexico and Puerto Rico, economic conditions and social integration were much less advanced.

[5] All citations refer to the text that appeared as a supplement to the *Chicago Catholic* of June 24, 1983. The text has also been reprinted in Mornion 1983. For Catholic commentary, see Lawler (1983, 1984); Dougherty (1984); Dwyer (1984). The report has inspired two volumes by evangelicals: Curry (1984) and Bernbaum (1984).

[6] The data for Figure 8.1 were taken from a General Social Survey question asking if the United States was spending "too much money, too little money, or about the right amount" on a series of program areas. In 1983, the subject of military spending was introduced with the phrase "the military, armaments and defense." About one-third of 1984 respondents were asked about "national defense" and another third about "strengthening national defense"; the remaining third received the same question as in 1983. Because the distribution of responses was similar using all three question forms, they were combined as one for analysis in Figure 8.1.

[7] As Michael Novak (1984) acknowledged, the bishops also strongly en-

dorsed such capitalist practices and motivations as tax incentives, small business, multinational corporations, and policies designed to promote entrepreneurial activity.

[8] Terms such as liberal and conservative may not fit well on issues such as abortion. In describing support for legalized abortion as "liberal" and opposition as "conservative," I do not mean to suggest that there is anything intrinsically liberal about supporting abortion as a right or anything inherently conservative about a restrictive policy.

[9] In *Roe* v. *Wade,* the Supreme Court argued that because of the constitutional right to privacy, states could not limit abortion during the first three months of pregnancy. Concerns for maternal health could justify medical regulations in the second trimester, and the government's interest in encouraging "normal childbirth" permitted restrictive policies in the last three months.

[10] This encyclical is better known for its insistence that all forms of artificial birth control violate the sanctity of human life.

[11] Opponents of abortion have debated the relative merits of constitutional amendments that would restore the criminal status of abortion nationwide versus proposals that would simply return the issue to the jurisdiction of the states rather than the federal government. Given the numerous obstacles to constitutional change, many observers feel that the *Roe* decision is most likely to be overturned by a judicial change of mind. Though the Court has repeatedly confirmed its 1973 decision, most recently in the *Thornburgh v. American College of Obstetricians and Gynecologists* ruling of June 1986 the statute was struck down by a narrow 5–4 vote, and the antiabortion wing has been strengthened by the promotion of William Rehnquist to chief justice and the appointment of Antonin Scalia to Rehnquist's seat on the court.

[12] Luker (1975) found that Catholics constituted about one third of the women seeking abortions in a Northern California clinic. An elaborate study in Hawaii, which had liberalized abortion laws well before most of the nation, showed that Catholic women made extensive use of elective abortion but were also less likely than pregnant women from other denominations to terminate pregnancy artificially (Leon and Steinhoff 1975).

[13] There were similar results in 1972 when George McGovern's liberalism on abortion was one of the factors reducing Catholic support for the Democratic ticket even though the vice-presidential nominee, R. Sargent Shriver, was a member of the church.

[14] Keep in mind that researchers have mostly discovered insignificant differences between the two sides. If antiabortion advocates are not more liberal, neither are they generally much more conservative except where the issue ties in to abortion.

[15] Use of the social abortion scale, where Catholics are much less supportive of abortion, would not materially alter the conclusion reached after inspection of Figure 8.2.

[16] Throughout this chapter, "liberal Protestantism" refers to the theologically liberal denominations that made up the nonevangelical or "mainline" wing in Chapter 4. On the religious beliefs that distinguish them from their evangelical counterparts, see Stark and Glock (1970).

[17] Interestingly, the historian Richard Hofstadter (1955, 148–152) offered a similar explanation to account for the initial surge of mainline activism during the Progressive era.

[18] Prior to Gray's election, former representatives Adam Clayton Powell and Charles Diggs probably represented the pinnacle of black power in the House. Both were ministers of large, influential churches.

[19] The other group was the unemployed.

[20] De facto segregation occurs not because of law but because of segregation in other areas of life.

[21] Kahane eventually left New York for Israel, where he heads a similar movement to "defend" Jews in West Bank settlements against Arabs.

[22] Of course, the neoconservative movement also attracted prominent non-Jewish members such as Daniel Patrick Moynihan, Jeanne Kirpatrick, and James Q. Wilson.

[23] For black reaction to the Farrakhan movement, see the special polls of a national black sample in Simon Wiesenthal Center (1986).

[24] Jackson has since gone out of his way to mend fences with the Jewish community. See the account in Gross (1985).

REFERENCES

Ammerman, Nancy T. 1981. "The Civil Rights Movement and the Clergy in a Southern Community." *Sociological Analysis*. 41: 339–350.

Associated Press. 1985. "Church Says Media Are Obsessed with Sex, Violence." *Gainesville Sun*. September 21: 9A.

Barker, Lionel. 1985a. "Family Planning Funds Will Go Only for 'Natural' Methods." *Washington Post Weekly Edition*. August 26: 34.

Barker, Lionel. 1985b. "Shultz Is on the Spot over Funds for Family Planning." *Washington Post Weekly Edition*. September 30: 17.

Berenson, William, Kirk W. Elifson, and Tandy Tollerson, III. 1976. "Preachers in Politics: A Study of Political Activism Among the Black Ministry." *Journal of Black Studies*. 6: 373–392.

Berger, Peter, and Richard John Neuhaus, editors. 1976. *Against the World, for the World*. New York: Seabury Press.

Bernbaum, John A., editor. 1984. *Perspectives on Peacemaking*. Ventura, CA: Regal Books.

"The Black Church." 1982. *Crisis*. 89:5–50.

Blau, Peter M. 1953. "Orientation of College Students Toward International Relations." *American Journal of Sociology*. 59: 205–214.

Briggs, Kenneth. 1984a. "Activism Affirmed by Catholic Order." *New York Times*. December 10: A5.

Briggs, Kenneth. 1984b. "Catholic Group Extols Capitalism as Bishops Ready Economy Study." *New York Times*. November 7: 1, 21.

Briggs, Kenneth. 1976. "The Sporadic Activism of U.S. Churches." *New York Times*. January 11: 20 (section 4).

Califano, Joseph, Jr. 1984. "Moral Leadership Is Not Partisanship." *Washington Post National Weekly Edition*. September 3: 28.

Callahan, Daniel. 1970. *Abortion: Law, Choice, and Morality*. New York: Macmillan.

Campbell, Ernest Q., and Thomas F. Pettigrew. 1959. *Christians in Racial Crisis.* Washington, DC: Public Affairs Press.

Carson, Claybourne, Jr. 1984. "Blacks and Jews in the Civil Rights Movement." In *Jews in Black Perspectives: A Dialogue,* ed. Joseph Washington. Rutherford, NJ: Fairleigh Dickinson University Press, 113–131.

Carter, Paul A. 1954. *The Decline and Revival of the Social Gospel.* Ithaca, NY: Cornell University Press.

Cohen, Sharon. 1984. "Islam in America: Different Words from the Same Book." *Gainesville Sun.* July 5: 7B.

Cohen, Steven M. 1984. "The Political Attitudes of American Jews, 1984." New York: American Jewish Committee.

Cohodas, Nadine. 1983. "Campaign to Overturn Ban on Abortion Funding Begun." *Congressional Quarterly Weekly Report.* August 20: 1689–1693.

Cole, Leonard. 1976. *Blacks in Power.* Princeton, NJ: Princeton University Press.

Connors, John F., Richard C. Leonard, and Kenneth E. Burnham. 1968. "Religion, Church Attitudes, Religious Education, and Student Attitudes to War." *Sociological Analysis* 29: 211–219.

Cooney, John. 1984. *The American Pope.* New York: Times Books.

Costelloe, Kevin. 1985. "Pope: Wage War for Social Justice." *Gainesville Sun.* May 20: 4C.

Cox, Harvey. 1968. "The 'New Breed' in American Churches: Sources of Social Activism in American Religion." In *Religion in America,* ed. William G. McLaughlin and Robert N. Bellah. Boston, MA: Beacon Press, 368–383.

Crosby, Donald, S.J. 1978. *God, Church, and Flag.* Chapel Hill, NC: University of North Carolina Press.

Cuomo, Mario. 1984. "Excerpts from Cuomo Talk on Religion and Public Morality." *New York Times.* September 14: 13.

Curran, Charles E. 1982. *American Catholic Social Ethics: Twentieth Century Approaches.* Notre Dame, IN: University of Notre Dame Press.

Curry, Dean C., editor. 1984. *Evangelicals and the Bishops' Pastoral Letter.* Grand Rapids, MI: William B. Eerdmans.

Dickenson, James R. 1984. "Almighty Politics." *Washington Post National Weekly Edition.* October 1: 11.

Dougherty, James E. 1984. *The Bishops and Nuclear Weapons.* Hamden, CT: Archon Books.

Drinan, Robert F., S.J. 1970. *Vietnam and Armageddon.* New York: Sheed and Ward.

Dwyer, Judith A., editor. 1984. *The Catholic Bishops and Nuclear War.* Washington, DC: Georgetown University Press.

Fenno, Richard F., Jr. 1978. *Home Style.* Boston, MA: Little, Brown.

Feuerlicht, Roberta Strauss. 1983. *The Fate of the Jews: A People Torn Between Israeli Power and Jewish Ethics.* New York: Times Books.

Fox, Mario. 1985. "New Head of NCC Promises More Lay Involvement in Its Agenda." *Gainesville Sun.* June 1:3B.

Friedman, Lawrence M. 1983. "The Conflict over Constitutional Legitimacy." In *The Abortion Dispute and the American System,* ed. Gilbert Y. Steiner. Washington, DC: Brookings Institution, 13–29.

Furlow, Robert. 1985. "Catholic Bishops Call for More Aid to Farm Families." *Gainesville Sun.* May 15: 12C.

Furlow, Robert. 1984. "Bishop: Politicians Can't Separate Moral Views from Public Policy." *Gainesville Sun.* August 11: 3B.

Garrett, William R. 1973. "Politicized Clergy: A Sociological Interpretation of the 'New Breed.' " *Journal for the Scientific Study of Religion.* 12: 383–397.

Gaustad, Edwin S. 1968. "America's Institution of Faith." In *Religion in America,* ed. William G. McLoughlin and Robert N. Bellah. Boston, MA: Beacon Press, 111–133.

Gilkey, Langdon. 1968. "Social and Intellectual Sources of Contemporary Protestant Theology in America." In *Religion in America,* ed. William G. McLoughlin and Robert N. Bellah. Boston, MA: Beacon Press, 137–166.

Granberg, Donald. 1982a. "Comparison of Pro-Choice of Pro-Life Activists: Their Values, Attitudes, and Beliefs." *Population and Environment.* 5: 75–94.

Granberg, Donald. 1982b. "Family Size Preferences and Sexual Permissiveness as Factors Differentiating Abortion Activists." *Social Psychology Quarterly.* 45: 15–23.

Granberg, Donald. 1981a. "Comparison of Members of Pro- and Anti-Abortion Organizations in Missouri." *Social Biology.* 28: 239–252.

Granberg, Donald. 1981b. "The Abortion Activists." *Family Planning Perspectives.* 13: 157–163.

Granberg, Donald, and James Burlison. 1983. "The Abortion Issue in the 1980 Elections." *Family Planning Perspectives.* 15: 231–238.

Granberg, Donald, and Beth Wellman Granberg. 1981. "Pro-Life Versus Pro-Choice: Another Look at the Abortion Controversy in the U.S." *Sociology and Social Research.* 65: 424-433.

Greer, William R. 1985. "Catholic Bishops Say Women's Role Should Be Larger." *New York Times.* September 16: 1, 14.

Gross, Jane. 1985. "Jackson Calls for Coalition of Blacks, Jews After Europe Trip." *Gainesville Sun.* May 20: 3A.

Grupp, Fred W., and William M. Newman. 1973. "Political Ideology and Religious Preference: The John Birch Society and the Americans for Democratic Action." *Journal for the Scientific Study of Religion.* 12: 401–413.

Hadden, Jeffrey K. 1969. *The Gathering Storm in the Churches.* Garden City, NY: Doubleday-Anchor.

Hadden, Jeffrey K., and Raymond C. Rymph. 1971. "The Marching Ministers." In *Religion in Radical Transition,* ed. Jeffrey K. Hadden. New Brunswick, NJ: Transaction Books, 99–110.

Hadley, Charles D. 1985. "Black Ministers, Black Political Organizations, and the Continuing Transformation of Their Role in Louisiana Politics." Paper presented to the annual meeting of the Southern Political Science Association, Nashville, TN.

Hall, Carla. 1985. "How a Philadelphia Preacher Won Converts to His Budget Gospel." *Washington Post National Weekly Edition.* June 10: 12–13.

Hamilton, Charles V. 1972. *The Black Preacher in America.* New York: William Morrow.

Hanna, Mary. 1985. "The Catholic Bishops' Pastoral Letter on Poverty." Paper presented to the annual meeting of the American Political Science Association, New Orleans, LA.

Hanna, Mary. 1979. *Catholics and American Politics.* Cambridge, MA: Harvard University Press.

Harris, Louis, and Bert E. Swanson. 1970. *Black-Jewish Relations in New York City.* New York: Praeger.

Hawk, Kathleen. 1985a. "Catholics Respond to Bishop's Call for Input on Women's Issues." *Gainesville Sun.* September 21: 1–2B.

Hawk, Kathleen. 1985b. "Nun Speaks Out About Repercussions over Signing Abortion Ad." *Gainesville Sun.* September 14: 1–2B.

Herbers, John. 1984a. "Catholic Activism: Reasons and Risks." *Gainesville Sun.* September 23: 5B.

Herbers, John. 1984b. "55 Scholars Say Church's Abortion Stand Is Not Monolithic." *New York Times.* September 15: 29.

Hofstadter, Richard. 1965. *The Paranoid Style in American Politics.* New York: Vintage Books.

Hofstadter, Richard. 1955. *The Age of Reform.* New York: Vintage Books.

Hornblower, Margot. 1985. "Now a Suburb Grows in Brooklyn—and Without Federal Help." *Washington Post Weekly Edition.* July 29: 31–32.

Hornblower, Margot. 1984. "The Catholic Church's Political Role: A Growth Industry." *Washington Post National Weekly Edition.* November 26: 11.

Hunt, Larry L., and Janet G. Hunt. 1977. "Black Religion as Both Opiate and Inspiration of Civil Right Militance: Putting Marx's Data to the Test." *Social Forces.* 56: 1–14.

IEA and Roper Center. 1982. "Theology Faculty Survey." *This World.* 1: 27–108.

Jaffe, Frederick S., Barbara Lindheim, and Philip R. Lee. 1981. *Abortion Politics: Private Morality and Public Policy.* New York: McGraw-Hill.

Jelen, Ted G. 1984. "Respect for Life, Sexual Morality, and Opposition to Abortion." *Review of Religious Research.* 25: 220–231.

Kane, Joseph N. 1974. *Facts About the Presidents.* New York: H. H. Wilson.

Katznelson, Ira. 1976. *Black Men, White Cities.* Chicago, IL: University of Chicago Press.

Kelley, Dean M. 1977. *Why Conservative Churches Are Growing.* Second edition. San Francisco, CA: Harper and Row.

Kennedy, Edward M. 1984. "Excerpts from Speech by Kennedy." *New York Times* September 11: 10.

Kennedy, Eugene. 1985. *Reimagining American Catholicism.* New York: Vintage Books.

Kissling, Frances. 1985. "The Catholics Who Support Choice." *Washington Post Weekly Edition.* September 2: 28.

Kleppner, Paul. 1985. *Chicago Divided: The Making of a Black Mayor.* Dekalb, IL: Northern Illinois University Press.

Koller, Norman B., and Joseph D. Retzer. 1980. "The Sounds of Silence Revisited." *Sociological Analysis.* 41: 155–161.

Lawler, Philip F. 1984. *The Ultimate Weapon.* Chicago, IL: Regnery Gateway.

Lawler, Philip F., editor. 1983. *Justice and War in the Nuclear Age.* Lanham, MD: University Press of America.

Legge, Jerome S. 1985. "Self-Interest Versus Symbolic Politics: The Formulation of Attitudes Toward Abortion Policy." Paper presented to the Southern Political Science Association, Nashville, TN.

Leon, Joseph J., and Patricia G. Steinhoff. 1975. "Catholics' Use of Abortion." *Sociological Analysis.* 36: 125–136.

Liebman, Arthur. 1979. *Jews and the Left.* New York: Wiley-Interscience.

Lipset, Seymour Martin. 1985. "Most Jews Are Still Both Democratic and Liberal." *Washington Post National Weekly Edition.* January 14: 22–23.

Lipset, Seymour Martin. 1964. "Three Decades of the Radical Right: Couglinites, McCarthyites, and Birchers." In *The Radical Right,* ed. Daniel Bell. Garden City, NY: Doubleday-Anchor, 373–446.

Luker, Kristin. 1984. *Abortion and the Politics of Motherhood.* Berkeley, CA: University of California Press.

Luker, Kristin. 1975. *Taking Chances: Abortion and the Decision Not to Contracept.* Berkeley, CA: University of California Press.

Madison, Christopher. 1984. "Mondale Walks Tightrope to Hold Black Support Without Risking Jewish Vote." *National Journal.* September 8: 1654–1658.

Malone, James W. 1984a. "Excerpts from Address to Bishops on Shaping Public Policies." *New York Times.* November 13: 1,16.

Malone, James W. 1984b. "Text of Bishops' Statement on Role of the Church in Politics." *New York Times.* October 14: A1.

Margolis, Michael, and Kevin Neary. 1980. "Pressure Politics Revisited: The Anti-Abortion Campaign." *Policy Studies Journal.* 8: 698–716.

Marty, Martin E. 1984. "Mainline Churches Kept Fairly Quiet During Campaigns." *Miami Herald.* December 28: 1E, 5E.

Marx, Gary T. 1967. *Protest and Prejudice.* New York: Harper and Row.

Matthews, Donald R., and James W. Prothro. 1966. *Negroes and the New Southern Politics.* New York: Harcourt, Brace and World.

Matthews, Jay. 1985. "California's Antiabortion Initiative." *Washington Post Weekly Edition.* August 12: 12.

May, Henry F. 1963. *Protestant Churches and Industrial America.* New York: Octagon Books.

McMillan, Margaret. 1927. *The Life of Rachel McMillan.* London: J. M. Dent.

Meconis, Charles A. 1979. *With Clumsy Grace: The American Catholic Left, 1961–1975.* New York: Seabury Press.

Menendez, Albert J. 1977. *Religion at the Polls.* Philadelphia, PA: Westminster Press.

Merton, Andrew H. 1981. *Enemies of Choice: The Right-to-Life Movement and Its Threat to Abortion.* Boston, MA: Beacon Press.

Meyer, Donald B. 1961. *The Protestant Search for Political Realism, 1919–41.* Berkeley, CA: University of California Press.

Mornion, Philip J., editor. 1983. *Catholics and Nuclear War.* New York: Crossroads.

Morris, Aldon. 1984. *The Origins of the Civil Rights Movement.* New York: Free Press.

Morris, Aldon. 1981. "Black Southern Student Sit-In Movement: An Analysis of Internal Organization." *American Sociological Review.* 46: 744–767.

Mueller, John E. 1973. *Wars, Presidents, and Public Opinion.* New York: John Wiley.

Nelsen, Hart M. 1975. "Why Do Pastors Preach on Social Issues?" *Theology Today.* 32: 56–73.

Nelsen, Hart M., Thomas Madron, and Raytha Yokley. 1975. "Black Religion's Promethean Motif: Orthodoxy and Militancy." *American Journal of Sociology.* 81: 139–148.

Nelsen, Hart M., Raytha L. Yokley, and Thomas W. Madron. 1973. "Ministerial Roles and Social Actionist Stance: Protestant Clergy and Protest in the Sixties." *American Sociological Review.* 38: 375–386.

New York Times. 1984. "Voters Found Uneasy over Religion as Issue." *New York Times.* September 19: 13.

New York Times Service. 1985. "Poll Finds American Catholics Leaving Church Teachings." *Gainesville Sun.* November 25: 6A.

Noble, Kenneth B. 1984. "D.C.'s Shiloh Baptist Is a Symbol of Black Political Activism." *Gainesville Sun.* September 1: 1C.

Novak, Michael 1984. "The Bishops and the Poor." *Washington Post National Weekly Edition.* November 26: 29.

O'Brien, David J. 1968. *American Catholics and Social Reform: The New Deal Years.* New York: Oxford University Press.

O'Connor, John J. 1984. "Key Portions of Archbishop's Speech on Abortion and Politics." *New York Times.* October 16: 14.

"Opinion Round-Up." 1985. *Public Opinion.* 7: 23–42.

"Opinion Round-Up." 1983. *Public Opinion.* 5: 21–40.

Paige, Connie. 1983. *The Right to Lifers.* New York: Summit Books.

Paris, Peter J. 1978. *Black Leaders in Conflict.* New York: Pilgrim Press.

Piehl, Mel. 1982. *Breaking Bread: The Catholic Worker and the Origin of Catholic Radicalism in America.* Philadelphia, PA: Temple University Press.

Pratt, Henry J. 1972. *The Liberalization of American Protestantism.* Detroit, MI: Wayne State University Press.

Quinley, Harold E. 1974. *The Prophetic Clergy: Social Activism Among Protestant Ministers.* New York: Wiley-Interscience.

Rainey, Jane G. 1985. "Religious Involvement in the Pro-Choice Movement: Challenging Some Stereotypes of the Abortion Debate." Paper presented to the annual meeting of the American Political Science Association, New Orleans, LA.

Reagan, Ronald. 1984. *Abortion and the Conscience of the Nation.* Nashville, TN: Thomas Nelson.

Roof, Wade Clark. 1978. *Community and Commitment: Religious Plausibility in a Liberal Protestant Church.* New York: Elsevier.

Salamon, Lester M. 1973. "Leadership and Modernization: The Emerging Black Political Elite in the American South." *Journal of Politics.* 35: 615–646.

Sawyer, Darwin O. 1982. "Public Attitudes Toward Life and Death." *Public Opinion Quarterly.* 46: 521–533.

Schindler, Alexander M. 1984. "Jewish Voters Are Placed in a Dilemma." *Gainesville Sun.* July 9: 11A.

Schneider, William. 1985. "The Jewish Vote in 1984: Elements in a Controversy." *Public Opinion.* 7: 18–19, 58.

Silk, Leonard. 1984a. "Bishop's Letter and U.S. Goals." *New York Times.* November 14: 32.

Silk, Leonard. 1984b. "In Celebration of Creative Capitalism in Society." *New York Times.* November 7: 21.

Simon Wiesenthal Center. 1986. "The Farrakhan Phenomenon." *Response.* 13: 2–3.

Smith, Robert C. 1981. "The Black Congressional Delegation." *Western Political Quarterly.* 34: 203–221.

Stark, Rodney, Bruce D. Foster, Charles Y. Glock, and Harold E. Quinley. 1971. *Wayward Shepherds.* New York: Harper and Row.

Stark, Rodney, and Charles Y. Glock. 1970. *American Piety: The Nature of Religious Commitment.* Berkeley, CA: University of California Press.

Starr, Jerrold. 1975. "Religious Preference, Religiosity, and Opposition to War." *Sociological Analysis.* 36: 323–334.

Surrey, David S. 1982. *Choice of Conscience: Vietnam Era Military and Draft Resisters in Canada.* New York: Praeger.

Tamney, Joseph B., and Stephen D. Johnson. 1985. "Christianity and the Nuclear Issue." *Sociological Analysis.* 46: 321–328.

Traugott, Michael W., and Maris A. Vinovskis. 1980. "Abortion and the 1978 Congressional Elections." *Family Planning Perspectives.* 12: 238–246.

Tygart, Clarence E. 1977. "The Role of Theology Among Other 'Belief' Variables for Clergy Civil Rights Activism." *Review of Religious Research.* 18: 271–278.

Vinovskis, Maris A. 1979. "Abortion and the Presidential Election of 1976: A Multivariate Analysis of Voting Behavior." In *Michigan Law Review.* 7: 1750–1771.

Wagenaar, Theodore C., and Patricia E. Bartos. 1977. "Orthodoxy and Attitudes of Clergymen Towards Homosexuality and Abortion." *Review of Religious Research.* 18: 114–125.

Walton, Hanes, Jr. 1985. *Invisible Politics: Black Political Behavior.* Albany, NY: State University of New York Press.

Washington, Joseph R., Jr., editor. 1978. *Black Religion and Public Policy: Ethical and Historical Perspectives.* Papers of a symposium held at the University of Pennsylvania in March 1978.

Weber, Paul J., and John L. Anderson. 1985. "The Impact of the Bishops' Pastoral on the Primary and Secondary Media." Paper presented to the annual meeting of the American Political Science Association, New Orleans, LA.

Williams, Juan. 1984. "Catholic Bishops' Pastoral Draft Jolts Community." *Washington Post.* November 19: A8.

Wilmore, Gayraud S. 1983. *Black Religion and Black Radicalism.* Second edition. Maryknoll, NY: Orbis Books.

Wilson, James Q. 1965. *Negro Politics: The Search for Leadership.* New York: Free Press.

Wolf, Donald J., S. J. 1968. *Toward Consensus: Catholic-Protestant Interpretations of Church and State.* Garden City, NY: Doubleday-Anchor.

Wood, James R. 1981. *Leadership in Voluntary Organizations: The Controversy over Social Action in Protestant Churches.* New Brunswick, NJ: Rutgers University Press.

9

Religion and American Political Life

Viewed against the backdrop of history, the recent rise in political activism among some religious groups is not a departure from national tradition but only the renewal of a long-standing pattern in American political life. As previous chapters have documented, religion—in the guise of sacred values, institutions, and social groups—has operated at several levels of politics. The religious factor was present at the creation of the American political system, one of several elements contributing to the design of governmental institutions and to the core of beliefs that grew into the national political culture. The place of religion in a pluralistic society has generated a seemingly endless supply of court cases about the proper relationship between church and state. Religious affiliation has long been a potent influence on mass partisan loyalties and has been a factor inspiring the positions taken by political elites upon a wide range of pressing national issues. If the past few years are any indication, religion has retained a potency that will keep it among the social forces likely to fuel political conflict.

What may not be so clear are the political consequences of the interaction between the spheres of religion and politics. In referring to "consequences," I do *not* mean either the impact of political activism upon religion nor the effect of religious intervention on the disposition of particular policies. Both are legitimate issues that have been examined. elsewhere in the book. Rather, this chapter's theme is the effect of religious activism upon the general tenor of political life in the United States. Specifically, I will assess the benefits and costs to democracy and the functioning of the political system of the religious presence in public life. My conclusion, that religion in politics is neither an unvarying source of good nor a consistent evil influence, is unlikely to please either the most ardent advocates of a "Christian America" or secularists who want to keep religion safely outside the public arena. It is consistent, however, with the historical record, which has shown that religion has the capacity both to ennoble and to corrupt political life.

THE CASE AGAINST RELIGIOUS INFLUENCE IN POLITICS

Even if they were to lower their profile, religious groups would still be important actors in American political life. Does this reality bode good or evil for the future of politics in the United States? The question is not merely academic, for although certain forms of religious influence cannot be controlled, the government has some limited power to encourage or discourage organized political involvement by the churches (Kelley 1982, 64–83, 111–28, 151–64). To cite one important example, the tax-free status of churches is conditional upon their refraining from endorsement of candidates or devoting more than a certain percentage of resources to lobbying and political action. Currently interpreted to give churches substantial leeway for public involvement, the laws could be tightened to make it more difficult for clergy to engage in political action or to use their congregations as a base for movements with public goals.[1] Considering the strong public sentiment for keeping the churches "out of politics," such a restrictive policy might enjoy broad support. That makes it even more important to assess the pros and cons of active religious involvement by churches and religiously inspired activists.

The rise of religious activism has been a source of concern and apprehension to many observers, including many who are sympathetic to religion as an institution (see, for example, Maguire 1982). At the heart of that concern lies the fear that religious controversy in politics will lead to extremism and polarization, injecting the body politic with unhealthy doses of fanaticism and ill will. Carried to extremes, critics have contended, the entry of religious issues into the public agenda may produce violence, undermining the foundations of democratic politics.

Why should religion have such dire consequences for the stability of government? Many commentators have insisted that democratic government depends on a willingness to negotiate, to bargain, to approach politics in the spirit of compromise. Some issues naturally lend themselves to this type of treatment. Conflicts over money—demands for pay raises, proposals to increase taxes, competition for federal funding—are inherently subject to bargaining, because financial benefits are divisible in terms of dollars. Economic conflicts can usually be managed within the framework of a stable political system. But when conflicts take on an either/or dimension, the impediments to compromise can prompt antagonists to subvert the political system by resorting to armed violence. On the one occasion in American history when such an all–or–nothing issue—slavery—dominated the national agenda, the result was a complete breakdown of the political system and a bloody civil war.

Like slavery, religious issues may challenge the normal system of governance. Policy debates with a moral dimension do not readily lend themselves to compromise solutions. If you regard abortion as murder and I see it as a neutral medical procedure, it will be hard to find a middle ground that either one of us will accept as a legitimate public policy. The same type of problem arises in the context of debates over prayer in public schools, the rights of homosexuals, traditional sex roles, and other policy areas in which religious groups have been active. Without realistic hope for a compromise solution that is minimally acceptable to all sides, such issues are likely to fester and breed support for extremist action. When intertwined with religious values, political issues may take on a dangerous characteristic—namely, a lack of bargainability that impedes the peaceful resolution of conflict.

A related problem raised by critics of church activism involves the potential impact of religious values on the *style* of political activists. As religious issues do not easily admit of compromise, so, too, religious values may produce an orientation that can lead to rigidity and dogmatism. Because they are imparted at an early age and constitute a critical element of one's identity, religious values can exercise a very strong grip on the human mind. Deep faith may be accompanied by close-mindedness, dogmatism, and contempt for alternative points of view. Carried to extremes, confidence in one's own viewpoint can poison the political atmosphere and endanger social stability. A person who believes that he or she is acting under God's direct command may be prone to look upon compromise as a betrayal of divine intention. Activists who believe that God is on their side are likely to perceive their opponents as not merely misguided or confused but as evil and malevolent. Against opponents who are transformed into symbols of iniquity, the normal courtesies and respect due an antagonist will be suspended. Religious enthusiasm may lead to fanaticism on behalf of causes deemed conservative or liberal.

This apprehension about the potentially destabilizing effects of religious values on political conflict has been reinforced by the experience of other countries. Sadly, world history does not lack examples of inquisitions, crusades, and massacres resulting from the fusion of religious passion with secular authority. In the contemporary era, there have been troubling reports from Iran about the pathetic eagerness of children to offer themselves up as virtual human sacrifices in a "holy war" for Islam (Hansen 1984). The political consequences of religiously oriented politics also present evidence in the carnage of Northern Ireland, Lebanon, India, and other trouble spots around the globe. Closer to home, there has been the appalling example of mass suicide in Jonestown and the disturbing reports about the rise of "Christian" paramilitary cults in the depressed farming country (King 1985). From time to time—but always too often—we read newspaper accounts about churches or congregations that evolve into totalitarian cults, practicing horror in the name of God and undermining social harmony.

On a less dramatic level, a systematic study of seventeen Western nations by Rose and Urwin (1966) confirmed the dangers of a strong religious presence in party politics.[2] In approximately half the countries, the principal line of electoral conflict was defined by religious affiliation or practice; the remaining nine nations lacked a strong religious dimension to party competition. According to Rose and Urwin, the countries with the strongest religious divisions had experienced much more strain, violence, and political instability than had the nations whose politics were largely free of religious controversy. In some cases, religious conflict in the former group had even contributed to the collapse of governmental systems and the emergence of antidemocratic politics. The correlation between the strength of "ethnocultural" cleavages and political instability appears to have persisted to the present day (Powell 1982, 44–47).

Do these findings necessarily apply to the United States? Does the entry of religious groups in the political arena threaten the stability of the political system? Reasonable people can disagree over the answer to this question, but there can be no denying that some of the symptoms attributed to religiously based politics have appeared in American life. To demonstrate the basis for that conclusion and to show how the problem is not restricted to any one side of the religious spectrum, I offer accounts of two experiences that helped bring me to an awareness of the possible costs of recent trends in religious-political interaction.

In the summer of 1980, while supervising the work of two student interns at the Republican National Convention in Detroit, I happened to encounter a Texas delegate in a hotel lobby. Stopping and pointing to the large pro-ERA button on my lapel, she challenged me to justify my support for an amendment that, she declared, would undoubtedly lead to incest. Astonished by the question, I asked her how the constitutional amendment could possibly encourage incest. Instead of answering, she looked me coldly in the eye, scowled, and asked if I was a Christian. When I answered no, she announced loudly that there was no point in talking any further, pointedly turned her back on me, and strode away angrily—as if escaping a leper.

About five years later, I was attending a national conference of political scientists in Chicago when I fell into a conversation with a distinguished colleague from another university. In the course of discussing my work on this book, I tried to make a case for some of the positive consequences of religious involvement in American political life. For every example of an ignoble or repressive movement that she brought up, I countered with an example that I thought illustrated religion at its best. As I was defending Moral Majority from a charge of bigotry, she suddenly exploded with the ferocious declaration, "I *hate* religion and politics!" After an awkward pause, the conversation moved to another, safer topic.

What these two anecdotes convey, aside from my own puzzling ability to provoke outbursts in otherwise calm people, is the degree of passion that religion can inspire in political life. It does not bode well for political discourse when a political activist declares publicly that there is no point in discussing a policy issue with an interested onlooker. And to literally turn one's back physically on another person, as the Texas delegate did to me, is the first step in a process that can lead to treating a fellow human being as a mortal enemy. Similarly, two professional political scientists ought to be able to discuss a recent development in national life without one of them expressing hatred for the argument of another. In both cases, the strength of convictions about matters of deep personal concern destroyed calm and reasoned debate. Though neither the Texas delegate nor the political scientist would be likely to throw bombs, their actions gave me a glimpse of the thought process that might lead to the kind of behavior that disfigures countries such as Lebanon and Northern Ireland. As no academic research ever could, they brought home to me the danger of public conflicts about matters of conscience and moral outlook.

Even though it lacks the dramatic impact of a personal encounter, academic research can offer guidance on the question of whether such experiences are typical. Aside from anecdote, is there persuasive evidence that strong religious convictions (of whatever kind) promote rigidity and dogmatism, the elements of an antidemocratic outlook? Many social scientists have interpreted the weight of evidence to support a link between the intensity of religious belief and various indicators of an antidemocratic orientation. That conclusion has been based on comparison of the expressed political and social attitudes of people with different reported levels of exposure to religious influence.

The link between religious attachment and political intolerance was supported by one of the first major academic surveys of American attitudes toward civil liberties (Stouffer 1966). Using a format that would be widely imitated in subsequent research, the investigator gauged tolerance in 1954 by asking members of a national sample if they would support various forms of freedom for unpopular groups—socialists, communists, and atheists. The results indicated that general attachment to religion was associated with low levels of support for basic civil liberties. Specifically, a high level of tolerance characterized 28 percent of respondents who had attended church in the month before the survey but a substantially higher 36 percent of the people who were not churchgoers (Stouffer 1966, 142). The difference held up with controls for social factors related to religion that might independently reduce political tolerance. Stouffer also discovered that some kinds of religion were less conducive to tolerance than others (1966, 143–44). At one extreme, only 21 percent of southern Protestants fell into the "most tolerant" category whereas 73 percent of

Jewish respondents were so classified. Northern Catholics and Protestants, who scored about the same on the tolerance scale, held a position midway between the extremes.

In the three decades since Stouffer's findings were first published, they have been repeatedly confirmed by other researchers. The General Social Survey has included questions about the willingness to extend civil liberties to five relatively unpopular groups: advocates of racism, communism, atheism, militarism, and homosexuality. As Figure 9.1 shows, religious group differences during the 1980s produced essentially the same patterns observed in 1954. The nonaffiliated were substantially more likely than persons attached to religion to score high on a scale of support for civil liberties. Among religious groups, the same ordering reported by Stouffer was in evidence: low tolerance among evangelical Protestants (black and white alike), intermediate support for civil liberties by Catholics and mainline Protestants, the highest commitment to democratic norms among Jews. These findings have also been extended to other antidemocratic orientations. Thus, researchers have found that hostility to blacks, Jews, and other minority groups has most often been expressed by adherents of theologically conservative churches and has been least common in persons outside the churches.

As empirical evidence linking religious attachment with antidemocratic orientations accumulated, researchers began to look for explanations of the relationship in the more durable aspects of religion itself. Whereas Stouffer attributed the connection to the religiously threatening nature of noncomformity and others linked it to the social background of churchgoers, some observers pointed to features of religious belief that either promoted exclusivity or attracted persons with an intolerant style of thought. Milton Rokeach (1971) called attention to the mixed nature of religious messages—their dual emphasis upon the oneness of humankind and the rigid separation between true believers and heathen. He

Figure 9.1 Support for Civil Liberties by Religious Groups

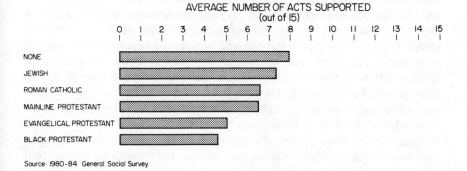

Source: 1980-84 General Social Survey

argued that the latter tendency frequently overwhelmed the benevolent impulse at the root of religious traditions. Other investigators, influenced by Rokeach's work on styles of thinking, hypothesized that conventional religion attracted people who could not accept doubt, ambiguity, or challenges to their belief systems, and who were prone to reject people who did not share their attitudes or outlooks (Budner 1962, 38–40; Raschke 1973). This tendency to ascribe intolerance to the very nature of religious commitment can be captured in the conclusion of an influential study by Nunn and colleagues (1978, 140): "Traditional Christians, who participate actively in their churches and who find themselves with limited resources to comprehend and affect the larger world, closely link God and political authority and are also likely to see political nonconformity as the work of the Devil."

ASSESSING THE EVIDENCE

These results paint a disturbing portrait of the capacity for democratic thinking and action among deeply religious people and lead to concern about the implications of their increasing involvement in political life. Dogmatism, close-mindedness, and intolerance are not traits that promote civility or the free exchange of ideas. If such traits are pronounced among religious activists and their opponents, there is a solid basis for concern about the increasing politicization of religious issues. In my view, however, the evidence supporting a link between religiosity and the propensity to intolerance is not strong enough to warrant alarm.

In the first place, studies on the relationship between religious commitment and various forms of antidemocratic orientations have not uniformly pointed to a strong connection. In his careful review of relevant research published during the 1960s, Wuthnow (1973, 122) found that religious commitment was positively related to social conservatism in only about one-half of the reported analyses; more commonly, the variables were unrelated or negatively associated.[3] Wuthnow further demonstrated substantial methodological deficiencies in many of the studies that contributed to the conventional wisdom. Typical weaknesses included a lack of appropriate controls for external influences, the use of unrepresentative samples, and reliance on overly simple measures of complex political and religious orientations. An additional flaw has recently been noted in studies that have purported to measure the impact of religious affiliation upon political tolerance. Even though they have claimed to measure general orientations toward civil liberties, most studies have commonly asked respondents about their willingness to extend constitutional rights to left wing groups or other organizations perceived as especially threatening to Christian values. When the target groups have included those that threaten the values of liberal religious groups, the interdenominational differences in tolerance have narrowed appreciably (Sullivan et al. 1982, 137–39; Beatty and Murphy 1984, 322–27). Even with such elaborations, however, persons outside the churches seem substantially more tolerant of opposing viewpoints than church members (Smidt and Penning, 1982).

A second problem has been the reliance of all such studies on attitudes rather than on behavior. People do not always act consistently with their expressed beliefs. The crisis that enveloped the American Civil Liberties Union (ACLU) over the Skokie case in 1977 showed that the attitude–behavior gap can be especially large in the realm of civil liberties. In Skokie, a Chicago suburb with a high concentration of Jewish refugees from the European Holocaust, local authorities tried to block a planned march by members of a Nazi organization. When the ACLU provided support for the Nazis' legal challenge to the Skokie ordinance— an action for which there was ample precedent in its history—the organization lost thousands of members and a vital proportion of financial resources. Even for supporters of an organization whose sole purpose was the defense of civil liberties, it was easier to express tolerance in the abstract than in practice (Gibson and Anderson 1985). The higher levels of tolerance expressed by the nonreligious might erode under similar pressure—as, indeed, religious activists have charged.[4]

Morover, those who have viewed religious commitment as a source of antidemocratic sentiment have not always distinguished among different types of commitment. Most studies have simply examined the attitude differences between church members and nonaffiliates, or between different denominations, or, in a few cases, between churchgoers of varying frequency. These are poor approximations of what might well turn out to be the real source of variation in the linkage between religious commitment and tolerance—differences in the manner in which people absorb religious values. In a pioneering survey of democratic attitudes in the United States, researchers from the University of California stressed that people hold their religious values in different ways (Adorno et al. 1950, chap. 18). For example, some attend church only out of a sense of duty to parental expectations or because it conforms to social practice in their community. What is missing from such conventional or nominal religiosity is deeply rooted acceptance of the nobler values associated with major religious traditions—love, charity, compassion, and forgiveness. Some adherents do not hear these messages either because they are not physically present often enough or, more likely, because they do not try to listen to what is being said or implied. But other persons who take religion seriously—meaning that they embrace the ethical messages transmitted by a religious tradition—internalize the content of the tradition and assign the highest priority to acting righteously. Before condemning individuals for falling short of biblical standards, they are likely to recall the admonition to hate the sin but love the sinner. Hence, it was predicted, "The more 'human' and concrete a person's relation to religion, the more human his approach to those who 'do not belong' is likely to be: their sufferings remind the religious subjectivists of the idea of martyrdom inseparably bound up with his thinking about Christ" (Adorno et al. 1950, 731).

In a moving illustration of precisely that style of deep commitment, the psychiatrist Robert Coles (1985) reported about six-year-old Ruby. The first black child to integrate a New Orleans school in 1960, she had to march every day past a howling and vicious mob threatening her life: "As she walked by the mob, sometimes a hundred or so strong, protected by federal marshals on her way to a sadly deserted classroom, she said, 'Please, dear God, forgive those folks, because they don't know what they're doing.' She'd heard in Sunday school that Jesus had once reached out similarly and she was trying to follow suit." That type of religious commitment—which is precisely what is meant by "taking religion seriously"—could very likely militate against the arrogance that threatens democratic interchange.

This argument about a link between "genuine" religious commitment and thoughtful, reasoned behavior, has attracted some research support. Gordon Allport (1958, 421–22) reported an intriguing study in which standard prejudice scales were administered to Catholic and Baptist laymen. The process of selecting respondents was designed to produce persons who exhibited diverse styles of religiosity—commitment to the essence of the faith versus commitment for social or professional reasons. The Catholic participants were selected by a knowledgeable parishioner who was asked to recommend some church members who were deeply influenced by faith and others who participated for secular advantages. In an attempt to match this distinction between "devout" and "institutional" church members, the Protestant participants were recruited from regular and irregular attenders at Bible class. In both cases, "the most devout, more personally absorbed in the religion, were far less prejudiced than the others."

The negative association between "intrinsic" religious commitment and prejudice has been found to hold in larger and more systematic studies (Gorsuch and Aleshire 1974; Studlar 1978; Wilson and Bagley 1973). The findings point to a curvilinear pattern: the most pro-democratic values are expressed by people on the extremes of religious commitment—those outside the churches and those most deeply involved in religious groups—and the association between religion and various forms of prejudice is manifested by people who are only moderately involved with churches.[5] Recent work by H. Wesley Perkins (1983, 1985) has further rehabilitated strong religious commitment by linking it empirically to social compassion and concern for inequality, as well as to lower levels of racial prejudice. Hence, it seems reasonable to maintain that religion vs. irreligion is not the crucial dimension underlying political attitudes but that religious people differ principally by the nature and motivation of their religiosity. Unfortunately, I have not yet come across studies that examine the relationship between political tolerance and styles of religious commitment. Until such studies become available, it will remain arguable whether intense religious commitment—measured in qualitative rather than quantitative terms—actually promotes democratic orientations.

Finally, I am comforted by the belief that political participation may actually teach religious activists to moderate their style and tame their expectations. There is fairly consistent evidence that political activists are more tolerant than nonparticipants.[6] Although it has not yet been shown that political participation actually *causes* more tolerant outlooks, a logical case can be made for such a relationship. From the perspective of social learning theory, political participation should bring the individual into contact with others who value the opportunity to influence policy through democratic means. This experience might enhance the individual's respect for a system that facilitates such opportunities. The only evidence relevant to the argument has been provided by Guth and Green's (1984) mail survey of financial contributors to various party and ideological political action committees (PACs). Contributors to religiously oriented PACs and antiabortion electoral efforts were not less tolerant than the sample as a whole or than some mainstream groups. In fact, the (admittedly) small number of "religiously" conservative activists were more supportive of political liberties than were many "secular" conservative givers—contributors to anti-tax, gun ownership, libertarian, and Republican causes. Though far from proving the assertion about the moderating influence of political involvement, such fragmentary findings give hope that religious extremists will learn the rules of the game as a consequence of participation in conventional political action.

For all these reasons, some observers have retreated from earlier predictions about the baleful effect of religious activism on the political system. Of course, people tend to find what they are looking for, so I want to point with caution at some signs that the American political system can indeed accommodate religiously inspired campaigns for candidates or issues. The essence of the argument is that while such issues may strain the system by making compromise difficult and attracting the attention of persons with passionate commitments, the system can cope with this situation. To some extent, such activity may even enhance the vitality of political life.

The abortion issue provides perhaps the best illustration of how the political system adapts to the pressure applied by deeply committed activists. Advocates on both sides of the issue will usually admit that the rhetoric used to advance the cause does not elevate the tone of political discourse. The debate has often been conducted in harsh and uncompromising language in which phrases such as "baby killer" and "Nazi" are used in place of thought. Such a style of argument is more likely to open wounds than to persuade. In Congress, too, the opposing sides have sometimes used their power to deny free expression to the "enemy." When the prochoice wing was ascendant in the Senate, proposed constitutional amendments did not receive the amount of floor debate they warranted; later, the prolife wing used its majority status to support some dubious assaults on congressional procedures. The issue has also intruded on governmental decision-making in areas that appear to be far removed from any substantive relationship to abortion. The fear about abortion's disruptive potential has certainly been intensified by the alarming outbreaks of violence on the fringes of the prolife movement. Taken together, these trends have persuaded some observers, such as Senator Barry Goldwater, that the abortion debate might threaten "the perpetuation of our form of government."

Despite such fears, careful study suggests that most of the abortion-related activity has stayed well within the bounds of democratic norms (Steiner 1983). Despite the excesses alluded to, most leaders have seemed committed to defusing the issue, channeling it in ways that do not threaten the political process. Without abandoning their beliefs, some staunch supporters of abortion restriction have nevertheless foregone the use of certain weapons out of a concern for the larger health of the political system. Senator Mark Hatfield, the chair of the Senate Appropriations Committee, has resisted attempts to attach antiabortion bills to appropriations legislation, and Senator Jake Garn, a leader of the antiabortion movement in Congress, resigned from the advisory board of a prolife political action committee because of its decision to target several incumbents for defeat solely because they voted against restrictive policies on abortion. In both cases, techniques that might have advanced the cause were rejected because their use seemed to undermine procedural norms that contributed to effective governance. The prochoice coalition has also demonstrated concern for the maintenance of accepted procedure by approving several prolife nominees for federal jobs.

It is noteworthy that despite its bitterly divisive nature, the abortion issue has engendered a willingness to compromise. The advocates of restriction by constitutional amendment have seemingly withdrawn from a position of favoring only an absolute prohibition on abortion to one that would permit abortion under certain conditions. Supporters of liberalized policies might not appreciate the magnitude of these compromises nor their divisive impact on prolife activists, but they do in fact constitute a significant revision of earlier positions, indicating the willingness of antiabortion forces to adapt to political realities.

The search for compromise is also apparent in the courts and the legislative branch. Ever since *Roe* v. *Wade,* the Supreme Court has steered a middle course by rejecting the extreme options of allowing abortion on demand or returning to the pre-1973 situation. Instead, the Court has granted its approval to some limitations on access to abortion while continuing to uphold the principle of abortion as a constitutionally protected right of privacy. Similarly, Congress has moved the issue to the familiar terrain of the budgetary process, debating whether federal funds should be used to pay for abortion. This conflict follows a well-established precedent of using control over appropriations as a means for settling policy debates. In both the legislative and judicial arenas, the debate has focused on bargainable questions of implementation of the law.

To go one step further, it can be argued that the abortion debate has actually invigorated public life in the United States. This argument challenges the standards of democracy used by critics of religiously in-spired political activism. Those who have criticized the place of such passionate issues on the public agenda sometimes have argued from a conception of democracy that treats mass involvement in policy-making as suspect or potentially dangerous to governmental stability. Influenced by the collapse of democracy in several nations, they have contended that high-energy issues like abortion may promote an excess of public excitement and involvement, leading to a surge of high hopes followed by disillusionment when the system yields an ambiguous compromise. Rather than treating active citizen participation as a requirement of the democratic process, these "revisionist" democrats have tended to approach it as a threat to the stability of democratic governance. Correspondingly, far from deploring apathy and limited citizen action, they see them as useful for diminishing the intensity of political conflict. Without the oversight of intense activists, political elites should have the opportunity to forge policy in a more orderly and manageable atmosphere.

But this particular view of democracy is not the only conceivable model available from the history of political thought. Another view defines the continuous and active involvement of the people in public decision-making as the key characteristic of a democratic system (Pateman 1970; Tesh 1984). In this view, issues like abortion enhance democracy by forcing ordinary men and women to take a stand on issues of public significance and by encouraging them to act upon their beliefs in the public realm. In the process of advocacy, mobilization, and negotiation, citizens learn the skills necessary to maintain a democratic political system. If it is possible that mass involvement will disturb existing arrangements, it should also strengthen belief in principles that support a democratic political system. The rise of the abortion issue challenges not democracy per se, but rather a particular conception of democracy that keeps important issues off the agenda, or limits their focus, or leaves decision-making to political elites. Groups motivated by passionate conviction on issues like abortion "try to politicize that which had been private, to broaden that which had been narrow, and to bring ordinary citizens into that which had been the province of professionals" (Tesh 1984, 44). That may not be orderly—but it is not clear that orderliness is an appropriate standard for democratic politics.

THE CASE FOR RELIGION IN POLITICS

In the last section, I evaluated the case against religious activism in politics and found it wanting. Though the rise of religiously based political issues may present challenges to the capacity of a democratic political system, the American political process seems adequate to the task. Now it is time to consider the positive claims for religion in politics.

Earlier in this book, I reported the belief of some scholars that religion contributed to the development of democratic values and the acceptance of democratic practices in the United States.[7] Some observers have gone well beyond that statement, debatable as it is, to make an even larger claim for religion. They have argued that religion is an *essential* support for a democratic political orientation and have warned that the decay of religious values or their exclusion from policy debate will weaken the health of the American political system. While acknowledging that problems accompanying political debate over moral values, they have asserted that the absence of faith from the political realm is far more dangerous to democracy than is an excess of passion.

Whatever its role in the past, how might religion today be expected to sustain democratic political institutions? According to some advocates, the dominant religions in the United States uphold beliefs that are essential to the maintenance of democratic values. Consider the notion of "human rights," a fundamental element of American political culture. On what basis can we assert that human beings, simply because they are human beings, are entitled to the various liberties spelled out in the U. S. Constitution? Although the idea of human rights is so deeply embedded in American thought that it almost seems "natural," it has usually been justified in religious terms. The religious traditions that have dominated American life commonly assert the equality of human beings before God. By virtue of humankind's common link to God, it is declared, all people deserve to be treated with a minimum of decency and respect. The Bill of Rights, supported by public opinion, embodies a religiously grounded teaching.

Other elements in the American creed have been said to originate in some conception of a divine presence. The political scientist Ernest Griffith (1956, 113) once attempted to list the beliefs essential to the survival of democracy and to show how each one depended upon the Judeo-Christian heritage:

1. Love for and belief in freedom: best based upon belief in the sacredness of the individual as a child of God.
2. Active and constructive participation in community life: best based upon the obligation of the Christian, the Jew, and other believers to accept responsibilities, cooperating with and working for their brother men [*sic*].
3. Integrity in discussion: best based upon the inner light of truth being primary in a world God meant to be righteous.
4. The freely assumed obligation of economic groups to serve society: best based upon the Christian insight into the nature of society as set forth, for example, by the parable of the body and its members.
5. Leadership and office holding regarded as public trusts: best based upon or inspired by the example and teachings of religious prophets, such as Jesus, who accepted such a service "to the death."
6. Attitudes assuring that passion will be channeled into constructive ends: best based upon religious faiths that unite an obligation to love and serve with a recognition of the primacy of individual personality.
7. Friendliness and cooperation among nations: best based upon the vision of world brotherhood derived from a faith that we are all children of a common Heavenly Father.

In this view, religion provides the standards for judgment that are necessary to give meaning to concepts such as fairness, justice, goodness, and dignity.

The bald claim that religion is essential to maintain democratic values immediately inspires two critical questions. First: Is religion the only basis for supporting the democratic outlook, or are other secular systems of belief capable of performing the same task? If alternatives are available, then religion can hardly be treated as essential to the survival of democratic government. But even if religious values do undergird freedom, that does not necessarily suggest that religious groups should enter the political arena. Hence the second question: Should religion fulfill its public function only by speaking to the consciences of individuals or should it enter the political arena more directly?

To maintain that religion is the only basis for morality, a position that President Reagan appeared to endorse during the 1984 campaign, is to ignore the existence of secular philosophies that also support respect for human rights and liberties. In fact, the research of many political scientists has suggested that the health of democracy depends less on public opinion of any sort than on favorable social and economic conditions (Lipset 1960, chap. 2) Nonetheless, advocates of religion have argued that it supplies a more powerful rationale for democracy than does any competing system of thought. In particular, they have claimed, religion—and religion alone—has the capacity to impart a sacred character to democratic values, to make them objects of faith that can resist all threats. By grounding a respect for human dignity in a force beyond human comprehension, like religion, the values rise above debate and are protected from the whims of public opinion or the challenges of competing philosophies. Only religion can provide a standard of judgment that transcends human authority. In the United States, the major religious groups thus contribute to the preservation of a democratic order by making support for political liberty an article of faith.

But does this necessarily mean that religious groups should enter the political order? Can't they contribute to the defense of democratic values without becoming embroiled in political activity and partisan debate? The advocates of a strong religious presence have answered these questions by pointing to the danger of a rigid separation between private conscience and public activity. When religious groups refrain from taking stands on controversial public issues, they may give the impression that religion speaks only to the concerns of private life. If religion is rigidly confined to the sphere of private morality, it has been argued, society runs the risk of enacting public policy without regard for moral consequences. It is important that religious claims enjoy a legitimate status in political debate, if only to guard against the danger of amoral government actions. This argument recalls the emphasis upon the prophetic role of the churches, a familiar theme in the American civil religion discussed in Chapter 3.

Religious groups thus perform the important task reminding us that public decisions inescapably involve and reflect values. Without such reminders, political conservatives have warned us, society might be willing to sacrifice the aged and the ill in the name of "efficiency" or some other standard.[8] Liberals have relied just as much upon transcendent values when they demanded protection for the poor and oppressed, even at the cost of economic growth. The values operating in these examples—respect for life and compassion—will carry greater force in public consciousness when they are defended with the same resources as are competing secular values. The political activity of religious groups can thus be seen as necessary for the defense of moral judgment in public policy-making. Even in a society in which commitment to religion is widespread, the churches have a duty to insist on its application to the problems of the day. Contentious though that might be, the alternative is even less satisfactory for the health of society.

In the modern world, Richard J. Neuhaus has argued tirelessly, religion supplies a counterweight to the greatest threat faced by democracy—a slide into totalitarianism. In a passage worth quoting at length, Neuhaus (1984, 82) summarized the importance of religion in keeping government under popular control:

Once religion is reduced to nothing more than privatized conscience, the public square has only two actors in it—the state and the individual. Religion as a mediating structure—a community that generates and transmits moral values—is no longer available. Whether in Hitler's Third Reich or in today's sundry states professing Marxist-Leninism, the chief attack is not upon individual religious belief. Individual religious belief can be dismissed scornfully as superstition, for it finally poses little threat to the power of the state. No, the chief attack is upon the *institutions* that bear and promulgate belief in a transcendent reality by which the state can be called to judgment. Such insititutions threaten the totalitarian proposition that everything is to be within the state, nothing is to be outside the state.

If that analysis is correct, the church alone stands between the individual and the government, preventing the latter from swallowing up the former.

In truth, world history has supplied notable examples of religious values inspiring stubborn resistance to governments that demand complete obedience. Although the German churches as a group did not cover themselves with glory during the rise of Nazism, some of the most courageous resisters to Hitler were motivated by belief in divinely inspired values transcending the norms of national loyalty. More recently, the Catholic church has preached on behalf of the autonomy of individuals against both leftist governments—as in Poland and Nicaragua—and right-wing regimes in countries such as El Salvador and the Philippines. The contemporary movements mentioned previously in this book—Sanctuary, the nuclear freeze, antidraft activity, refusal to pay taxes for military programs—seem to draw disproportionately from Catholics attuned to the message that emanated from the Vatican Council of the 1960s. In all such cases, religion can provide a sense of perspective that may prompt the individual to challenge the authority of the state. By forcefully reminding individuals that their behavior must conform to higher standards, a religious tradition can promote disobedience to the excessive demands of government or other authority figures.

Religious values may guard against totalitarian sympathies in yet another manner. One great source of evil behavior is certainty—the unshakeable conviction that the individual posseses some higher Truth. Armed with certainty about the one true master or the inevitable destiny of communism, human beings have committed some of the greatest crimes in history. Doubt is a potential antidote to such monstrousness, because it activates the conscience. A person who is *not* wholly certain may question the rightness or appropriateness of behavior—including his or her own actions.

Christianity may engender doubt by its insistence on the fallen state of humankind. The doctrine of original sin teaches that humans are depraved and cannot be certain even of the righteousness of their own behavior. Sustained by this assumption, the founders of the United States devised a governmental system that would make it difficult for would-be tyrants to accumulate enough power to overwhelm democratic institutions. One who assumes that humans are imperfect may counsel against the type of utopianism that has occasionally disfigured the world. While doubt can lead to confusion and paralysis, it may also prompt a pause that enables people to rethink the possible consequences of a particular course of action. In that way, the doctrine of original sin may serve as a hedge against extremism (Marty 1980; Niebuhr 1944).

Each facet of religion may contribute to the protection of a democratic political system. Religious *values* can supply a basis for rejecting the claims of the state by giving precedence to sacred obligations. For example, slavery and other systems of oppression have been condemned by some church leaders as incompatible with the dictates of religion and the content of the Bible. Religious *institutions* transmit the beliefs that can stand as a buffer between individuals and the state. They expose congregants to standards of right and wrong and may preach about how best to apply values to concrete situations. And when the individual is deeply attached to a religious *community,* he or she may prove more resistant to recruitment by political causes that threaten human rights. People bonded to others by social ties are probably less susceptible to the allure of totalitarian movements than are social isolates (Kornhauser 1959).

I believe that the foregoing argument provides the strongest case for an active religious presence in all aspects of society including the political arena. Like the case against religious activism in politics, it is best treated as a hypothesis. Note that I described religion's impact upon democracy in terms that emphasized potential—*can, may, might,* and *could.* Those terms were used because they convey the conditional impact of religion. To put it bluntly, although religion may enhance freedom in many respects, it can also undermine it. According to one eminent historian (Muller 1963), the record of religion with regard to human freedom is remarkably mixed. As has just been pointed out, religious values have in some instances supported the spirit and practice of democratic government. Yet the concept of democracy arose with the Greeks, well before the beginning of the Judeo-Christian era, and the church has often been a bulwark of resistance to the spread of democratic values. In a conclusion that dramatically calls attention to the coexistence of democratic and antidemocratic impulses in Western religion, Mueller concluded (1963, 3) that "Christianity did more to promote the growth of freedom than did any other of the higher religions . . . while it also opposed freedom of thought, speech, and conscience more fiercely than did any other religion except Mohammedanism."

If religion is to fulfill its promise as a bulwark against tyranny, it must encourage its followers to resist rulers who demand actions that are inconsistent with religious values. The evidence on that point does not suggest that religious commitment necessarily works to produce more reasoned behavior. The ambivalent relationship between religion and support for constituted authority was revealed in a disturbing study conducted by two psychologists from Atlanta (Bock and Warren 1972). They built upon the famous experiments devised by another psychologist, Stanley Milgram (1974), who put laboratory subjects in a situation where an authority figure encouraged them to help with an experiment that involved inflicting pain upon other subjects. Specifically, the participants were ordered to administer what they thought were electrical shocks to fellow subjects who had been unsuccessful in what was portrayed as a learning experiment. Milgram's finding that most persons obeyed the commands—even in the face of loud protests from the "victim" of the shocks—raised fundamental questions about what human qualities accounted for refusal to go along with destructive behavior.

The scenario devised by Milgram seemed an excellent opportunity to investigate one issue not carefully considered in his original experiments, the role of religious values in distinguishing between compliance and acceptance. The Atlanta psychologists thus recruited thirty college students, measured their religious values and commitment, and then put them through what amounted to a facsimile of the original Milgram experiments. In findings that will recall the studies of prejudice described earlier in the chapter, Bock and Warren discovered a strong but nonlinear relationship between religious commitment and willingness to inflict pain on others. Those with low or high levels of attachment to religion were substantially more likely than persons of moderate attachment to resist the instructions to administer shocks. To explain this finding, the investigators suggested that the nature of religious commitment—rather than its amount—was a critical factor in whether subjects complied or refused:

> In the Judeo-Christian tradition, a high value is placed on a strong, well-defined response to "the will of God." In fact, a decisive response even if negative is to be preferred over neutrality. The Biblical position is that the man who is undecided about basic religious issues is unable to be decisive when confronted by an ethical dilemma. His tendency is to forfeit his choice to any impinging power. On the other hand, having taken a definite religious stance, one is in a position to act in accord with conscience.

If the findings of this study can be assumed to hold for the general population in real-world settings—both untested assumptions—then they should diminish our confidence that religious commitment will automatically inspire resistance to tyranny. Once again, it depends upon the quality of religious commitment that brings people into the public sphere. People who appear to have internalized the ethical principles of religion—along with those who have minimal contact with religious institutions—will probably prove most likely to resist orders that conflict with widely accepted ethical principles. Based on the limited experimental data, those whose religious commitment is moderate do not seem endowed with a tendency to challenge rulers who demand that citizens abdicate conscience.

As we saw in Chapter 7, white evangelical Protestants have greatly increased their political involvement during the past few years. Critical observers have argued that the style of religious commitment exemplified by some of the evangelical activists possesses dangerous authoritarian tendencies. This charge has been more often made than substantiated, in part because of weaknesses in the empirical measurement of "authoritarianism."[9] Lacking better evidence, there are signs that some of the politically minded evangelical leaders do not practice democracy very actively in the institutions they control. Thus, the dynamic evangelical churches that have provided leadership for the New Christian Right conform to fairly rigid and hierarchical authority patterns that give members very little experience of democratic decision-making to carry with them into the public arena (Fitzgerald 1981). At the Christian university he founded and continues to lead, Reverend Jerry Falwell has provided a code of conduct that is similarly weighted toward authority (Baker 1985). Under the rules, students at Liberty Baptist may not participate in unauthorized demonstrations, are obliged to attend church, and may be expelled for participation in demonstrations or petition drives not approved by university authorities. Students are thus asked to waive a number of rights guaranteed under the Constitution, including protection against warrantless searches of their rooms. Again, we cannot know for certain if these practices are widespread in evangelical Protestantism or common among all types of religions; nor is it guaranteed that adherents of such churches draw lessons about governance from religious institutions or that such lessons would carry over to the behavior of church members in other settings. Nonetheless, these tendencies should dissuade observers from asserting too confidently that religious commitment in politics necessarily acts as a brake upon totalitarian tendencies.

What, then, can we finally conclude about the impact of religion upon democracy in the contemporary situation? There is little alternative but to conclude that religion may sometimes sustain democratic values and sometimes undermine them. The source of the paradox is simply that religious values are ambiguous with regard to politics. They contain messages that can lead persons of common faith in different directions. The multiple political uses of religious ideas have been demonstrated repeatedly in specific policy conflicts. In the period leading up to the Civil War, northerners and southerners alike found ample justification for slavery and abolition in the same religious document. During the Prohibition era in this century, learned clergymen argued earnestly about the message of scripture with regard to intoxicating beverages. The problem arises today even in the unlikely context of environmental policy, a subject of conflicting biblical images. Just as some interpret God's intention that people should have dominion "over all the earth" (Genesis 1:26) as a call to exploit the environment in the interests of human happiness, others cite the 24th Psalm, "The Earth is the Lord's," to promote reverence for the natural environment and support a preservationist ethic (Blackburn 1972). The problem is no less vexing at the general level of democracy. The call in Matthew XXII, "Render therefore unto Caesar the things which are Caesar's; and unto God the things that are God's," does not define precisely what it is that humanity owes to state and to church. Depending upon how responsibility is allocated, that biblical injunction may be interpreted as a call to revolution or, at the other extreme, as a plea for servility.

The problem of limited guidance extends even to such fundamental questions as the best form of human government. The doctrine of original sin has been interpreted by some theologians as a call to caution, an injunction against committing evil in the name of higher values. As such, it may promote a belief in the wisdom of limited government. Yet it has also been used as an argument against the human capacity for self-government. If mortals are prone to greed, jealousy, rapaciousness, envy, pride, and other expressions of sinfulness, then they are simply not worthy of basic rights or opportunities to exercise their free will in politics. Even today, people of faith continue to argue if the Bible is capitalistic or socialistic, supportive of abortion or not, militaristic or pacifistic. The most careful students of religious thought simply cannot agree on the precise relevance of Christian doctrine to specific issues or if Christianity is inherently conducive to democracy or dictatorship (Wolin 1956). I submit that the obstacle is not deficient understanding, but the mixed political messages contained in the major religious creeds.

Given the ambiguity of religious texts and teachings, the mixed historical record, and the empirical evidence cited earlier in the chapter, it would be foolhardy to assert that religious faith necessarily upholds democratic values. In some contexts and for some types of people, it may enhance freedom. Or it may encourage particular types of freedom while enforcing conformity in other realms of human endeavor. It seems to matter less whether people are religious than how they hold their religious values and attempt to apply them in concrete situations. An upsurge in religiously based political activity is neither to be welcomed uncritically nor condemned out of hand.

*   *   *   *   *

It seems appropriate to end this work by stressing that science cannot establish whether religious claims are true or false. But science, especially social science, can attempt to discover the consequences of religious values, institutions, and communities for the political system. This book described how religion interacts with the political system in one country and has explained why some patterns recur. Because of the limitations of previous research and the inherent tentativeness of science, I have emphasized the provisional status of my conclusions. More and better research might clarify the patterns of religious influence in politics, and might even provide a basis on which to offer confident predictions about the future of the relationship between the two domains. The impact of religion on American political life is surely important enough to warrant the effort.

NOTES

[1] In that regard, a federal district court is currently preparing to hear a lawsuit demanding that the Internal Revenue Service withdraw tax-exempt status from the Roman Catholic church. The plaintiffs charge that the church's deep involvement in the antiabortion movement puts it in violation of the requirement that tax-exempt institutions refrain from devoting a "substantial" share of their resources to influencing public policy. Should the case be won—and even if it is lost—the legislative branch might have to confront the issue of whether churches should be allowed to enter deeply into political action without sacrificing their tax advantages.

[2] The study examined nations with regular elections and national survey data in Western Europe, Scandinavia, and North America.

[3] Lest it be thought that I am treating conservative preferences as antidemocratic sentiments, let me emphasize that most of the scales Wuthnow examined really measured what has aptly been called "pseudo-conservatism," surface agreement with right-wing goals but usually involving means that most conservatives would reject. What passes for mass conservatism often lacks the subtlety and respect for democratic means that characterizes the conservative intellectual tradition (McClosky 1958).

[4] From a social learning perspective, the differences of expression might only reflect the greater familiarity of nonaffiliates with democratic norms and their ability to recognize the socially desirable response (McClosky and Zaller 1984).

[5] Wade Clark Roof (1974) has suggested that the apparent prejudice of churchgoers is principally an outgrowth of their localistic orientation, a consequence of their limited exposure to agents of modernity.

[6] In an interesting study that compared different types of activists, Sharon Presley (1985) showed that party activists tended to be recruited from conventional religious backgrounds, whereas political resisters reported either no religious affiliation or membership in an unconventional church. As the resisters

included persons who had committed acts of civil disobedience or otherwise exposed themselves to legal sanctions, the results suggested that membership in mainstream churches is associated with adherence to democratic norms and that defiance of legally constituted authority is more common among persons outside the established churches.

[7]The same argument has been made about countries undergoing modernization. In such societies, it has been argued (Smith 1970), religious values may contribute to a democratic outlook and help to draw citizens into political action. As I noted in Chapter 2, active involvement in a church may serve to encourage the development of political skills and promote electoral participation.

[8]Opponents of liberalized abortion make just such an argument when they contend that the prochoice position is grounded on values that lead to disrespect for human life and dignity. Supporters of liberalized abortion would respond that forcing women to bear unwanted children is a greater denial of respect for human life and dignity. Hence, the abortion debate is a conflict between different interpretations of what is right rather than a clash between advocates of morality versus amorality.

[9]Specifically, the scales that purport to measure unquestioning support for authority and related signs of intellectual rigidity are loaded with items that tap support for traditional religious values. Thus a five-point scale purporting to measure "conventionality," a construct associated with authoritarianism, included participation in church activities and a belief in the truth of religion as elements of a conventional outlook (Raden 1982). Worse yet, another study labeled respondents as "religious dogmatists" if they agreed with such statements as "Regular attendance of services is a necessary part of religion" or "Parents should make every effort to ensure that their children develop strong religious convictions" (Fagan and Breen 1970). When authoritarianism is thus equated with attachment to traditional religion, it is not possible to determine if the two concepts are actually linked. For evidence that authoritarianism is a personality trait independent even of sociopolitical values, see Ray (1979).

REFERENCES

Adorno, T. W., Else Frenkel-Brunswik, Daniel J. Levinson, and R. Nevitt Sanford. 1950. *The Authoritarian Personality.* New York: Harper and Brothers.

Allport, Gordon W, 1958. *The Nature of Prejudice.* Abridged edition. Garden City, NY: Doubleday-Anchor.

Baker, Donald. 1985. "It's Not Exactly 'Animal House.' " *Washington Post Weekly Edition.* May 27: 7–8.

Beatty, Kathleen Murphy, and Oliver Walter. 1984. "Religious Preference and Practice: Reevaluating Their Impact on Political Tolerance." *Public Opinion Quarterly.* 48: 318–329.

Blackburn, Joyce. 1972. *The Earth Is the Lord's?* Waco, TX: Word Books.

Bock, David C., and Neil Clark Warren. 1972. "Religious Belief as a Factor in Obedience to Destructive Commands." *Review of Religious Research.* 13: 185–191.

Budner, Stanley. 1962. "Intolerance of Ambiguity as a Personality Variable." *Journal of Personality.* 30: 29–50.

Coles, Robert. 1985. "Out of the Mouths of Babes: When Ethics and Reality Collide." *Washington Post Weekly Edition.* September 2: 24.

Fagan, John, and George Breed. 1970. "A Good, Short Measure of Religious Dogmatism." *Psychological Reports.* 26: 533–534.

Fitzgerald, Frances. 1981. "A Disciplined, Charging Army." *New Yorker.* May 18: 53–141.

Gibson, James L., and Arthur J. Anderson. 1985. "The Political Implications of Elite and Mass Tolerance." *Political Behavior.* 7: 118–146.

Gorsuch, Richard L., and Daniel Aleshire. 1974. "Christian Faith and Ethnic Prejudice: A Review and Interpretation of Research." *Journal for the Scientific Study of Religion.* 13: 281–307.

Griffith, Ernest S., John Plamenatz, and J. Roland Pennock. 1956. "Cultural Prerequisites to a Successfully Functioning Democracy: A Symposium." *American Political Science Review.* 50: 101–137.

Guth, James L., and John C. Green. 1984. "Political Activists and Civil Liberties: The Case of Party and PAC Contributors." Paper presented to the annual meeting of the Midwest Political Science Association, Chicago, IL.

Hansen, Karsten. 1984. "Where the Martyrs Come Running." *Manchester Guardian Weekly.* March 25: 9.

Kelley, Dean M., editor. 1982. *Government Intervention in Religious Affairs.* New York: Pilgrim Press.

King, Wayne. 1985. "Racist Aryan Nation Group Inducts New Disciples." *New York Times.* October 20: 31.

Kornhauser, William. 1959. *Politics of Mass Society.* Glencoe, IL: Free Press.

Lipset, Seymour Martin. 1960. *Political Man.* Garden City, NY: Doubleday-Anchor.

Maguire, Daniel C. 1982. *The New Subversives: Anti-Americanism of the Religious Right.* New York: Continuum.

Marty, William R. 1980. "The Search for Realism in Politics and Ethics: Reflections by a Political Scientist on a Christian Perspective." *Logos.* 1: 93–124.

McClosky, Herbert. 1958. "Conservatism and Personality." *American Political Science Review.* 52: 27–45.

McClosky, Herbert, and John Zaller. 1984. *The American Ethos: Public Attitudes Toward Capitalism and Democracy.* Cambridge, MA: Harvard University Press.

Milgram, Stanley. 1974. *Obedience to Authority.* New York: Harper and Row.

Muller, Herbert J. 1963. *Religion and Freedom in the Modern World.* Chicago, IL: University of Chicago Press.

Neuhaus, Richard John. 1984. *The Naked Public Square: Religion and Democracy in America.* Grand Rapids, MI: William B. Eerdmans.

Niebuhr, Reinhold. 1944. *The Children of Light and the Children of Darkness.* New York: Scribner's.

Nunn, Clyde Z., Harry J. Crockett, Jr., and J. Allen Williams, Jr. 1978. *Tolerance for Nonconformity.* San Francisco, CA: Jossey-Bass.

Pateman, Carole. 1970. *Participation and Democratic Theory.* Cambridge, England: Cambridge University Press.

Perkins, H. Wesley. 1985. "A Research Note on Religiosity as Opiate or Prophetic Stimulant Among Students in England and the United States." *Review of Religious Research.* 26: 269–280.

Perkins, H. Wesley. 1983. "Organized Religion as Opiate or Prophetic Stimulant: A Study of American and English Assessments of Social Justice in Two Urban Settings." *Review of Religious Research.* 24: 206–224.

Powell, G. Bingham, Jr. 1982. *Contemporary Democracies: Participation, Stability, and Violence.* Cambridge, MA: Harvard University Press.

Presley, Sharon. 1985. "Moral Judgment and Attitudes Toward Authority in Political Resisters." Paper presented to the annual meeting of the Midwest Political Science Association, Chicago, IL.

Raden, David. 1982. "Dogmatism and Conventionality." *Psychological Reports.* 50: 1020–1022.

Raschke, Vernon. 1973. "Dogmatism and Committed and Consensual Religiosity." *Journal for the Scientific Study of Religion.* 12: 339–344.

Ray, John J. 1979. "Does Authoritarianism of Personality Go with Conservatism?" *Australian Journal of Psychology.* 31: 9–14.

Rokeach, Milton. 1971. "Paradoxes of Religious Belief." In *Religion in Radical Transition,* ed. Jeffrey K. Hadden. New Brunswick, NJ: Transaction Books, 15–24.

Roof, Wade Clark. 1974. "Religious Orthodoxy and Minority Prejudice: Causal Relationship or Reflection of Localistic World View?" *American Journal of Sociology.* 80: 643–664.

Rose, Richard, and Derek Urwin. 1969. "Social Cohesion, Political Parties, and Strains in Regimes." *Comparative Political Studies.* 2: 7–67.

Smidt, Corwin D., and James M. Penning. 1982. "Religious Commitment, Political Conservatism, and Political and Social Tolerance in the United States: A Longitudinal Analysis." *Sociological Analysis.* 43: 231–246.

Smith, Donald Eugene. 1970. *Religion and Political Development.* Boston, MA: Little, Brown.

Steiner, Gilbert Y., editor. 1983. *The Abortion Dispute and the American System.* Washington, DC: Brookings Institute.

Stouffer, Samuel A. 1966. *Communism, Conformity, and Civil Liberties.* New York: John Wiley.

Studlar, Donley. 1978. "Religion and White Racial Attitudes in Britain." *Ethnic and Racial Studies.* 1: 306–315.

Sullivan, John L., James Pierson, and George E. Marcus. 1982. *Political Tolerance and American Democracy.* Chicago, IL: University of Chicago Press.

Tesh, Sylvia. 1984. "In Support of 'Single-Issue' Politics." *Political Science Quarterly.* 99: 27–44.

Wilson, Glenn D., and Christopher Bagley. 1973. "Religion, Racism, and Conservatism." In *The Psychology of Conservatism,* ed. Glenn Wilson. New York: Academic Press, 117–128.

Wolin, Sheldon. 1956. "Politics and Religion: Luther's Simplistic Imperative." *American Political Science Review.* 50: 24–42.

Wuthnow, Robert. 1973. "Relitious Committment and Conservatism: In Search of an Elusive Relationship." In *Religion in Sociological Perspective,* ed. Charles Y. Glock. Belmont, CA: Wadsworth, 117–132.

Index